FIRST EDITIONS
A FIELD GUIDE FOR COLLECTORS OF ENGLISH AND AMERICAN LITERATURE

FIRST EDITIONS
A FIELD GUIDE FOR
COLLECTORS OF ENGLISH AND
AMERICAN LITERATURE

K. Anthony Ward

Published by
SCOLAR PRESS
Gower House
Croft Road
Aldershot
Hants GU11 3HR
England

Ashgate Publishing Company
Old Post Road
Brookfield
Vermont 05036
USA

British Library Cataloguing in Publication Data

Ward, K. Anthony
    First Editions: A Field Guide for Collectors of English and American Literature
    I. Title
    094.4

Library of Congress Cataloging-in-Publication Data

Ward, K. Anthony
    First editions: a field guide for collectors of English
and American literature / by K. Anthony Ward.
        p. cm.
    ISBN 0-85967-980-2
    1. English literature—Bibliography—First editions.   2. American
literature—Bibliography—First editions.   3. Book collecting—
Handbooks, manuals, etc.   I. Title
Z2011.W27   1994
[PR83]
016.8208—dc20   93-34580
                            CIP

ISBN 1 85928 128 1 (Pbk)
ISBN 0 85967 980 2 (Hbk)

Phototypeset in 10 point Bembo by Intype, London
Printed and bound in Great Britain by
Biddles Ltd, Guildford and King's Lynn

CONTENTS

PREFACE   vi

INTRODUCTION AND HOW TO USE THE GUIDE   vii

LIST OF PSEUDONYMS   xxii

CHECKLISTS A–Z   1

PREFACE

When I entered the book trade over 30 years ago, I immediately felt
the need for a handy guide to take with me on buying trips. No such
guide being available, I made do with a notebook into which I transcribed snippets of bibliographical data which I thought might be useful.
For all its limitations, it proved to be invaluable, and I know now that
similar notebooks are carried by many collectors and dealers.

Why no field guide had been published for collectors of first editions
remained a mystery to me for over 30 years. But having finally got
round to compiling one myself, I now understand why no-one else
has undertaken the task. It is fraught with difficulties, some predictable
and some unexpected. And the plain fact is, the subject is so vast, it is
virtually impossible to do it justice in a single volume. However, the
task completed, I am sure that many collectors will find this guide a
useful addition to their libraries.

The information it contains has been gleaned from many sources, so
it seems appropriate that I couch my acknowledgements in the broadest
possible terms. Thanks then are due to the numerous bibliographers,
cataloguers, journalists, and fellow dealers alive and dead, who have
collectively and faithfully documented the wares of the trade. In
addition, I must specifically thank Mr Ron Cook for making his own
collection of reference books so freely available, and for the patience
he showed when I kept them overlong.

K. Anthony Ward

INTRODUCTION AND HOW TO USE THE GUIDE

For the serious book collector, there is no substitute for a good reference library. But 'in the field' with no library at hand, even the experienced collector may sometimes find himself in need of an *aide memoir*. For the novice-collector (probably without a good reference library anyway) the need for a handy reference book may be acute. This present volume, within its limitations, should meet the needs of both.

It will be appreciated that no single volume could deal comprehensively with all first editions, and that this volume must inevitably be highly selective in both the authors covered and in its treatment of those authors. For a start, then, it is concerned solely with first editions in the field of English and American literature. There is no date limitation. The aim has been to include the most important works of the major figures in literature, while not entirely forgetting those authors who may not have much claim on the heights of literature, but who nevertheless have a substantial following among present day collectors. There is some slight bias against living authors. Given that all could not be included, it seemed reasonable to leave out most living authors, if only on the grounds that their publications are more familiar and tend to be far less problematical than earlier volumes, bibliographically speaking. There is, on the other hand, a good selection of twentieth century authors who are no longer with us.

Authors of the nineteenth century figure prominently. There are a number of reasons for that. The interest of collectors in the nineteenth century has been growing steadily during the last 50 years, and writers of the period who have largely been overlooked are now attracting serious attention. In many cases, authors of that century have been included and dealt with at some length, specifically in the hope of giving added stimulus to the trend. Bibliographically, the nineteenth century is a fascinating area for collectors, and a complicated one. It embraced the transition from paper-covered boards to publisher's cloth.

There was constant innovation in production and marketing techniques, and the development of decorative cloth bindings. The attempts of publishers to meet the demands of the circulation libraries and an expanding Empire-wide market had important consequences in the book trade. There was the rise of the novel as the dominant literary form, and so on – all these developments, and many others, make the nineteenth century a thoroughly fascinating period for the book collector. And crucially, we have now reached a point in time where nineteenth century books are starting to disappear at an alarming rate. There is still time for the collector of modest means to put together a decent collection of nineteenth century literature, but that time is fast running out. Many of the books which have, through most of the twentieth century, seemed readily available (and in little demand) will very soon be all but impossible to find.

Time has already run out as far as books published before 1800 are concerned. The well-heeled collector who frequents only the shops of the leading dealers may not think so, but pre-1800 books are now rare in most 'antiquarian' bookshops, with their massed ranks of twentieth century dust wrappers. Volumes by unconsidered authors and on unpopular subjects can sometimes be seen, alone or in tiny clusters on the shelves. But only a mopping-up operation is now open to the collector of modest means. In view of this, it was tempting to exclude all pre-1800 writers; but that seemed too drastic, even defeatist. Great rarities do turn up from time to time. And what would be the use of a reference book of this kind, if it failed entirely to cater for the situation in which the improbable actually happens? So, though the inclusion of such authors as Chaucer and Shakespeare may raise some eyebrows, they simply could not be left out entirely.

Some of the factors mentioned above have helped to determine not only which authors to include, but the treatment they have individually received. It did not seem sensible (even if possible) to treat all of them in exactly the same way. For example, an important and fashionable author like Anthony Trollope, whose first editions are, broadly speaking, available but not too common, seemed to call for a fairly comprehensive checklist. Whereas Shakespeare, though of immense importance, called for something different. A checklist of his quarto plays in particular would be pointless. Some brief, general comments appeared sufficient. Information of this kind (directed in this case purely at the uninformed novice) is always useful, and can be as crucial as the bare bones of a bibliographical checklist.

In the main, however, it is the bare bones which are here given. More often than not, they will be sufficient to assure the collector that he has a first edition in prospect. Or, on the other hand, that the possible first edition he has been mulling over is nothing of the kind, but merely an undeclared reprint.

How to identify a first edition is a subject about which whole books have been written, and there is no simple formula available to the novice (or indeed to anyone else). In a nutshell, the only safe way is to consult a bibliography – though it has to be said that even a full descriptive bibliography needs to be used with intelligence. And that is even more the case with minimal checklists of the kind found in this volume, which is why it must be regarded primarily as an *aide memoir*. The user need not be an expert, but it is taken for granted that he knows something of the ways of the rare book trade and will appreciate the inevitable limitations of basic bibliography. If he does, he should have no difficulty in using this guide to good effect.

Terminology and abbreviations

The terminology and abbreviations employed are the standard ones in the trade. The traditional term 'dust wrapper', frequently abbreviated to 'd/w', has been used throughout, rather than the publishers' term 'jacket'. The traditional term 'verso title-page' (or simply 'verso title') has been used, rather than 'copyright page'. The latter term is increasingly used nowadays by dealers in modern first editions, but is not appropriate where earlier books are concerned. Where the place of publication is not given, London should be assumed in the case of United Kingdom editions. The term 'English Edition', though widely used in the trade, has not been adopted for general use in this guide. The term implies 'English language' which is rarely the intention, and in any case appears to ignore the important role played by Scottish publishers in 'English' literature. The term 'United Kingdom' (or 'U.K.') has been preferred.

The normal bibliographical practice of placing matter in parentheses to indicate that it does not appear on the title-page, has been adopted. However, as far as dates of publication are concerned, the principal has not been rigorously applied to modern books. It is increasingly the practice of modern publishers not to date the title-page, but to give the date (and/or edition indicator) in one form or another, elsewhere in the book. 'First Published in . . .' on the verso-title is commonly used in the U.K., and absence of any mention of further printings is usually indicative of a first printing. The practice of using a series of numbers including a '1' to indicate a first printing is more widespread in the United States than it is in Britain.

Collectors (in the U.K. especially) should take note of the American practice of identifying Book-of-the-Month-Club editions by a very small black or blind device on the back cover, usually in the lower righthand corner. This device should be taken as over-ruling any other indications which suggest (or state) that the books are first editions.

Book sizes

As a general rule, sizes have not been given for standard octavo (8vo) volumes. Book sizes, by the way, as the newcomer will discover soon enough, can be a little confusing. The same book, he will observe, can be described in one place as say 12mo, and in another as small 8vo. Another book may be described here as quarto and elsewhere as folio. Basically, there are two reasons for this (not counting sheer ignorance). The first is that lazy cataloguers are tempted to make assumptions about sizes. And the second is that the size of a book, technically speaking, derives from its collation – the result of folding the sheets of paper on which the book is printed, a specified number of times (the sheet itself being of standard dimensions). Thus the expression 'octavo' (for example) indicates both the collation (8 leaves) and the size. The potential for confusion lies in the fact that sheets of different dimensions can be used in the first place. Thus a small sheet may be folded to produce eight leaves, while a larger sheet may be folded to produce twelve leaves – resulting in an 8vo and a 12mo respectively, and two booklets of very similar size. Both are liable to be called 8vo or 12mo. If the fractionally larger one is then trimmed at the binders more heavily than the smaller one, the difference between them could disappear completely. The problem, in a nutshell, is that there is no independent vocabulary of sizes. There is only the vocabulary of collation.

It is not only cataloguers who promote the confusion over sizes. Some eccentric 'sizes' can be observed in some standard bibliographies. (Martindell's KIPLING for example). But collectors quickly become immune to the shock of seeing different sizes allocated to the same book. Little harm results as a general rule. As far as this guide is concerned, where sizes are given at all, their accuracy will depend upon the source of the information. It has not (of course) been possible to study every book described.

Bindings

The term 'wrappers' means paper covers (i.e. paperback) and 'boards' means only paper-covered boards. Cloth-covered boards are described simply as 'cloth'. As a general rule, binding materials have not been given without good reason. Where no binding is mentioned it can be assumed that the book is bound in the standard materials of the period. Broadly speaking, that means publishers cloth after about 1840, boards or wrappers from about 1800 to 1840. Books dated earlier than 1800 are sometimes found in original boards or wrappers, and sometimes in bespoke bindings, some sort of exotic material, or in no binding at all. But generally, nowadays, they are found in calf or some other leather or half-leather, and the best that can be hoped for is a good contemporary binding of some sort.

While on the subject of bindings, it is perhaps worth reminding the reader that the colour detail of a cloth binding can be highly significant or it can be unimportant. Victorian publishers in particular were inclined to issue the same title in a variety of coloured cloths. These are usually a puzzle to bibliographers and attempts to establish priorities often end in failure. In some cases, the sequence in which different colours were used has been firmly established, but in many other cases the priority remains a mystery – if indeed there is any priority to be discovered. In this guide, the colour of the first binding is given as a matter of course, where any binding description is called for. Alternative colours used subsequently are mentioned in appropriate cases. Collectors coming upon a cloth binding (especially if it is a Victorian binding) of a colour different from the usual one, should view it with caution while at the same time considering that variants occur quite frequently, priorities (as said above) have not always been firmly established, and indeed, unrecorded variants do turn up quite often and can be of great interest. On the other hand, an unfamiliar binding colour on a very modern book indicates, more often than not, that the copy concerned was remaindered, or has simply been rebound by a former owner. The first consideration, however, in all cases of different-coloured bindings, is whether or not the copy concerned really is the first edition, or a different edition entirely.

Copyright editions

Another point to bear in mind is that publishers (and authors) of the nineteenth century and early twentieth century were constantly fighting to protect their copyrights against pirates, both at home and abroad. In the course of this battle, it was quite usual for them to 'publish' a small number of copies of a title well in advance of the main edition, in an attempt to establish legal copyright. These 'copyright editions' frequently had greatly abbreviated texts, and were almost invariably issued in a binding quite different from that of the eventual standard first editions. Wrappers were used as often as not. Copies of these editions are naturally very rare indeed, and hardly ever appear on the market. On the other hand, the pirated editions which they were intended to forestall are, in the main, not so scarce.

Binding embellishment

The colour of a cloth binding is one thing, but the embellishments upon it are quite another. Variations in the lettering and decorations of bindings are nearly always significant. In many particular cases, the significance has not always been discovered, but publishers and binders do not, and never have, made a habit of altering embellishments without good reason. Stocks of cloth of a particular colour might easily run out during a binding-up, and be replaced by another of a similar shade, or even of a totally different colour. But brasses for stamping on bindings and art work in general, are expensive and are not replaced willy-nilly. And of course they do not 'run out' as might a quantity of cloth.

So, even a small variation in the embellishment of a binding will, as likely as not, signify some intention on behalf of the publisher. There are many possibilities. A quantity of the sheets may have been destined for a different market from the bulk. A Colonial Edition might fall into this category. It may have been (and frequently was) that sales of the original edition appeared to be exhausted, and the publisher was anxious to revive them by bringing out a cheaper edition. That was in fact the standard practice of many publishers during the nineteenth century, and was not unknown before that. In such a case, the binding would be a cheaper one – thinner boards, cheaper cloth, and less embellishment. In such cases, if first edition sheets were still in stock at the time, they might be bound-up in the new, cheaper casing. If the first edition sheets ran out, and sales were booming, new sheets would be printed and the book would continue to be issued in the same cheaper binding until those ran out – and so on. It is easy to see how this process could result in a series of issues, impressions or editions – and of course, the variant first edition binding with different (i.e. less) embellishment.

As it happens, the process of issuing a book first in an expensive binding (or edition) and then in a cheaper one to reach a poorer (but increasingly large) market, was a deliberate policy of publishers in the late nineteenth century. It was not a process left to chance, but one which was planned. Nor did it necessarily stop at one cheaper edition. An even cheaper edition might follow the first cheap one, and then yet another, still cheaper. The process usually came to an end with an edition in paperback, or a 'yellowback'. But this is rather a different matter from the case of the first edition in a differently-embellished binding.

Remainders

Remaindering in sheets is a very different process from the standard modern practice of clearing out ready-bound books for sale at a lower price, and has more serious implications for the collector. In modern publishing, good-housekeeping is the order of the day. But in the past, unsold sheets could lie abandoned in a publishers warehouse for many a long year. Eventually, they might be destroyed, or they might be reprieved by the publisher, or perhaps sold on to another publisher. In the last two cases, they would almost certainly see the light of day in a binding different from the original. In other circumstances, the same sheets could be revived much earlier. If the original publisher, for example, ran into financial difficulties, the unbound stock might pass to a successor very soon after first publication. If there happened to be unused binding cases available, the new publisher might take those too. A good example of the consequences of this kind of situation is the case of the Bronte Sisters' first book. (q.v.)

Binding lettering

The lettering on a binding, especially on the spine, and particularly the publisher's imprint, can be an important clue to events such as those just hypothesized. And here, we are not concerned with the sending of sheets from England to America, or *vice versa*, for a foreign edition to be put out. That was standard practice. Two possibilities are of interest. Firstly, the case where different versions of a publisher's imprint have been used on the spine. And secondly, the case where the imprint of a totally different publisher appears on the spine. And in both cases, we are assuming the sheets to be of the first printing.

The second case – different publisher's imprints – is almost certainly an indication that the sheets were remaindered in one sense or another.

There have been publishers who specialized in buying up unwanted sheets (or indeed ready-bound volumes). These 'jobbing publishers', as they are called, were flourishing in the nineteenth century. The stock which they bought was put onto the market in various forms. The usual one would be the original sheets with a new title-page and a new binding. But it is easy to see, taking account of the possible economies which might be open to the jobbing publisher (and sheer hazard), how variants might result. However, regardless of the variations which have been generated by the process, 'remainder issues' of first editions, while not having the same attraction to collectors as the *bona fide* first issues, ought not to be despised. They are interesting at least insofar as they shed light on a corner of publishing history. There is also another consideration. If first edition sheets are passed on to a jobbing publisher, perhaps a longish time after the original publication date, then the implication is that the book did not sell well in the first place. And that means, of course, that the first issue will be rare. It may in fact be so rare as to make the jobbing publisher's later issue of some value. But this will not apply if the original publisher was over-optimistic about the book's prospects, and ordered a vast number of sheets to be printed – of which only a relatively small number remained unsold.

Imprints

The use by one publisher of different imprints on the same book is also an interesting reflection of publishing practices and history. What it normally indicates is that some development has occured in the publishing house concerned. It may be that the firm has taken on a new partner (or lost one), or it may simply be that a new 'image' has been devised. Whatever the circumstances, the resulting variants can nearly always be placed in historical sequence and priorities allocated. Always assuming, of course, that the matter has been successfully researched and the sequence of events has been established.

All this goes to show that in the identification of first editions, the name of the publisher must figure prominently. More often than not, it is the most crucial piece of information after the date. In a book which is not dated it has to be the starting point. In the checklists in this guide, therefore, the name of the publisher is given in the great majority of cases. It has frequently been abbreviated to avoid constant repetition of long-winded imprints, but no confusion should result from this.

Dust wrappers

What was said above about cloth bindings is also true of dust wrappers. Variations can be due to remaindering, changes of some sort at the publishing house, or to the publisher's marketing decisions. Chance can also play a part. An interesting modern example is the case of John Fowles' first book THE COLLECTOR. Dealers have set great store by the fact that one version of the dust wrapper carries quotes from reviews and another does not. First editions in the 'first issue' dust wrapper (without the reviews) are priced very much higher than those in the 'second issue' dust wrapper. And yet that same 'first issue' dust wrapper is frequently seen on books of the second impression. How this might have come about is easy to imagine. But the actual reason in this specific case is less important than the general principle it demonstrates. A likely scenario is that, with the book already on sale in the first dust wrapper, the publisher ordered a new wrapper to be printed, incorporating quotes from some of the favourable reviews which appeared after publication. In the new dust wrapper, the book sold well and ran into a second impression. At some point, the stock of new dust wrappers was exhausted, so the unused copies of the abandoned first dust wrapper were brought back into play. Thus the earliest dust wrapper appeared not only on the earliest copies of the book, but also on much later ones.

That is one possible scenario. Another is that at some stage a batch of the abandoned dust wrappers got mixed up with the new ones and were used by mistake. In either case, there is no certainty about the timing of the change. The old dust wrappers could have been brought back into play, either deliberately or by accident, while the first impression books were still being issued. Finally, it is not beyond the bounds of possibility that the first dust wrapper was not used at all, until the second and preferred dust wrapper ran out of stock. And if that had happened, it would make a mockery of the collector's preference for the 'first issue' dust wrapper.

The essential point in all this is that book production is a process whereby different elements of the product are brought together by different individuals or firms, and that the process therefore lends itself to vagaries of fate. Dust wrappers, moreover, being physically separate from the rest of the product even at the point of sale, can have an ultimate fate never intended by the publisher. In other words, they can be switched from one copy to another.

The date at which dust wrappers came into use has never been firmly established. What is certain is that they originated quite some time before the end of the nineteenth century, though of course examples are rarely seen nowadays. In fact, early dust wrappers are considerably rarer than the books on which they appeared. This is because they were, as a matter of course, quickly discarded by purchasers, just as paper bags are discarded today. The modern view that dust wrappers are an essential part of the book as published, was not taken in former times – not, in fact, until well into the twentieth century.

More may be discovered in due course about the history of dust wrappers. A prime consideration will be to define the term. Because it is almost certain that the modern printed dust wrapper stemmed from a plain piece of paper wrapped around the book for purely protective purposes – still seen today, especially on books from private presses. Some very attractive pictorial dust wrappers were in use early in the twentieth century, but for the first two or three decades, a very plain printed dust wrapper was the norm, especially for 'literary' works. They were frequently white or cream, so that nowadays, if they are found at all, they are nearly always found badly soiled or browned – the spines especially (which, since they have lived through the age of cigarette-smoking, is no great surprise).

Dust wrappers are not very well documented. Probably as a result of their being regarded as disposable, they were not automatically recorded in bibliographies until recent times. Now, there is much uncertainty about whether particular books ever had them. Such doubts arise especially in connection with books published around the end of the nineteenth and the beginning of the twentieth centuries. There is little doubt, however, that they were in widespread use at this time.

Collectors of modern first editions take a dim view of the general public's habit of clipping prices from dust wrapper flaps. Concern over this matter has in fact only arisen very recently (in the last two or three decades) and began in America – from whence came the expression 'price-clipped', Other collectors (and dealers), who are not much interested in modern first editions, sometimes regard this as a fuss about nothing. But it is not. The price on a dust wrapper can be a vital piece of bibliographic evidence. Progressive prices on the same book must correspond with the publishing sequence, and may provide the first hint of a series of print runs or impressions. As likely as not, an increased price merely reflects rampant inflation while the first printing was still in stock. But in any case, the price is not necessarily the only thing lost when the dust wrapper is clipped. It has sometimes been the infuriating habit of some publishers to have the impression number printed in the immediate proximity of the price (and nowhere else), so that when the price is cut off, the impression number goes with it. And a second impression (for example) is then indistinguishable from a first impression. But the point already made about the different elements of the physical book and the use of them to deduce historical sequence, should not be forgotten. It cannot be taken for granted that the first sheets printed were the first to be bound-up and the first to be put into dust wrappers.

Advertisements

Similar considerations apply to the advertisements or catalogues, which are frequently found in books, usually at the end. Whether they are dated or not, there is rarely absolute certainty about the sequence of events by which they got into the book in the first place. It is always tempting to assume that, in the case of dated advertisements, those with the earliest date were bound into the earliest copies of the book. But this need not have been the case. Whatever the original intention of the publisher, fate may have played a part somewhere along the line.

Typographical variation

Typographical quirks are another case in point. Like advertisements, variations in typesetting are frequently quoted as indicators of issue priority. The thorough bibliographer will have investigated such matters and may have discovered some evidence to support an assertion that particular variations occurred in a particular sequence. But it is often the case that a typographical variation occurred without rhyme or reason, and in such a way that no priority can safely be ascribed to it. Consider, for example, the frequently quoted case of an individual letter in the text appearing only faintly on the printed page. In many copies of the book, it may appear thus, while in other copies it may appear in perfect register, consistent with the other letters around it. Some external evidence may exist to prove that the earliest copies of the book have the letter faintly impressed, and that later copies have it perfectly impressed. This would suggest that the letter had been incorrectly positioned when the printing began, that the fault was eventually noticed during the machining and the letter adjusted before the end of the run. However, it may also have been the case that the letter was printing perfectly at the start, became loose at some stage, and the fault was not noticed at all.

Such vicissitudes are part and parcel of book production and publishing, and collectors should be aware of the possibilities. Any copy of a book varying in some way from the description given in a bibliography, should never be rejected out of hand. It may not be 'wrong'. It may be an interesting variant, perhaps not recorded, perhaps even not 'wrong' at all, but absolutely 'right'.

Rarity

The present volume is not a price guide. Here and there, however, prices or 'values' have been mentioned, sometimes merely as a side-remark, but usually with the intention of giving some general indication of the rarity (or otherwise) of the book concerned, be that rarity absolute or merely demand-induced.

On the subject of rarity, a useful if dangerous rule of thumb is that an author's first book is frequently his rarest, and that all of an author's books preceding his most famous one tend to be scarce, while his subsequent ones tend to be relatively common. That is very far from being an infallible rule, but is a useful one to bear in mind. There are naturally many other factors which play a part in making books rare – catastrophies such as war and warehouse fires, to name but two. The publications of obscure, short-lived publishers also tend to be rare. Rarity can be deliberately manufactured, by publication in a limited edition – sometimes a self-defeating ploy, because limited editions tend to be preserved carefully. Which is why many so-called 'limited' editions, of perhaps 1500 copies, can be positively common 50 years after publication. The physical nature of a book can underlie its eventual rarity. Books in wrappers, like pamphlets, tend to have a shortish life. Gutta-percha bindings tend to fall apart. Thick books without correspondingly thick bindings tend to crack open, thin books get lost, heavy books break easily if dropped, and so on.

The factors responsible for rarity are almost endless. But for practical purposes, the collector need only be concerned with two possibilities. Firstly, that a book might be rare because (whatever the reason) few copies have survived. And secondly, that a book might be rare merely because the demand exceeds the supply. It is often difficult to be sure which of these applies in specific cases. And for obvious reasons, the second has more serious implications for the collector, than the first. To put it bluntly, he may be faced with the possibility of paying a very high price for a book which is not really as rare as it seems. If he thinks about it, he will realize that this situation is the crux of the whole business of collecting, whatever the field. Collectors create rarity, and without them, most 'collector's items' would not be rare.

But the fear must be that the book might only be rare (and expensive) because it is at the crest of a wave of fashionable demand, which could fall as quickly as it rose. The dilemma is pretty well normal in the field of modern first editions, where authors in vogue are pursued by one and all until prices have risen to the point where hardly anyone can afford them. The crowd then moves on rapidly to a new favourite.

The worried newcomer may take some comfort from the curious fact that prices hardly ever come down again, except perhaps in the sense that over a long period of time, constant inflation in the economy eventually catches up with them. (If inflation were squeezed out of the economy, prices might then visibly decline.) The events of the great depression (the one which followed the roaring twenties) are often quoted as a warning to investors in books. The collector who, for example, invested heavily in the first editions of Galsworthy in the twenties, would now, about 70 years later, be sitting on a collection which is virtually worthless. That is a sobering thought, but the circumstances were exceptional (one hopes). Since the war, despite repeated recessions, no comparable calamities have occurred in the world of books. But there is one little factor in the present situation which might make a difference. Until very recently, investors in modern first editions tended to put their money on runners in the literary stakes. Today, quite a lot of money is being put into authors with no literary pretensions whatsoever. And who can tell what might happen in these cases

Demand-induced rarity is inextricably bound up with monetary values and, for sociological reasons, tends to remain constant for a longish period of time. (Collectors who have bought at the top of the market are naturally reluctant to sell at a loss, and hoard the books in the hope that prices will eventually rise.) In other words, books which have become rare due to a surge in demand do not reappear on the market the minute they go out of fashion. Thus, even out of vogue, they remain rare. The time will eventually come, of course, when (perhaps due to the death of the collector) they emerge from their sanctuary. What happens then will depend upon what has happened in the meantime in the collecting world, and what the attitude then is towards the author concerned. They may be avidly snapped up, or totally ignored. One cannot help reflecting on the fact that books published while their author is at the peak of popularity must be hoarded in very large numbers. And if they should ever be all tipped out onto the market at the same time, their reputation for rarity would vanish instantly. But that is perhaps merely a collector's nightmare.

In the main, limited editions have been ignored in the checklists in this volume. Their nature is self-evident, and they do not normally present the collector with problems of identification.

Pseudonyms

Pseudonyms are one of the hazards of book collecting. Nothing is more irritating than having the real name behind a pseudonym buzzing obscurely at the back of the mind, especially when a quick decision is needed. A list of the pseudonyms employed by writers covered by this volume is therefore provided (see pp. xxii to xxiv). Anonymous publications are more of a problem. Many of them do appear in this guide – far too many for listing separately. General familiarity with the contents of the guide is recommended as the only possible solution.

Definitions

In this guide, the terms edition, impression, issue, state, and so on, have been applied as found in the standard bibliographies for each author. In the absence of a standard bibliography, they have been applied in accordance with established usage in the trade. In a few cases, where the traditional designations appear to be dubious, a more appropriate description has been suggested. But by and large, no attempt has been made to update or alter well-established designations, even where current thinking calls for a change.

The beginner, by the way, who has any doubts about the definitions of the terms, is urged to obtain a copy of the late John Carter's *ABC FOR BOOK COLLECTORS*, in which these and other terms of the trade are defined. In the meantime, an 'edition' comprises all the copies printed from the same typesetting. An 'impression' (essentially a publisher's term) comprises all the copies from a single print-run – second and subsequent impressions being printed from the same typesetting. 'Issues' and 'states' are groups of copies within a single edition (or impression), which have characteristics distinguishing them (collectively) from other copies of the same edition (or impression). Those characteristics are commonly referred to as 'points'. Thus, for example, if a typographical error is corrected during a print-run, the early copies with the error will form the 'first issue' and the corrected copies will form the 'second issue'.

It has to be said that, though the standard definitions of these terms are well-established and universally accepted, they are not entirely satisfactory from everyone's point of view. Thus doubts are frequently expressed about whether certain 'second issues' should really be called 'second editions' – the crux of the matter being the extent of the typographical changes involved.

Writing in 1956, John Carter pointed out the implications of printing from plates – in particular, that copies printed from plates 50 years after first publication would still form part of the first edition. The same, of course, would be true of copies printed from typesetting stored on computer disk. There is something inherently unsatisfactory about this, and the difficulty stems essentially from terminology. What collector is going to be happy with a 'first edition' printed half a century (or more) after the first copies were on sale in the bookshops?

In point of fact, a publisher marketing a book printed from plates or stored typesettings 50 years after initial publication would almost certainly offer it as a 'new edition' or at least a 'new impresssion'. The academic would say he was wrong to do so, but the collector would be perfectly happy with such a misuse of the terminology. But then collectors of 'first editions' are really collectors of first impressions, and always have been. The term 'first edition' though, as applied to the quarry of the book collector, has become deeply ingrained in the culture, and has acquired a kind of glamour which would be completely lost if we all now started talking about collecting 'first impressions'.

LIST OF PSEUDONYMS

Pseudonym	Real Name
ALEXANDER, Drawncansir	Tobias Smollett (probably)
ALLEYN, Ellen	Christina Rossetti
ALTANGI, Lien Chi	Oliver Goldsmith
ASTON, James	T. H. White
BELL, Acton	Anne Brontë
BELL, Currer	Charlotte Brontë
BELL, Ellis	Emily Brontë
BOLDREWOOD, Rolf	T. A. Browne
Bostonian, a	Edgar Allan Poe
BOZ	Charles Dickens
British Officer in the Service of the Czar, a	Daniel Defoe
C.3.3.	Oscar Wilde
CADMUS	John Buchan
CARROLL, Lewis	C. L. Dodgson
CHAUCER, Daniel	Ford Madox Ford
Chinese Philosopher, a	Oliver Goldsmith
CLEISHBOTHAM, Jebediah	Sir Walter Scott
CLERK, N. W.	C. S. Lewis
CLOUT, Colin	Edmund Spenser
CORVO, Baron	Fredericke Rolfe
CROWLEY, Aleister	Edward Alexander
DAVISON, Lawrence H.	D. H. Lawrence
DEDALUS, Stephen	James Joyce
D.E.D.I.	W. B. Yeats
Derry Down Derry	Edward Lear
DOYLE, John	Robert Graves
Dramatist, a	J. K. Jerome (probably)
EASTAWAY, Edward	Edward Thomas
ELIOT, George	Marian Evans
English Opium Eater, The	Thomas De Quincey

Pseudonym	Real Name
EPSILON	John Betjeman
FAIRFIELD, Flora	Louisa M. Alcott
FARREN, Richard M.	John Betjeman
FITZVICTOR, John	P. B. Shelley
Four Anglo-Indian Writers	R. Kipling & family
GANCONAGH	W. B. Yeats
Gentleman of the University of Oxford	P. B. Shelley
GRAHAM, Viva	Edith Somerville
HAMILTON, Clive	C. S. Lewis
HARFORD, Henry	W. H. Hudson
HARMONIA	Susan Buchan
HERRING, Geilles	Edith Somerville
INGOLDSBY, Thomas	R. H. Barham
J.D.	John Donne
KAIN, Saul	Siegfried Sassoon
KEROUAC, John	Jack Kerouac
Lay-Hand in the Country, a	Daniel Defoe
LEE, William	William S. Burroughs
LUCAS, Victoria	Sylvia Plath
LYRE, Pinchbeck	Siegfried Sassoon
MACDIARMID, Hugh	C. M. Grieve
MALLOWAN, A. C.	Agatha Christie
MALONE, Louis	Louis MacNeice
McK	J. K. Jerome
MEREDITH, Owen	Sir Edward Bulwer Lytton
MESNAGER, Monsr.	Daniel Defoe (probably)
MURALTO, Onuphrio	Horace Walpole
NEWMAN, Col. A.	Daniel Defoe (probably)
NIMROD	C. J. Apperley
NORDEN, Charles	Lawrence Durrell
Old Boy, an	Thomas Hughes
PALINURUS	Cyril Connolly
P.B.S.	P. B. Shelley
PEESLAKE, Gaffer	Lawrence Durrell
PORSON, Prof.	S. T. Coleridge
PROSPERO and CALIBAN	Fr. Rolfe & Col. Pirie-Gordon
RAMAL, Walter	Walter de la Mare
R.C.B.	Rupert Brooke
ROSS	Violet Martin
ROSS, J. H.	T. E. Lawrence

Pseudonym	Real Name
ROWLEY, Thomas	Thomas Chatterton
SAKI	H. H. Munro
SAPPER	Cyril McNeile
SECUNDUS, Scriblerus	Henry Fielding
SHAW, T. E.	T. E. Lawrence
SILURIENSIS, Leolinus	Arthur Machen
SPARKS, Timothy	Charles Dickens
TICHBURN, Cheviot	W. H. Ainsworth
TITMARSH, M. A.	W. M. Thackeray
TWAIN, Mark	Samuel Langhorne Clemens
Two Brothers	Alfred & Charles Tennyson
Two Writers	R. Kipling & his sister
VICTOR & CAZIRE	P. B. & Eliz. Shelley
WAGSTAFF, Simon	Jonathan Swift
WESTMACOTT, Mary	Agatha Christie
WINTERSTRAW, John	William Hope Hodgson
Ye Grey Quill	Fr. Rolfe
YORICK, Mr.	Laurence Sterne

A

À BECKETT, Gilbert Abbott (1811–1856)

He was a prolific playwright and journalist, editing and contributing to publications such as *Illustrated London News* and *Punch*. He edited and contributed to GEORGE CRUIKSHANK'S TABLE BOOK, which was published at the *Punch* Office, originally in 12 monthly parts, and then as a book in 1845. That work is, of course, collected as a Cruikshank item. Interest in À Beckett himself is minimal. His very popular Comic Histories, currently selling for about £50 per volume, are mainly collected for the sake of the Leech illustrations. These are listed below, along with a less well-known and scarcer item, which also has illustrations by Leech.

THE COMIC BLACKSTONE.   Punch Office 1844–46 in four parts. Fcap 8vo. Yellow boards lettered in red and black, with a comic cut of a 'Bill of Costs' on the side.
  The earliest issue of Part One has an engraved title-page of two councel playing battledore and shuttlecock (sic.). Bradbury & Agnew issued a revised edition, in the parts, from 1846, before issuing the whole work in one volume.

THE QUIZZIOLOGY OF THE BRITISH DRAMA.   Punch Office 1846. 12mo. Reddish brown cloth, lettered in gilt. Frontispiece and eight woodcuts (including one on the title page) by John Leech.

THE COMIC HISTORY OF ENGLAND   was first published at the Punch Office, 1847–48, in 19/20 parts. Book: Punch Office 1847–48. 2 vols. Purple or brown cloth with gilt vignettes by Leech on the covers and spine. Leech also contributed 20 coloured plates (10 in each volume) and numerous woodcuts in the text. New Edition: Bradbury, Agnew & Co. 1863. One volume. Edition de Luxe: Bradbury, Agnew & Co. n.d. 2 vols. 4to. Illustrations on China paper. Another Edition: Edinburgh 1881. 2 vols. Imp.8vo.

THE COMIC HISTORY OF ROME   was originally issued in 10 parts. Book: Bradbury & Evans n.d. (1852). One vol. Leech contributed a pictorial title, 10 coloured plates and many woodcuts. New Edition: Bradbury, Agnew & Co. 1863. One vol. Edition de Luxe: Bradbury, Agnew & Co. n.d. One vol.

4to. Illustrations on China paper. Another Edition: Edinburgh 1881. One vol. Imp.8vo.

ADAMS, Richard (b. 1920)

Collectors were not slow to notice that his first book, WATERSHIP DOWN, was on its way to becoming a phenomenal success. As the book went into a rapid succession of new impressions, the 2000 copies of the first printing were quickly hunted down by collectors. And now, only 20 years later, the first edition is hard to get hold of and being priced at anything over £300 in a decent dust wrapper. The American edition fetches far less.

After the enormous success of that first book, the rest were inevitably printed in large numbers and are consequently easy to obtain. They present no challenge to the collector, and with one exception the first editions are bibliographically uninteresting and easy to identify. The one exception is THE GIRL IN A SWING. After it had been printed and review copies sent out, there was a fear that the book might be considered libellous, and it was hastily withdrawn. Appropriate changes were made, including a change of name for the heroine. I do not know how many copies of the original version ('first issue') have survived, but it does not appear to be particularly scarce. Copies presently sell for £30 or £40, and of course, hardly any collectors want the second issue.

WATERSHIP DOWN. Rex Collins 1972. U.S.: Macmillan 1972.

THE GIRL IN A SWING. Allen Lane 1980. The first issue has 'Allen Lane' on the title-page, the second issue does not. U.S.: Knopf 1980.

AINSWORTH, William Harrison (1805–1882)

Ainsworth produced an enormous body of work. His novels were extremely popular during his lifetime and were printed in very large numbers. However, his popularity with readers has not endured and the interest of collectors is not great. Some interest undoubtedly stems from the fact that many of his novels were in the form of three-deckers and that many were illustrated by the best book illustrators of the period (Cruikshank, Phiz, and so on). On the matter of illustrations, however, it should be noted that not all the novels were illustrated at the first edition stage. In some cases, the illustrations were added in the green cloth edition published by Routledge in the 1870s, and in the slightly later edition in red cloth with a facsimile signature on the front cover. AINSWORTH'S MAGAZINE first appeared in February 1842 and lasted for 11 years.

It is difficult now to assess the degree of rarity of Ainsworth's novels in first edition form. Decent copies appear to be fairly hard to come by, despite the enormous numbers published. The circulating libraries would have purchased many copies, effectively removing them from the collectors' market. And the comparative lack of interest from collectors throughout the twentieth century may have resulted in many copies being allowed to disappear which might otherwise have been preserved. Currently, the first editions fall mainly within a price band of £50–£150.

WORKS OF CHEVIOT TICHBURN. London 1822.
This pseudonymous volume of poetry was reprinted in Manchester in 1825. Both the London and Manchester editions are rare.

DECEMBER TALES. Whittaker 1823. Fcap 8vo. Boards.
This, his second book, is scarce. I recently saw a rebound copy offered at £150.

CONSIDERATIONS ON THE BEST MEANS OF AFFORDING IMMEDIATE RELIEF TO THE OPERATIVE CLASSES IN THE MANUFACTURING DISTRICTS. John Ebers 1826. 24pp pamphlet.
Rare, but few collectors desire it.

LETTERS FROM COCKNEY LAND. John Ebers 1826. 12mo. Boards.

SIR JOHN CHIVERTON, a Romance. John Ebers 1826. Small demy 8vo. Boards.
This work was the subject of a dispute. A Manchester solicitor named J. P. Aston claimed it as his work. (Ainsworth, by the way, was the son of a Manchester solicitor.) In the late 19th century, it was generally thought that both Ainsworth and Aston probably had a hand in it. I am not sure what view is taken (if any) by modern scholars.

ROOKWOOD. Bentley 1834. 3 vols.
His first great success with the reading public.

CRICHTON. Bentley 1837. 3 vols.

JACK SHEPPARD. Bentley 1839. 3 vols.

THE TOWER OF LONDON. 13 monthly parts in wrappers, followed by the book edition – Bentley 1840.
Some copies were bound from the parts with all the illustrations (by Cruikshank). Those which were not bound from the parts, contain an extra plate 'The Escape of Courtenay'.

GUY FAWKES. Bentley 1841. 3 vols.

OLD SAINT PAUL'S. First issued in 1841, as 12 monthly parts with 20 plates by Franklin. The book edition brought out by Hugh Cunningham in 1847, contains the 20 plates by Franklin and two new ones by 'Phiz'. But only 21 plates are included in the list of illustrations, the plate at page 28 being omitted.

THE MISER'S DAUGHTER. Cunningham & Mortimer 1842. 3 vols.

WINDSOR CASTLE. Henry Colburn 1843. 3 vols, each with a frontispiece by Cruikshank, but with no other illustrations.
Also issued in monthly parts with 18 full page illustrations and 87 woodcuts by Cruikshank. And this latter version was also issued by Colburn in 1843, in one volume, pictorial cloth.

SAINT JAMES'S. Mortimer 1844. 3 vols.

AURIOL. Colburn 1845. Two parts, being the July and August issues of The New Monthly Magazine. Book edition: Routledge 1865.

JAMES THE SECOND. 'Edited by W. Harrison Ainsworth'. Colburn 1848. 3 vols.

THE LANCASHIRE WITCHES. Colburn 1849. 3 vols.
This, one of his best known works, had appeared in The Times, during 1848. From the type set up for this purpose, an edition was privately printed in 1849 and bound as a folio in purple cloth.

THE STAR CHAMBER. Routledge 1854. 2 vols.

THE FLITCH OF BACON. Routledge 1854.

BALLADS, ROMANTIC, FANTASTICAL, AND HUMOUROUS. Routledge 1855.

THE SPENDTHRIFT. Routledge 1857.

MERVYN CLITHEROE. Routledge 1858
The original issue in '12 monthly parts' in wrappers, suffered remarkable delays. The first part was issued in December 1851 and part 4 duly appeared in March 1852. Part 5 was then delayed until December 1857, and the final part appeared in June 1858.

OVINGDEAN GRANGE. Routledge 1860.

THE CONSTABLE OF THE TOWER. Chapman & Hall 1861. 3 vols.

THE LORD MAYOR OF LONDON. Chapman & Hall 1862. 3 vols.

CONSTABLE POLE.   Chapman & Hall 1863. 3 vols.

JOHN LAW.   Chapman & Hall 1864. 3 vols.

THE SPANISH MATCH.   Chapman & Hall 1865. 3 vols.

THE CONSTABLE OF BOURBON.   Chapman & Hall 1866. 3 vols.

OLD COURT.   Chapman & Hall 1867. 3 vols.

MYDDLETON POMFRET.   Chapman & Hall 1868. 3 vols.

THE SOUTH SEA BUBBLE.   Chapman & Hall 1868.

TOWER HILL.   Chapman & Hall 1870.

TALBOT HARLAND.   John Dicks n.d. (1870). Pictorial wrappers.
   Very difficult to find in acceptable condition.

HILARY ST. IVES.   Chapman & Hall 1870. 3 vols.

BOSCOBEL.   Tinsley 1872. 3 vols.

THE GOOD OLD TIMES.   Tinsley 1873. 3 vols.

MERRY ENGLAND.   Tinsley 1874. 3 vols.

PRESTON FIGHT.   Tinsley 1875. 3 vols.

THE GOLDSMITH'S WIFE.   Tinsley 1875. 3 vols.

THE LEAGUER OF LATHAM.   Tinsley 1876. 3 vols.

CHETWYND CALVERLEY.   Tinsley 1876. 3 vols.

THE FALL OF SOMERSET.   Tinsley 1877. 3 vols.

BEATRICE TYLDERSLEY.   Tinsley 1878. 3 vols.

BEAU NASH.   Routledge (1879). 3 vols.

STANLEY BRERETON.   Routledge (1881). 3 vols.

AKENSIDE, Mark (1721–1770)

THE PLEASURES OF IMAGINATION. A Poem. (Anonymous). For Dodsley 1744. 4to. 125pp. Vignette title in red and black. Advert leaf at end. His most important work. There were two further issues in 1744.

ODES ON SEVERAL SUBJECTS. (Anonymous). for Dodsley & sold by M. Cooper 1745. 4to. 54pp. Engraved title vignette.

THE POEMS. W. Bowyer & J. Nichols, sold by Dodsley 1772. 4to. Portrait. Also issued in 8vo. The first collected edition.

ALCOTT, Louisa M. (1832–1888)

Born into a good family with an impractical father, Louisa began writing short pieces while still a teenager, in an attempt to help support the family. Her first published piece was a poem entitled 'Sunlight' which was taken by Petersen's Magazine for the issue of September 1851. It appeared under the pseudonym of Flora Fairfield.

Other pieces followed, but she finally achieved financial security with LITTLE WOMEN which has become one of the best loved children's books of all time. GOOD WIVES was purely a U.K. title for the second part of LITTLE WOMEN. Other titles used for the same book are given below.

The following checklist is merely a small selection of her best known publications.

LITTLE WOMEN. Boston: Roberts Bros. 1868 (Part I) & 1869 (Part II). The first edition of Volume One does not have 'Part One' on the spine, and in the second volume there is no reference on preliminary page iv to 'Little Women, Part First'. The work contains four plates including a frontispiece.
Not a common book, especially in fine condition. A decent copy today is worth £2,000–£3,000 or $4,000.

LITTLE WOMEN/GOOD WIVES. Sampson Low 1868 (Part I) & 1869 (Part II).
The U.K. Edition of the two volumes is worth quite a lot less than the Boston Edition – about £500. The use of the title GOOD WIVES for Part II occurred only in the U.K. In subsequent editions by various publishers, it was also called LITTLE WOMEN WEDDED, LITTLE WOMEN MARRIED, NICE WIVES and LITTLE WIVES.

LITTLE MEN. Sampson Low 1871. U.S. (later): Roberts Bros 1871.

JO'S BOYS. Sampson Low 1886. U.S.: Roberts Bros 1886.

COMIC TRAGEDIES WRITTEN BY 'JO' AND 'MEG' AND ACTED BY THE 'LITTLE WOMEN'. Boston: Roberts Bros 1893. 8vo. Peacock-blue cloth and gilt.

AUNT JO'S SCRAP-BAG. This was the series title for a stream of little volumes. The first in the series had the title MY BOYS and was published by Sampson Low in 1871, and later by Roberts Bros. The second was SHAWL STRAPS, 1873, and the third CUPID AND CHOW CHOW, also 1873.

UNDER THE LILACS. 11 monthly parts during 1877–1878. Book: Sampson Low 1878.
One of her novels for adults.

ALDINGTON, Richard (1892–1962)

Aldington was a member of the Imagist group of poets, which flourished in the early years of the twentieth century, and whose main spokesman was Ezra Pound. Along with Pound, Joyce and eight others, he contributed to the first of the movement's anthologies DES IMAGISTS (1914), and was for a time editor of the Imagist periodical THE EGOIST.

His most celebrated work is his anti-war novel DEATH OF A HERO. The first edition had a dust wrapper designed by Paul Nash, and its presence is essential for the current value of £50–£100 to be achieved. The book is fairly common without it.

I give below a selection of his earliest, most interesting and scarcest first editions. Most of his publications after c. 1925 are fairly easy to obtain, even in the limited signed issues.

IMAGES (1910–1915). The Poetry Bookshop (1915). Pictorial wrappers with a hand-coloured design by John Nash. U.S.: Boston. Four Seas Company 1916.
His first book.

THE POEMS OF ANYTE OF TEGEA. (trans.). Egoist 1915.

IMAGES OLD AND NEW. Boston: Four Seas Company. 1916. Wrappers.

REVERIE, A Little Book of Poems for H.D. Cleveland: The Clerk's Press 1917. Square 12mo. Wrappers. Limited to 50 copies on Tuscany hand-made paper.

One of his rarest publications. 'H.D.' was the American writer Hilda Doolittle, whom Aldington married in 1913.

LATIN POEMS OF THE RENAISSANCE.   Egoist 1919. Wrappers.

IMAGES OF DESIRE   Elkin Mathews 1919. Wrappers.

IMAGES OF WAR.   Beaumont Press 1919. Limited Edition. Trade Edition: Allen & Unwin 1919. Thin boards. U.S.: Boston. Four Seas Company 1921. Allen & Unwin sheets with a new title page.
The American edition is not in Kershaw's bibliography.

GREEK SONGS IN THE MANNER OF ANACREON.   Egoist 1919. Blue-lettered cream boards.

LATIN POEMS OF THE RENAISSANCE.   Egoist 1919. Blue-lettered cream boards.

DEATH OF A HERO.   Chatto & Windus 1929. Thickish royal 8vo, black cloth and d/w (by Paul Nash).
The first edition was expurgated. The American edition of the same year was also expurgated, though less so. The first completely unexpurgated edition was published in Paris by Babou & Kahane in 1930. This was in two quarto volumes in wrappers with tissue dust wrappers. There were only 300 copies.
The full text was not published in England until 1965, in a paperback edition.

LIFE QUEST.   Chatto & Windus 1935. Blue cloth, also black buckram with decorated boards.
As far as I know, neither binding has priority.

ANDERSEN, Hans Christian (1805–1875)

Andersen's fairy tales were first published in his native Denmark, from 1835 onwards. The English editions, by various translators and illustrators, began to appear about a decade later. They were issued by various publishers in various translations, variously illustrated, in numerous issues and editions. The following list of First U.K. Editions of selected 'fairy tale' books, with a few other works by Andersen, may cast a helpful ray of light on a rather dark and complicated scene.

THE IMPROVISATORE, or Life in Italy.   Translated by Mary Howitt. Bentley 1845. 2 vols.
Published later (from c. 1870) in various editions by Ward, Lock & Tyler

(later Ward, Lock & Co.) illustrated with varying numbers of mounted photographs. These editions are not usually dated. In America, Houghton Mifflin issued the book in 1898, with entirely different photographs.

ONLY A FIDDLER.   H. G. Clarke 1845. 2 vols. 32mo. 12pp adverts at end. (Vols 3 & 4 of 'Andersen's Danish Novels' (– see the adverts).

ONLY A FIDDLER! AND O.T., or Life in Denmark.   Bentley 1845. 3 vols. 12mo.

WONDERFUL STORIES FOR CHILDREN.   Trans. Mary Howitt. Chapman & Hall 1846. Illustrated with hand coloured wood engravings. Gilt dec blue cloth.

DANISH FAIRY LEGENDS AND TALES.   (trans. Caroline Peachey). Pickering 1846. Linen spine, boards, 3pp adverts.

A DANISH STORY-BOOK.   Trans. Charles Boner. Cundall 1846. With 4 lithographed plates (hand-coloured) and wood engravings after Count Pocci. Dec. cloth gilt.

THE NIGHTINGALE AND OTHER TALES.   Trans. Charles Boner. Cundall 1846. With four lithographed plates (hand-coloured) and wood engravings by Count Pocci.
A companion volume to A DANISH STORY-BOOK.

A POET'S BAZAAR.   Bentley 1846. 3 vols.

TALES FROM DENMARK.   Cundall 1847. Small 4to.
This volume combines the previously published A DANISH STORY-BOOK and THE NIGHTINGALE AND OTHER TALES, with all the original illustrations. Reissued by Grant & Griffith, 1848–49.

THE SHOES OF FORTUNE AND OTHER TALES.   Trans. Charles Boner. Chapman & Hall 1847. 12mo. With 4 plates after Otto Speckter, and wood-engravings in the text.

A PICTURE BOOK WITHOUT PICTURES.   Trans. (from the German) Meta Taylor. David Bogue 1847. Dec. cloth.

THE TRUE STORY OF MY LIFE.   Longman, Brown, Green and Longmans 1847. 12mo.

TALES FOR THE YOUNG.   Burns 1847. 12mo. One plate by William Bell Scott, three by Dalziel Bros. Light blue cloth.

A CHRISTMAS GREETING TO MY ENGLISH FRIENDS. Trans. Lock-meyer, Bentley 1847.

THE UGLY DUCK AND OTHER TALES. Grant and Griffith, n.d. (c. 1847).
This is a re-issue of A DANISH STORY-BOOK with a new title-page.

THE DREAM OF LITTLE TUK AND OTHER TALES. trans. Charles Boner. Grant & Griffiths 1848. With 4 plates by Pocci. U.S.: Boston & Cambridge: Munroe 1848.

THE TWO BARONESSES, A Romance. Bentley 1848. 2 vols. 12mo.
This preceded the Danish edition. The Second Edition was published in the following year by Bentley in a single volume.

TALES AND FAIRY STORIES. Trans. Madame de Chatelain. Routledge 1853. With plates after H. Warren.

TALES FOR CHILDREN. Trans. Wehnert. Bell and Daldy 1861. With 47 plates by E. H. Wehnert, and 57 illustrations in the text (various artists).
The plates are 'electrotyped by a new process, recently discovered by Mr. W. J. Lynton'.

THE WILD SWANS. Ipswich: J. Haddock. Not dated (1863). With 7 litho-graphed plates.

THE ICE MAIDEN (and other tales). Trans. Mrs Bushby. Bentley 1863. 4to. Blue pictorial cloth. Wood-engravings by Pearson after Zwecker.

STORIES AND TALES. Trans. Dulcken. Routledge, Warne & Routledge 1864. Illus after Bayes.

WHAT THE MOON SAW AND OTHER TALES. Trans. Dulcken. Rout-ledge 1866. Illus Bayes. Issued in New York by James Miller 1867.

STORIES FROM THE HOUSEHOLD. Frontispiece & text illustrations by Dalziel after Bayes. Routledge 1866. Dec. cloth.

THE HANS ANDERSEN LIBRARY. Routledge (1866–90). 20 vols, 8vo. Various coloured clothes. Each volume has a coloured frontispiece and black & white text illustrations.
The series is based on previous Routledge publications of Andersen's work.

OUT OF THE HEART. Trans. Dulcken. Routledge 1867. 16mo. Frontis-piece & 15 plates in colour, etc.

THE WILL O' THE WISPS ARE IN TOWN, and other New Tales. Trans.

Plesner & Rugeley-Powers. Strahan (1867). 16mo. seven plates by Swain after Eltze.

THE WOOD NYMPH. Trans. Plesner. Sampson Low 1870. Wood-engraved title and 3 plates in colour. Pictorial cloth.

FAIRY TALES. A new translation by Mrs H. B. Paull. 12 wood-engraved plates after Mrs Kemp and Miss Runciman. Warne 1869. 8vo. 671pp. Dec. cloth.
> Re-issued many times in the ensuing years, in various bindings, with varying numbers of plates (usually less than 12), and in due course with extra stories.

FAIRY TALES. Translated by Ward & Plesner. With 12 coloured plates by 'E. V. B.' (i.e. E. V. Boyle) Sampson Low 1872. Large 4to.
> The first edition illustrated by Duncan Carse was published by Black in 1912. The first with illustrations by W. Heath Robinson was in 1913. (Hodder & Stoughton). With illustrations by Harry Clarke in 1916 (Harrap). Illustrated by Kay Nielsen in 1924 (Hodder & Stoughton), by Arthur Rackham in 1932 (Harrap), and as FAIRY TALES AND LEGENDS by Rex Whistler in 1935 (Cobden-Sanderson).

APPERLEY, Charles James (pseud. 'NIMROD') (1778–1843).

Apperley and Surtees are the two most popular sporting writers, and there is always a ready market for their books, especially those with coloured plates. The first editions however, are not all illustrated, as will be seen from the checklist below.

A book not in the list but of interest to Apperley fans, is Captain Malet's ANNALS OF THE ROAD published by Longman in 1876. This includes Nimrod's ESSAYS ON THE ROAD (from the Sporting Magazine). It is a thick 4to in pictorial red cloth, and has 10 plates and 3 woodcuts.

The principal 'Nimrod' publications are:

REMARKS ON THE CONDITION OF HUNTERS, THE CHOICE OF HORSES, AND THEIR MANAGEMENT. By Nimrod. M. A. Pittman 1831.
> Articles from The Sporting Magazine 1822–1828. Not illustrated, but sometimes found with Turner's plates inserted.

NIMROD'S HUNTING TOURS, interspersed with Characteristic Anecdotes, Sayings, and Doings of Sporting Men ... to which are added Nimrod's Letters on Riding to Hounds ... M. A. Pittman 1835.

Not illustrated. Originally a series of articles in The Sporting Magazine entitled 'Letters on Hunting'. Matter not connected with foxhunting was omitted from the book.

THE CHACE, THE TURF, AND THE ROAD.   By Nimrod. John Murray 1837. Portrait frontispiece by Maclise & 13 plates (uncoloured) by H. Alken. Papers from the Quarterly Review. Other Editions: 1843, 12mo.; 'Murray's Reading For the Rail' series, 1852, 8vo.; 1870, 8vo. Coloured Plates.

MEMOIRS OF THE LIFE OF THE LATE JOHN MYTTON, ESQ. OF HALSTON, SHROPSHIRE. By Nimrod. Rudolph Ackermann 1837. Engraved title (sometimes found coloured) and 18 coloured plates by Alken & Rawlins. Second Edition: 1837. Contents same as first edition.

SPORTING, Embellished by Large Engravings and Vignettes Illustrative of British Field Sports.   Edited by Nimrod. H. Baily & Co. 1838. Imperial 4to. Engraved title, steel plates and woodcuts (38 in all) after Gainsborough, Landseer, Cooper, etc. Text by Thomas Hood, etc.

NIMROD'S NORTHERN TOUR, DESCRIPTIVE OF THE PRINCIPAL HUNTS IN SCOTLAND AND THE NORTH OF ENGLAND.   Walter Spiers, at the New Sporting Magazine Office 1838, Pictorial cloth. Not illustrated.

NIMROD ABROAD.   By C. J. Apperley, Esq. Henry Colburn. 1842. 2 vols.

THE HORSE AND THE HOUND: Their Various Uses and Treatment. By Nimrod. Edinburgh: Adam & Charles Black 1842. Engraved frontispiece by Dobbie and 7 plates, vignette on title, and woodcuts. Another Edition: Black 1858.

THE LIFE OF A SPORTSMAN.   By Nimrod. Rudolph Ackermann 1842. Royal 8vo. Blue cloth (later, in brick-red cloth). With 36 coloured plates by Alken. Coloured frontis, coloured title. Another Edition: Routledge 1874. With all the col plates.
   One of the most sought after of all sporting books. Alken's illustrations in this volume are considered to be his finest book-work. The first edition in the blue binding is rare and worth about £1,250.

HUNTING REMINISCENCES: Comprising Memoirs of Master of Hounds; Notices of the Crack Riders . . .   By Nimrod. Rudolph Ackermann 1843. Eng frontis. & title. 32 plates and maps by Wildrake. Alken, and Henderson – not coloured.

ARABIAN NIGHTS ENTERTAINMENTS, or The Thousand and One Nights.

The stories in this celebrated collection have their origins in various parts of the orient and in different periods. They first appeared in Europe at the beginning of the 18th century, translated from the Arabic by Antoine Galland. At about the same time (1705–1708) an anonymous hack-translation appeared in England.

A scholarly edition was published in 1838–1840, in the translation by Edward William Lane, but this was expurgated. The first complete edition in English, translated by John Payne, was issued in a limited edition in 1882–1884. The translation by Sir Richard Burton followed in 1885–1888, and this is now regarded as the best version.

AUDEN, W. H. (1907–1973)

Apart from certain privately printed publications, Auden's first editions are not rare. However, the very first book, or more accurately booklet, is of legendary rarity, and worth something in excess of £5000. Facsimile editions have been published, but none of these is likely to be mistaken for the real thing. A number of similar very small editions of Auden's poems were published in subsequent years, and these too are rare and valuable. But his first commercially published volume (POEMS, published by Faber in 1930) can only be called scarce at best. It includes the poems from the earlier privately printed booklet with the same title. Faber went on to publish virtually all Auden's works in the U.K. and Random House issued them in America. From 1940, some of the Random House editions preceded the Faber editions.

Most of Auden's first editions currently cost no more than £20–£30. He published very few limited editions, and inscribed copies of trade editions are not often seen, making them particularly desirable and expensive when they do appear.

Below, is a small selection from a very long list of publications.

POEMS.   Privately Printed by Stephen Spender, Hampstead 1928. Orange wrappers. Number of copies uncertain, but probably less than 30. Only 12 copies are known.

POEMS.   Faber & Faber 1930. Wrappers. 1000 copies printed.
Includes the poems from the earlier booklet of the same name, along with others. Usually found rather worn and soiled. A really fine copy should be worth £150–£200.

THE ORATORS.   Faber 1932. Black boards, d/w.

THE DANCE OF DEATH.   Faber 1933. Green boards, d/w.

POEMS.   New York: Random House 1934. Orange boards, d/w.
Not merely the American edition of the Faber volume. It includes other work published by Faber up to 1934.

LOOK, STRANGER!   Faber 1936 Boards, d/w.

ON THIS ISLAND.   New York: Random House 1937. The American edition of LOOK, STRANGER!

SPAIN.   Faber 1937. Slim booklet in red wrappers.
Considered to be one of his scarcer publications. Generally priced at around £50, but a lot depends on the condition which is often not very good.

EDUCATION TODAY AND TOMORROW.   By Auden & T. C. Worsley.
Hogarth Press 1939, Wrappers.
One of the scarcer publications of his 'middle period'. Worth about £40.

AUSTEN, Jane (1775–1817)

Jane Austen's five major books (NORTHANGER ABBEY and PER-SUASION counting as one book) were all originally published anonymously – the first being 'By A Lady', the rest 'By the Author of . . .'. They were all 12mo and in paper-covered boards (variant colours). Needless to say, many were immediately rebound in leather, and consequently first editions in the original boards are extremely rare. Nowadays, even copies in early leather bindings are scarce. Half titles, if present, should be carefully checked, to ensure that they are not on stubs; because when the books were more common than they are now, half-titles from later editions were sometimes inserted into the first editions to enhance their value. And it should be noted that the half-title for volume one of EMMA was printed at the end of the book and left for the binder to transfer to the front. He may not have done this in some cases.

In accordance with the custom of the time, more than one printer was used for the printing of Jane Austen's multi-volume novels, with the exception of SENSE AND SENSIBILITY. This fact provides a useful check in estab-lishing the integrity of a presumed first edition, and the role of the printers is given in the list below. Their imprints may (in some cases) be found on the verso of the half-titles and at the end of the text.

All five major works are now valued at several thousand pounds each in the original boards. A few other publications of interest appeared long after the author's death. These are appended to the checklist below.

SENSE AND SENSIBILITY. London: Printed for the Author, by C. Roworth (all three vols) and published by T. Egerton 1811. 3 vols. It is thought that no more than a thousand copies were printed. In the first issue, there is no printers imprint on the half-titles, which have ruled lines measuring four fifths of an inch in volume one and in volume two. In later issues these lines are very much longer.

PRIDE AND PREJUDICE. T. Egerton 1813. 3 vols. The first volume was printed by Roworth, the others by Sidney.

MANSFIELD PARK. T. Egerton 1814. 3 vols. Volumes one and three were printed by Roworth, volume two by Sidney.
(This is the Keynes version, which I believe is now the accepted one.)

EMMA. John Murray 1816. 3 vols. Vols 1 and 2 were printed by Roworth, Vol 3 by Moyes.

NORTHANGER ABBEY and PERSUASION. John Murray 1818. 4 vols. Half-titles immediately before the texts (i.e. after the prelims). NORTHAN-GER was printed by Roworth, PERSUASION by Davison.

A MEMOIR OF JANE AUSTEN By James E. Austen Leigh. Mathews & Marot 1870.
The second edition of 1871 includes the first appearance of LADY SUSAN, which was published separately by Clarendon Press in 1925.

LETTERS. Edited by Lord Brabourne. Bentley 1884. 2 vols.
The letters were censored by Jane's sister Cassandra. The Definitive Edition entitled LETTERS TO HER SISTER CASSANDRA AND OTHERS was published by the Clarendon Press in 1932. This was also in 2 volumes.

LOVE AND FREINDSHIP AND OTHER EARLY WORKS. Chatto & Windus 1922.
Note the erroneous spelling of 'Friendship'.

FRAGMENT OF A NOVEL. Oxford University Press 1925.
This was the first printing of the unfinished novel SANDITON. The same press issued a facsimile of the manuscript in 1975. And Peter Davies published it completed by 'Another Lady' in 1975.

VOLUME THE FIRST. Oxford University Press 1933.

VOLUME THE THIRD. Oxford University Press 1951.

LADY SUSAN.   See A MEMOIR OF JANE AUSTEN.

SANDITON.   See FRAGMENT OF A NOVEL.

B

BALLANTYNE, R. M. (1825–1894)

Many of Ballantyne's books, typically of children's books of the period, were issued in variant bindings, with no apparent priority. The first editions are usually dated, but reprints rarely give any indication of an earlier edition. Ballantyne's classic is:

THE CORAL ISLAND: a Tale of the Pacific Ocean.   Nelson 1858. Pictorial cloth. Illustrated by the author, with frontispiece, pictorial title, and six plates, in full colour. Another issue has the illustrations in two colours only.

BARHAM, Richard Harris (1788–1845)

The pieces now known in their collected form as THE INGOLDSBY LEGENDS first appeared (from 1837) in 'Bentley's Miscellany' and 'The New Monthly Magazine'. Collected into book form, they first appeared from 1840 onwards, as set out below. Since then they have appeared in numerous editions, with various illustrators, and indeed a number of the legends have appeared separately in various attractive forms. A complete collection of The Ingoldsby Legends in all their various guises, would form an interesting (and quite large) selection of volumes, epitomizing Victorian book production.

Barham's fame rests on this one work, but he did also write a novel which is of interest to collectors, principally (I imagine) because it came out as a three-decker. Details below.

THE INGOLDSBY LEGENDS.   Richard Bentley 1840 (first series, 1000 copies), 1842 (second series, 1500 copies) & 1847 (third series, 1500 copies). All three vols, in brown cloth, were illustrated by various artists (Cruikshank, Leech, etc.) the first series having 6 plates, the second having 7, and the third having 6. There were specially bound Private Editions of the First and Second

Series (but not the Third) consisting of 12 copies in each case. In volume one, page 236 is blank. In volume 3, page 350 has the misprint 'topot'.

A set of the three volumes, in the original brown cloth, is worth around £300–£400. Each series was reprinted separately, several times, before the first one-volume edition in 1866 (with 72 illustrations). There was an edition in two vols, in 1870, with 25 plates.

SOME ACCOUNT OF MY COUSIN NICHOLAS by Thomas Ingoldsby Esq . . . To which is added 'The Rubber of Life'. Richard Bentley 1841. 3 vols, cloth.

BARNES, William (1801–1886)

Barnes, remembered mainly for his dialect poetry, published a number of works on other subjects – philology, grammars, etc., all of which are very hard to find. Particularly scarce are two early booklets – A CATECHISM OF GOVERNMENT . . . (etc), 21pp. in wrappers, published by Charles Bastable of Shaftesbury in 1833; and a 23pp. booklet A FEW WORDS ON THE ADVANTAGES OF A MORE COMMON ADOPTION OF THE MATHEMATICS . . . (etc) which was published by Whittaker in 1834. These are each worth £500 or so. This is quite a lot more than his later volumes of poetry generally fetch (about £50), but less than his more keenly desired earliest literary work. This is a reflection of their absolute rarity (the demand being comparatively modest). The later poetry volumes, though in great demand, are relatively easy to track down.

ORRA, A LAPLAND TALE. 1822.
Apart from some poems published in his local Dorchester newspaper, this was his earliest literary publication. It is rare and worth in the region of £1000.

POEMS OF RURAL LIFE IN THE DORSET DIALECT. John Russell Smith 1844.
The collected dialect poems came out under the same title, in 1879.

POEMS, PARTLY OF RURAL LIFE (in National English). John Russell Smith 1846. Green cloth, also blue cloth, also brown cloth, with label on spine.

HWOMELY RHYMES a Second Collection of Poems in the Dorset Dialect. John Russell Smith 1859. Purple cloth. Adverts on the endpapers.

POEMS OF RURAL LIFE in Common English. Macmillan 1868. Blue cloth with variants – some with Macmillan's imprint at the foot of the spine, some with Macmillan's medallion at the foot of the spine, and some without either.

All versions are worth about £50.

BECKETT, Samuel (b. 1906)

A number of Beckett's works were first published in French and subsequently translated into English. I am concerned here only with the English language editions.

Though he has written fiction and poetry as well as plays, he is principally a playwright, and as such, one of the very few who have caught the attention of collectors in a big way. Many of his books have been published in smallish limited editions as well as trade editions, and he is consequently one of the more expensive modern authors to collect.

His first published story was called ASSUMPTION and appeared in the journal 'transition' in 1929. This journal, launched in Paris in 1927 and edited by Maria Jolas and Elliot Paul, was an important outlet for experimental writing, and published work by many important modern authors – James Joyce, Gertrude Stein, Dylan Thomas, Lawrence Durrell, etc., as well as Beckett.

After the huge success of WAITING FOR GODOT (the performed play, that is, rather than the publication) Beckett's works were very keenly collected, so that his publications from the mid-fifties on are not scarce. I have therefore curtailed the checklist at that point.

OUR EXAGMINATION ROUND HIS FACTIFICATION FOR INCAMI-NATION OF WORK IN PROGRESS. Paris: Shakespeare & Co. 1929. Wrappers. 300 copies, including 96 on large paper. U.K.: Faber 1936. U.S.: New Directions 1939.
    Beckett was a contributor to this anthology. From copies of the Paris edition which I have seen in recent times, it appears that both the text paper and the wrappers are tending to go brown, so that really fine copies may be extremely hard to come by in future years. Meanwhile, the present 'going rate' is about £300 for the ordinary copies, and twice as much for the 96 on large paper. The U.K. edition, using French sheets and with a somewhat 'normalized' title, is almost as scarce as the Paris edition. Prices vary quite a lot, but generally seem to be around £100.

WHOROSCOPE. Paris: Hours Press 1930. Wrappers. Limited to 300 copies, of which 100 were signed.
    The first book of which he was sole author. It is difficult to find in fine condition. It was stapled and the staples are now, over 60 years later, being

found to have rusted, leaving the booklet inclined to fall apart. So this already scarce and expensive publication is likely to become even scarcer and even more expensive in the future, in well-preserved condition. Prices are currently around £700 for the unsigned copies and over £1000 for the signed ones.

PROUST. Chatto & Windus, Dolphin series 1931. Dolphin-decorated boards and dust wrapper. U.S.: Grove Press 1957. Limited to 250 signed.

MORE PRICKS THAN KICKS. Chatto & Windus 1934. U.S.: Grove Press 1970.

ECHO'S BONES. Paris: Europa Press 1935.

MURPHY. Routledge 1938. U.S.: Grove Press 1957.
His first novel.

WAITING FOR GODOT. New York: Grove Press 1954. U.K.: Faber 1956.

MOLLOY. Paris: Olympia Press 1955. U.S.: Grove Press 1955. U.K.: Calder 1959.

MALONE DIES. New York: Grove Press 1956. U.K.: Calder 1958.

BECKFORD, William (1759–1844)

His classic work VATHEK was originally published anonymously under the title AN ARABIAN TALE (q.v.). Beckford had written the work in French and had intended the French language edition to be published first. However, it was translated into English by the Rev. Samuel Henley who, against the author's express wishes, went ahead with the London edition. This stung Beckford into action and he had the French language edition published as quickly as possible, in Lausanne, in 1787. After revising the manuscript, he had it published in Paris, later the same year.

It is not generally appreciated that Beckford published many other works, most (if not all) of which are rarer than VATHEK. Some are extremely rare – for example, DREAMS, WAKING THOUGHTS AND INCIDENTS (1783) which was suppressed, and EPITAPHS (1823). Only a few copies of each are known.

In a letter of 1832 to the bookseller George Clarke, Beckford maintained that he had not been idle and that certain anonymous publications would be the proof of this, if 'the world discovers the key'. Since then, a number of anonymous works have been attributed to Beckford, but these have not all been universally accepted. Others may still await discovery.

Beckford was a great collector, and books from his vast library can often be recognised by the binding ornaments which were based on elements of the Beckford coat of arms. The library was dispersed in 1882–83 (Hamilton Palace sales). Many volumes were bought by Lord Rosebury, and these found their way back onto the market when the Rosebury collection was sold in 1931.

AN ARABIAN TALE, from an unpublished manuscript; with Notes Critical and Explanatory. J. Johnson 1786. 8vo.

The second edition of 1809 is considered to be rarer than the first.

French Language Edition: A Lausanne, chez Isaac Hognau & Compe 1787.

Revised (French Language): A Paris, chez Poincot. The rarest copies have an advert leaf at the end.

BEERBOHM, Max (1872–1956)

The writers and artists of the 1890s are still in vogue and Beerbohm, though he survived well into the twentieth century, is very much a product of the period. His witty caricatures and elegant prose have great appeal to modern collectors. It seems unlikely though, that any of them will be able to get hold of a copy of his first appearance in print. This was CARMEN BECCERIEUSE, a satiric piece in Latin, privately printed while he was a pupil at Charterhouse. There is a copy in the library at Charterhouse, but no others are known. Beerbohm's bibliographers, Gallatin and Oliver doubted it's existence, but it was reprinted in THE CARTHUSIAN, April 1912, in pink wrappers. Even this is all but impossible to find nowadays.

Other early works appeared in the Strand Magazine (1892), the English Illustrated Magazine (1894) and The Yellow Book (first issue in April 1894), and none of these is difficult to obtain. After Zuleika Dobson, 1911, his most sought after and valuable books are the 4to volumes of drawings published by Heinemann. The rest, with a few exceptions, are easy to obtain and inexpensive, and are omitted from the checklist.

THE WORKS OF MAX BEERBOHM. New York: Scribner's 1896. Brown cloth, decorated and lettered in gilt and white. 1000 copies printed. U.K.: John Lane 1896 (4 days later). Red (vermilion) cloth.
A bold title for a first book. The New York edition evidently did not sell

well, because 401 copies were pulped in 1901. It is now valued at about £200 – roughly twice that of the U.K. edition.

CARICATURES OF TWENTY-FIVE GENTLEMEN.   Leonard Smithers 1896. Limited to 500 copies. Purple cloth gilt. Title-page vignette by Aubrey Beardsley. The earliest copies had the publisher's name on the spine as simply 'Leonard Smithers'. On later copies '& Co.' was added.
   The book fetches about the same as Beerbohm's first, namely £200. The binding issue point makes only a small difference.

THE HAPPY HYPOCRITE.   Springfield, Massachusetts: Wayside Press. London: John Lane 1897. Decorated green wrappers, bearing the legend 'Bodley Booklet No. 1.'
   Though dated 1897 on the title-page, the Colophon gives the publication date as 'December 1896'. At all events, it was issued first in America.

MORE.   John Lane 1899.

THE POETS' CORNER.   Heinemann 1904. Folio. Pictorial boards (or 'stiffened wrappers'). 20 lithographic plates.
   Unlike the later King Penguin edition, the first edition is uncommon and commands a price of about £150.

A BOOK OF CARICATURES.   Methuen 1907. Red cloth.

YET AGAIN.   Chapman & Hall 1909.

THE SECOND CHILDHOOD OF JOHN BULL.   Stephen Swift 1911. Blue cloth spine and grey boards.
   Regarded as his least successful book of drawings.

ZULEIKA DOBSON.   Heinemann 1911. Smooth brown cloth, d/w. Of 4000 copies issued, 1390 were done in a rougher reddish-brown cloth for the libraries. U.S.: John Lane 1912. Buff cloth with a design in brown and gold.
   His most famous work, and his only completed novel. The d/w is scarce. Even without it, the book sells for about £100.

FIFTY CARICATURES.   Heinemann 1913. 4to. U.S.: Dutton 1913.

SEVEN MEN.   Heinemann 1919. Blue cloth, blue d/w.
   There were 5000 copies of this. It is frequently seen without the dust wrapper, and with the cloth looking very dull and worn. Fine copies in genuinely fine dust wrappers are quite scarce.

A SURVEY.   Heinemann 1921. 4to.

ROSSETTI AND HIS CIRCLE.   Heinemann 1922. 4to.

THINGS OLD AND NEW. Heinemann 1923. 4to.

OBSERVATIONS. Heinemann 1925. 4to.

THE DREADFUL DRAGON OF HAY HILL. Heinemann 1928. Cloth spine, boards, d/w.
An attractive volume in very fine condition, it seems particularly prone to foxing. Even the dust wrapper, if present at all, is quite often foxed.

THE HEROES AND HEROINES OF BITTER SWEET. Leadley 1931. 900 copies.

BENNETT, E. Arnold (1867–1931)

Most of Bennett's vast output is not currently popular with collectors and consequently not expensive. Even some of the limited signed editions are very moderately priced. His most popular and expensive book is the novel THE OLD WIVES' TALE, which has achieved the status of a modern classic. The U.K. First Edition, in the dust wrapper, has a value of around £500. And indeed, it is the novels, especially those in the Clayhanger series and those set in the 'Five Towns' (i.e. the Potteries district in Staffordshire) which hold most interest for collectors. The real enthusiast will want to search out his first stories to appear in print, which were in the magazine 'Tit-Bits' during 1890 and in the Yellow Book in 1895. But not many will have the enthusiasm to bother with issues of the journal 'Woman' of which he became assistant editor in 1893, and later editor.

The following checklist gives his earliest and most sought after works. Of his many minor works, a few are worth mentioning in so far as the publishers Hodder & Stoughton republished them under different titles. Thus MENTAL EFFICIENCY (1912) was a revised and expanded version of THE REASONABLE LIFE. FRIENDSHIP AND HAPPINESS (1914) was a new edition of THE FEAST OF ST FRIEND. And both MARRIAGE (1916) and MARRIED LIFE (1921) were new editions of THE PLAIN MAN AND HIS WIFE.

JOURNALISM FOR WOMEN by 'E. A. Bennett'. John Lane 1896. Pictorial blue cloth. The first issue has an 1897 Catalogue at the end.
His first book. Rare, but usually priced at only £50 or thereabouts.

A MAN FROM THE NORTH. John Lane 1898. There are variant bindings, but the earliest is red cloth stamped in white.
His first novel. Scarce, and valued at several hundred pounds.

POLITE FARCES FROM THE DRAWING ROOM. Lamley & Co. 1900. Pinkish red cloth. 4pp adverts at the end dated October 1898.

FAME AND FICTION.   Grant Richards 1901.

ANNA OF THE FIVE TOWNS.   Chatto & Windus 1902. Pictorial cloth, d/w.
A very important first edition and rare in fine condition. Copies in less than fine condition can occasionally be had for a little under £100, but a really fine copy would be worth a lot more. A fine copy in a fine dust wrapper would be quite something!

THE GRAND BABYLON HOTEL.   Chatto & Windus 1902.

HOW TO BECOME AN AUTHOR.   Pearson 1903.

THE TRUTH ABOUT AN AUTHOR.   (Anon). Constable 1903. The first issue binding is red cloth with a green cloth spine.

BURIED ALIVE.   Chapman & Hall 1908.

THE OLD WIVES' TALE.   Chapman & Hall 1908. Decorated lavender cloth. U.S.: Doran 1911.
His masterpiece and a modern classic. In 1927 Benn put out a facsimile of the manuscript, in an edition of 500 copies, all signed by the author. This was printed on Jap. vellum and bound in quarter parchment gilt, with black cloth sides, and was sold in a slipcase.

WHAT THE PUBLIC WANTS.   First issued in wrappers as a Supplement to The English Review, July 1909. Published later in the same year by Duckworth.

CLAYHANGER.   Methuen 1910.
The first volume in the celebrated Clayhanger series. The others were Hilda Lessways, These Twain and The Roll Call. The latter was omitted from Methuen's composite volume of 1925, The Clayhanger Family, of which there was a trade edition and a signed edition of 200 copies.

HILDA LESSWAYS.   Methuen 1911.

THESE TWAIN.   Methuen 1916.

THE ROLL CALL.   Hutchinson 1918.

THE MATADOR OF THE FIVE TOWNS.   Methuen 1912.

RICEYMAN STEPS.   Cassell 1923.

THE BRIGHT ISLAND.   Golden Cockerel Press 1924. Limited to 200 signed.

IMPERIAL PALACE. Cassell 1930. Also a special issue of 100 signed copies on hand-made paper in 2 volumes, bound in full yellow vellum and a slipcase.

VENUS RISING FROM THE SEA illustrated by E. McKnight Kauffer. Cassell 1931. Edition of 350 copies, signed by the artist.
   In 1932 Cassell published a trade edition combining two works – DREAM OF DESTINY & VENUS RISING FROM THE SEA.

BETJEMAN, John (1906–1984)

Betjeman's publishing career, in the fields of poetry and architecture, began at the start of the 1930s. An early poem appeared in the London Mercury in 1930, and his early writings on architecture appeared in the Architectural Review, to which he began contributing in 1931. None of his principal works are particularly rare, although demand clearly outstrips the supply where the early volumes are concerned. The pseudonymous privately printed SIR JOHN PIERS is perhaps the most difficult to obtain.

MOUNT ZION. James Press 1931. Blue and gold patterned boards, and d/w. Also issued in striped boards.
   The patterned binding is preferred to the striped binding, though both are hard to come by.

GHASTLY GOOD TASTE. Chapman & Hall 1933. Cloth spine, pink boards. Gatefold at end. In the second issue, pp. 119–120 are on a cancel leaf.

CORNWALL Illustrated in a series of views. Architectural Press 1934.

DEVON. Architectural Press 1936.

CONTINUAL DEW. Murray 1937. Decorated black boards.

AN OXFORD UNIVERSITY CHEST. Miles (1938). Cloth spine, marbled boards.

SIR JOHN PIERS. By 'Epsilon' (pseud.). Ireland: Mullingar 1938. Privately Printed. 150 copies. Wrappers.

A HANDBOOK ON PAINT. By Betjeman & Casson. Silicate Paint Co. J. B. Orr & Co. Ltd. 1939. Sm.8vo.

ANTIQUARIAN PREJUDICE. Hogarth Press 1939. Wrappers.

OLD LIGHTS FOR NEW CHANCELS. Murray 1940. Sm.8vo. Blue boards, paper label.

VINTAGE LONDON. Collins 1942. Slim 4to.

ENGLISH CITIES AND SMALL TOWNS. Collins 1943. Britain in Pictures series. Slim 4to. Boards & d/w.

JOHN PIPER. Penguin 1944. Modern Painters series. Sm.8vo. Wrappers.

NEW BATS IN OLD BELFRIES. Murray 1945. Sm. 8vo. Red cloth, paper label.

SLICK, BUT NOT STREAMLINED. New York: Doubleday 1947. 1,750 copies. Black cloth.

MURRAY'S BUCKINGHAMSHIRE ARCHITECTURAL GUIDE. By Betjeman & Piper. Murray 1948. Slim 4to.

SELECTED POEMS. Murray 1948. Red boards, paper label. Also 18 specials.

MURRAY'S BERKSHIRE ARCHITECTURAL GUIDE. Murray 1949. Slim 4to.

MURRAY'S SHROPSHIRE ARCHITECTURAL GUIDE. Murray 1951. Slim 4to.

FIRST AND LAST LOVES. Murray 1952. White boards.

A FEW LATE CHRYSANTHEMUMS. Murray 1954. Blue cloth, paper label.

POEMS IN THE PORCH. SPCK 1954. Pamphlet. Wrappers.

THE ENGLISH TOWN IN THE LAST HUNDRED YEARS. Cambridge University Press, 1956.

COLLINS GUIDE TO ENGLISH PARISH CHURCHES. Collins 1958.

COLLECTED POEMS. Murray 1958. White boards, d/w.

SUMMONED BY BELLS. Murray 1960. Green boards, d/w. U.S.: Houghton Mifflin 1960.

GROUND PLAN TO SKYLINE. By Richard M. Farren (pseud.). 1960.

A RING OF BELLS. Murray 1963. U.S.: Houghton Mifflin 1963.

ENGLISH CHURCHES. By Betjeman & Clarke. Studio Vista 1964.

THE CITY OF LONDON CHURCHES.   Pitkin 1965.

HIGH AND LOW.   Murray 1966. U.S.: Houghton Mifflin 1967.

SIX BETJEMAN SONGS.   Duckworth 1967.

VICTORIAN AND EDWARDIAN LONDON FROM OLD PHOTOGRAPHS.   Batsford 1969.

VICTORIAN AND EDWARDIAN OXFORD FROM OLD PHOTOGRAPHS.   By Betjeman & Vaisey. Batsford 1971.

A WEMBLEY LAD, AND THE CREM.   Poem of the Month Club 1971. Broadsheet, signed.

LONDON'S HISTORIC RAILWAY STATIONS.   Murray 1972.

A PICTORIAL HISTORY OF ENGLISH ARCHITECTURE.   Murray 1972. U.S.: Macmillan 1972.

VICTORIAN AND EDWARDIAN BRIGHTON FROM OLD PHOTOGRAPHS.   By Betjeman & Gray. Batsford 1972.

WEST COUNTRY CHURCHES.   Society of SS. Peter & Paul 1973. 19pp pamphlet.

VICTORIAN AND EDWARDIAN CORNWALL.   By Betjeman & Rowse. Batsford 1974.

A NIP IN THE AIR.   Murray 1974.

ARCHIE AND THE STRICT BAPTISTS.   Murray 1977. U.S.: Lippincott 1978.

THE BEST OF BETJEMAN.   Murray 1978.

CHURCH POEMS.   Murray 1981.

UNCOLLECTED POEMS   Murray 1982.

AH MIDDLESEX.   Warren 1984. Wrappers. 250 copies.

BLOOMFIELD, Robert (1766–1823)

His first work, The Farmer's Boy, was immensely successful. 26,000 copies were sold within three years of first publication.

THE FARMER'S BOY; a rural poem.   Bensley for Vernor and Hood 1800. 4to. 8 woodcut head- and tail-pieces by Nesbit and Anderson. Also issued in 8vo.

RURAL TALES, BALLADS AND SONGS.   (Printed by T. Bensley) for Vernor & Hood; and Longman and Rees 1802. Sm. 4to. Oval mezzotint portrait. 11 woodcuts after Thurston (by Charlton Nesbit, not Bewick). Issued in 8vo, later that year.

GOOD TIDINGS; or News from the Farm.   From the Parnassian Press . . . by James Swan 1804. 4to.

WILD FLOWERS; or pastoral and local poetry.   For Vernor, Hood, Sharpe; and Longmans 1806. Sm. 8vo. 8 wood-engraved cuts by Bewick. Second Issue has 'Angria' on p.81.

THE BANKS OF THE WYE. A Poem.   For the Author 1811. Sm. 8vo. Engraved frontispiece & 3 plates.

MAY DAY WITH THE MUSES.   for the Author, & Baldwin, Cradock & Joy 1822.

HAZELWOOD-HALL: A Village Drama.   for Baldwin 1823. 12mo.

THE REMAINS.   Thomas Davison for the Exclusive Benefit of the Family of Mr. Bloomfield 1824. 2 vols.

THE HORKEY.   A Ballad. Illustrated by George Cruikshank (the younger). Macmillan 1882. 4to. Cloth spine, pictorial boards.

BOLDREWOOD, Rolf (1826–1915) (pseudonym of T. A. Browne)

Boldrewood is celebrated as the author of one of the key books of Australian literature:

ROBBERY UNDER ARMS.   A Story of Life and Adventure in the Bush and in the Goldfields of Australia. Remington and Co. 1888. 3 vols. Green cloth. The earliest bindings have the author's name mis-spelt 'Bolderwood' on the spines.

BORROW, George Henry (1803–1881)

As a young man, Borrow was articled to a solicitor, and his first published work was as editor of CELEBRATED TRIALS, AND REMARKABLE CASES OF CRIMINAL JURISPRUDENCE published in 6 vols in 1825. Later, he travelled extensively in Europe, using his experiences to write books which are difficult to categorize, in that they combine autobiography and travel, fact and fiction.

Two of his early works of translation were privately printed in Russia and, as might be expected, these are extremely rare. They are TARGUM and THE TALISMAN, both published in Leningrad in 1835, and both limited to 100 copies. Earlier translations were FAUSTUS, published by Simpkin and Marshall in 1825 (various bindings); and ROMANTIC BALLADS ... AND MISCELLANEOUS PIECES. Norwich: S. Wilkin 1826. Boards. This work, with the Norwich imprint, is rare and worth in the region of £300–£400. There is a Second State with a cancel title-page bearing the London imprint of John Taylor, and a Third State bearing the imprint of Wightman and Cramp – both dated 1826.

His principal original works were:

THE BIBLE IN SPAIN. Murray 1843. 3 vols. Dark blue-green cloth, paper labels on spines. 1,000 copies printed.

THE ZINCALI: or, an Account of the Gypsies of Spain. Murray 1841. 2 vols. Dark blue cloth, paper labels on spines. 750 copies printed.

LAVENGRO; The Scholar-The Gypsy-The Priest. John Murray 1851. 3 vols. Dark greenish-blue cloth with paper labels. Collie & Fraser list 9 variants. 3,000 copies were printed (250 were eventually sold to Mudie, and about 500 to Smith & Son in 1868). The sixth edition, published in March 1900 is the definitive edition.

THE ROMANY RYE. Murray 1857. 2 vols. Dark blue-green cloth, paper labels on spines. 1000 copies printed.

WILD WALES. Murray 1862. 3 vols. Blue cloth, white paper labels on spines (variant brown labels). 1000 copies printed.

ROMANO LAVO-LIL ... English Gypsy Language. Murray 1874. Dark blue cloth, blind rules and paper label on spine. 16pp. adverts at end, dated June 1873. Some copies have 32pp adverts. Collie & Fraser note a binding variant which lacks the blind stamping on the spine and carries adverts for Home and Colonial Library, dated September 1880. 1000 copies were printed, of which 435 sets of sheets were used for a 'New Edition' in 1880, bound in red cloth.

BOSWELL, James (1740–1795)

Boswell published numerous anonymous pamphlets and verses, from 1760 on. I give below the first work to appear under his name, followed by his three most celebrated publications.

LETTERS BETWEEN THE HONOURABLE ANDREW ERSKINE, AND JAMES BOSWELL, ESQ. Printed by Samuel Chandler; for W. Flexney . . . 1763.

AN ACCOUNT OF CORSICA . . . Glasgow: Printed by Robert and Andrew Foulis for Edward and Charles Dilly . . . 1768. Folding map – in its earliest state, with no imprint; in the second state, it has the imprint; and in later states it has a scale of miles.

THE JOURNAL OF A TOUR OF THE HEBRIDES. Printed by Henry Baldwin, for Charles Dilly 1765.

THE LIFE OF SAMUEL JOHNSON, LL.D. Printed by Henry Baldwin, for Charles Dilly . . . 1791. 2 vols. 4to. Portrait frontispiece and 2 engraved plates in volume II. The earliest issue has the misprint 'gve' on p. 135 of Volume I. The Second Edition was Revised and Augmented, and was published in 3 volumes, in 1793.

BRONTË, Anne (1820–1849), Charlotte (1816–1855), Emily Jane (1818–1848)

The Brontës' works were originally published under pseudonyms – Currer, Ellis and Acton Bell (Charlotte, Emily and Anne, respectively. Note that the initials correspond.) The pseudonyms were retained through many editions, even when the identity of the authors was widely known.

POEMS by Currer, Ellis and Acton Bell. Aylott and Jones 1846. 1000 copies. Dark green cloth. Second binding: Lighter green cloth stamped in blind with a harp. Second Issue: Smith Elder & Co. 1846. Cancel title-page.
According to a letter written by Charlotte, only two copies were sold in the first twelve months. The sisters then gave a few copies away as presents. In all, 39 copies had been disposed of, one way or another, when 961 unsold copies were purchased in November 1848 by Smith, Elder & Co. and issued under their name with a cancel title-page, still dated 1846.

Those first 39 copies (i.e. those with the Aylott and Jones title page) constitute the first issue. Even within that very small number, there are binding variants. In September 1846, the binding was changed from a dark green to a lighter green cloth stamped in blind with a harp.

The second issue consists of the 961 with a Smith, Elder cancel title-page. Some of these are in the light green cloth with the blind-stamped harp (presumably purchased with the sheets from Aylott and Jones). A 4-line errata slip was inserted.

Both issues are rare. The first issue is worth a small fortune in any binding. (The copy in the British Library is not in the original binding.) The second issue gets about £500.

JANE EYRE, an autobiography. Edited by Currer Bell. Smith, Elder 1847. 3 vols. Blind-stamped purple cloth. All copies were issued with advertisements, but a few had a fly-title for the publisher's catalogue inserted in the first volume, and an advert for The Calcutta Review. The first issue has a 36pp catalogue at the end of volume one, dated June and October. Second Edition: Smith, Elder 1847. Gives Currer Bell as author, rather than editor. U.S.: Boston: Wilkins, Carter 1848.
   The first edition is rare in any binding. In the original, it is perhaps worth £8000–£10,000. Decently rebound, it would get something like £2000.

SHIRLEY By Currer Bell. Smith, Elder 1849. 3 vols. Purple cloth.

VILLETTE By Currer Bell. Smith, Elder of London, and Smith, Taylor, of Bombay 1853. 3 vols. Dark green cloth, also brown cloth.

THE PROFESSOR By Currer Bell. Smith, Elder 1857. 2 vols. 12mo. Purple cloth. Remaindered as one volume in green cloth.

WUTHERING HEIGHTS By Ellis Bell. Newby 1847. 3 vols. Purple cloth, also in half-cloth boards, with labels. The third volume contains Anne Bronte's novel AGNES GREY.
   WUTHERING HEIGHTS is one of the most charismatic novels in literature. It is rare, more so than JANE EYRE, and a really nice copy might be valued at £20,000 and possibly a lot more than that. The second edition of 1850 is important, in that it includes a biographical notice by Charlotte and new poems by Emily and Anne.

THE TENANT OF WILDFELL HALL By Acton Bell. Newby 1848. 3 vols. Purple cloth.
   The second edition of the same year has a preface by the author.

BROOKE, Rupert (1887–1915)

Brooke is still one of the most popular of the English poets, and the most conspicuous in the fashionable genre of war poetry. His first two publications, the privately printed poems he submitted to Rugby School poetry competitions, are extremely rare. So is the 'Appius and Virginia' piece. But his few volumes of real substance appear on the market quite frequently, and are not overly expensive. However, they are uncommon in really fine condition and (where applicable) with dust wrappers.

THE PYRAMIDS (1904).   pp.16. Pamphlet, printed on rectos only. No author's name on title-page.
This poem was entered in the poetry competition at Rugby School. It was not a prize winner, but his mother had about 20 copies printed.

THE BASTILLE (1905).   8pp. booklet in grey wrappers. Printed by A. J. Lawrence. The poet's name is not given, but 'R.C.B.' is printed on the back wrapper. There was a reprint in 1920, privately printed by George E. Over, with the author's name on the title-page, but not the date.
This poem won the poetry competition at Rugby School.

POEMS.   Sidgwick & Jackson 1911. Dark blue cloth with a paper label on the spine. Issued without a dust wrapper until the 13th impression. There were 500 copies of the first impression.

THE AUTHORSHIP OF THE LATER 'APPIUS AND VIRGINIA'.
Privately Printed (1913). 20 copies.

1914 AND OTHER POEMS.   Sidgwick & Jackson 1915. Dark blue cloth, d/w. 1,000 copies were issued.
The d/w is rarely seen. The volume includes 'The Soldier' which first appeared in the periodical New Numbers, same year.

LITHUANIA.   Chicago Little Theatre 1915. Wrappers. U.K.: Sidgwick 1935. Yellow cloth, d/w, and also in yellow boards.

1914: SONNETS I-V.   Sidgwick 1915. Pamphlet.

THE OLD VICARAGE GRANCHESTER.   Sidgwick 1916. Pamphlet.

LETTERS FROM AMERICA.   Sidgwick 1916.

JOHN WEBSTER AND THE ELIZABETHAN DRAMA.   Sidgwick 1916.

SELECTED POEMS.   Sidgwick 1917.

THE COLLECTED POEMS.   Sidgwick 1918. Limited Edition: Riccardi Press 1919. 13 copies on vellum & 1000 on Riccardi paper.

FRAGMENTS NOW FIRST COLLECTED. Hartford, U.S.A. 1925. Limited to 94 copies. There were 5 copies on vellum.

A LETTER TO THE EDITOR OF THE POETRY REVIEW. Watch Hill Press 1929. Limited to 50 copies.

TWENTY POEMS. Sidgwick 1935. Wrappers.

DEMOCRACY AND THE ARTS. Hart-Davis 1946 (1947).

THE PROSE. Sidgwick 1955.

THE LETTERS. Faber (1968).

BROWNE, Sir Thomas (1605–1682)

Browne published only a handful of works, some of them posthumously. His most celebrated work is RELIGIO MEDICI and his most ambitious is PSEUDOXIA EPIDEMICA. Three tracts are of some importance – HYDRIOTAPHIA, OR URN BURIAL (1658), its companion piece THE GARDEN OF CYRUS (1658), and the posthumous A LETTER TO A FRIEND (1690).

RELIGIO MEDICI. Andrew Crooke 1642. 190pp. Second Edition: same publisher and date. 159pp. First Authorized Edition (being the first with the complete text): Andrew Crooke 1643.

The two editions of 1642 were both published without Browne's consent. The shorter volume (159pp) was at one time thought to be the first edition, but priority is now given to the longer version (190pp). The 1643 edition is described on the title-page as 'A True and Full Copy'.

PSEUDOXIA EPIDEMICA. printed by T. H. for Edward Dodd 1646. Folio. Otherwise known as 'Vulgar Errors'. The Second Edition of 1650 was Corrected & Much Enlarged. In fact, Browne continued revising the work, the revisions culminating in the final edition before his death, namely the 'Sixth and Last Edition, Corrected and Enlarged' which was Printed by J. R. for Nath. Ekins, 1672.

CERTAIN MISCELLANY TRACTS. printed for Charles Mearne, & sold by Henry Bonwick 1684.

CHRISTIAN MORALS. John Jeffrey . . . Cambridge: University Press 1716. 12mo. The Second Edition, printed by Richard Hett for J. Payne in 1756 includes a Life of Browne by Samuel Johnson.

BROWNING, Elizabeth Barrett (1806–1861)

Mrs Browning was a popular poet in her day, from her fourth publication onwards (1838), and has remained a steady favourite ever since. Most of her first editions, after the first three, are not difficult to obtain and at present are moderately priced (mostly well under £100). Her first publication is extremely rare, but her second and third, perhaps surprisingly, do turn up occasionally, at £200–£300.

She is best known today for her Sonnets from the Portuguese which have appeared in many editions over the years. This famous work however was not one which appeared as an independent volume during her lifetime. The sonnets made their first appearance in print within the collection POEMS in 1850, and in America in 1851 in PROMETHEUS BOUND AND OTHER POEMS.

The First Collected Edition of her POETICAL WORKS is described on the title-page as the 'Seventh Edition'. It was published by Chapman & Hall in 1866, in 5 vols.

THE BATTLE OF MARATHON. (Anon.) Printed for W. Lindsell 1820. 72pp Pamphlet.
This was financed by her father, and there were only 50 copies.

AN ESSAY ON MIND, with Other Poems. (Anon.) James Duncan 1826. 12mo. Blue-grey boards, drab paper spine with paper label.
This, too, was paid for by her father. A facsimile edition of the work, along with Miscellaneous Poems, was issued anonymously, without publisher or date, in about 1880.

PROMETHEUS BOUND ... AND MISCELLANEOUS POEMS. (Anon.) Printed and Published by A. J. Valpy 1833. Blue cloth with a paper label on the spine.

THE SERAPHIM AND OTHER POEMS. By Elizabeth B. Barrett. Saunders & Otley 1838. Claret boards. Also known in brown cloth.

POEMS. Edward Moxon 1844. 2 vols. No half-titles. Green cloth. There are various states of the text, often found mixed.

A DRAMA OF EXILE AND OTHER POEMS. New York: Henry G. Langley 1845. 2 vols. Small 8vo. Embossed slate (blue-green) cloth.

SONNETS. By E.B.B. Reading: [not for publication] 1847. Small 8vo.
This was thought to be the first printing of the famous Sonnets from the Portuguese, but proved to be a forgery (by T. J. Wise).

THE RUNAWAY SLAVE AT PILGRIM'S POINT. Edward Moxon 1849. 26pp. in buff wrappers reproducing the title-page.
  A Wise forgery.

POEMS. Chapman & Hall 1850. Second Edition, Enlarged. Includes the first printing of Sonnets from the Portuguese.

CASA GUIDI WINDOWS. Chapman & Hall 1851. Blue cloth (primary binding).

PROMETHEUS BOUND AND OTHER POEMS. New York: C. S. Francis 1851. 12mo. Brown cloth.
  Contains the first American printings of Casa Guidi Windows & Sonnets from the Portuguese.

TWO POEMS by Elizabeth Barrett and Robert Browning. Chapman & Hall 1854. 15pp. Wrappers.
  A Wise forgery.

AURORA LEIGH. Chapman & Hall 1857. U.S.: C. S. Francis 1857.

POEMS BEFORE CONGRESS. Chapman & Hall 1860.

NAPOLEON IN ITALY AND OTHER POEMS. New York: C. S. Francis 1860. Embossed cloth.
  The U.S. edition of POEMS BEFORE CONGRESS.

LAST POEMS. Chapman & Hall 1862.

BROWNING, Robert (1812–1889)

Browning achieved a degree of acclaim and popularity during his lifetime, but was never as consistently popular as his wife, nor as commercially successful as Tennyson. Today, his fame rests mainly on the single poem THE PIED PIPER. His work is not widely read, and his first editions have been rather neglected by collectors for quite a long time, although the rarest works are still getting good prices. Most of them (from BELLS AND POMEGRANATES onwards) are easy to obtain and are not expensive, mostly being available for less than £50. His second, third and fourth books are quite scarce, and fetch sums up to £500. His first, PAULINE, is very rare. Jerome Kern's copy made $16,000 as long ago as 1929.

PAULINE: A FRAGMENT OF A CONFESSION. (Anon.) Saunders and Otley 1833. Drab boards, label on spine. No half-title.

PARACELSUS. Effingham Wilson 1835. 12mo. Drab boards, label on spine.

STAFFORD. Printed for Longman, Rees, Orme, Brown, Green, and Longman 1837. Drab wrappers with paper label on front. No half title.

SORDELLO. Edward Moxon 1840. Drab boards, label on spine. Also issued (later) in green cloth.

BELLS AND POMEGRANATES. Edward Moxon. Issued in 8 parts numbered on the title-pages i to viii. The first part (Pippa Passes) dated 1841, the second and third 1842, the fourth and fifth 1843, the sixth 1844, the seventh 1845, and the eighth 1846.

CHRISTMAS-EVE AND EASTER-DAY. Chapman & Hall 1850. Green cloth. Earliest issue has publisher's adverts dated August, 1849.

TWO POEMS. By Elizabeth Barrett and Robert Browning. Chapman & Hall 1854. Wrappers.
  A Wise forgery.

CLEON. Edward Moxon 1855. Small 8vo. 23pp Mauve wrappers.
  A Wise forgery.

THE STATUE AND THE BUST. Edward Moxon 1855. Small 8vo. 21pp. Red wrappers.
  A Wise forgery. Issued again (in 1888) without wrappers.

MEN AND WOMEN. Chapman & Hall 1855. 2 vols. Green cloth. No half-titles.

GOLD HAIR: A LEGEND OF PORNIC. 1864. 15pp. Pink wrappers. Sm. 8vo.
  A Wise forgery. There was a revised edition of which the first issue contained 27 stanzas, the second issue 30.

DRAMATIS PERSONAE. Chapman & Hall 1864. Pink cloth.

THE RING AND THE BOOK. Smith, Elder 1868–1869. 4 vols. Green cloth. No half-titles. Vols 1 and 2 are dated 1868, vols 3 and 4 are dated 1869. First issue binding: vols 1 and 2 are numbered on the spine '1' and '2' (i.e. with Arabic numerals) whereas vols 3 and 4 are numbered on the spine 'III' and 'IV' (i.e. with Roman numerals). Later issue binding: spines all have Roman numerals.

HELEN'S TOWER. April 26, 1870. 4pp. Leaflet. The text (a 14 line poem) is on the front, beneath the title and above the author's name. The remaining 3pp. are blank.

BALAUSTION'S ADVENTURE. Smith, Elder 1871. No half-title. Brown cloth.

PRINCE HOHENSTIEL-SCHWANGAU. Smith, Elder 1871. No half-title. Blue cloth.

FIFINE AT THE FAIR. Smith, Elder 1872. Brown cloth.

RED COTTON NIGHT-CAP COUNTRY. Smith, Elder 1873. No half-title. Green cloth.

THE INN ALBUM. Smith, Elder 1875. Green cloth.

LAS SAISIAZ: THE TWO POETS OF CROISIC. Smith, Elder 1878. Green cloth & variants.

PACCHIAROTTO AND HOW HE WORKED IN DISTEMPER: WITH OTHER POEMS. Smith, Elder 1876. Buff cloth.

DRAMATIC IDYLS. Smith, Elder 1879. Later binding has 'First Series' on spine. DRAMATIC IDYLS Second Series. Smith, Elder 1880.

JOCOSERIA. Smith, Elder 1883. Red cloth.

FERISHTAH'S FANCIES. Smith, Elder 1884. Green cloth. Some copies have 8pp adverts.

PARLEYINGS WITH CERTAIN PEOPLE OF IMPORTANCE IN THE THEIR DAY. Smith, Elder 1887. Brown cloth.

ASOLANDO: FANCIES AND FACTS. Smith, Elder 1890 (1889). Red bevelled cloth.

BUCHAN, John (1875–1940)

Buchan's earliest works are all now getting over £100. There does not appear to be any one especially rare and expensive book, unless it be THESE FOR REMEMBRANCE, which is sometimes valued at three or four hundred pounds. The one most in demand, of course, is THE THIRTY NINE STEPS. But this is neither his rarest nor his most expensive. As will be seen from the checklist below, Buchan produced a very large number of books, and THE THIRTY NINE STEPS appears quite a long way down the list. The earliest titles will usually be the hardest to get.

SIR QUIXOTE OF THE MOORS. Fisher Unwin 1895. The full title on the spine is sometimes given as an indication of the first issue. However, there were various bindings, and the priority is uncertain.

SCHOLAR GIPSIES. John Lane 1896.

SIR WALTER RALEIGH. Oxford: Blackwell 1897. Cloth.
The same title was used for a very different book (stories for children) published by Nelson in 1911.

THE PILGRIM FATHERS. Oxford: Blackwell 1898.

A HISTORY OF BRASENOSE COLLEGE. Robinson 1898.

JOHN BURNET OF BARNS. John Lane 1898.

GREY WEATHER. John Lane 1899.

A LOST LADY OF OLD YEARS. Lane 1899.

THE HALF-HEARTED. Isbister 1900. Green pictorial covers. Later issues have plain covers.

THE WATCHER BY THE THRESHOLD. Blackwood 1902.

THE AFRICAN COLONY. Blackwood 1903.

THE LAW RELATING TO TAXATION OF FOREIGN INCOME. Stevens 1905.

A LODGE IN THE WILDERNESS. Blackwood 1906.

SOME EIGHTEENTH CENTURY BYWAYS. Blackwood 1908.

NINE BRASENOSE WORTHIES. Clarendon 1909.

PRESTER JOHN. Nelson 1910.

THE MOON ENDURETH. Blackwood 1912.

WHAT THE HOME RULE BILL MEANS. Smyth 1912.

THE MARQUIS OF MONTROSE. Nelson 1913.

ANDREW JAMESON, LORD ARDWALL. Blackwood 1913.

THE THIRTY-NINE STEPS. Blackwood 1915.

BRITAINS WAR BY LAND. O.U.P. 1915.

SALUTE TO ADVENTURERS. Nelson (1915).

THE ACHIEVEMENT OF FRANCE. Methuen 1915.

NELSON'S HISTORY OF THE WAR. Nelson 1915–1919. 24 vols.

ORDEAL BY MARRIAGE. Clay 1915.

THE POWER HOUSE. Blackwood 1916.

GREENMANTLE. Hodder & Stoughton 1916.

THE FUTURE OF THE WAR. Boyle, Sons & Watchurst 1916.

THE PURPOSE OF THE WAR. Dent 1916.

THE BATTLE OF JUTLAND. Nelson 1916. Pamphlet.

THE BATTLE OF THE SOMME, FIRST PHASE. Nelson 1916.
SECOND PHASE. Nelson 1917.

POEMS, SCOTS AND ENGLISH. Jack 1917. Also, an Edition-de-Luxe.

MR STANDFAST. Hodder & Stoughton 1918.

THESE FOR REMEMBRANCE. Privately Printed 1919.

THE ISLAND OF SHEEP. By 'Cadmus' and 'Harmonia' (pseud. John &
Susan Buchan). Fictional political symposium. Hodder & Stoughton 1919. The
novel of the same name: Hodder & Stoughton 1936.

THE BATTLE HONOURS OF SCOTLAND. Outram 1919.

THE HISTORY OF THE SOUTH AFRICAN FORCES IN FRANCE.
Nelson 1920.

FRANCIS AND RIVERSDALE GRENFELL. Nelson 1920.

THE PATH OF THE KING. Hodder & Stoughton (1921).

A HISTORY OF THE GREAT WAR. Nelson 1921–22. 4 vols. A condensed version of the earlier NELSON'S HISTORY . . .

HUNTINGTOWER. Hodder & Stoughton 1922.

A BOOK OF ESCAPES AND HURRIED JOURNEYS. Nelson 1922.

MIDWINTER. Hodder & Stoughton (1923).

THE LAST SECRETS. Nelson 1923.

DAYS TO REMEMBER. By Buchan & Newbolt. Nelson 1923.

LORD MINTO. Nelson 1924.

SOME NOTES ON SIR WALTER SCOTT. English Association Pamphlet. O.U.P. 1924.

THE THREE HOSTAGES. Hodder & Stoughton (1924).

JOHN MACNAB. Hodder & Stoughton (1925).

THE HISTORY OF THE ROYAL SCOTS FUSILIERS, 1678–1918. Nelson 1925.

TWO ORDEALS OF DEMOCRACY. New York: Houghton Mifflin 1925.

THE MAN AND THE BOOK: SIR WALTER SCOTT. Nelson 1925.

HOMILIES AND RECREATIONS. Nelson 1926. Also, Limited Edition of 200.

THE FIFTEENTH (SCOTTISH) DIVISION. By Buchan & Stewart. Blackwood 1926.

THE DANCING FLOOR. Hodder & Stoughton (1926).

WITCH WOOD. Hodder & Stoughton 1927.

THE RUNAGATES CLUB. Hodder & Stoughton 1928.

MONTROSE. Nelson 1928.

THE COURTS OF THE MORNING. Hodder & Stoughton 1929.

THE CAUSAL AND THE CASUAL IN HISTORY. C.U.P. 1929.

THE KIRK IN SCOTLAND 1560–1929. By Buchan & George Adam Smith. Hodder & Stoughton 1930.

LORD ROSEBERY. British Academy, Milford 1930.

CASTLE GAY. Hodder & Stoughton 1930.

MONTROSE AND LEADERSHIP. O.U.P. 1930.

THE BLANKET OF THE DARK. Hodder & Stoughton 1931.

THE NOVEL AND THE FAIRY TALE. English Association Pamphlet 1931. Wrappers.

SIR WALTER SCOTT. Cassell 1932.

JULIUS CAESAR. Davies 1932.

THE GAP IN THE CURTAIN. Hodder & Stoughton 1932.

THE MAGIC WALKING STICK. Hodder & Stoughton 1932.

A PRINCE OF THE CAPTIVITY. Hodder & Stoughton 1933.

ANDREW LANG AND THE BORDER. O.U.P. 1933.

THE MASSACRE AT GLENCOE. Davies 1933.

THE MARGINS OF LIFE. Birbeck College 1933.

GORDON AT KHARTOUM. Davies 1934.

OLIVER CROMWELL. Hodder & Stoughton 1934.

THE FREE FISHERS. Hodder & Stoughton 1934.

THE HOUSE OF THE FOUR WINDS. Hodder & Stoughton 1935.

THE KING'S GRACE. Hodder & Stoughton 1935. Also, 500 signed. Also, School Edition.

MEN AND DEEDS. Davies 1935.

THE ISLAND OF SHEEP. Novel. Hodder & Stoughton 1936.
  For fictional political symposium with same title, see above, 1919.

AUGUSTUS. Hodder & Stoughton 1937.

NAVAL EPISODES OF THE GREAT WAR. Nelson 1938.

THE INTERPRETER'S HOUSE. Hodder & Stoughton 1938.

UNCHANGING GERMANY. Nelson 1939.

MEMORY HOLD THE DOOR. Hodder & Stoughton 1940.

COMMENTS AND CHARACTERS. Nelson 1940.

CANADIAN OCCASIONS. Hodder & Stoughton 1940.

SICK HEART RIVER. Hodder & Stoughton 1941.

THE LONG TRAVERSE. Hodder & Stoughton 1941.

BUNYAN, John (1628–1688)

Bunyan was arrested late in 1660 for preaching without a licence and spent most of the next twelve years in Bedford gaol. He was released in 1672, but imprisoned again for a short time in 1676. During the first long period of imprisonment, he wrote a number of works, including some of THE PILGRIM'S PROGRESS. This was probably continued after his release, and during his second, briefer spell in prison. The first part of the work was subsequently published in 1678. And the whole thing, being the first and second part together, was first published in 1684.

The typically elaborate title page of the first part, a mixture of capitals and lower case with long s's, reads as follows:

THE PILGRIM'S PROGRESS From This World, To That which is to come: Delivered under the Similitude of a Dream Wherein is Discovered, The manner of his letting out, His Dangerous Journey; And safe Arrival at the Desired Countrey . . . By John Bunyan. Licensed and Entred according to Order. LONDON. Printed for Nath. Ponder at the Peacock in the Poultry near Cornhil, 1678.

BURKE, Edmund (1729–1797)

A PHILOSOPHICAL ENQUIRY INTO THE ORIGIN OF OUR IDEAS OF THE SUBLIME AND BEAUTIFUL. Printed for R. and J. Dodsley . . . 1757. Anonymous. It is thought that about 500 copies were printed. 'Introduction on Taste' was added in 1759.

BURNETT, Frances Hodgson (1849–1924)

THAT LASS O'LOWRIES. New York: Scribner, Armstrong 1877. In its earliest state, the illustrator's name (Arthur Fredericks) appears on the title-page. The third printing has 'All Rights Reserved' on the title-page, and the adverts at the end incorporate reviews of the book. U.K.: Warne 1877.
Her first book.

LITTLE LORD FAUNTLEROY. New York: Charles Scribner's Sons 1886. The first issue has the imprint of the De Vinne Press at the end. The book has a frontispiece, a vignette title and 24 illustrations by Reginald B. Birch. U.K.: Warne 1886.
Her most famous book, now worth about $200.

THE SECRET GARDEN New York: Stokes 1911. U.K.: Heinemann (1911). Illus. Charles Robinson.

BURNEY, Fanny (Frances, Mme. D'Arblay 1752–1840)

Fanny Burney became a celebrity when her authorship of the anonymous EVELINA was revealed. This novel and the two which followed, were and still are highly regarded, but the much later WANDERER is considered to be of lesser quality. Her diaries and letters, which came out under her married name of Madame D'Arblay, and for which she is perhaps best known, came out in 1842–1846. The EARLY DIARY was not published until 1889.

The three early novels are not common and are not cheap (£300 plus, rebound). Even the more common WANDERER is usually priced at something in the region of £200, rebound. In original state, they are all very much more. Even early reprints of the first three novels fetch respectable prices of £100 or thereabouts.

EVELINA, or a Young Lady's Entrance into the World. In a Series of Letters. (anonymous) T. Lowndes 1778. 3 vols. 12mo. Second Edition: Lowndes 1779. 3 vols.

CECILIA, or Memoirs of an Heiress. By the author of Evelina. T. Payne and Son, and T. Cadell 1782. 5 vols. Sm. 8vo. Second Edition: T. Payne & Son 1783. 5 vols.

BRIEF REFLECTIONS relative to the Emigrant French Clergy: earnestly submitted to the Humane Consideration of the Ladies of Great Britain. T. Davison for T. Cadell 1793. 8vo.

CAMILLA; or, A Picture of Youth. By the Author of Evelina and Cecilia. Payne, Cadell & Davies 1796. 5 vols. 12mo. Dublin Edition: William Porter 1796. 3 vols.

THE WANDERER; or Female Difficulties. Printed for Longman, Hurst, etc. 1814. 5 vols. Large 12mo. Roan-backed boards. Her last novel.

BURNEY, Sarah Harriet (c. 1770–1844)

Sara was the half-sister of Fanny Burney. Not now as important a writer as Fanny, she was a popular society novelist in her day. Her first book was:

CLARENTINE. Printed for G. G. & J. Robinson 1796. 3 vols. Large 12mo. Errata-leaves at the end of each volume.
Not reprinted until 1816. The first edition, in a contemporary binding, is worth about £200. There was an American edition in 1818.

BURNS, Robert (1759–96)

Burns's first book, POEMS, CHIEFLY IN THE SCOTTISH DIALECT, is a major collector's item, but is not excessively rare. The first edition has a current value of a few thousand pounds. The second and subsequent editions are important in so far as additional material was incorporated. The Edinburgh Edition, for example (being the second edition), contains almost twice as many poems as the first edition, adding 27 poems to the original 36. The rarest Burns item is THE PRAYER OF HOLY WILLIE, published in 1789. Only one copy is known.

POEMS, CHIEFLY IN THE SCOTTISH DIALECT. Kilmarnock: Printed by John Wilson 1786. 240pp including 5pp Glossary. Blue wrappers, also in blue boards.
Slightly more than 600 copies were printed. Only a handful have survived in the original wrappers, one of which was acquired by the trustees of the Burns Cottage at Alloway in 1908, for £1,000.

Second Edition: Edinburgh 1787. First Issue has 'Boxburgh' in the list of subscribers – later 'Roxburgh'.
One of the most celebrated 'points' in bibliography occurs in the Address To A Haggis, on p.263. In one version, the word 'skinking' occurs, and in another the word is 'stinking'. This variation is regularly referred to as an 'issue point', but strictly speaking, because the type was entirely reset between the versions, the variation signifies two distinct editions. However, traditionally, the 'stinking' version has been favoured by collectors as the earliest (and

most expensive) 'issue'. Currently though, the 'skinking' version appears to be preferred. The word 'skinking' by the way, means 'thin'.

Other Editions: Belfast, Dublin, and London editions were all issued in 1787.

BURROUGHS, William S. (b. 1914)

There has been a very strong revival of interest in Burroughs during the last decade, but he originally caught the interest of collectors very early in his career, so that the majority of his books have been faithfully preserved and are not particularly rare. The checklist below includes all his major publications, but a number of broadsides have been omitted.

JUNKIE. By William Lee (pseud.) New York: Ace Books (1953). Wrappers. Bound with NARCOTIC AGENT by Maurice Helbrand.
An Ace Doublebook.

LETTER FROM A MASTER ADDICT TO DANGEROUS DRUGS. (Privately Published c. 1957). Stapled sheets – an offprint from THE BRITISH JOURNAL OF ADDICTION, VOL 53, No. 2, January 1957.

THE NAKED LUNCH. Paris: Olympia Press (1959). Wrappers & d/w. Later copies have the price on the back wrapper changed by rubber stamp. Revised Edition: New York: Grove Press (1962). Cloth, d/w. U.K.: Calder 1964. Cloth, d/w.
In the U.S.A. and the U.K. the title was simply NAKED LUNCH.

THE EXTERMINATOR. By Burroughs & Gysin. (San Francisco): Auerhahn Press 1960. Wrappers.

MINUTES TO GO. By Burroughs, Gysin, Corso & Beiles. (Paris): Two Cities (1960). Wrappers. Also, 5 numbered copies, signed by Burroughs & Gysin. U.S.: San Francisco: Beach Books 1968.

THE SOFT MACHINE. Paris: Olympia Press (1961). Wrappers & d/w. A new, revised, augmented edition was issued by the same publisher in 1963. New York: Grove Press (1966). Cloth, d/w. U.K.: Calder 1968.

THE TICKET THAT EXPLODED. Paris: Olympia Press (1962). Wrappers & d/w. New York: Grove Press 1967. Cloth, d/w. U.K.: Calder 1968.

DEAD FINGERS TALK. Paris: Olympia Press (1963). Wrappers. U.K.: Calder 1964. Cloth, d/w.

THE YAGE LETTERS. By Burroughs & Ginsberg. (San Francisco): City Lights (1963). Wrappers.

TAKIS. (New York: Iolas Gallery 1963). Wrappers.

ROOSEVELT AFTER INAUGURATION BY 'WILLIE LEE' ALIAS WILLIAM S. BURROUGHS. (New York: Fuck You Press 1964). Wrappers.

NOVA EXPRESS. New York: Grove Press (1964). Cloth, d/w U.K. Cape 1966.

TIME. New York: C Press 1965. There were 14 bound copies issued with a page of manuscript and an original drawing by Brion Gysin, and 986 copies in wrappers, of which 100 were signed by Burroughs and Gysin.

VALENTINE DAY'S READING. New York: East End Theatre 1965. Wrappers.

APO–33 BULLETIN: A METABOLIC REGULATOR. (San Francisco: Mary Beach 1967). Wrappers.

SO WHO OWNS DEATH TV. By Burroughs, Pelieu & Weissner. (San Francisco): Beach Books (1967). Wrappers (black or white).

THE DEAD STAR. San Francisco: Nova Broadcast Press 1969. Wrappers.

THE JOB: INTERVIEWS WITH WILLIAM BURROUGHS. Cape (1969). U.S.: Grove Press (1970).
   An edition in French was published by Belfond of Paris in 1969, in wrappers.

ACADEMY SERIES. Brighton, England: Urgency Press Rip Off (c. 1969). Wrappers. 650 copies.

THE THIRD MIND. New York: Grove Press (1970).

THE LAST WORDS OF DUTCH SHULTZ. Cape Golliard Press 1970. Also 100 signed copies. U.S.: Viking 1975.

THE WILD BOYS: A BOOK OF THE DEAD. New York: Grove Press (1971). U.K.: Calder 1972.

ELECTRONIC REVOLUTION 1970–71. (London: Henri Chopin 1971). Wrappers. 500 copies, of which 100 boxed were signed by the author and included two silkscreens signed by the illustrator, Brion Gysin.

ALF'S SMILE. (Brighton, England): Unicorn Books 1971. 'edition of 99 numbered and signed copies of which numbers 1 to 90 are for sale and numbers 1 to 99 are hors commerce' (sic).

EXTERMINATOR!. New York: Viking (1974). U.K.: Calder 1974.

WHITE SUBWAY. Aloes Books (1974). Wrappers. 975 copies. Also 25 signed copies. perfect-bound.

THE BOOK OF BREATHING. Ingatestone, England: Henri Chopin (1974). 50 bound copies, signed; also 350 numbered copies in wrappers; also an unlimited issue in wrappers.

PORTFOLIO 1. (Silkscreens by Burroughs, Cozette de Charmoy, and Henri Chopin). Ruby Editions 1974. Loose sheets in portfolio. 100 copies signed by the artists.

PORT OF SAINTS. London / Ollon, Switzerland: Covent Garden Press / Am Here Books 1973 (1975). Of 200 copies, 100 boxed were signed by the author. U.S.: Blue Wind Press 1980.

SNACK... By Burroughs and Mottram. London: Aloes Books (1975). Wrappers.

SHORT NOVELS. Calder 1978.

BLADE RUNNER; A MOVIE. Blue Wind Press 1979.
  Not 'a movie', but a novel.

AH POOK IS HERE AND OTHER TEXTS. Calder 1982.

CITIES OF THE RED NIGHT. New York: Holt Rinehart 1981. U.K.: Calder 1981.

BURTON, Robert (1577–1640)

The first edition of Burton's classic is scarce and commands high prices in fine condition. A copy recently in the stock of Quaritch was priced at £38,000 – but this was for an exceptionally fine copy with a distinguished provenance. An average copy would be priced very much lower. There were many reprints in the 17th Century and these can fairly easily be obtained for no more than a few hundred pounds.

THE ANATOMY OF MELANCHOLY, what it is. With all the Kindes, Causes, Symptomes, Prognostickes, and severall Cures of it... By Democritus Junior... At Oxford, printed by John Lichfield and James Short, for Henry Cripps, Anno Dom. 1621. Sm. 4to. Second Edition: same printers and publisher 1624. Folio.

BUTLER, Samuel (1613–1680)

This Samuel Butler, not to be confused with the Victorian novelist of the same name, wrote a number of works, mainly satirical, but is remembered nowadays only for the enormously popular HUDIBRAS. There were numerous early reprints, and new editions have continued to appear right up to modern times, though the work is little read nowadays.

HUDIBRAS. First published in three parts. Part I was issued in 1663, with the imprimatur dated November 11, 1662, and with an Errata list at the foot of the last page. Part II came out in 1664, with the imprimatur dated November 5th, 1663. And Part III was published in 1678, with a separate leaf of errata at the end.

BUTLER, Samuel (1835–1902)

The later of the two Samuel Butlers wrote many works which nowadays have little or no appeal to the collector, nor indeed any to the general reader. His best known and most important works were the two novels EREWHON and THE WAY OF ALL FLESH. These are still read and still highly regarded. He also published two travel books which attract the keen interest of collectors. Those four works are listed below.

A FIRST YEAR IN CANTERBURY SETTLEMENT. Longman 1863. Folding map.
Usually priced nowadays in the region of £200.

EREWHON OR OVER THE RANGE. (anonymous). Trubner & Co. 1872. Brown cloth.

ALPS AND SANCTUARIES OF PIEDMONT AND THE CANTON TICINO. David Bogue 1882 (1881). 4to. Brown cloth.

THE WAY OF ALL FLESH. Grant Richards 1903. Red cloth. T.e.g. 12pp. Grant Richards adverts at the end.

BYRON, (George Gordon Noel, Baron Byron 1788–1824)

Byron's first editions are in the main still readily available, and perhaps surprisingly can mostly be had for under £100 apiece. A collector prepared to go up to £300 a book could buy practically everything. However, the first FUGITIVE PIECES is very rare, and the next three or four books are not too easy. Some of the pamphlets published during the author's lifetime are rare and valuable. The availability of so many of his works no doubt stems from his lifetime popularity and the consequent printing of his books, especially the later ones, in quite large numbers. There were, for example, 8000 copies of MAZEPPA, and 6000 of THE PRISONER OF CHILLON.

FUGITIVE PIECES. A 66pp. booklet in greenish grey wrappers, undated (but 1806).

POEMS ON VARIOUS OCCASIONS. Newark: Printed by S. & J. Ridge 1807. Boards with a paper label saying 'Poems'.

HOURS OF IDLENESS. Newark: Printed and Sold by S. & J. Ridge. Sold also by ... Crosby ... Longman ... Rivington ... Mawman 1807. Boards. First issue: page 22, line 2 reads 'Those tissues of fancy ...'. In the second issue, the line reads 'Those tissues of falsehood ...' and the leaf is a cancel.

ENGLISH BARDS, AND SCOTCH REVIEWERS. Printed for James Cawthorn. n.d. (1809). (The paper is watermarked 1805). The second issue contains a Preface, not in the first issue. A Second Edition (Revised and augmented) was printed in 1809 (paper watermarked 1808). In this, on line 1007, page 80, 'Aberdeen' is misprinted 'Abedeen'.

IMITATIONS AND TRANSLATIONS ... Together with Original Poems never before published. Collected by J. C. Hobhouse. Printed for Longman etc. 1809. Boards.
   Contains nine new poems.

CHILDE HAROLD'S PILGRIMAGE. Printed for ... Murray ... Blackwood ... Cumming ... By Thomas Davison 1812. Boards. First issue: the poem on page 189 is headed 'Written beneath a Picture of J-V-D'. In the second issue, 'of J-V-D'; is omitted (cancel leaf).

CHILDE HAROLD'S PILGRIMAGE. CANTO THE THIRD. Printed for John Murray 1816. Plain wrappers.

CHILDE HAROLD'S PILGRIMAGE. CANTO THE FOURTH. Murray 1818. Paper-covered boards. First issue: page 155 ends with 'the impressions of': page 156 begins with the word 'despotism'; 157 begins with 'a fine of 8000 lira'; page 158 begins with 'penned in 1321'; 159 with 'triotic employment'.

THE CURSE OF MINERVA. Printed by T. Davison 1812. 25pp. in wrappers.

WALTZ: AN APOSTROPHIC HYMN. By Horace Hornem (pseud.). Sherwood, Neely and Jones 1813. 27pp. Wrappers.

THE GIAOUR, a Fragment of a Turkish Tale. Murray 1813. 41pp. Wrappers.

THE BRIDE OF ABYDOS. Murray 1813. 72pp. Wrappers. First issue: page 47 has 20 lines. Second issue: page 47 has 22 lines.

THE CORSAIR. Murray 1814. Wrappers. First issue ends at page 100; the second issue at page 108.

ODE TO NAPOLEON BUONAPARTE. Murray 1814. Pamphlet. pp.14.

LARA (and) JACQUELINE. Murray 1814. Boards.

HEBREW MELODIES. Murray 1815. 53pp. Wrappers. First issue: has a notice of Roger's 'Jacqueline' (verso of sig.E4) – omitted from the second issue.

THE SIEGE OF CORINTH (and) PARISINA. Murray 1816. 91pp. Wrappers.

THE PRISONER OF CHILLON. Murray 1816. 60pp. Wrappers. First issue: recto of sig.E8 (i.e. last leaf) is blank, and verso carries adverts. In the second issue, the adverts appear on the recto.

POEMS. Murray 1816. 38pp. Boards. First issue: has Notes on page 39. In the second issue, the Notes are moved to page 40, and page 39 is occupied by a poem 'To Samuel Rogers'.

MANFRED. Murray 1817. 80pp. Plain wrappers. First issue: verso title-page has printer's imprint in 2 lines. Second issue: verso title-page has printer's imprint in one line. Third issue: has a quotation from Hamlet on the title-page.

BEPPO Murray 1818. 49pp. Wrappers.

MAZEPPA. Murray 1819. 71pp. Unlettered wrappers. First issue: imprint on page 70. Second issue: imprint on verso of page 71 (advert leaf).

DON JUAN. London: Printed by Thomas Davison 1821. 4to. Boards.
Subsequent Cantos were all published in 8vo.

DON JUAN, CANTOS III, IV AND V. Printed by Thomas Davison 1821. Boards.

DON JUAN, CANTOS VI, VII AND VIII. Printed for John Hunt 1823. Boards.

DON JUAN. CANTOS IX, X AND XI.   Printed for John Hunt 1823. Boards.

DON JUAN, CANTOS XII, XIII AND XIV.   Printed for John Hunt 1823. Boards.

DON JUAN. CANTOS XV AND XVI.   Printed for John and H. L. Hunt 1824. Boards.

MARINO FALIERI (and) THE PROPHECY OF DANTE.   Murray 1821. Boards. First issue: on page 151, the speech of the Doge begins 'What Crimes?'. Second issue: the same speech begins 'His Crimes!' and is longer.

SARDANAPALUS (and) THE TWO FOSCARI (and) CAIN.   Murray 1821. Boards.

LETTER TO **** ******.   Murray 1821. 55pp. Wrappers. 8pp. adverts dated March, 1821. The second issue has 4 leaves inserted before the adverts, on paper water-marked '1819'.
    The asterisks represent the publisher John Murray.

THE ISLAND.   Printed for John Hunt 1823. 94pp. Unlettered wrappers. The paper is watermarked '1822'.

THE AGE OF BRONZE.   Printed for John Hunt 1823. 36pp. Unlettered wrappers.
    About a thousand copies were printed – considerably fewer than many of Byron's other works.

WERNER.   Murray 1823. Unlettered wrappers. Advertisement for 'Werner' on page 188. Second issue: Page 188 has no advert for 'Werner' but has 'The End' followed by the imprint.

THE DEFORMED TRANSFORMED.   Printed for J. and H. L. Hunt 1824. 88pp. Wrappers.

THE PARLIAMENTARY SPEECHES.   Printed for Rodwell and Martin 1824. 44 pp. Wrappers.

CORRESPONDENCE OF LORD BYRON.   n.d. (1824). 168pp. Plain boards.
    The correspondence with Robert Charles Dallas and Byron's mother.

WORKS.   John Murray 1815. 4 vols.

WORKS.   With Letters & Journals & Moore's Life of Byron. Murray 1832/33. 17 vols.

C

CARROLL, Lewis. (pseud. of C. L. Dodgson 1832–1898)

The key book ALICE'S ADVENTURES IN WONDERLAND is a classic collectors' item, the circumstances of its first publication having all the ingredients which make book collecting such a fascinating business. Basically, publication was already under way when the author, unhappy with the printing of the illustrations, caused the edition to be withdrawn. Changes were made, and publication then went ahead. But as is usually the case in such circumstances, all the original copies were not destroyed. Thus a rarity was created right from the outset.

Copies of the suppressed edition occur for sale so infrequently, it is impossible to put a meaningful value on it. The subsequent First Published Edition (i.e. Second Edition) is itself very scarce and fetches prices well in excess of £1000, everything depending, of course, on the condition, which is not usually very good. The same is true of the first American edition. The later THROUGH THE LOOKING GLASS is very much cheaper, generally going for a few hundred pounds – the condition again being crucially important. THE HUNTING OF THE SNARK has in the past been very modestly priced, but in recent times this book has been achieving a high public profile and an enhanced status. It looks certain to increase greatly in value.

Of the many pamphlets, booklets, and 'games' which Carroll published, the WONDERLAND POSTAGE-STAMP-CASE is of particular interest and is extremely rare in its complete form. I have appended a note on this at the end of the checklist.

ALICE'S ADVENTURES IN WONDERLAND. With 42 illustrations by John Tenniel. Macmillan and Co. 1865. 8vo. (7½ × 5ins). Frontispiece. 192pp text. Red cloth, lettered in gold on the spine. Picture of Alice and the Pig on the front, the Cheshire Cat on the back. Some copies (for presentation) were bound in white vellum. 2000 copies were printed. Second Edition (type reset): Macmillan 1866. Same binding as first edition. U.S.: Appleton 1866.
  Some copies of the first edition had already left the binders and been sent out when the book was suppressed and copies recalled. Those returned were given to homes and hospitals. The remaining sheets went to Appleton's in New York, where they were published with a new title page (cancel leaf) dated 1866. The binding was the same as the London issue, but with 'Appleton' at the foot of the spine, instead of 'Macmillan & Co.'.

The third U.K. edition of 1867 is in great demand, the earlier editions being either unobtainable or impossibly expensive for many collectors.

PHANTASMAGORIA AND OTHER POEMS. Macmillan 1869. Blue cloth.

THE SONGS FROM ALICE'S ADVENTURES IN WONDERLAND.
Music by William Boyd. Weekes & Co. Not dated (1870) but the Preface is dated 'London 1870'. 10pp. in white wrappers, the front wrapper serving as title page.

THROUGH THE LOOKING-GLASS, AND WHAT ALICE FOUND THERE. With 50 illustrations by John Tenniel. Macmillan 1872. Red cloth with Red Queen on front and White Queen on back. The first issue has an error on page 21 – the last word of the second line of 'Jabberwocky' being 'wade' instead of 'wabe'. This error is also found in the First American Edition (Boston 1872) but not in subsequent U.K. or American editions.

THE HUNTING OF THE SNARK. With 9 illustrations by Henry Holiday. Macmillan 1876. Issued in cloth of various colours – buff, white, blue, green, red – all illustrated with the Bellman aboard ship (on the front) and a buoy (on the back). Some copies were done in vellum for presentation. U.S.: Osgood 1876.

RHYME? AND REASON? With 65 illustration by Arthur B. Frost & 9 by Henry Holiday. Macmillan 1883. Green cloth with a ghost on the front and the Bellman on the back.

A TANGLED TALE. With 6 illustrations by Arthur B. Frost. Macmillan 1885. Red cloth with a dragon on the front and two knights' heads on the back.

ALICE'S ADVENTURES UNDER GROUND. Being a facsimile . . . with 37 illustrations by the author. London & New York: Macmillan 1886. Red cloth with the title on the front and the Mock Turtle on the back.

THE GAME OF LOGIC. Macmillan 1886. Red Cloth. The book was accompanied by a printed envelope containing a card and 9 counters. Second Edition: Macmillan 1887.

SYLVIE AND BRUNO. With 46 illustrations by Harry Furniss. Macmillan 1889. Red cloth with Sylvie's head on the front and Bruno's on the back. Some copies were done in green cloth with a coloured illustration on the front.

THE NURSERY 'ALICE'. containing 20 coloured enlargements from Tenniel's illustrations . . . text adapted to nursery readers. Macmillan 1889. 4to.

Illustrated yellow boards. Called, on the title page, the 'People's Edition' this is the true First Edition. There was another edition in 1890.

SYLVIE AND BRUNO CONCLUDED. With 46 illustrations by Harry Furniss. Macmillan 1893. Red cloth, with the Professor on the front and the Chancellor on the back. Some copies were done in white cloth, for presentation. In the Contents, Chapter 8 is incorrectly given as starting at page 110.

THREE SUNSETS AND OTHER POEMS. With 12 Fairy fancies by E. Gertrude Thomson. Macmillan 1898. Green cloth.

THE LEWIS CARROLL PICTURE BOOK. T. Fisher Unwin 1899. Red cloth with the title and the Gryphon and the March Hare on the front. Contains some previously unpublished material.

FEEDING THE MIND. Chatto 1907. Grey boards, also in grey wrappers, and also in maroon leather.

THE WONDERLAND POSTAGE-STAMP-CASE. Small, buff coloured, cloth lined, paper case containing four buff coloured 'pages' two of which have pockets for holding stamps. Oxford: Emberlin and Son (1890). Along with a booklet entitled EIGHT OR NINE WISE WORDS ABOUT LETTER WRITING, 1890. The 2 items enclosed in a printed pink envelope. The whole item was done in 1890 despite the envelope bearing the date 1888 and the Case 1889.

CHANDLER, Raymond (1888–1959)

Chandler's first editions are extremely popular at present. The first four are getting prices in excess of $1000, but dust wrappers are essential.

THE BIG SLEEP. New York: Knopf 1939. 'First Edition' on verso title. U.K.: Hamilton (1939).

FAREWELL MY LOVELY. New York: Knopf 1940. U.K.: Hamilton (1940).

THE HIGH WINDOW. New York: Knopf 1942. U.K.: Hamilton (1943).

THE LADY IN THE LAKE. New York: Knopf 1943. 'First Edition' on verso title. U.K.: Hamilton (1944).

FIVE MURDERERS. New York: Avon 1944. Wrappers.

FIVE SINISTER CHARACTERS. New York: Avon 1945. Wrappers.

THE FINGER MAN.   New York: Avon 1946. Wrappers.

THE LITTLE SISTER.   Hamilton (1949). U.S.: Knopf 1949.

TROUBLE IS MY BUSINESS.   Penguin (1950). Wrappers. New York: Houghton Mifflin 1951.

THE SIMPLE ART OF MURDER.   Houghton Mifflin 1950. U.K.: Hamilton (1950).

THE LONG GOODBYE.   Hamilton (1953). U.S.: Houghton Mifflin 'March 1st 1954' on verso title.

PLAYBACK.   New York: Houghton Mifflin 'October 16th 1958' on verso title. U.K.: Hamilton (1958).

RAYMOND CHANDLER SPEAKING.   New York: Houghton Mifflin 1962. U.K.: Hamilton (1962).

KILLER IN THE RAIN.   New York: Houghton Mifflin 1964. U.K.: Hamilton (1964).

THE SMELL OF FEAR.   Hamilton (1965).

THE BLUE DAHLIA.   S. Illinois University Press 1976. U.K.: Elm Trees Press 1976.

CHATTERTON, Thomas (1752–1770)

Felix Farley's Bristol Journey, published in 1768, includes a passage of pseudo-archaic prose which Chatterton (then 16 years old) claimed to have found in a chest in St Mary Redcliffe Church. This was the start of the series of forgeries which culminated in the poems and letters of the 15th Century monk Thomas Rowley. Other Chatterton forgeries appeared in the Town and Country Magazine, during 1769, including 'Elinoure and Juga' (May) – the only piece by 'Thomas Rowley' to be published before Chatterton's suicide. The three important early publications, all posthumous, are:

POEMS, supposed to have been written at Bristol, by Thomas Rowley.   T. Payne & Son 1777. There are two states, the first very rare, the second much less so. The second state has a cancelled and reworded advert leaf (signed C4).
The Third Edition of 1778 was the first to include an Appendix by Thomas Tyrwhitt 'tending to prove, that they were written, not by any Ancient Author, but entirely by Thomas Chatterton'.

MISCELLANIES IN PROSE AND VERSE.   Fielding & Walker 1778.

THE WORKS. Edited by Robert Southey and Joseph Cottle. Biggs & Cottle for Longman 1803. With 7 plates. 3 vols, 8vo.
The first and only complete collection.

CHAUCER, Geoffrey (c.1343–1400).

There is no longer a realistic chance of a collector stumbling upon a Chaucer first edition. But for the record, CANTERBURY TALES was first published by William Caxton in 1478. There were several other editions before 1500, and of course, countless editions have appeared since. Editions of the collected works began to appear in the sixteenth century. The very earliest of these are extremely rare and beyond the pockets of most collectors. Editions from the second half of the sixteenth century, do still appear on the market occasionally, and at this point prices start to become affordable. I give below two editions from this period.

WOORKES.   The 'Stowe Edition'. Jhon Kyngston for Jhon Wright 1561. Folio. Black letter. Some woodcuts.
The earliest Chaucer seen with reasonable frequency on the market. Four figure prices are usual.

WORKES.   Edited by Speght. Printed by Adam Islip, at the charges of Thomas Wight. Anno 1598. Folio.
This, the sixth edition, being the first edited by Speght (with the assistance of John Stowe and others) has much additional material, including a copperplate portrait of Chaucer by John Speed after Hoccleve, a Glossary of 'Old and obscure words explaned' and 'Two Books of his, neuer before Printed'.

CHESTERFIELD, Philip Dormer Stanhope, Fourth Earl of (1694–1773)

Chesterfield's famous letters to his natural son Philip Stanhope were not written for publication but to instruct the boy in the social graces. After the death of Chesterfield (who outlived his son by five years) Stanhope's widow promptly published them. They were well received and soon became the accepted guide to good manners, though Samuel Johnson declared that they taught 'the morals of a whore and the manners of a dancing-master'.

LETTERS WRITTEN TO HIS SON, PHILIP STANHOPE, ESQ;   late Envoy Extraordinary at the Court of Dresden: together with several Other pieces on various Subjects. Published by Mrs. Eugenia Stanhope, from the

Originals now in her Possession . . . Printed for J. Dodsley 1774. 2 vols, large 4to. (frequently described as folio). Frontispiece portrait in volume I.
Not an excessively rare book. In a good contemporary binding it is usually priced somewhere in the range of £300–£500. A second edition was published in the same year, as four 8vo volumes, and in this form it was reprinted many times. An edition was also published in Dublin in 1874, and this too was in four 8vo vols.

SUPPLEMENT TO THE LETTERS. Printed for J. Dodsley 1787, 4to.

MISCELLANEOUS WORKS. Consisting of Letters to his Friends . . . and various other Articles. To which are prefixed, Memoirs of his life, tending to illustrate the Civil, Literary, and Political, History of his Time. Printed for Edward and Charles Dilly 1778. 2 vols. 4to.

CHESTERTON, G. K. (1874–1936)
Though there is some interest in his other works, the greatest interest nowadays is in his Father Brown stories.

GREYBEARDS AT PLAY. R. Brimley Johnson 1900. Small 4to. Linen spine, illustrated boards.
His first book. A volume of poetry.

THE NAPOLEON OF NOTTING HILL. Bodley head 1904. Pictorial cloth.
His first novel.

THE INNOCENCE OF FATHER BROWN. Cassell 1911.

THE WISDOM OF FATHER BROWN. Cassell 1914.

THE INCREDULITY OF FATHER BROWN. Cassell (1926).

THE SECRET OF FATHER BROWN. Cassell (1927).

THE SCANDAL OF FATHER BROWN. Cassell (1935).

CHRISTIE, Agatha (1890–1976)
Most of Christie's works were first published in London, with the American editions following soon afterwards. The exceptions can be seen in the checklist below. After the first book, the American publisher of the crime fiction (as opposed to the plays, verse and pseudonymous works) was

invariably Dodd Mead of New York. After the first half-dozen titles, I have only given the American editions where there seemed a particularly good reason for doing so.

Her first book (U.S. and U.K. editions) is now fetching several hundred pounds without the dust wrapper, and several thousand pounds with it (in decent condition). Agatha Christie is a prime example of an author who did not attract the attention of serious collectors early in her career. The inevitable consequence being that her works, especially the earliest, were not preserved in the finest condition. So copies in fine condition are at a premium, and the dust wrappers are rare. Her post-war works however, have survived in large numbers and are not difficult to obtain.

It should be noted that it was not the normal habit of Collins, who published the majority of her works, to date title-pages. They were, however, generally scrupulous about giving accurate copyright dates (i.e. dates of first publication) on the verso title-page, and in identifying reprints. And the novice-collector (who is frequently uncertain on this point) should note that Collins Crime Club was not a book club in the usual sense.

THE MYSTERIOUS AFFAIR AT STYLES.   New York: Lane 1920. U.K.: Lane 1921.

THE SECRET ADVERSARY.   Lane 1922. U.S.: Dodd Mead 1922.

MURDER ON THE LINKS.   Lane 1923. U.S.: Dodd Mead 1923.

THE MAN IN THE BROWN SUIT.   Lane 1924. U.S.: Dodd Mead 1924.

POIROT INVESTIGATES.   Lane 1924. U.S.: Dodd Mead 1925.

THE SECRET OF CHIMNEYS.   Lane 1925. U.S.: Dodd Mead 1925.

THE ROAD OF DREAMS.   (poetry). Bles 1925.

THE MURDER OF ROGER ACKROYD.   Collins 1926. U.S.: Dodd Mead 1926.

THE BIG FOUR.   Collins 1927. U.S.: Dodd Mead 1927.

THE MYSTERY OF THE BLUE TRAIN.   Collins 1928.

THE SEVEN DIALS MYSTERY.   Collins 1929.

PARTNERS IN CRIME.   Collins 1929.

THE UNDERDOG. Reader's Library 1929. The volume also contains BLACKMAN'S WOOD by E. Phillips Oppenheim.
  A surprising number of fine copies in fine d/ws surfaced in the 1980s.

THE MURDER AT THE VICARAGE. Collins 1930.

THE MYSTERIOUS MR QUINN. Collins 1930.

GIANT'S BREAD. By Mary Westmacott (pseud.). Collins 1930.

THE SITTAFORD MYSTERY. Collins 1931.

THE MURDER AT HAZELMOOR. New York: Dodd Mead 1931.
  The U.S. edition of THE SITTAFORD MYSTERY.

PERIL AT END HOUSE. Collins 1932.

THE THIRTEEN PROBLEMS. Collins 1932.

THE TUESDAY CLUB MURDERS. New York: Dodd Mead 1933.
  The U.S. edition of THE THIRTEEN PROBLEMS.

LORD EDGWARE DIES. Collins 1933.

THIRTEEN AT DINNER. New York: Dodd Mead 1933.
  The U.S. edition of LORD EDGWARE DIES.

THE HOUND OF DEATH AND OTHER STORIES. Odhams 1933.

PARKER PYNE INVESTIGATES. Collins 1934.

MR PARKER PYNE, DETECTIVE. New York: Dodd Mead 1934.
  The U.S. edition of PARKER PYNE INVESTIGATES.

THE LYSTERDALE MYSTERY AND OTHER STORIES. Collins 1934.

BLACK COFFEE. (play). Ashley 1934.

WHY DIDN'T THEY ASK EVANS? Collins 1934.

MURDER ON THE ORIENT EXPRESS. Collins 1934.

MURDER ON THE CALAIS COACH. New York: Dodd Mead 1934.
  The U.S. edition of MURDER ON THE ORIENT EXPRESS.

MURDER IN THREE ACTS. New York: Dodd Mead 1934.

UNFINISHED PORTRAIT. By Mary Westmacott (pseud.). Collins 1934.

BOOMERANG CLUE. New York: Dodd Mead 1935.
  The U.S. edition of WHY DIDN'T THEY ASK EVANS?

THREE ACT TRAGEDY. Collins 1935.
  The U.K. edition of MURDER IN THREE ACTS.

DEATH IN THE CLOUDS. Collins 1935.

DEATH IN THE AIR. New York: Dodd Mead 1935.
  The U.S. edition of DEATH IN THE CLOUDS.

THE A.B.C. MURDERS. Collins 1936.

CARDS ON THE TABLE. Collins 1936.

MURDER IN MESOPOTAMIA. Collins 1936.

MURDER IN THE MEWS AND OTHER STORIES. Collins 1937.

DEAD MAN'S MIRROR AND OTHER STORIES. New York: Dodd
Mead 1937.
  The U.S. edition of MURDER IN THE MEWS AND OTHER
  STORIES.

DEATH ON THE NILE. Collins 1937.

DUMB WITNESS. Collins 1937.

POIROT LOSES A CLIENT. New York: Dodd Mead 1937.
  The U.S. edition of DUMB WITNESS.

APPOINTMENT WITH DEATH. Collins 1938.

THE REGATTA MYSTERY AND OTHER STORIES. New York: Dodd
Mead 1939.

HERCULE POIROT'S CHRISTMAS. Collins 1939.

MURDER FOR CHRISTMAS. New York: Dodd Mead 1939.
  The U.S. edition of HERCULE POIROT'S CHRISTMAS.

MURDER IS EASY. Collins 1939.

EASY TO KILL. New York: Dodd Mead 1939.
  The U.S. edition of MURDER IS EASY.

TEN LITTLE NIGGERS. Collins 1939.

AND THEN THERE WERE NONE. New York: Dodd Mead 1940.
The U.S. Edition of TEN LITTLE NIGGERS.

ONE, TWO, BUCKLE MY SHOE. Collins 1940.

SAD CYPRESS. Collins 1940.

THE PATRIOTIC MURDERS. New York: Dodd Mead 1941.
The U.S. edition of ONE, TWO, BUCKLE MY SHOE.

EVIL UNDER THE SUN. Collins 1941.

N OR M. Collins 1941.

THE BODY IN THE LIBRARY. Collins 1942.

THE MOVING FINGER. New York: Dodd Mead 1942. U.K.: Collins
1943.

FIVE LITTLE PIGS. Collins 1942.

MURDER IN RETROSPECT. New York: Dodd Mead 1942.
The U.S. edition of FIVE LITTLE PIGS.

DEATH COMES AS THE END. New York: Dodd Mead 1942. U.K.:
Collins 1945.

TOWARDS ZERO. Collins 1944.

ABSENT IN THE SPRING. By Mary Westmacott (pseud.). Collins 1944.
New York: Farrar & Rinehart 1944.

TEN LITTLE NIGGERS. (play). French 1944.

SPARKLING CYANIDE. Collins 1945.

REMEMBERED DEATH. New York: Dodd Mead 1945.
The U.S. edition of SPARKLING CYANIDE.

APPOINTMENT WITH DEATH. (play). French 1945.

THE HOLLOW. (novel). Collins 1946.

COME TELL ME HOW YOU LIVE. Collins 1946.

TEN LITTLE INDIANS.   New York: French 1946.
   The U.S. Edition of the play TEN LITTLE NIGGERS.

MURDER ON THE NILE.   (play). French 1946.

THE LABOURS OF HERCULES.   Collins 1947. New York: Dodd Mead
1947 (THE LABORS OF HERCULES).

TAKEN AT THE FLOOD.   Collins 1948.

THERE IS A TIDE . . .   New York: Dodd Mead 1948.
   The U.S. edition of TAKEN AT THE FLOOD.

THE ROSE AND THE YEW TREE.   By Mary Westmacott (pseud.). Heinemann 1948. U.S.: Rinehart 1948.

WITNESS FOR THE PROSECUTION.   New York: Dodd Mead 1948.

CROOKED HOUSE.   Collins 1945.

A MURDER IS ANNOUNCED.   Collins 1950.

THREE BLIND MICE AND OTHER STORIES.   New York: Dodd Mead
1950.

UNDER DOG AND OTHER STORIES.   New York: Dodd Mead 1951.

THEY CAME TO BAGHDAD.   Collins 1951.

THE HOLLOW.   (play). French 1952.

THEY DO IT WITH MIRRORS.   Collins 1952.

MURDER WITH MIRRORS.   New York: Dodd Mead 1952.
   The U.S. edition of THEY DO IT WITH MIRRORS.

MRS MCGINTY'S DEAD.   Collins 1952.

A DAUGHTER'S A DAUGHTER.   By Mary Westmacott (pseud.). Heinemann 1952.

AFTER THE FUNERAL.   Collins 1953.

FUNERALS ARE FATAL.   New York: Dodd Mead 1953.
   The U.S. edition of AFTER THE FUNERAL.

A POCKET FULL OF RYE.   Collins 1953.

WITNESS FOR THE PROSECUTION. (play). French 1954.

DESTINATION UNKNOWN. Collins 1954.

SO MANY STEPS TO DEATH. New York: Dodd Mead 1955.
   The U.S. edition of DESTINATION UNKNOWN.

HICKORY, DICKORY, DOCK. Collins 1955.
   Entitled HICKORY, DICKORY, DEATH in the U.S. (Dodd Mead 1955).

THE MOUSETRAP. (play). French 1956.

DEAD MAN'S FOLLY. Collins 1956.

THE BURDEN. By Mary Westmacott (pseud.). Heinemann 1956.

THE SPIDER'S WEB. (play). French 1957.

TOWARDS ZERO. (play). French 1957. New York: Dramatists Play Service
1957.

4.50 FROM PADDINGTON. Collins 1957.

WHAT MRS MCGILLICUDDY SAW! New York: Dodd Mead 1957.
   The U.S. edition of 4.50 FROM PADDINGTON.

VERDICT. (play). French 1958.

THE UNEXPECTED GUEST. (play). French 1958.

ORDEAL BY INNOCENCE. Collins 1958.

CAT AMONG THE PIGEONS. Collins 1959.

THE ADVENTURE OF THE CHRISTMAS PUDDING. Collins 1960.

GO BACK FOR MURDER. (play). French 1960.

DOUBLE SIN AND OTHER STORIES. New York: Dodd Mead 1961.

13 FOR LUCK. New York: Dodd Mead 1961. U.K.: Collins 1966.

THE PALE HORSE. Collins 1961.

THE MIRROR CRACK'D FROM SIDE TO SIDE. Collins 1962.
   Simply THE MIRROR CRACK'D in New York (Dodd Mead 1963).

RULE OF THREE.   (plays). French 1963.

THE CLOCKS.   Collins 1963.

A CARIBBEAN MYSTERY.   Collins 1964.

STAR OVER BETHLEHEM AND OTHER STORIES.   By A. C. Mallowan. (pseud.). Collins 1965.

SURPRISE! SURPRISE!   New York: Dodd Mead 1965.

13 CLUES FOR MISS MARPLE.   New York: Dodd Mead 1965.

AT BERTRAM'S HOTEL.   Collins 1965.

THIRD GIRL.   Collins 1966.

ENDLESS NIGHT.   Collins 1967.

BY THE PRICKING OF MY THUMBS.   Collins 1968.

PASSENGER TO FRANKFURT.   Collins 1970.

NEMESIS.   Collins 1971.

THE GOLDEN BALL AND OTHER STORIES.   New York: Dodd Mead 1971.

ELEPHANTS CAN REMEMBER.   Collins 1972.

POSTERN OF FATE.   Collins 1973.

AKHMATON.   (play). Collins 1973.

POEMS.   Collins 1973.

HERCULE POIROT'S EARLY CASES.   Collins 1974.

MURDER ON BOARD.   New York: Dodd Mead 1974.

CURTAIN.   Collins 1975.

SLEEPING MURDER.   Collins 1976.

MISS MARPLE'S FINAL CASES AND OTHERS.   Collins 1979.

AUTOBIOGRAPHY.   Collins 1979.

CHURCHILL, Rt. Hon. Sir Winston Leonard Spencer (1874–1965)

Churchill had scores of single speeches published as pamphlets or booklets. Some are exceedingly rare. Only a few are included in the following check-list. The 'F' numbers found on the verso titles of the collections of speeches published by Cassell, were planned as publication date codes (F Month Year) – thus 'F 543' represents May 1943. There are cases, however, as may be observed in the list, where the codes and actual publication dates vary slightly.

THE STORY OF THE MALAKAND FIELD FORCE. Longmans, Green 1898. Apple-green cloth, d/w. The second issue has an Errata slip. There was a Colonial Edition of 2000 in grey-green cloth

THE RIVER WAR. Longmans, Green 1899. 2 vols. Blue cloth with gilt gunboat on front. 2000 copies.
Published in America in the same year, and in a one-vol Revised Edition in 1902.

SAVROLA. New York: Longmans, Green 1900 (February 3rd). Dark blue cloth. 4,000 copies. U.K.: same publisher 1900 (February 13th). Blue-green cloth. 1500 copies. First Illustrated Edition: Newnes (1908). Wrappers.
His only novel. Frederick Woods records a copy of the U.K. Edition with a Cancel title-page (verso blank), possibly made up from Colonial Edition sheets.

LONDON TO LADYSMITH. Longmans, Green 1900. Fawn cloth, black armoured train on front. 10,000 copies printed.

IAN HAMILTON'S MARCH. Longmans, Green 1900. Dark red cloth. 5000 copies printed.

MR WINSTON CHURCHILL ON THE EDUCATION BILL. Reprinted from the Lancashire Post 11 November 1902. Burnley: Express Printing Works. 8pp. Pamphlet speech.
Very rare.

MR BRODRICK'S ARMY. Arthur L. Humphries 1903. 44pp. Wrappers.
A rare volume of speeches – possibly not officially published. The second edition of the same year has 104pp. This also is rare.

FOR FREE TRADE. Arthur L. Humphries 1906. Wrappers.
A facsimile exists.

LORD RANDOLPH CHURCHILL. Macmillan 1906. 2 vols. Plum cloth. 8000 copies.

MY AFRICAN JOURNEY.   Hodder & Stoughton 1908. Pictorial red cloth. 12,500 copies.

LIBERALISM AND THE SOCIAL PROBLEM.   Hodder & Stoughton 1909. Plum buckram.

THE PEOPLE'S RIGHTS.   Hodder & Stoughton (1910). Red cloth, also wrappers. The first issue has an index. For the second issue, this was removed and a second appendix was added.

MY EARLY LIFE.   Thornton Butterworth (1930). On verso title, a list of 11 works by Churchill. For the second issue, a twelfth title was added – The World Crisis.
    Entitled A ROVING COMMISSION in America.

INDIA – SPEECHES.   Thornton Butterworth (1931). Orange cloth, also orange wrappers. Reprint in green wrappers.

THE WORLD CRISIS.   Thornton Butterworth. 6 vols (1923, 1923, 1927, 1927, 1929, 1931).

THOUGHTS AND ADVENTURES.   Thornton Butterworth (1932). Sandy brown cloth.

MARLBOROUGH.   Harrap (1933–38). 4 vols.

GREAT CONTEMPORARIES.   Thornton Butterworth (1937). Dark blue buckram, top edges blue. Revised edition in 1938.

ARMS AND THE COVENANT.   Harrap (1938). Dark blue cloth, top edges blue.
    The same sheets were used for a cheaper edition. In America the book was entitled WHILE ENGLAND SLEPT (1938).

STEP BY STEP 1936–1939.   Thornton Butterworth (1939). Green cloth.

A SPEECH BY THE PRIME MINISTER.   The Right Honourable Winston Churchill in the House of Commons August 20th. 1940. (Ministry of Information) 16pp. Light blue wrappers, maroon lettering.
    The famous (but not rare) speech, known as 'The Few' speech.

INTO BATTLE.   Cassell (1941) 'F 141' on verso title.

THE UNRELENTING STRUGGLE.   Cassell (1942) 'F 642' on verso title..

THE END OF THE BEGINNING.   Cassell (1943) 'F 543' on verso title.

ONWARDS TO VICTORY. Cassell (1944). 'F 544' on verso title.

DAWN OF LIBERATION. Cassell (1945) 'F 345' on verso title.

VICTORY. Cassell (1946) 'F 246' on verso title.

SECRET SESSION SPEECHES. Cassell (1946).

WAR SPEECHES 1940–1945. Cassell (1946). Definitive Edition: Cassell (1952). 3 vols. 'F 151' on verso title.

MAXIMS AND REFLECTIONS. Eyre & Spottiswoode 1947. Previously published miscellanea.

PAINTING AS A PASTIME. Odhams Press/Ernest Benn (1948).

SINEWS OF PEACE. Cassell 1948

THE SECOND WORLD WAR. Cassell. 6 volumes: 1. THE GATHER-ING STORM, 1948. 2. THEIR FINEST HOUR, 1949. 3. THE GRAND ALLIANCE, 1950. 4. THE HINGE OF FATE, 1951. 5. CLOSING THE RING, 1952. 6. TRIUMPH AND TRAGEDY, 1954.
   Vol. 1 of the U.S. Edition (Houghton, Mifflin) came out four months before the U.K. edition. It contains many errors and lacks the folding maps.

EUROPE UNITE. Cassell (1950).

IN THE BALANCE. Cassell (1951) 'F 851' on verso title.

STEMMING THE TIDE. Cassell (1953) 'F 353' on verso-title.

THE WAR SPEECHES. Cassell 1951–52. 3 vols.

A HISTORY OF THE ENGLISH-SPEAKING PEOPLES. Cassell. 4 vols: 1. THE BIRTH OF BRITAIN, 1956. 2. THE NEW WORLD, 1956. 3. THE AGE OF REVOLUTION, 1957. 4. THE GREAT DEMOCRACIES, 1958.

THE AMERICAN CIVIL WAR. Cassell (1961).
   A reprinted extract from A HISTORY OF THE ENGLISH-SPEAKING PEOPLES.

THE UNWRITTEN ALLIANCE. Cassell (1961). 'F 1261' on verso title.

THE ISLAND RACE. Cassell (1964).
   Abridged version of THE HISTORY OF THE ENGLISH-SPEAKING PEOPLES.

CLARE, John (1793–1864)

Clare's few published works are extremely popular nowadays. The first edition of his first book is very scarce and commands prices in excess of £500. His others are not usually more than £200.

POEMS DESCRIPTIVE OF RURAL LIFE AND SCENERY. London: Taylor & Hessey (and) Stamford: E. Drury 1820. 12mo. Boards. There should be 4 leaves of adverts at the end (called for by Hayward) but copies exist with 5 leaves.
 His first book. Second & Third Editions came from the same publishers in the same year.

THE VILLAGE MINSTREL AND OTHER POEMS. London: Taylor & Hessey (and) Stamford: E. Drury 1821. 2 vols. 12mo. Boards.

THE SHEPHERD'S CALENDAR. for John Taylor 1827. 12mo.

THE RURAL MUSE. Whittaker & Co. 1835. Variant bindings.

SKETCHES IN THE LIFE OF JOHN CLARE. written by himself. Now first published. Edited by Blunden. Cobden-Sanderson 1931. Cloth, d/w.

COLERIDGE, Samuel Taylor (1772–1834)

Coleridge's famous poem 'The Rime of the Ancient Mariner' first appeared in the LYRICAL BALLADS (q. v.) which consists of poems by Coleridge and Wordsworth. This is one of the key books in English poetry, and one of the rarest in first edition form. Its current value is around £5000.

He published many works including a lot of pamphlets which are now rare and valuable. The list below contains all his important literary works, but omits the political/moralistic publications – though it is not always easy to distinguish one from the other. Some posthumous publications are also omitted.

THE FALL OF ROBESPIERRE. Cambridge: Printed by Benjamin Flower, For W. H. Lunn, and J. & J. Merrill; and sold by J. March, Norwich 1794, 37pp. Pamphlet.
 This verse drama was written partly by Coleridge (Act I) and partly by Southey (Acts II & III).

POEMS ON VARIOUS SUBJECTS. Printed for G. G. and J. Robinsons, and J. Cottle, Bookseller, Bristol 1796. Boards.

Poems by Charles Lamb and Charles Lloyd were added in the second edition of 1797 (same publishers).

ODE ON THE DEPARTING YEAR.   Bristol; Printed by N. Biggs, and Sold by J. Parsons 1796. 16pp. Pamphlet.

LYRICAL BALLRDS.   Bristol: Printed by Biggs and Cottle for T. N. Longman . . . London 1798. Pink boards. No half-title. Uncancelled leaf at p.97–98. Second Issue: London: Printed for J. & A. Arch . . . 1798. p.97–98 is a cancel leaf. Errata leaf at end.

The authors were Coleridge and Wordsworth. The second edition of 1800 (January 1st 1801) contains new poems in volume 2. There was a third edition in 1802.

FEARS IN SOLITUDE.   Printed for J. Johnson 1798. 23pp. Wrappers.

OMNIANA, OR HORAE OTIOSIORES.   Printed for Longman, Hurst, Rees, Orme, and Brown 1812. 2 vols. Drab boards.

REMORSE.   Printed for W. Pople 1813. Drab wrappers.

CHRISTABEL; KUBLA KHAN, A VISION; THE PAINS OF SLEEP. Printed for John Murray . . . By William Bulmer and Co. 1816. 64pp. Drab wrappers.

BIOGRAPHIA LITERARIA.   Rest Fenner 1817. 2 vols. Grey boards, drab paper spine, paper labels. Also, a large paper edition.

SIBYLLINE LEAVES.   Rest Fenner 1817. Grey boards, paper label on spine.

ZAPOLYA.   Rest Fenner 1817. Green boards with pink paper spine. Not labelled.

THE DEVIL'S WALK.   A Poem by Professor Porson. Edited . . . by H. W. Montagu. London: Marsh & Miller . . . And Constable & Co., Edinburgh. (1830). No half-title. First issue: page numbers 21–22 missing.

The authors were Coleridge & Southey.

SPECIMENS OF THE TABLE TALK OF THE LATE SAMUEL TAYLOR COLERIDGE.   John Murray 1835. 2 vols, each with a frontispiece. Drab boards with paper label.

LETTERS CONVERSATIONS & RECOLLECTIONS.   Edward Moxon 1836. 2 vols. Drab boards.

THE LITERARY REMAINS.   Collected & Edited by Henry Nelson Coleridge. William Pickering. 4 vols, dated 1836, 1836, 1838, and 1839. Blue cloth.

CONFESSIONS OF AN ENQUIRING SPIRIT. William Pickering 1840.
Blue cloth, paper label

COLLINS, Wilkie (1824–1889)

The comparative rarity and value of Collins's books appears uncertain at present. I have seen his first book, the MEMOIRS valued at £1000, but also priced at £220. In 1951, the bibliographer Sadleir judged the rarest novels to be firstly MAN AND WIFE, then QUEEN OF HEARTS, then (joint third) ARMADALE and THE MOONSTONE. Today, his judgement looks pretty sound, although the going rate for ARMADALE does not appear to reflect its relative scarcity. Both the U.K. and (possibly earlier) U.S. editions have been available recently for well under one hundred pounds, while later titles in no better condition, have been well over that. However, the two best known titles – WOMAN IN WHITE and THE MOON-STONE – seem to be settling around a current valuation of about £2000. This no doubt reflects their popularity and importance, as much as their scarcity.

MEMOIRS OF THE LIFE OF WILLIAM COLLINS, R.A. (etc). By his Son. Longmans 1848. 2 vols.

ANTONINA, OR THE FALL OF ROME. Bentley 1850. 3 vols.
His first novel.

RAMBLES BEYOND RAILWAYS: Notes in Cornwall Taken A-Foot. Bentley 1851

MR WRAY'S CASH-BOX. Bentley 1852.

BASIL. Bentley 1852. 3 vols. Half-cloth boards & labels, or bright blue cloth. Revised Edition: Sampson Low 1862.

HIDE AND SEEK. Bentley 1854. 3 vols. Half cloth boards, labels. Also light pinkish-brown cloth.

AFTER DARK. Smith, Elder 1856. 2 vols. Dark green cloth. 16pp catalogue at end of volume 1. Prelims of volume II on whiter paper.

THE DEAD SECRET. Bradbury & Evans 1857. 2 vols. Grey-purple cloth.

THE QUEEN OF HEARTS. Hurst & Blackett 1859. 3 vols. Sage-green cloth. 16pp undated Catalogue at end of vol I.

THE WOMAN IN WHITE. New York: Harper 1860. One vol. Brown

cloth with woman stamped in white on the spine. Second state binding: the woman is stamped in blind. U.K.: Sampson Low 1860. 3 vols. Violet cloth.
The U.K. edition was one month later than the U.S. edition. Sampson, Low issued the first U.K. one-vol edition in 1861.

NO NAME. Sampson Low 1862. 3 vols. Orange-scarlet cloth. U.S.: Harper 1863.
Not a rare book. It was probably over-produced after the great success of THE WOMAN IN WHITE.

MY MISCELLANIES. Sampson Low 1863. 2 vols. Green cloth. 16pp Catalogue at end of each volume, dated November 1863.

ARMADALE. Smith Elder 1866. Illustrated by George H. Thomas. 2 vols. Bright brown cloth, with pictorial gold blocking. U.S.: Harper 1866.

THE MOONSTONE. Tinsley Brothers 1868. 3 vols. Purple cloth. U.S.: Harper 1868 (The First Illustrated Edition).

MAN AND WIFE. F. S. Ellis 1870. 3 vols.

POOR MISS FINCH. Bentley 1872. 3 vols. Chocolate cloth.

THE NEW MAGDALEN. Bentley 1873. 2 vols. Brown cloth.

MISS OR MRS? AND OTHER STORIES. Bentley 1873. Brown cloth.

THE FROZEN DEEP AND OTHER STORIES. Bentley 1874. 2 vols. Blue cloth, bevelled edges. U.S.: Boston: William F. Gill 1875. One vol. Pictorial green cloth. (The First Illustrated Edition).

THE LAW AND THE LADY. Chatto & Windus 1875. 3 vols. Green cloth. 40pp Catalogue dated December 1874 at end of volume I.

THE TWO DESTINIES. Chatto & Windus 1876. 2 vols.

THE HAUNTED HOTEL and MY LADY'S MONEY. Chatto & Windus 1879 (1878). 2 vols.

A ROGUE'S LIFE. Bentley 1879. Scarlet cloth. No. VII in Half Crown Empire Library series.

THE FALLEN LEAVES. Chatto & Windus 1879. 3 vols.

JEZEBEL'S DAUGHTER. Chatto & Windus 1880. 3 vols.

THE BLACK ROBE. Chatto & Windus 1881. 3 vols.

HEART AND SCIENCE.   Chatto & Windus 1883. 3 vols.

I SAY NO.   Chatto & Windus 1884. 3 vols.

THE EVIL GENIUS.   Chatto & Windus 1886. 3 vols.

THE GUILTY RIVER.   Bristol: Arrowsmith's Christmas Annual 1886.
Wrappers.
   Re-issued the next year in the same publisher's Bristol Library.

LITTLE NOVELS.   Chatto & Windus 1887. 3 vols. Blue cloth. 32pp Catalogue dated April 1887 at end.

THE LEGACY OF CAIN.   Chatto & Windus 1889. 3 vols. Ultramarine
cloth. 32pp Catalogue dated October 1888 at end of vol III.

BLIND LOVE.   Chatto & Windus 1890. 3 vols.
   Completed by Walter Besant.

THE LAZY TOUR OF TWO IDLE APPRENTICES.   By Collins & Dickens. Chapman & Hall 1890.

COMBE (or COOMBE), William (1741–1823)

Combe was a prolific writer – a journalist and pamphleteer, as well as a
satirical poet. For much of his adult life, he was a prisoner of the King's
Bench (for debt), and this is probably why his works were published anonymously during his lifetime. His most celebrated works are the three tours of
Dr. Syntax. These however are probably collected more for their illustrations
than for Combe's texts. Dr. Syntax, by the way, is simply a character in the
books, and not a pseudonym. The character inspired other works not written
by Combe (THE TOUR OF DR. SYNTAX THROUGH LONDON and
THE TOUR OF DR. SYNTAX THROUGH PARIS, both first published
in 1820).

THE TOUR OF DR. SYNTAX IN SEARCH OF THE PICTURESQUE:
a poem. R. Ackermann's Repository of Arts 1812. Imperial 8vo. Frontispiece,
illustrated title, and 29 other plates (all hand-coloured) by Rowlandson.
   Reprinted several times with the same illustrations, and in 1838 with new
illustrations by Crowquill (issued in cloth). A miniature edition (16mo) along
with the second and third tours (see below), with all the illustrations by
Rowlandson was published by Ackermann in 1833. Another, undated but
later edition (8vo) of the three vols, with the Rowlandson plates, was
published by Nattali & Bond.

THE SECOND TOUR OF DR SYNTAX IN SEARCH OF CONSOLATION. Ackermann 1820. With 24 coloured plates by Rowlandson.

THE THIRD TOUR OF DR SYNTAX IN SEARCH OF A WIFE. Ackermann 1821. With 24 coloured plates by Rowlandson.

THE HISTORY OF JOHNNY QUAE GENUS. the Little Foundling of the Late Doctor Syntax: a Poem. Ackermann 1822. Royal 8vo. Boards. Frontispiece and 23 other plates (all coloured) by Rowlandson.

COMPTON-BURNETT, Ivy (1884–1969)

Ivy Compton-Burnett financed her first three books herself. She paid Blackwoods to publish her first, and the second and third were issued by the vanity publishers Heath Cranton Limited. Through her will, she financed the De-Luxe edition of her Collected Works (19 vols. 500 copies each) which was issued by Gollancz in 1972. Those first three novels are now hard to find. The rest are not difficult. DOLORES, her first book, attracts a few hundred pounds.

DOLORES. Blackwood 1911.

PASTORS AND MASTERS. Heath Cranton 1925.

BROTHERS AND SISTERS. Heath Cranton 1929.

MEN AND WIVES. Heinemann 1931.

MORE WOMEN THAN MEN. Heinemann 1933.

A HOUSE AND ITS HEAD. Heinemann 1935.

DAUGHTERS AND SONS. Gollancz 1937.

A FAMILY AND ITS FORTUNE. Gollancz 1939.

PARENTS AND CHILDREN. Gollancz 1941.

ELDERS AND BETTERS. Gollancz 1944.

MANSERVANT AND MAIDSERVANT. Gollancz 1947.

TWO WORLDS AND THEIR WAYS. Gollancz 1949.

DARKNESS AND DAY. Gollancz 1951.

THE PRESENT AND THE PAST. Gollancz 1953.

MOTHER AND SON. Gollancz 1955.

A FATHER AND HIS FATE. Gollancz 1957.

A HERITAGE AND ITS HISTORY. Gollancz 1959.

THE MIGHTY AND THEIR FALL. Gollancz 1961.

A GOD AND HIS GIFTS. Gollancz 1963.

THE LAST AND THE FIRST. Gollancz 1971.

CONGREVE, William (1670–1729)

The first book by this celebrated playwright was not a play but a novel of intrigue entitled INCOGNITA. It was first published in 1691 and is a great rarity. Two years later, he published his first comedy, THE OLD BATCHELOUR. This brought him fame and (eventually) fortune. The first edition is scarce, but his subsequent first editions are relatively common. All the same, they mostly fetch the best part of a thousand pounds, and his masterpiece THE WAY OF THE WORLD is usually priced at about £2000. In the fashion of the time, the plays were generally published as quartos in boards or wrappers.

THE OLD BATCHELOUR. a Comedy. Peter Buck 1693.

THE DOUBLE-DEALER. a Comedy. Jacob Tonson 1694. Second issue: GI cancelled.

LOVE FOR LOVE. Jacob Tonson 1695.

THE MOURNING MUSE OF ALEXIS. Jacob Tonson 1695. Folio.

THE MOURNING BRIDE, A Tragedy. Jacob Tonson 1697.

AMENDMENTS OF MR. COLLIER'S FALSE AND IMPERFECT CITATIONS. J. Tonson 1698.

THE WAY OF THE WORLD. Jacob Tonson 1700.

A PINDARIQUE ODE... Jacob Tonson 1706. Folio.

AN IMPOSSIBLE THING.   A Tale. J. Roberts 1720.

POEMS ON SEVERAL OCCASIONS.   Glasgow: R. & A. Foulis 1752. 8vo (in 4's).

THE WORKS. . .   Plays and Poems. Birmingham: Baskerville 1761. 3 vols. Frontispiece & 5 plates. Contains the first issue of SEMELE.

CONNOLLY, Cyril (1903–1974)

The Paris edition of THE ROCK POOL, his first book, currently fetches two or three hundred pounds. The rest of his first editions get a lot less than that, but there is a continuing firm interest in his work.

THE ROCK POOL.   Paris: Obelisk Press 1936. Wrappers. New York: Scribner 1936. London: Hamilton, 1947.

ENEMIES OF PROMISE.   Routledge 1938.

THE UNQUIET GRAVE.   By Palinurus (pseud.). Horizon 1944. Limited to 1000 copies – 500 in wrappers, 500 in boards. Unlimited Edition: Hamish Hamilton of London, and Harper of New York, both in 1945.

PUT OUT THE LIGHT.   (Trans. of Vercors). Macmillan 1944.

SILENCE OF THE SEA.   New York: Macmillan 1944.
   The U.S. edition of PUT OUT THE LIGHT.

THE CONDEMNED PLAYGROUND.   Routledge 1945.

THE MISSING DIPLOMATS.   Queene Anne Press 1952. Wrappers with d/w.

IDEAS AND PLACES.   Weidenfeld 1953.

LES PAVILLONS.   By Connolly & Zerbe. 4to. New York: Macmillan 1962. U.K.: Hamilton 1962.

PREVIOUS CONVICTIONS.   Hamilton 1963.

THE MODERN MOVEMENT.   Deutsch (and) Hamilton 1965.

THE EVENING COLONNADE.   Bruce & Watson 1973.

A ROMANTIC FRIENDSHIP: THE LETTERS ... TO NOEL
BLAKISTON. Constable 1975.

JOURNAL AND MEMOIR. Collins 1983. (The Memoir by David Pryce-
Jones).

CONRAD, Joseph (1857–1924)

Conrad's first editions, even the early ones, are reasonably easy to find, most
of them having been published in quite large numbers. However, the challenge is to find the early books in dust wrappers. Their presence can change
the price from a few hundred pounds to more than a thousand pounds.
Copies with good inscriptions by the author are also scarce.

He is not a particularly fashionable author at the present time, but has long
been a steady favourite, with a good following in each new generation of
collectors. More importantly perhaps, his position as a significant figure in
English Literature seems very secure, and no collector investing good money
in his first editions is likely to find his money wasted.

ALMAYER'S FOLLY. T. Fisher Unwin 1895. Green cloth. 2000 copies
printed.

AN OUTCAST OF THE ISLANDS. T. Fisher Unwin 1896. Green cloth.
3000 copies printed.

THE CHILDREN OF THE SEA. New York: Dodd Mead 1897. Blue-grey
cloth. Probably 1000 copies were printed.
   Published a few days before the U.K. edition, which was entitled THE
   NIGGER OF THE 'NARCISSUS' (q.v.).

THE NIGGER OF THE 'NARCISSUS'. Heinemann 1898. (December
1897). Grey cloth. 16pp. adverts. The second issue has 32pp. adverts. 1500
copies printed.
   The U.K. edition of THE CHILDREN OF THE SEA. A preliminary
   edition of 7 copies only in grey wrappers was 'published' by Heinemann in
   August, 1897 to establish copyright. An inscribed copy of this 'copyright'
   edition was sold in the U.S.A. in 1928 for $4900, but it is unlikely that
   another copy will ever appear on the open market.

TALES OF UNREST. T. Fisher Unwin 1898. Green cloth. The first issue
has uncut edges, some copies having top edges gilt. Later copies have all edges
trimmed. 3000 copies printed.

LORD JIM. Edinburgh & London: Blackwood 1900. Grey-Green cloth.
2893 copies printed.

THE INHERITORS. By Conrad & Ford. New York: McClure, Phillips 1901. Yellow cloth. 32pp adverts at end. U.K.: Heinemann 1901. Yellow cloth. 1500 copies printed. First Issue has black ornament on front, untrimmed edges, and 32pp adverts at end.

YOUTH. A Narrative And Two other stories. Edinburgh & London: Blackwood 1902. Green cloth. 3150 copies printed.

TYPHOON. New York & London: Putnam, The Knickerbocker Press 1902. Green cloth, red letters. Later issues in maroon cloth.
In the U.K., the work was included in TYPHOON AND OTHER STORIES (q.v.). It was issued separately by Heinemann in 1912.

TYPHOON AND OTHER STORIES. Heinemann 1903. Dark slate-coloured cloth. Of 3000 copies printed, half were used for a Colonial Edition.

ROMANCE. By Conrad & Hueffer. Smith, Elder 1903. Blue cloth. 8pp. adverts. 2000 copies printed.

NOSTROMO. London & New York: Harper 1904. Blue cloth. 3000 copies printed, of which 1000 were used for a Colonial Edition.

THE MIRROR OF THE SEA. Methuen n.d. (1906 on verso title). Dark green cloth, gold letters on spine, gilt top, other edges untrimmed. 40pp. publisher's catalogue at end. 1500 copies printed.

THE SECRET AGENT. Methuen n.d. (1907 on verso title). Red cloth. 40pp. publisher's adverts at end, dated September 1907.

A SET OF SIX. Methuen n.d. (1908 on verso title). 40pp. publisher's adverts at end, dated either February 1908 or June 1908. Pale claret cloth, gold lettering on spine and front. Also, dark blue cloth, lettered in gold on the spine and in red on the front. 1500 copies printed. First issue: On the verso half-title, alongside 'The Secret Agent' are the words '(with Ford M. Hueffer)' in lower case. Second Issue: the words 'WITH FORD M. HUEFFER' appear below 'The Secret Agent' and are in capitals.
The issues derive from a straightforward error which was noticed during the printing and put right before many copies of the sheet had been printed. Thus copies of the first issue are very rare indeed.

UNDER WESTERN EYES. Methuen n.d. (1911 on verso title). Red cloth. 32pp. publisher's adverts (on thin paper) at end. 3000 copies printed.

SOME REMINISCENCES. Eveleigh Nash 1912. Blue cloth. 1000 copies printed.

A PERSONAL RECORD. New York: Harper 1912.

The U.S. edition of SOME REMINISCENCES.

TWIXT LAND AND SEA. Dent 1912. Green cloth. 3500 copies printed. First binding: The titles of the tales printed on the front cover (in black) include 'Freya of the Secret Isles'. On the second binding, this becomes 'Freya of the Seven Isles'.

The binding priorities should not be attributed to the book as a whole. The sheets in the second bindings might easily have been printed first. Strictly speaking, there are three versions of the binding. The error was noticed after some copies had been bound and gone out (first binding). At that point, the cases already stamped but still on hand, had the word 'secret' erased and overstamped with the word 'Seven' (second binding). From then on, new cases were stamped correctly (third binding). Eighty years later, the corrected bindings can still be identified by close inspection, if the cloth is still clean and bright. On some copies however, the evidence may have been obliterated by the ravages of time.

CHANCE. Methuen n.d. (1913 or 1914 on verso title). Green cloth. 3000 copies printed. First issue: The words 'First Published in 1913' on verso title. Second issue: 'First Published in 1914' on verso title, which is a cancel leaf. Third issue: 'First Published in 1914' on verso title, which is not a cancel leaf, the entire half-sheet having been reprinted.

The issues arose from a postponement of publication after printing and after some copies had gone out. Only about 50 copies of the first issue went out, and these are naturally rare. Faked first issues may have the date skilfully altered. Copies dated 1913, with 31pp. adverts dated 'July 1913' at the end, should be genuine first issues. Copies dated 1913, with only 8pp. adverts dated 'Autumn 1913' may also be first issues, although the same 8pp. adverts were used for the later issues.

WITHIN THE TIDES. London & Toronto: Dent 1915. Green cloth. 3500 copies printed.

VICTORY. New York: Doubleday 1915 (March). Blue cloth. 10,000 copies printed. U.K.: Methuen n.d. (September 1915. Dated on verso title). Red cloth. 35pp. adverts at end. 8000 copies printed.

In view of the numbers printed, the U.K. edition should be somewhat scarcer than the American, but the numbers being so high, neither is really scarce.

ONE DAY MORE. Beaumont Press (1919). Canvas spine, boards. Limited to 250 copies, plus 24 copies on Japanese vellum.

This was the first published edition, an edition of 25 copies having been privately printed by Clement Shorter in 1917.

THE SHADOW LINE. London & Toronto & Paris: Dent ('March 1917' on verso title). Green cloth. 18pp. publisher's adverts at end. 5000 copies printed.

THE ARROW OF GOLD.   New York: Doubleday 1919. Blue cloth. 15,000 copies printed. U.K.: T. Fisher Unwin (later in 1919. Dated on the verso title). Green cloth. 20,000 copies. The first issue has a dropped 'A' on p.67.
   The U.K. Edition has corrections to the text which were not made in the American edition.

THE RESCUE.   New York: Doubleday 1920. Blue cloth. 25,000 copies printed. U.K.: Dent 1920. Limp red cloth. 40 copies printed and distributed privately. First U.K. Published Edition: Dent 1920. Green cloth. 23,750 copies printed.

NOTES ON LIFE AND LETTERS.   London & Toronto: Dent 1921. Light Olive Green cloth. 'Privately Printed 1921' on verso title. 33 copies printed. First Published Edition: Dent 1921. Dark sage-green cloth. 9500 copies printed.

THE ROVER.   T. Fisher Unwin 1923. U.S.: Doubleday 1923.

LAUGHING ANNE & ONE DAY MORE.   John Castle 1924.

THE NATURE OF A CRIME.   By Conrad & Hueffer. Duckworth (1924).

SUSPENSE.   Dent 1925.

TALES OF HEARSAY.   T. Fisher Unwin 1925. U.S.: Doubleday 1925.

LAST ESSAYS.   Dent 1926.

CORNFORD, Frances (1886–1960)

Her first book is not recorded in Anderson's bibliography, nor in the British Library Catalogue. It is given below, followed by her first regularly published book.

THE HOLTBURY IDYLL.   An Heroic Comedy in thirteen Letters, six Telegrams and two Newspaper Paragraphs. Edited by F. D. C. No place, publisher or date. Printed by the Women's Printing Society (1908). 48pp. Brown wrappers.
   A satirical epistolary novel, and extremely rare. The editor was Frances Crofts Darwin. Its value is perhaps about £1000.

POEMS.   Hampstead: The Priory Press 1910. Sm.4to. Cloth spine, grey boards.

CORVO, Baron (Frederick Rolfe 1860–1913)

Two books in the list below are collaborations between Rolfe and Col. Pirie-Gordon under the pseudonyms of Prospero and Caliban. Another volume arising from this collaboration was published with Pirie-Gordon given as the sole author. This was INNOCENT THE GREAT, published by Longmans in 1907 (scarlet cloth). Rolfe claimed to have revised and edited the book. But the degree of Rolfe's involvement in this, and other collaborative projects, is a matter of some uncertainty.

Rolfe used many pseudonyms other than Baron Corvo, though these are not relevant to the list below, which is concerned only with his principal works. Some of the other pseudonyms he adopted were Frank English, Frederick Austin, Nicholas Crabbe, A Crab Maid, Uriele de' Ricordi and Fradulph Authades.

THE WINTONIAN was a magazine produced (mimeographed) at Winchester Modern School (no longer in existence). In the early 1880s, Rolfe was a master at the school and is known to have contributed to the magazine. A copy of the issue for February 4th, 1882 is in the Bodleian Library, Oxford, and this has three contributions ascribed to Rolfe – two anonymous and one under the pseudonym 'Ye Grey Quill'. Other issues of this elusive school magazine await discovery.

TARCISSUS: The Boy Martyr of Rome, In the Diocletian Persecution. (Printed at Saffron Walden, Essex 1880) Grey paper covers. 12pp. No title page other than the front cover. No author's name, but the initials 'F.W.R.' are given on the Dedication page immediately preceding the text.
    The number of copies printed is unknown. A. J. A. Symons apparently believed there were 50 copies, but Cecil Woolf suggests 'considerably more than fifty'. Whatever the number, the book is now a great rarity.

STORIES TOTO TOLD ME. By Baron Corvo. London & New York: John Lane: The Bodley Head 1898. Green wrappers. Number six in the series Bodley Booklets.

THE ATTACK ON ST. WINEFRIDE'S WELL. or The Holywell Gone Mad. No. 1. An anonymous 8pp. pamphlet in green wrappers. Front wrapper serves as title-page. Published by F. W. Hochheimer, Holywell. n.d. (1898).
    Very rare. Cecil Woolf knew of only one copy – the one he discovered in the British Museum.

IN HIS OWN IMAGE. By Frederick Baron Corvo. London & New York: John Lane: The Bodley Head 1901. Bound in cloths of various colours (no certain priority) & d/w.
    Printed in America, but published first in London. 1000 copies were issued in the U.K., and 500 in the colonies.

CHRONICLES OF THE HOUSE OF BORGIA. By Frederick Baron Corvo. London: Grant Richards (and) New York: Dutton 1901. Red buckram, d/w. 1,250 copies printed – 730 for the U.K., 520 for America.

Published in American about a month after the U.K. A few copies which include an essay on homosexuality among the Borgias (Appendix III) have survived suppression, but are extremely rare.

A HISTORY OF THE BORGIAS. New York: Modern Library (1931 on verso title). Limp leatherette, also cloth (various colours).

This is a new edition of CHRONICLES OF THE HOUSE OF BORGIA. It is a collector's item in its own right, partly because of an informative introduction by Shane Leslie, but mainly because of the scarcity of the original edition. However, it is not itself scarce.

THE RUBAIYAT OF UMAR KHAIYAM. Done into English from the French of J. B. Nicolas By Frederick Baron Corvo. London & New York: John Lane, The Bodley Head 1903. Grey cloth spine, green boards, paper label on spine, d/w. Also (perhaps the American issue) in red cloth spine, grey boards. 500 copies were published in the U.K. from American sheets.

A surprisingly rare book – Cecil Woolf knew of only two copies (one in each binding). This gives added importance to the second edition, which was the first illustrated: John Lane, The Bodley Head (1924). 16 illustrations in colour by Hamzeh Carr. Fawn cloth, d/w. 2500 copies printed, of which 260 were published in Boston, U.S.A. by Small, Maynard in 1925, in the same binding style. 1784 copies were remaindered in 1928–1930 (these are lettered in black rather than the original gold, and the dust wrapper, unlike the original, does not bear the price of 21/- on the spine). It follows that less than 500 copies of the original U.K. issue are available for collectors, and consequently even this second edition is not easy to obtain.

HADRIAN THE SEVENTH By Fr. Rolfe. Chatto & Windus 1904. First issue: Maroon cloth, illustrated in white on front, with 'Chatto and Windus' on spine, d/w. 32pp. catalogue at end, dated September 1903. Second issue: purple cloth, illustrated in blind on front, with 'Chatto & Windus' on spine (note the ampersand), d/w. Title page is a cancel leaf, and the catalogue is not dated.

The first issue consisted of 700 copies, the second of 450. A further 350 copies were remaindered or destroyed.

DON TARQUINIO By Fr. Rolfe. Chatto & Windus 1905. Violet cloth, d/w. 32pp. publisher's catalogue at end. 650 copies issued in the original form, some with gilt top edges, some with plain top edges (possibly issued later). Remainder issues: A further 250 sets of the original sheets were issued in 1912 by Caxton Publishing Co. in red cloth. Another 101 were issued in 1924 by Chatto in dark blue cloth, some copies with the date 1905 erased from the title page.

DON RENATO. By Fr. Rolfe. Francis Griffiths 1909. Oatmeal cloth, decorated in purple.
  Printed but not published. An exceedingly rare book, only five copies being known to exist.

THE WEIRD OF THE WANDERER... Here produced by Prospero & Caliban. William Rider & Son 1912. Dark blue cloth, d/w. 1475 copies printed.
  The authors were Rolfe and Col. Pirie-Gordon.

THE BULL AGAINST THE ??? OF THE ANGLICAN RACE. By Frederick Baron Corvo. Privately Printed (for A. J. A. Symons) 1929. Crown 4to. 18pp. in white wrappers with paper label on front. 50 copies only.

THE DESIRE AND PURSUIT OF THE WHOLE. By Frederick Rolfe Baron Corvo. Cassell (1934 on verso title). Veridian cloth, d/w. 2020 copies printed, of which 536 were remaindered in 1938 in light green cloth without d/w.

HUBERT'S ARTHUR... Here produced by Prospero and Caliban. London, Toronto, Melbourne and Sydney: Cassell (1935). Scarlet cloth, lettered on the spine in scarlet on a gold panel, d/w. 1515 copies printed. Remainder issue: In 1938, 515 copies were bound in similar scarlet cloth, but lettered on the spine in purple, and issued in the original d/w.
  Rolfe and Col. Pirie-Gordon were joint authors.

THE SONGS ... OF MELEAGER. By Frederick Baron Corvo (Fr. Rolfe) in collaboration with Sholto Douglas. The First Edition Club (1937). Limited to 750 copies. Green cloth with gold rules, plain cellophane d/w.
  Rolfe extensively revised the original translations by Douglas.

THREE TALES OF VENICE. By Fr. Rolfe (Baron Corvo). Thames Ditton, Surrey: The Corvine Press (1950). Limited to 150 copies, of which 10 (not for sale) were on goatskin parchment and specially bound by Sangorski, and 140 were on handmade paper bound in green basil (spine and corners) and green cloth.

AMICO DI SANDRO. By Frederick Baron Corvo. Privately Printed 1951. Limited to 150 copies, of which 10 were on goatskin parchment specially bound by Sangorski, and 140 were on handmade paper bound in quarter khaki buckram, white boards.

LETTERS TO GRANT RICHARDS. By Frederick Baron Corvo. Hurst, Berkshire: The Peacocks Press (1952). Limited to 200 copies, of which 10 were printed on handmade paper specially bound by Sangorski, and 190 were bound in cream handmade paper boards.

COWLEY, Abraham (1616–1687)

VERSES LATELY WRITTEN UPON SEVERAL OCCASIONS. Herringman, 1663. Sm.8vo. Second issue has cancel title.

COWPER, William (1731–1800)

His well-known poem JOHN GILPIN first appeared in THE PUBLIC ADVERTISER, before being put out as a chapbook. It was included in the collection of 1785, along with Cowper's other famous work THE TASK.

OLNEY HYMNS, In Three Books. (Anonymous. By Cowper & John Newton). W. Oliver, J. Buckland, J. Johnson 1779. 12mo.

POEMS . . . Printed for J. Johnson . . . 1782. 8vo. Second volume published in 1785.
A very important collection, and very rare indeed – less than 50 copies are known. It is especially rare with the Preface by John Newton, which was suppressed.

THE ILIAD AND ODYSSEY OF HOMER. Translated into English Blank Verse by William Cowper. for J. Johnson 1791. 2 vols. 4to.

PRIVATE CORRESPONDENCE. Now first published . . . Colburn 1824. 2 vols.

POEMS, the Early Productions . . . now first published. for Baldwin, Cradock & Joy 1825. 12mo.

THE WORKS. Edited by Robert Southey. for Baldwin & Cradock 1835–37. 15 vols. Sm. 8vo. The first issue of the first volume does not have the volume number on the title-page. A corrected title-page for volume one was included at the end of volume 2.

CRABBE, George (1754–1832)

His first work INEBREITY was published anonymously at Ipswich in 1775, while he was apprenticed to a Suffolk doctor. This work and THE CANDIDATE (also anonymous) of 1780, are very scarce. He wrote some novels which were never published and which he apparently destroyed, but many other previously unpublished works were discovered after his death and published posthumously. Some of these were included in the 1834 collection; some later discoveries did not appear until NEW POEMS in 1960.

THE LIBRARY: a Poem.   (anon). J. Dodsley 1781. 4to.

THE VILLAGE: a Poem.   J. Dodsley 1783. 4to.

THE NEWS-PAPER: a Poem.   J. Dodsley 1785. 4to. Advert leaf at end.

A DISCOURSE ON 2 CORINTHIANS, I, 9, READ IN THE CHAPEL AT BELVOIR CASTLE AFTER THE FUNERAL OF THE DUKE OF RUTLAND.   J. Dodsley 1788. 4to.

POEMS.   J. Hatchard 1807. U.S.: Philadelphia: Bradford & Inskeep 1808.
   This collection includes previously published works and much new material.

THE BOROUGH: a Poem.   Hatchard 1810. First issue: on line 20 of page 5, the word 'fingers' is in lower-case type.

TALES IN VERSE.   J. Hatchard 1812.

THE ENTIRE WORKS OF GEORGE CRABBE.   1816. 4 vols 12mo, & 4 vols 8vo.

A VARIATION OF PUBLIC OPINION . . . 1817.

TALES OF THE HALL.   Murray 1819, 2 vols. In the earliest state, P6 is a cancel. Advert leaf at end of vol 2. Boards, paper labels.

THE POETICAL WORKS.   1822. 7 vols.

THE POETICAL WORKS . . . LETTERS AND JOURNALS . . . Murray 1834.   8 vols.
   Includes previously unpublished material.

POSTHUMOUS SERMONS.   Ed. J. D. Hastings. Hatchard 1850.

CRANE, Stephen (1871–1900)

The bookseller Dr Jacob Schwartz, writing in 1931, commented that a small shipment of Crane's first book had just been discovered and that a copy had fetched £240 at Sotheby's. That was a good price then, but imagine the value of a small shipment today, when copies are valued at prices like $10,000 or more! His first three books, all of them valuable, were:

MAGGIE, A GIRL OF THE STREETS.   By Johnston Smith (pseudonym). No publisher or date. (New York 1893). 164pp. Yellow wrappers. 'Copy-righted' at the foot of the title-page. Second Edition (slightly revised): by Stephen Crane. New York: Appleton 1896. 12pp adverts. Cream-yellow buckram. First issue: Watermarked paper printed in Roman type. Title-page in mixture of Capitals and lower-case. Second issue: printed in Old English type. Title-page in capitals only.

THE BLACK RIDERS AND OTHER LINES. Boston: Copeland & Day 1895. Yellow cloth, also grey decorated boards. 500 copies. Also 50 on vellum.

THE RED BADGE OF COURAGE. New York: Appleton 1895. Cream-yellow buckram. 4pp adverts. Later printing mentions the present book in the adverts.

CRASHAW, Richard (c. 1612–1649)

A posthumous collection was published in 1652 with the title CARMEN DEO MOSTRO, but the only collection of his English verse to be published during his lifetime was:

STEPS TO THE TEMPLE. Sacred Poems, with other Delights of the Muses. Printed by T. W. for Humphrey Moseley 1646. 12mo. Second Edition, with additions: 1648.
A scarce book, worth around £1000.

CROWLEY, Aleister (Edward Alexander 1875–1947)

Published many fugitive and ephemeral pieces, often privately printed in small editions, and frequently anonymous or under one exotic pseudonym or another. The problem for the collector is not so much to identify the first editions (most were not reprinted) as to know that they exist and to track them down. But there are many collectors on the trail nowadays, and not much is available under £100. The selection below excludes posthumous publications, of which there have been quite a few. The letters. O.T.O. in the imprint of some publications, stands for Ordo Templis Orientis.

ACELDAMA – A PLACE TO BURY STRANGERS IN. A Philosophical Poem by a Gentleman in the University of Cambridge. Privately Printed by Leonard Smithers (1898).

SONGS FOR THE SPIRIT. Kegan Paul (1898). Blue linen, red lettering.

JEPHTHAH AND OTHER MYSTERIES LYRICAL AND DRAMATIC. Kegan Paul (1899). Quarter linen, boards.

CARMEN SECULARE. By St. E. A. of M. and S. Privately Issued, 1901. pp. (ii) 30. Green wrappers. Second issue has imprint of Kegan Paul (1901).

THE SOUL OF OSIRIS. A History. Kegan Paul (1901). Cloth spine, boards, paper label.

AHAB AND OTHER POEMS. Intro & Epilogue by Count Vladimir Svareff. Privately Printed at the Chiswick Press (1903).

ALICE: AN ADULTERY. No publisher or date. Privately Printed (1903). Wrappers.

BERASHITH – AN ESSAY IN ONTOLOGY WITH SOME REMARKS ON CEREMONIAL MAGIC BY ABHAVANANDA. Paris: Privately Printed for the Sangha of the West (1903). Wrappers.

THE GOD-EATER. A Tragedy of Satire. Watts (1903). Black wrappers.

ARGONAUTS – A STUDY OF SOCIETY AND THE GRACE OF GOD. Boleskine, Foyers, Inverness: Society for the Propagation of Religious Truth (1904). Black wrappers.

IN RESIDENCE: The Don's Guide to Cambridge. Cambridge: Elijah Johnson 1904. Blue Wrappers.

WHY JESUS WEPT. Privately Printed (1904). Jap. paper wrappers.

ORACLES. The Biography of an Art. Boleskine, Foyers, Inverness: Society for the Propagation of Religious Truth (1905).

COLLECTED WORKS OF ALEISTER CROWLEY. Boleskine, Foyers, Inverness: 1905, 1906 & 1907. 3 vols. Wrappers. Issued in one volume, 1907, in white linen. Also on India paper in limp vellum.

GARGOYLES. Being Strangely Wrought Images of Life and Death. Foyers: Society for the Propagation of Religious Truth (1906). 50 copies. White wrappers.

KONX OM PAX: Essays in Light. London & New York: Walter Scott Pub. Co. (1907). Black buckram.

RODIN IN RHYME. Seven Lithographs . . . with a Chaplet of Verse by Crowley. Chiswick Press for the author (1907). White buckram.

TANNHAUSER. A Story of All Time. Boleskine, Foyers, Inverness: Society for the Propagation of Religious Truth (1907). Blue cloth.

AMPHORA.   Privately Printed for the Authoress and her Intimates. (1908)

777. Walter Scott Pub. Co. (1909). 500 copies. Errata leaf. Red buckram. Revised Ed.: Neptune Press (1955). 1100 in qtr. vellum, blue buckram.

CLOUDS WITHOUT WATER.   Edited from a Private MS. by the Rev. C. Verey. Privately Printed for Circulation among the Ministers of Religion. (1909). Wrappers.

THE WINGED BEETLE; poems.   Privately Printed (1910). 300 copies. 50 copies were printed on handmade paper.

AMBERGRIS – A SELECTION OF THE POEMS OF ALEISTER CROWLEY.   Elkin Mathews (1910).

THE SCENTED GARDEN OF ABDULLAH THE SATIRIST OF SHIRAZ.   Translated . . . by the late Major Lutiy and another. Privately Printed (1910).

BOOK FOUR – PART I (YOGA).   Wieland & Co. (c. 1911). Thin yellow boards.

HAIL MARY! The Equinox (1912).   Blue wrappers.

HOUSEHOLD GODS. A Comedy.   Pallanza: Privately Printed (1912). White buckram.

MORTADELLO. THE ANGEL OF VENICE. A COMEDY.   Wieland & Co. (1912). Red buckram, also in white linen.

BOOK FOUR – PART II.   Wieland & Co. (c. 1913). Boards.

LIBER CCCXXXIII. THE BOOK OF LIES.   Wieland & Co. 1913. Errata sheet. Gilt dec cloth.

THE LAW OF LIBERTY.   A Tract of Therion, that is a Magus.   O.T.O. (c. 1917). Singled folded sheet. 4pp.

DIARY OF A DRUG FIEND.   Collins (1922). Dark blue cloth, lettered in red. U.S.: Dutton (1923).

SONGS FOR ITALY.   No publication details. (1923). 15pp. Pamphlet.

CONFESSIONS OF ALEISTER CROWLEY.   Mandrake Press (1929). 800 copies. 2 vols. White buckram. U.S.: Hill & Wang (1970).

MAGICK IN THEORY AND PRACTICE.   By The Master Therion.

London & Paris: Privately Printed at the Lecram Press. For Subscribers Only. (1929). Issued in 4 parts in wrappers. Also issued in one volume, cloth.

MOONCHILD, A Prologue.   (a novel, in fact). Mandrake Press 1929. Green cloth, d/w.

THE STRATAGEM AND OTHER STORIES.   Mandrake Press (1930). 16mo. Qtr black cloth, dec boards, d/w.

THE BANNED LECTURE – GILLES DE RAIS.   P. R. Stevenson (1930). Blue Wrappers.

ONE STAR IN SIGHT. Sanctuary of the Gnosis in the Valley of Los Angeles by Authority of To Mega Therion.   (1935). Black card, silver lettering.

LITTLE ESSAYS TOWARDS TRUTH.   O.T.O. (1938). Leaf of Addenda follows p. 23.

THE BOOK OF THE LAW.   O.T.O. (1938). Wrappers.

THE HEART OF THE MASTER.   By Khaled Khan. O.T.O. (1938). Dec. yellow buckram.

EIGHT LECTURES ON YOGA.   Being Equinox Vol III, No. 4. By the Mahatma Guru Sri Paramahamsa Shivagi. O.T.O. (1939). Dec tan buckram, d/w.

ENGLAND STAND FAST – A POEM.   O.T.O. (1939). Single sheet folded. 4pp.

THUMBS UP. A PENTAGRAM. A PANTANGLE TO WIN THE WAR. O.T.O. (1951). 100 signed. Blue wrappers.

THE CITY OF GOD – A RHAPSODY.   O.T.O. (1943). One of 200. Signed frontis. Wrappers.

THE BOOK OF THOTH – A SHORT ESSAY ON THE TAROT OF THE EGYPTIANS.   Being the Equinox Vol III, No. 5. By the Master Therion. O.T.O. 1944. 200 signed by the author. Illustrations, including 8 coloured plates.

OLLA. An Anthology of Sixty Years of Song.   O.T.O. (1946). 500 copies, also 20 on handmade paper.

THE LAST RITUAL.   Brighton: Privately Printed 1948. Wrappers.

D

DAY-LEWIS, Cecil (1904–1972)

His rare first book was:

BEECHEN VIGIL and other poems.   Fortune Press 1925. Wrappers.

DEFOE, Daniel (1660–1731)

Defoe (simply 'Foe' until he was 35) was a prolific author, publishing well over 500 books, pamphlets and journals. Many were anonymous or pseudonymous, and many were printed discreetly, giving neither publisher nor printer.

The large number of his publications and the obscurity of so many, make Defoe an ideal author for the specialist collector, and a difficult one for the amateur. Everyone will of course be familiar with ROBINSON CRUSOE, MOLL FLANDERS and perhaps one or two other titles. These are not likely to be found sleeping in a miscellaneous lot at auction, nor undervalued on a bookseller's shelves. But many others are, and it is the specialist who is likely to spot them and 'make a killing'. For all of Defoe's works, even the minor pieces are scarce and valuable.

In the minimal checklist below, I have given the key works, to enable the collector to safely identify the first editions or (more likely) to rule out a 'possible' first edition. And to these I have added just a few examples of his other works to give the non-specialist some idea of the 'flavour' of his satires and some indication of the scope of his publications in general. I repeat that many were anonymous, pseudonymous, and without the publisher or printer being given.

A LETTER TO A DISSENTER.   1688. Sm. 4to.
His anonymous first publication.

REFLECTIONS ON THE LATE GREAT REVOLUTION.   Ric. Chiswell 1689. Sm. 4to.
His anonymous second publication. 'Written by a Lay-Hand in the Country, for the Satisfaction of some Neighbours'.

AN ESSAY UPON PROJECTS.   1697.

His first important signed work.

THE TRUE-BORN ENGLISHMAN. 1701.
An anonymous and very popular verse satire, or 'Satyr' as the title-page has it.

THE SHORTEST-WAY WITH DISSENTERS. Printed in the Year MDCCII. (i.e. 1702). Sm. 4to.
This famous prose tract was published anonymously, but he nevertheless spent three days in the pillory for it. It was suppressed and officially burned, and is consequently very scarce. £2000–£3000 might buy a copy.

MORE SHORT WAYS WITH DISSENTERS. 1704.

AN ELEGY ON THE AUTHOR OF THE TRUE-BORN-ENGLISH-MAN. With an Essay on the late Storm. By the Author of the Hymn to the Pillory. Printed in the Year, 1704. Sm. 4to.
Verse throughout. The printer was H. Hills.

THE EXPERIMENT: or the Shortest Way . . . B. Bragg 1705. Sm. 4to.

THE DYET OF POLAND. Printed at Dantzick 1705. Sm. 4to.
An anonymous attack upon the High-Church Party, clandestinely printed in London.

JURE DIVINO. By the Author of the True-Born-Englishman. Printed . . . 1706. Sm. 8vo.
Published by Benjamin Bragg, this was pirated and preceded the authorized first edition (folio) by one day. Altogether, four editions of the work appeared in 1706.

MINUTES OF THE NEGOTIATIONS OF MONSR. MESNAGER AT THE COURT OF ENGLAND. Written by Himself. Done out of French. S. Baker 1717.
Disclaimed by Defoe, but probably by him.

THE LIFE AND STRANGE SURPRIZING ADVENTURES OF ROBIN-SON CRUSOE, OF YORK. MARINER: . . . Written by Himself. Printed for W. Taylor at the Ship in Pater-Noster-Row. 1719.
Today worth in the region of £4000–£5000. The second and third editions of the same year, are worth considerably less. The book was an immediate success, and Defoe promptly began work on a sequel, THE FARTHER ADVENTURES. Four months later, it was ready for publication. Meanwhile (October 7th 1719), serial publication of both works had begun in the ORIGINAL LONDON POST, OR HEATHCOTES INTELLIGENCER. This ran until October 19th 1720, and has been regarded by some (i.e. Dibdin) as the true first edition. The book was of course subsequently printed in many editions and indeed many languages. One of the rarest

editions is an English/French interlineary edition 'A Dampierre: par G.E.J., M.A.L., 1797'. The French translation was by Madame de Montmorency Lavale, and the work was in 2 vols, royal 8vo. Only 25 copies were printed (according to Lowndes).

The book sparked off a stream of imitations, now known as 'Robinsonades'. Among these are THE HERMIT by 'Edward Dorrington', 1727, later entitled THE ADVENTURES OF PHILIP QUARLL; THE LIFE AND ADVENTURES OF PETER WILKINS, A CORNISHMAN by Robert Paltock, 1751; and the best-known among them, THE SWISS FAMILY ROBINSON by Johann David Wyss, first published (in German) in Zurich, 1812–13 (2 vols), with the first U.K. edition in 1814. The real life adventure of Alexander Selkirk, on which ROBINSON CRUSOE was based, is related in a book by Captain Woodes Rogers, entitled A CRUISING VOYAGE ROUND THE WORLD. This was published by Bell and Lintot in 1712. An eccentric, satiric biography of Defoe was published as THE LIFE AND STRANGE SURPRISING ADVENTURES OF Mr. D– De F–, of London, Hosier . . . In a Dialogue between Him, Robinson Crusoe, and his Man Friday . . . (etc). This anonymous work by Charles Gildon, was published by J. Roberts as early as 1719.

THE FARTHER ADVENTURES OF ROBINSON CRUSOE. Taylor 1719.

THE SERIOUS REFLECTIONS DURING THE LIFE AND SURPRISING ADVENTURES OF ROBINSON CRUSOE. Taylor 1720.

MEMOIRS OF A CAVALIER . . . Written Threescore Years ago by an English Gentleman . . . Printed for A. Bell . . . J. Osborn . . . W. Taylor . . . and T. Warner. n.d. (1720)
    A work of fiction, almost certainly by Defoe. The book appeared later under the name of 'Col. Andrew Newman'.

THE FORTUNES AND MISFORTUNES OF THE FAMOUS MOLL FLANDERS, &c. Who was born in Newgate, and during a Life of continu'd Variety for threescore Years, besides her Childhood, was twelve Year a Whore, five times a Wife (whereof once to her own Brother), twelve Year a Thief, eight Year a transported Felon in Virginia, at last grew rich, liv'd honest, and died a Penitent. Written from her own Memorandums. London: Printed for, and Sold by W. Chetwood . . . and T. Edling . . . MDDCXXI (sic) i.e. 1721 (January 1722). 8vo.
    Nowadays worth perhaps £4000.

A JOURNAL OF THE PLAGUE YEAR. 1722.

COLONEL JACK. 1722.

AN IMPARTIAL HISTORY OF THE LIFE AND ACTIONS OF PETER ALEXOWITZ. Written by a British Officer in the Service of the Czar. W. Chetwood 1723 (1722).

A TOUR THRO' THE WHOLE ISLAND OF GREAT BRITAIN, divided into Circuits or Journies . . . By a Gentleman. Printed and sold by G. Strahan 1724–27. 3 vols. 8vo. Errata-leaf in volume one, and advertisment leaves in volumes two and three. Folding plan of Colchester & 2 large folding maps.
    A popular guide book. The first edition is worth about £1000. After 1837, the work was revised by Samuel Richardson.

ROXANA. 1724.

THE GREAT LAW OF SUBORDINATION CONSIDERED. 1724.
    An important sociological work.

A NEW VOYAGE ROUND THE WORLD, by a Course never sailed before. for A. Bettesworth, 1725. Engraved frontispiece and three plates.
    A work of fiction.

A SYSTEM OF MAGICK; or, a History of the Black Art. Being an Historical Account of Mankind's most early Dealing with the Devil; and how the Acquaintance on both Sides first began . . . Printed: and Sold by J. Roberts . . . 1727. Frontispiece of a magician.
    A much wanted book, worth £400–£500.

CONJUGAL LEWDNESS: or, Matrimonial Whoredom. Printed for T. Warner . . . 1727. 8vo.
    The title gave offence and for the second issue (same year, same publisher) a cancel title-page was inserted, giving the title as A TREATISE CONCERNING THE USE AND ABUSE OF THE MARRIAGE BED. Both issues are very scarce.

THE MEMOIRS OF AN ENGLISH OFFICER by Capt. George Carleton. 1728.
    This work has been attributed to Swift and also to the real Captain George Carleton (see Sir Walter Scott's edition of 1808), but is now most often attributed to Defoe.

DE LA MARE, Walter (1873–1956)

De La Mare is not particularly fashionable at present, but there has always been a steady interest in his work. The earliest books, up to 1912, are now getting very scarce. Listed below are the first editions which are attracting the most interest from collectors.

SONGS OF CHILDHOOD. By Walter Ramal (pseud.). Longmans, Green 1902. Small 8vo. T.e.g. Vellum spine, blue cloth gilt. Frontispiece after Richard Doyle.
His first book, a volume of verse.

HENRY BROCKEN. Murray 1904.
His first novel. It appeared under his real name, but the pseudonym used for his first book is given immediately below his name on the title-page, in brackets. During the printing, the righthand bracket dropped out, and copies with this bracket missing are regarded as second issues.

POEMS. Murray 1906.

THE THREE MULLA-MULGARS. Duckworth 1910.

THE LISTENERS and Other Poems. Constable 1912.

A CHILD'S DAY. Constable 1912.

PEACOCK PIE. Constable 1913.
The first edition was not illustrated. W. Heath Robinson illustrated it in the edition from Constable in 1916 and Lovat Fraser 'embellished' it in 1924 (same publisher). The familiar modern version with illustrations by Ardizzone, first appeared in 1946.

DE QUINCEY, Thomas (1785–1859)
CONFESSIONS OF AN ENGLISH OPIUM-EATER. Taylor & Hessey 1822. Advert leaf at the end.
Anonymous, and today worth about £700. The Second Edition came in 1823, as did the first American Edition.

WALLADMOR. Taylor & Hessey 1825. 2 vols. Boards.
An anonymous translation.

KLOSTERHEIM: or, The Masque. By the English Opium-Eater. Edinburgh: Blackwood 1832.

DICKENS, Charles (1812–1870)
The novels were generally first published in monthly parts, in illustrated paper covers, with the last two parts combined into a double number. Normally there were 20 parts (expressed as 19/20) but there are exceptions (given below). The first book editions were published on completion of the

monthly parts. In the case of SKETCHES BY BOZ, bound vols were issued before and after the parts. Some of the parts were reprinted at an early date. The advertisements they bore are significant. The finer points are set out in Hatton & Cleaver's BIBLIOGRAPHY OF THE PERIODICAL WORKS OF CHARLES DICKENS, published in 1933 and recently reprinted.

Dickens' novels have been scrutinized very thoroughly indeed by bibliographers of several generations, and countless points have been identified (though their full significance has not always been established to everyone's satisfaction). I could not list all of them below, but I hope I have listed enough to give the uncertain collector in the field, a better than fifty-fifty chance of getting it right.

SKETCHES BY 'BOZ' (First Series). John Macrone 1836. 2 vols. 12mo. Dark green cloth. Preface dated 'Furnival's Inn, February 1836'. 16 plates by Cruikshank (Frontispiece & 7, in each volume). The Second Edition, published in the same year, has the Preface dated 'August, 1836'.

SKETCHES BY 'BOZ' Second Series. John Macrone 1837. Preface dated 'December 17, 1836'. 1 vol. 12mo. Pink cloth. 10 plates by Cruikshank. 10 leaves of adverts dated Dec. 1836 at end. The first issue does not have the list of illustrations on the lower half of the second page of contents, the second issue does (This implication by Eckel, was queried by Sadleir). The Second Edition, published later in 1837, has two additional plates by Cruikshank – 'The Last Cab-driver' and 'The First of May'. These two plates may sometimes be found added to the first edition.

SKETCHES BY 'BOZ' (First & Second Series together) issued by Chapman & Hall in 20 monthly parts from November 1837 to June 1839. 40 illustrations by Cruikshank (2 per issue). Book: Chapman & Hall 1839. One vol. Green cloth. Unsold copies of the parts were also issued in this form. The 40 plates include 27 of the 28 used in the earlier editions (re-engraved and slightly larger than the originals) plus 13 new ones. The original plate not included is 'The Free and Easy'. In their earliest state, the plates preceeding 'Greenwich Fair' do not have the publisher's imprint (Chapman & Hall) at the bottom, the remainder do.

SUNDAY UNDER THREE HEADS. By Timothy Sparks. Chapman & Hall 1836. Pamphlet. Illustrated buff wrappers. 3 illustrations (plus that on the wrapper) by H. K. Browne. In this first edition, the title appears as a heading to Chapter III on page 35 (it is missing in a facsimile reprint by Jarvis & Son) and the word 'Hair' is correctly printed on page 7, line 15 (but misprinted as 'Air' in a facsimile reprint by Edwin Pearson).

THE VILLAGE COQUETTES. Richard Bentley 1836. 71pp. Wrappers.

THE STRANGE GENTLEMAN. By 'Boz'. Chapman & Hall 1837. 46pp.

Wrappers. Frontispiece by 'Phiz'. Should have a preliminary unpaged 'Costume' leaf.

THE POSTHUMOUS PAPERS OF THE PICKWICK CLUB. Edited by 'Boz'. 19/20 monthly parts in wrappers from April 1836. Book: Chapman & Hall 1837. Green or purple cloth. Some copies were bound from the parts. First issue: In the title vignette, 'Veller' on the signboard. Later issues: 'Weller' on the signboard.

Earliest Issue Plates: There are 45 plates – 7 by Seymour, 2 by 'Buss' (Cricket Match p. 69, and Arbour Scene p. 74) and 36 by 'Phiz' (of which the first four were signed 'Nemo'). Originally, none of the plates had titles.

Later Issue Plates at various stages – i) the 2 plates by 'Buss' were dropped. ii) the 4 plates signed 'Nemo' were signed 'Browne'. iii) the plates were given titles (inscriptions).

Author's Addresses: As the parts were published, 'addresses' (communications from Dickens to the reader) were inserted. There were four of these – in parts 2, 3, 10, and 15.

OLIVER TWIST. By 'Boz'. Richard Bentley 1838. 3 vols. 24 plates by Cruikshank. The first issue has a 'Fire-side' plate (Oliver and others sitting before a fireplace) facing page 313 in vol 3. This plate was dropped for the second issue.

SKETCHES OF YOUNG GENTLEMEN. (Anonymous). Chapman & Hall 1838. Pictorial cover and 6 illustrations by 'Phiz'.

THE MEMOIRS OF JOSEPH GRIMALDI. Edited by 'Boz'. Richard Bentley 1838. 2 vols. Pink cloth. Portrait frontis (Vol 1) and 12 plates by Cruikshank. The First Issue has no border around 'The Last Song' (final plate) and the sixth plate listed is misbound. Second Issue: In brown cloth. 'The Last Song' plate has a pictorial 'pantomimic' border by Crowquill. Both issues are scarce. An edition published in 1846 (2 vols) has a coloured 'Mother Goose' plate, appearing for the first time.

NICHOLAS NICKLEBY. 19/20 monthly parts in wrappers from April 1838. Book: Chapman & Hall 1839. Portrait after Maclise and 39 illustrations by 'Phiz'.

THE LOVING BALLAD OF LORD BATEMAN. (Anonymous, but by Dickens & Thackeray). Charles Tilt 1839. 32mo. Pictorial green cloth. 11 illustrations and a sheet of music by Cruikshank. First issue: Page numbers in middle of upper margin. Second issue: Page numbers in top right corner.

SKETCHES OF YOUNG COUPLES. By the Author of 'Sketches of Young

Gentlemen'. Chapman & Hall 1840. 12mo. Pictorial boards and 6 illustrations by 'Phiz'. Second Edition same year.

MASTER HUMPHREY'S CLOCK. 88 weekly parts in wrappers; also 19/20 monthly parts in wrappers, from April 4th 1840. Book Edition: 3 vols. Chapman & Hall 1840, 1841, & 1841. Brown cloth with a gilt clock on front and back. Some copies were bound from the parts. Some of the remaining sheets were used for the separate issues of BARNABY RUDGE and THE OLD CURIOSITY SHOP.

THE OLD CURIOSITY SHOP. Originally contained within Master Humphrey's Clock, in the parts from April 25th 1840; Issued as a separate volume by Chapman & Hall in 1841.

BARNABY RUDGE. Originally contained within Master Humphrey's Clock, in the parts from February 13th 1841; Issued as a separate volume by Chapman & Hall in 1841.

AMERICAN NOTES. Chapman and Hall 1842. 2 vols. Purple cloth. First issue: Preliminary pages numbered to xvi, the text to viii having been suppressed. Second issue: Preliminary pages numbered to viii. Two further editions in the same year.

MARTIN CHUZZLEWIT. 19/20 monthly parts from January 1843. Book: Chapman & Hall 1844. Green cloth. There should be an errata leaf with 13 lines (earliest issue) and '100£' on the signpost in the engraved title vignette. Second Issue: '£100' on the signpost.

A CHRISTMAS CAROL. Chapman & Hall 1843. Sm. 8vo. Cloth with a blind-stamped decorative border on front and back, and a gilt-stamped wreath on the front, encircling title and author. Hand-coloured frontispiece, three hand-coloured plates, and four vignettes, all by John Leech.
There are many variant states of this book and opinions differ about priorities. The basic issue points are (i) Titlepage dated 1843 (early) or 1844 (later). (ii) brown cloth (early) or pink cloth (later). (iii) 'STAVE I' at start of text (early) or 'STAVE ONE' (later), (iv) text uncorrected (early) or corrected (later).

Other points are: (v) the endpapers may be green or yellow, (vi) the half-title may be printed in green or blue, (vii) the title page may be printed in red and blue, or red and green, (viii) some variations in the 'D' for Dickens on the front cover have been observed. And so on, almost *ad infinitum*. It should be appreciated that various combinations of the above-mentioned points can appear in one copy of the book, and the exact status of that copy may be a matter for conjecture. There is no single authority to be consulted in respect of all the points. Contributions have been made (and continue to be made) in various books and periodicals.

THE CHIMES. Chapman & Hall 1845. Sm. 8vo. Red cloth with goblins and bells in gilt. The first issue has the publisher's name incorporated in the title vignette. Later issues have the publisher's name below the vignette and not part of the engraved plate. There are also issue points in the text, but the point mentioned above is the crucial one.

THE CRICKET ON THE HEARTH. Bradbury & Evans 1846. Sm. 8vo. Red cloth with blind borders. Gilt block on front. Advert leaf at end (issue point). Reprinted several times in the first year.

THE BATTLE OF LIFE. Bradbury and Evans 1846. Sm. 8vo. Red cloth with blind borders. Gilt block on front. First Issue: On the engraved title-page, the words 'A Love Story' are not supported by cupids, and the publisher's name appears at the bottom of the page. Second Issue: 'A Love Story' is supported by cupids, and the publisher's name appears at the bottom of the page. Third Issue: 'A Love Story' is supported by cupids, and the publisher's name does not appear at the bottom of the page.
Some issue points in the prelims are not firmly established.

PICTURES FROM ITALY. Bradbury and Evans, 1846. Illustrations by Samuel Palmer. Sm. 8vo. Cloth.

DOMBEY AND SON. 19/20 monthly parts in wrappers from October 1846. Book: Bradbury & Evans 1848. Green cloth.

THE HAUNTED MAN AND THE GHOST'S BARGAIN. Bradbury & Evans 1848. Sm. 8vo. Red cloth with blind borders. Gilt blocked on front. A few early copies had the date on the title-page in Roman numerals, thus 'MDCCCXLVIII'.

DAVID COPPERFIELD. 19/20 monthly parts in wrappers from May 1849. Book: Bradbury & Evans 1850. Green cloth.

A CHILD'S HISTORY OF ENGLAND. 3 vols. Bradbury & Evans 1852–3–4. Advert leaves at the end of each vol.

TO BE READ AT DUSK. London 1852. 20pp. Wrappers.
   A T. J. Wise forgery.

BLEAK HOUSE. 19/20 monthly parts in wrappers from March 1852. Book: Bradbury & Evans 1853. Green cloth.

HARD TIMES. Bradbury & Evans 1854. Green cloth. Not illustrated.

LITTLE DORRIT. 19/20 monthly parts in wrappers from December 1855. Book: Bradbury & Evans 1857. Green cloth. A slip with 9 lines should precede the text.

REPRINTED PIECES. 1858. Being vol 8 of the Library Edition.
Articles originally published in Household Words.

A TALE OF TWO CITIES. 7/8 monthly parts in wrappers from June 1859.
Book: Chapman & Hall 1859.
The part issue is one of the rarest of all Dickens part issues.

A CURIOUS DANCE ROUND A CURIOUS TREE. No date or publisher. Pamphlet. 19pp. Mauve wrappers (front wrapper serving as title-page, giving the title and the author) and an envelope.
A copy has been recorded in pink wrappers and a white envelope with a pink penny stamp embossed in one corner. Copies lacking the envelope may have a vertical crease due to folding for insertion into the smaller envelope (65 × 180mm approx.). The text first appeared in Household Words, January 1852. It was issued in this pamphlet form in aid of St. Luke's Hospital, and in this form is very rare.

GREAT EXPECTATIONS. Chapman & Hall 1861. 3 vols. 32pp. adverts at end, dated May 1861. Not illustrated.

THE UNCOMMERCIAL TRAVELLER. Chapman & Hall 1861.
17 Essays from All The Year Round. The 1868 Edition has 11 extra essays; the 1875 Illustrated Library Edition has 8 more added; and the 1908 Gadshill Edition has just one more added.

OUR MUTUAL FRIEND. 19/20 monthly parts in wrappers from May 1864. Book: Chapman & Hall 1865. 2 vols.

EDWIN DROOD. 6 monthly parts in wrappers from April 1870. Book: Chapman & Hall 1870. One vol. Green cloth. 32pp. catalogue at end dated 31.8.1870.

HUNTED DOWN. John Camden Hotten (1870). Green wrappers.

THE LIFE OF OUR LORD. Associated Newspapers 1934. Maroon cloth with d/w.

THE LETTERS. Edited by his sister-in-law and eldest daughter. Chapman & Hall 1880–1882. 3 vols.

DONNE, John (1572–1631)

Everything by Donne, including his sermons, is of great interest to scholars and to Donne specialists, but his poems attract the greatest interest from collectors. His son John collected these for publication after the author's death. The result was one of the most important volumes in the whole of English Poetry and, needless to say, the first edition is rare and valuable.

POEMS . . . with Elegies on the Author's Death.   London. Printed by M. F. for Iohn (sic) Marriot . . . 1633. (The author given as 'J. D.'). 4to. Portrait of Donne by Lombard.
    The Second Edition of 1635 has additional poems, and a portrait by W. Marshall. This edition was in 12mo.

POEMS &c. . . . With Elegies on the Author's Death.   To which is added divers Copies under his own hand, never before Printed. In the Savoy, Printed by T. N. for Henry Herringman . . . 1669.
    This is the fifth collected edition, with five poems not printed in previous collections.

DOYLE, Arthur Conan (1859–1930)

The first Sherlock Holmes publication is rare. Here we have a clear-cut case of demand far outstripping the supply, and a copy in anything like fine condition would almost certainly make something over £10,000. The facsimile produced by the Sherlock Holmes Society in 1960 (500 copies) is also getting rather scarce. The first separate edition – a paperback issued by Ward Lock in 1887 is almost as rare as the original annual, and is worth several thousand pounds.

A STUDY IN SCARLET.   28th Beeton's Christmas Annual 1887. Illustrated wrappers. The Holmes story occupies the first 95pp. First Separate Edition: Ward Lock 1888. Wrappers. The second impression, also dated 1888 (though in fact issued early in the following year), has an additional two lines on the front wrapper, stating 'This design, with the exception of this lettering, is composed with the "Patent Kalido Mosaic Type".'

THE MYSTERY OF CLOOMBER.   Ward & Downey 1889 (1888). Illustrated wrappers with 'Price One Shilling' across the top of the front wrapper. Very scarce.

MICAH CLARKE.   Longman etc. 1889.

THE SIGN OF FOUR.   Pages 147–223 of Lippincott's Magazine, February 1890. Wrappers. Issued in the U.S. and in London. The novel was included in the subsequent omnibus volumes from Lippincott's (distributed by Ward Lock in the U.K.) entitled 'Six Complete Novels by Famous Authors, from Lippincott's Monthly Magazine' (1890, blue cloth), and in 'Five Complete Novels by Famous Authors, from Lippincott's Monthly Magazine' (1891, brown cloth, and later in blue cloth). Book Form / Separate Edition: Blackett, 1890

(October). Red cloth. Second Issue has 'Griffith Farran & Cos. Standard Library' at foot of spine.

THE FIRM OF GIRDLESTONE.   Chatto & Windus 1890. Maroon cloth.

MYSTERIES AND ADVENTURES.   Walter Scott (1890). Green cloth. Also issued in wrappers. Continental Edition (enlarged): Heinemann & Balestier 1893.

THE CAPTAIN OF THE POLESTAR.   Longmans 1890. Dark green cloth, bevelled edges. The second issue has adverts dated 3/90.

THE WHITE COMPANY.   Smith, Elder 1891. 3 vols.

THE DOINGS OF RAFFLES HAW.   Cassell 1892. Dark blue cloth.

THE GULLY OF BLUEMANSDYKE.   Walter Scott (1892).
   This is a new edition of MYSTERIES AND ADVENTURES.

THE ADVENTURES OF SHERLOCK HOLMES.   The Strand Magazine (monthly, in wrappers) 1891–92. Book form: Newnes 1892. Bevelled pictorial pale blue cloth, with no name on the street sign. Dust wrapper. There are variant endpapers, including a light orangey-beige floral pattern.

THE GREAT SHADOW.   Bristol: Arrowsmith. (1892). Fcap 8vo. Brown cloth.

THE MEMOIRS OF SHERLOCK HOLMES.   The Strand Magazine (monthly, in wrappers) 1892–93. Book form: Newnes, 1894 (1893). Bevelled pictorial dark blue cloth, d/w.

THE PARASITE.   Constable 1894. Acme Library. Narrow fcap 8vo. Blue cloth, and simultaneously in wrappers.

ROUND THE RED LAMP.   Methuen 1894.

THE STARK MUNRO LETTERS.   Longmans, Green 1895.

THE EXPLOITS OF BRIGADIER GERARD.   Newnes 1896. Scarlet ribbed cloth, pictorial black blocking, gold lettering on front & spine, black device on back. First issue has catalogue dated 10.2.96.
   The work was re-issued later as a small cr. 8vo in smooth red cloth, with no mention of a previous edition.

RODNEY STONE   Smith, Elder 1896.

THE LAST ADVENTURES OF SHERLOCK HOLMES.   Newnes Cabinet
Edition 1897.
This is a re-titled reprint of THE MEMOIRS OF SHERLOCK HOLMES.

UNCLE BERNAC.   Smith, Elder 1897.

A DESERT DRAMA.   Philadelphia: Lippincott 1898. Dec blue cloth.

THE TRAGEDY OF THE KOROSKO.   Smith, Elder 1898.
Published earlier in U.S. as A DESERT DRAMA.

SONGS OF ACTION.   Smith, Elder 1898.

A DUET WITH AN OCCASIONAL CHORUS.   Grant Richards 1899.
First issue has 2pp integral adverts & 12pp catalogue dated 1899 with this
work listed as 'In Preparation'.

THE GREEN FLAG.   Smith, Elder 1900.

THE GREAT BOER WAR.   Smith, Elder 1900.

THE HOUND OF THE BASKERVILLES.   The Strand Magazine (monthly,
in wrappers) 1901–02. Book form: Newnes 1902. Red cloth with black
'hound' silhouette on front, and d/w. 25,000 copies were printed.
The book is not rare, but the d/w certainly is.

ADVENTURES OF GERARD.   Newnes (1903). Gilt dec blue cloth.

THE RETURN OF SHERLOCK HOLMES.   The Strand Magazine
(monthly, in wrappers) 1903–4. Book form: Newnes, 1905. Blue cloth, d/w.
U.S.: Collier's weekly magazine (wrappers) 1903–1905; Book Form: McClure
Phillips 1905.

THROUGH THE MAGIC DOOR.   Smith, Elder 1907.

ROUND THE FIRE STORIES.   Smith, Elder 1908.

THE LAST GALLEY.   Smith, Elder 1911.

SONGS OF THE ROAD.   Smith, Elder 1911.

THE LOST WORLD.   Hodder & Stoughton (1912). Also, a large paper
edition. A second large paper edition was issued by Frowde/Hodder (1914).

THE POISON BELT.   Hodder & Stoughton 1913.

THE VALLEY OF FEAR.   Strand Magazine (monthly, in wrappers) 1914–15.

Book form: Smith, Elder 1915 (June). Red cloth, d/w. Remaining stock issued later by John Murray with a new title-page dated 1915. U.S.: Collier's weekly magazine (wrappers) 1914. Book Form: Doran 1915 (February).
   The U.S. publications preceded the U.K. editions.

THE SPECKLED BAND. (play) French 1912. Light green wrappers. The second impression was in darker green wrappers.

DANGER! John Murray 1918.

THE GUARDS CAME THROUGH AND OTHER POEMS. Murray 1919. Wrappers.

THE COMING OF THE FAIRIES. Hodder & Stoughton (1922).

THREE OF THEM. Murray 1923.

THE LAND OF MIST. Hutchinson 1926.

HIS LAST BOW. Murray, 1927 (October). Cloth, d/w.
   Stories from various issues of The Strand Magazine.

THE CASE-BOOK OF SHERLOCK HOLMES. Murray (1927). Cloth, d/w.
   Stories from various issues of The Strand Magazines.

THE COMPLETE SHORT STORIES. Murray 1928.

THE COMPLETE LONG STORIES. Murray 1929.

THE MARACOT DEEP. Murray (1929).

THE EDGE OF THE UNKNOWN. Murray (1930).

DRYDEN, John (1631–1700)

   The following checklist is a small selection of Dryden's huge output. It includes some rare and important works, and some which collectors will encounter fairly often. His rarest works are very expensive, but some of the commoner first editions can be obtained for a few hundred pounds. Early reprints are often under £100.

THREE POEMS UPON THE DEATH OF HIS LATE HIGHNESSE, OLIVER, LORD PROTECTOR . . . by Edmund Waller, John Dryden and Mr Sprat. Printed by William Wilson . . . 1659. Sm. 4to.

An important early work and the first with Dryden's name on the title-page.

OF DRAMATIC POESIE, an Essay. Printed for Henry Herringman 1668. Sm. 4to.
His earliest major critical work. Shakespeare, he says, 'had the largest and most comprehensive soul'.

MARRIAGE A-LA-MODE. A Comedy. As it is Acted at the Theatre-Royal. Printed by T. N. for Henry Herringman 1673. 4to.
Perhaps his best-known play.

THE SATIRES OF DECIMUS JUNIUS JUVENALIS. Translated into English Verse by Mr. Dryden. for Tonson 1693. Folio.

TROILUS AND CRESSIDA, or, truth found too late. A Tragedy as it is acted at the Duke Theatre. for Abell Swall 1697. 4to.

THE SPANISH FRYER, or, the Double Discovery. for Richard Tonson & Jacob Tonson 1681. Sm. 4to.

ABSALOM AND ARCHITOPHEL, A Poem. (Anonymous). Printed for J. T. and are to be Sold by W. Davis 1681. Folio. First issue has sheet C corrected in manuscript.
Included in the Grolier Club's One Hundred Books Famous in English Literature. The 'J. T.' in the imprint was Jacob Tonson.

THE SECOND PART OF ABSALOM AND ARCHITOPHEL. (Anonymous). Jacob Tonson 1682. Folio. The second state has 'Fleet-Street' in the imprint and 12 lines on the final page.
Written in fact by Nahum Tate, but including 200 lines by Dryden.

THE VINDICATION: or, The Parallel of the French Holy-League and the English League and Covenant. for Jacob Tonson 1683. 4to.

BRITANNIA REDIVIVA: a Poem on the Birth of the Prince. for J. Tonson 1688. Folio.

ELEONORA: A Panegyrical Poem Dedicated to the Memory of the Late Countess of Abingdon. for Tonson 1692. 4to.

LOVE TRIUMPHANT; or, Nature will Prevail. A Tragi-Comedy. for Tonson 1694. 4to.

FABLES ANCIENT AND MODERN, translated into Verse . . . with Original Poems. for Tonson 1700. Folio.
This first edition is usually priced at two or three hundred pounds. Almost

as popular with collectors, is the Bensley folio edition of 1797, with engravings by Lady Diana Beauclerc.

THE COMEDIES, TRAGEDIES, AND OPERAS.   Now first Collected . . . for Tonson 1701. 2 vols. Folio. Portrait frontispiece.

THE MISCELLANEOUS WORKS . . . Now First Collected . . . Account of his Life and Writings (by Samuel Derrick).   Tonson 1760. 4 vols. 8vo.

DURRELL, Lawrence (1912–1992)

All of Durrell's early (pre–1940) publications are rare or at least scarce. A copy of QUAINT FRAGMENT would almost certainly be valued at well over a thousand pounds. The others are in the area of £500 to £1000. After that, from A PRIVATE COUNTRY onwards, values fall rapidly. Those published in the final two decades are very common indeed. The cornerstone of his achievement is the Alexandria Quartet. The four volumes, first published separately, are already hard to get in fine dust wrappers. and are certain to get even harder. No representative collection of modern fiction could afford to be without them.

QUAINT FRAGMENT.   Privately Published. Cecil Press 1931. Copies are known in red boards with cloth spine, and also in blue wrappers.
There are probably only a few copies in existence.

TEN POEMS.   Caduceus Press 1932. Wrappers. There were also 12 copies in buckram, signed by the author.
Many copies were destroyed in the Blitz.

BROMO BOMBASTS: A Fragment from a Laconic Drama.   By Gaffer Peeslake (pseudonym). Caduceus Press 1933. Black boards with paper label. 100 copies.

TRANSITION.   Caduceus Press 1934.
Few copies appear to have survived.

PIED PIPER OF LOVERS.   Cassell 1935.
His first novel, and thus an important book. It was not a commercial success, and has virtually disappeared from sight.

PANIC SPRING.   By Charles Norden (pseudonym). Faber (1937). U.S. Edition: Covici-Friede 1937.

THE BLACK BOOK.   Paris: Obelisk Press (1938). Wrappers. New York: Dutton 1960. Cloth & d/w. U.K.: Faber 1973. Cloth & d/w.

A PRIVATE COUNTRY.   Faber 1943. Grey boards.

PROSPERO'S CELL.   Faber 1945.
Not published in America until 1960, by Dutton.

CITIES, PLAINS AND PEOPLE.   Faber 1946.

ZERO AND ASYLUM IN THE SNOW; two excursions into reality.
Privately Printed, Rhodes 1946. (50 copies). Wrappers.
The second of these two sketches was 'Reprinted from SEVEN, 1946'. An
American edition was published in 1947, with the sub-title as the main title,
by Circle Editions, Berkeley, California.

SIX POEMS FROM THE GREEK OF SEKILIANOS AND SEFERIS.
(Translated, with an Introductory Note by) Lawrence Durrell. Privately
Printed, Rhodes 1946. Wrappers.
According to Durrell, there were about 50 copies.

CEFALU.   Editions Poetry (London) 1947. Brown cloth, also green cloth.

ON SEEMING TO PRESUME.   Faber 1948. Red boards.

SAPPHO.   Faber 1950. Grey boards. U.S.: Dutton 1958.

DEUS LOCI.   Ischia, Italy 1950. Greenish wrappers. 200 signed.

KEY TO MODERN POETRY.   Nevill 1952.

A KEY TO MODERN BRITISH POETRY.   Oklahoma Press 1952.
The U.S. edition of KEY TO MODERN POETRY.

REFLECTIONS ON A MARINE VENUS.   Faber 1953. U.S.: Dutton 1960.

POPE JOAN.   (trans.). Verschoyle (1954). U.S.: Dutton 1961.

PRIVATE DRAFTS.   (Nicosia, Cyprus) Proodos Press 1955. Pictorial wrappers. 100 signed.

THE TREE OF IDLENESS.   Faber 1955.

SELECTED POEMS.   Faber 1956. U.S.: Grove Press 1956.

BITTER LEMONS.   Faber 1957. U.S.: Dutton 1958.

ESPRIT DE CORPS.   Faber 1957. U.S.: Dutton 1958.

JUSTINE.   Faber 1957. U.S.: Dutton 1957.

WHITE EAGLES OVER SERBIA.   Faber 1957. U.S.: Criterion 1957.

THE DARK LABYRINTH.   New York: Ace 1958. Wrappers.
The U.S. edition of CEFALU. The title was adopted by Faber for their new edition of 1961.

BALTHAZAR.   Faber 1958. U.S.: Dutton 1958.

MOUNTOLIVE.   Faber 1958. U.S.: Dutton 1959.

STIFF UPPER LIP.   Faber 1958. U.S.: Dutton 1959.

ART AND OUTRAGE.   By Durrell and Perles. Putnam 1959. U.S.: Dutton 1960.

CLEA.   Faber 1960. U.S.: Dutton 1960.

COLLECTED POEMS.   Faber 1960. U.S.: Dutton 1960.

THE ALEXANDRIA QUARTET.   Faber 1962. Trade edition, also 500 signed copies. U.S.: Dutton 1962.

LAWRENCE DURRELL AND HENRY MILLER: A PRIVATE CORRESPONDENCE.   New York: Dutton 1963. U.K.: Faber 1963.

BECCAFICO.   Montpellier, France: La Licorne 1963. Limited to 150 signed copies. Wrappers.

AN IRISH FAUSTUS.   Faber 1963. U.S.: Dutton 1964.

LA DESCENTE DU STYX.   France: La Murene 1964. Limited to 250 signed. 4to. Wrappers.

SELECTED POEMS 1935–1963.   Faber 1964. Wrappers.

ACTE.   Faber (1965). U.S.: Dutton (1966).

SAUVE QUI PEUT.   Faber 1966. U.S.: Dutton 1967.

THE IKONS.   Faber 1966. U.S.: Dutton 1967.

NOTHING IS LOST, SWEET SELF.   Turret Books (1967). Pictorial wrappers. 100 signed.

IN ARCADIA.   Turret Books 1968. Wrappers. 100 signed.

TUNC.   Faber 1968. U.S.: Dutton 1968.

SPIRIT OF PLACE. Faber 1969. U.S.: Dutton 1969.

NUNQUAM. Faber 1970. U.S.: Dutton 1970.

THE RED LIMBO LINGO. Faber 1971. Limited Edition, including 100 signed. Red cloth, slipcase.

DOWN THE STYX. Santa Barbara, California: Capricorn Press 1971. Wrappers. 1000 copies. Also 200 bound specials, signed by the author.

ON THE SUCHNESS OF THE OLD BOY. Turret Books 1972. Limited Edition. 226 signed.

VEGA AND OTHER POEMS. Faber 1973.

THE BIG SUPPOSER. By Durrell & Alyn. New York: Abelard-Schuman 1973.
    Published in French under the title LE GRAND SUPPOSITOIRE, by Editions Pierre Belfond, Paris 1972.

THE PLANT MAGIC MAN. Santa Barbara, California: Capra Press 1973. Limited Edition. 200 signed.

THE REVOLT OF APHRODITE. Faber 1974.

THE BEST OF ANTROBUS. Faber 1974.

MONSIEUR. Faber 1974. U.S.: Viking 1974.

SICILIAN CAROUSEL. Faber 1977. U.S.: Viking 1977.

THE GREEK ISLANDS. Faber 1978. 4to. U.S.: Viking 1978.

LIVIA. Faber 1978. U.S.: Viking 1979.

COLLECTED POEMS: 1931–1974. Faber 1980. U.S.: Viking 1980.

A SMILE IN THE MIND'S EYE. Wildwood House 1980.

LITERARY LIFELINES. (Letters by Durrell and Aldington). Faber 1981. U.S.: Viking 1981.

CONSTANCE. Faber 1982. U.S.: Viking 1982.

SEBASTIAN. Faber 1983. U.S.: Viking 1984.

QUINX. Faber 1985. U.S.: Viking 1985.

HENRI MICHAUX. The Poet of Supreme Solipsism. Delos Press 1990. 226 copies, including 50 signed.

E

EDGEWORTH, Maria (1768–1849)

Her rarest first editions are probably A RATIONAL PRIMER and THE PARENT'S ASSISTANT, but her most popular works nowadays are the novels. Most of her works were originally issued in boards with paper labels. A few were issued in roan. The following selection includes her most important works.

LETTERS TO LITERARY LADIES. (anonymous). Johnson 1795. Boards. Second Edition (Enlarged): Johnson 1799. The second issue gives the author's name.

THE PARENT'S ASSISTANT. (anonymous) Johnson 1796. 6 vols sm. 8vo. The author's name first appeared in the Third Edition, 1800.

PRACTICAL EDUCATION. (By R. L. & Maria Edgeworth). Johnson 1798. 2 vols. 4to. Second Ed. (Revised): 1801. 3 vols.
Earlier editions of this title were written by Richard Lovell Edgeworth alone.

A RATIONAL PRIMER. By the Authors of Practical Education. Johnson 1799. Sm. 8vo.

CASTLE RACKRENT. (anonymous). Johnson 1800. Boards, label. Dublin Edition: P. Wogan etc. 1800.

BELINDA. Johnson 1801. 3 vols. Boards and labels.

EARLY LESSONS by the author of 'The Parents Assistant, Six Volumes.' Johnson 1801. 10 vols, sm. 12mo.
The Edition of 1809, also in 10 vols, gives the name of the author on all but the first two vols.

MORAL TALES FOR YOUNG PEOPLE. Johnson 1801. 5 vols.

ESSAYS ON IRISH BULLS. (By R. L. & Maria Edgeworth). Johnson 1802.

POPULAR TALES. Johnson 1804, 3 vols.

THE MODERN GRISELDA. Johnson 1805. Second Edition same year.

LEONORA. Johnson 1806. 2 vols. Boards and labels.

ESSAYS ON PROFESSIONAL EDUCATION. Johnson 1809.

TALES OF FASHIONABLE LIFE. Johnson 1809–12. 6 vols.

CONTINUATION OF EARLY LESSONS. Johnson 1814. 2 vols. Sm. 12mo. Half roan, marbled boards, labels.

PATRONAGE. Johnson 1814. 4 vols.

COMIC DRAMAS. R. Hunter 1917. Boards and label.

HARRINGTON & ORMOND. Hunter 1817. 3 vols. Boards and labels.

MEMOIRS OF RICHARD LOVELL EDGEWORTH, ESQ. Hunter 1820. 2 vols. 8vo.
  Begun by himself and concluded by his daughter Maria.

ROSAMUND. Hunter 1821. 2 vols. Sm. 12mo.

FRANK: A SEQUEL TO 'FRANK', IN EARLY LESSONS. Hunter 1822. 3 vols, Sm. 12mo. Half roan, marbled boards.

HARRY AND LUCY CONCLUDED. Hunter 1825. 4 vols. Boards, labels.

TALES AND MISCELLANEOUS PIECES. Hunter; Baldwin, Cradock & Joy; etc. 1825. 14 vols. Fcap 8vo.
  The First Collected Edition.

LITTLE PLAYS FOR CHILDREN. Hunter 1827. Sm. 12mo.

GARRY OWEN, OR THE SNOW WOMAN. First appeared in THE CHRISTMAS BOX, Ebers 1829. First Separate Ed.: Murray 1832.

TALES AND NOVELS. Baldwin & Cradock, etc. 1832–33. 18 vols.
  The Second Collected Edition.

HELEN. Bentley 1834. 3 vols. Boards, labels. U.S.: Philadelphia: Carey, Lea & Blanchard 1834. 2 vols.

ORLANDINO. Edinburgh: Chambers 1848. Sm. square 16mo. Variant bindings.

ELIOT, George (Marian Evans 1819–1880).

George Eliot has always been keenly collected and is currently very much in favour. Like so many Victorian authors, she was greatly undervalued during the middle of the 20th Century, but has gained a lot of ground during the last few decades. Her first two publications are rather obscure and frankly not very exciting for the average collector, though they are essential to the specialist. After those two however, all her publications are important works of English Literature. She is rare among authors in that she did not publish much that is trivial or superfluous. The first editions of her novels are generally priced at a few hundred pounds in the original cloth and in average condition.

THE LIFE OF JESUS. By David Friedrich Strauss. Chapman 1846. 3 vols. Some copies have adverts at the end. Green cloth with blind decoration on the front and the spine. Also, lilac cloth with blind decoration and (unlike the green binding) with the publisher in gilt at the foot of the spine.

The translation of this book, from the German, was begun by a Miss Brabant and completed by George Eliot. This is not acknowledged on the title-page, which merely says 'Translated from the Fourth German Edition'.

THE ESSENCE OF CHRISTIANITY. By Ludwig Feuerbach. Translated by Marian Evans. Chapman 1854.

The London bookseller Jarndyce has identified two issues – the first in black cloth with a half-title stating 'Chapman's Quarterly Series. No. VI.' and a later, remainder issue in purple cloth, without the 'Chapman' half-title. This is her only work published under her real name.

SCENES OF CLERICAL LIFE. Edinburgh: Blackwood 1858. 2 vols. Dark maroon cloth. 1050 copies published.

As might be expected of a pseudonymous first work of fiction, published in a smallish edition, it is rare.

ADAM BEDE. Edinburgh: Blackwood 1859. 3 vols. Bright brown (orange?) cloth. 2100 copies printed.

Reprinted several times in the same year, in 3 vols (2nd and 3rd editions) and then in 2 vols. These are clearly identified as new editions and should present no problem to the collector.

THE MILL ON THE FLOSS. Edinburgh: Blackwood 1860. 3 vols. Bright brown (orange?) cloth. About 4,000 copies printed.

Reprinted several times in the same year.

SILAS MARNER. Edinburgh: Blackwood 1861. One vol. Bright brown (orange?) cloth.

Six further editions were published in the same year.

ROMOLA. Smith, Elder 1863. 3 vols. Green cloth. U.S.: Harper 1863.
According to Sadleir, this is the second rarest of her first editions, and the rarest of all in fine condition. The second edition, also in 3 vols and published in the same year, is identified as such on the title page. The novel originally appeared in the Cornhill Magazine (July 1862-August 1863). For the book edition, minor revisions were made to the text.

FELIX HOLT THE RADICAL. Edinburgh: Blackwood 1866. 3 vols. Bright brown (red?) cloth. U.S.: Harper 1866. One vol. Brown cloth.

THE SPANISH GYPSY. Edinburgh: Blackwood 1868. Blue cloth. U.S.: Boston. Ticknor & Fields 1868. Green cloth.
Second edition, same year, identified on the title-page.

HOW LISA LOVED THE KING. Boston: Fields, Osgood 1869. Apparently issued in various cloths – terracotta, green, purple (etc.?).

AGATHA. Trubner & Co. 1869. 16pp. Pamphlet. Extremely rare.
The 'Second Edition' is a Wise forgery.

BROTHER AND SISTER: Sonnets by Marian Lewes. 1869. Blue wrappers.
A Wise forgery.

MIDDLEMARCH. Edinburgh: Blackwood n.d. (1871–72). 8 parts in green wrappers. Also, 4 vols in blue cloth. Also, as the 8 parts in 8 clothbound vols, with or without the wrappers bound in.
Title pages were printed for parts 1, 3, 5, and 7 only – evidence of the intention to publish in four bound vols rather than eight. The remaining parts are preceded by half-titles.

WISE, WITTY, AND TENDER SAYINGS. Edinburgh: Blackwood 1872.
Many reprints followed. Published in USA as WIT AND WISDOM OF GEORGE ELIOT. Boston: Roberts 1873.

THE LEGEND OF JUBAL AND OTHER POEMS. Edinburgh: Blackwood 1874. Cloth.

DANIEL DERONDA. Edinburgh: Blackwood n.d. (1876). 8 parts in slate-coloured wrappers. Also, 4 vols in dark maroon cloth. Also as the 8 parts in 8 clothbound vols. The first issue has pp.(iv) prelims in each of the four volumes. The second issue has pp.(vi) in each volume due to the insertion of a Contents leaf.
Title-pages were only printed for parts 1, 3, 5 & 7. With regard to the 'issue point' prelims, Sadleir believed their presence to be 'somewhat fortuitous'.

THE GEORGE ELIOT BIRTHDAY BOOK. Edinburgh: Blackwood n.d. First published in 1878.

IMPRESSIONS OF THEOPHRASTUS SUCH. Edinburgh: Blackwood 1879. Slate-coloured cloth. U.S.: Harper 1879. Green cloth.

THE ESSAYS. New York: Funk & Wagnalls 1883.

ESSAYS AND LEAVES FROM A NOTE-BOOK. Edinburgh: Blackwood 1884.
Basically the U.K. edition of the preceding item, but the contents are not identical.

GEORGE ELIOT'S LIFE AS RELATED IN HER LETTERS AND JOURNALS. Edinburgh: Blackwood 1885. 3 vols.

LETTERS FROM GEORGE ELIOT TO ELMA STUART 1872–80. Simpkin 1909.

EARLY ESSAYS. Privately Printed 1919. Limited Edition of 220 copies.

THE LIFTED VEIL. Holerth Press (1924). Wrappers.
The first separate edition of a story originally published in Blackwood's Magazine.

THE LETTERS. Bodley Head (1926).

ELIOT, T. S. (1888–1965)

There can be no doubt about Eliot's importance in 20th century poetry, and he is certain to remain of significant interest to collectors for a long time to come. Many of his later works, having been produced in fairly large numbers, will probably not become rare in the immediate future; but his earlier books, particularly the key books of poetry, are already very scarce and are bound to get positively rare before long.

His first book PRUFROCK, along with a few others – the first issue of POEMS (Hogarth Press), the 30 signed of ARA VOS PREC, the first issue of THE WASTE LAND, etc. – have a current value in the region of £2000. The 1000 copies of his second work, EZRA POUND, seem to have survived in decent numbers and are modestly valued at about $500. The great majority of his first editions can still be had for under £50. I believe the list below contains all the major works in his large output.

PRUFROCK AND OTHER OBSERVATIONS. Egoist Ltd 1917. 40pp in buff wrappers. 500 copies.

EZRA POUND: HIS METRIC AND POETRY. (anon). New York: Knopf 1917 (January 1918). Rose boards, plain buff d/w. 1000 copies.

POEMS. Hogarth Press 1919. Wrappers, paper label on front. 'Fewer than 250' copies. Earliest copies have misprints on page (13) – 'aestival' for 'estivale' (line 6) and 'capitaux' for 'chapitaux' (line 12). Later copies are in marbled wrappers.

ARA VUS PREC. (i.e. ARA VOS PREC). Ovid Press (1920). 264 copies, including 30 signed. Various bindings, most being yellow cloth spine & black boards (black cloth later), paper label on spine (lettered ARA VOS PREC).

POEMS. New York: Knopf 1920. Tan boards, yellow d/w. The U.S. edition, with some minor changes, of ARA VOS PREC.

THE SACRED WOOD. Methuen (1920). Later d/ws have the subtitle 'Essays on Poetry and Criticism' on the front. Copies bound later have 8pp adverts at end. U.S.: Knopf 1921.

THE WASTE LAND. New York: Boni & Liveright 1922. Flexible black cloth (later stiff), d/w. 1000 copies. Later copies have 'a' dropped out of 'mountain' on page 41, line 339. U.K.: Hogarth Press 1923. Boards. About 460 copies.

HOMAGE TO JOHN DRYDEN. Hogarth Press 1924. Wrappers. About 2000 copies.

POEMS 1909–1925. Faber & Gwyer 1925. Blue cloth, paper label, d/w. 1460 copies. U.S.: Harcourt Brace 1932.

JOURNEY OF THE MAGI. (Faber and Gwyer) 1927. 5000 copies. Wrappers. Later (unsold) copies issued in mauve envelope. Also 350 copies in yellow boards. U.S.: Rudge 1927. 27 copies only. Wrappers.

SHAKESPEARE AND THE STOICISM OF SENECA. O.U.P. 1927. Wrappers.

A SONG FOR SIMEON. (Faber and Gwyer 1928). Wrappers. 3500 copies. Later (unsold) copies issued in envelope. Also, 500 signed, in boards.

FOR LANCELOT ANDREWES. Faber & Gwyer (1928). U.S.: Doubleday 1929.

DANTE. Faber (1929). Boards, d/w.

ANIMULA. (Faber 1929). 3000 in wrappers; also 400 signed, in boards.

ASH-WEDNESDAY. New York: Fountain Press / London: Faber 1930. Limited to 600 copies. Ordinary Edition: Faber 1930.

ANABASIS. (Trans.) Faber 1930. Also 350 signed. U.S.: Harcourt Brace 1938.

MARINA. (Faber 1930). Wrappers. Also 400 signed, in boards.

THOUGHTS AFTER LAMBETH. Faber (1931). Wrappers. Also 300 in boards.

TRIUMPHAL MARCH. (Faber, 1931). Wrappers. Also 300 signed, in boards.

CHARLES WHIBLEY. O.U.P. 1931. Wrappers.

SELECTED ESSAYS 1917–1932. Faber (1932). Also 115 signed. U.S.: Harcourt Brace 1932.

JOHN DRYDEN. New York: Holliday 1932. Boards, d/w. 1000 copies. Also 110 signed.

SWEENEY AGONISTES. Faber (1932). Blue boards, d/w (later, blue-green boards, d/w).

THE USE OF POETRY AND THE USE OF CRITICISM. Faber (1933). U.S.: Harvard U.P. 1933.

AFTER STRANGE GODS. Faber (1934). U.S.: Harcourt Brace 1934.

THE ROCK. Faber (1934). 2000 in wrappers & 1000 in boards. U.S.: Harcourt Brace 1934.

ELIZABETHAN ESSAYS. Faber (1934). Earliest copies have misprint 'No. 21' on half-title, later changed to 'No. 24' (initially a cancel leaf, later integral).

MURDER IN THE CATHEDRAL. Acting Edition. Goulden 1935. Wrappers. Complete edition: Faber (1935). U.S.: Harcourt Brace 1935.

ESSAYS ANCIENT AND MODERN. Faber (1936). U.S.: Harcourt Brace 1936.

COLLECTED POEMS 1909–1935. Faber (1936). U.S.: Harcourt Brace 1936.

THE FAMILY REUNION. Faber (1939). U.S.: Harcourt Brace 1939.

OLD POSSUM'S BOOK OF PRACTICAL CATS.   Faber (1939). U.S.:
Harcourt Brace 1939. Illustrated Edition: Faber (1940).

THE IDEA OF A CHRISTIAN SOCIETY.   Faber (1939). U.S.: Harcourt
Brace 1940.

THE WASTE LAND AND OTHER POEMS.   Faber (1940). Boards, d/w.

EAST COKER.   Unbound stapled supplement to The New English Weekly
Easter Number 1940. In the same year, there was a reprint of 500 copies
(identified as a reprint on the front). The issue by Faber (1940) in yellow
wrappers, was the third edition.

BURNT NORTON.   Faber (1941). Wrappers.

POINTS OF VIEW.   Faber (1941).

THE DRY SALVAGES.   Faber (1941). Wrappers.

THE CLASSICS AND THE MAN OF LETTERS.   O.U.P. 1942. Wrap-
pers. In later copies, the middle letter of 'the' on line 6 of the title-page, is
very faint.

THE MUSIC OF POETRY.   Glasgow: Jackson 1942. Wrappers.

LITTLE GIDDING.   Faber (1942). Wrappers.

FOUR QUARTETS.   New York: Harcourt Brace (1943). 'first American
edition' on verso title. 788 copies. U.K.: Faber (1944).

REUNION BY DESTRUCTION.   The Council for the Defence of Church
Principles Pamphlet 7. (1943). Wrappers.

WHAT IS A CLASSIC?   Faber (1945). Green wrappers. 500 copies. This,
known as the Virgil Society issue, contains a statement of the objects of the
Society. An Ordinary Issue of 4500 copies was published in grey boards.

A PRACTICAL POSSUM.   Cambridge (Mass.): Harvard Printing Office and
Department of Graphic Arts, 1947. Wrappers. '80 copies' (in fact, only 60).

ON POETRY.   Massachusetts: Concord 1947. Wrappers. 750 copies.

MILTON.   Cumberlege 1947. Wrappers. 500 copies.

A SERMON.   C.U.P. 1948. Pamphlet. 300 copies.

NOTES TOWARDS THE DEFINITION OF CULTURE. Faber (1948). U.S.: Harcourt Brace 1949.

FROM POE TO VALERY. New York: Harcourt Brace (1948). Boards & envelope. 1500 copies.

THE UNDERGRADUATE POEMS. Massachusetts: Harvard Advocate (1949). Wrappers. About 1000 copies. Not authorized.

THE AIMS OF POETIC DRAMA. Poets' Theatre Guild 1949. Pamphlet. 5000 copies.

THE COCKTAIL PARTY. Faber (1950). U.S.: Harcourt Brace 1950.

POEMS WRITTEN IN EARLY YOUTH. Stockholm: Privately Printed 1950. Boards. 12 copies. U.K.: Faber (1967).

POETRY AND DRAMA. Cambridge, Mass.: Harvard U.P. 1951. U.K.: Faber (1951).

THE VALUE AND USE OF CATHEDRALS IN ENGLAND TODAY. (Chichester 1952). Wrappers. About 2000 copies.

AN ADDRESS TO MEMBERS OF THE LONDON LIBRARY. (1952). Wrappers. 500 copies.

THE COMPLETE POEMS AND PLAYS (1909–1950). New York: Harcourt Brace (1952).

AMERICAN LITERATURE AND THE AMERICAN LANGUAGE. Washington University (1953). Wrappers. 500 copies.

THE THREE VOICES OF POETRY. C.U.P. 1953. Wrappers.

THE CONFIDENTIAL CLERK. Faber (1954). Priced on d/w at 10s.6d and later at 12s.6d. U.S.: Harcourt Brace 1954.

RELIGIOUS DRAMA. New York: House of Books 1954. Limited to 300 numbered, plus 26 signed.

THE CULTIVATION OF CHRISTMAS TREES. Faber (1954). Wrappers & envelope. U.S.: Farrar Straus 1956.

THE LITERATURE OF POLITICS. Conservative Centre (1955). Wrappers.

THE FRONTIERS OF CRITICISM.   Minneapolis: Minnesota U.P. (1956). Wrappers & envelope.

ON POETRY AND POETS.   Faber (1957). U.S.: Farrar Straus 1957.

THE ELDER STATESMAN.   Faber (1959). U.S.: Farrar Straus 1959.

GEOFFREY FABER 1889–1961.   Faber (1961). Boards, d/w (later in box). 100 copies.

COLLECTED PLAYS.   Faber (1962).

GEORGE HERBERT.   Longmans, Green (1962). Wrappers.

COLLECTED POEMS 1909–1962.   Faber (1963). U.S.: Harcourt Brace 1963.

KNOWLEDGE AND EXPERIENCE IN THE PHILOSOPHY OF F. H. BRADLEY.   Faber (1964). U.S.: Farrar Straus 1964.

TO CRITICIZE THE CRITIC.   Faber (1965). U.S.: Farrar Straus 1965.

THE COMPLETE POEMS AND PLAYS.   Faber (1968).

F

FARQUHAR, George (1678–1707)

Farquhar gave up acting after wounding a fellow player, and took to writing comedies. His best-known work, still frequently performed today is:

THE BEAUX' STRATAGEM.   A Comedy. As it is Acted at the Queen's Theatre in the Hay-Market. By Her Majesty's Sworn Comedians. Printed for Bernard Lintott n.d. (1707). 4to.

FAULKNER, William (1867–1962)

All Faulkner's early works are getting scarce, but his first, the privately printed MARBLE FAUN, is extremely rare and worth in the region of $20,000. Demand for his first editions remains very strong, especially in America.

THE MARBLE FAUN. Privately Printed. Boston (1924).

SOLDIER'S PAY. New York: Liveright 1926. U.K.: Chatto & Windus 1930.

MOSQUITOES. Privately Printed. New York 1927. The earliest dust wrapper was red and green, with a mosquito. Later issued in a dust wrapper bearing the imprint of Boni & Liveright on the spine, and with a design representing card players on a yacht. Revised Edition: Garden City 1937.

SATORIS. New York: Harcourt Brace (1929). U.K.: Chatto & Windus 1933. Blue cloth. Top edges blue. Later, tan cloth, and top edges plain.

THE SOUND AND THE FURY. New York: Harcourt Smith (1929). On the back of the d/w, HUMANITY UPROOTED is priced at $3.00. Later, the price became $3.50. U.K.: Chatto & Windus 1931. Black cloth. Top edges red. Later, red-stamped mustard cloth; top edges plain; no imprint on spine.

AS I LAY DYING. New York: Harcourt Smith (1930). On some bindings, the lettering is imperfect. On page 11, line 1, the initial letter 'I' is misaligned. This is taken as an indication of an early copy. U.K.: Chatto & Windus 1935. White-stamped blue cloth. Top edges blue.

SANCTUARY. New York: Harcourt Smith (1931). U.K.: Chatto & Windus 1931. Gold-stamped red cloth. Later, black-stamped (brighter) red cloth.

THESE 13. New York: Harcourt Smith (1931). U.K.: Chatto & Windus 1933. Gold stamped blue cloth. Top edges green.

LIGHT IN AUGUST. New York: Random House (1932). Glassine d/w over paper d/w. U.K.: Chatto & Windus 1933.

A GREEN BOUGH. New York: Harcourt Smith 1933.

DOCTOR MARTINO AND OTHER STORIES. New York: Harcourt Smith 1934. U.K.: Chatto & Windus 1934.

PYLON. New York: Harcourt Smith 1935. Dust wrappers with a blank back are later. U.K.: Chatto & Windus 1936. Reddish-brown cloth; later, bright red.

ABSALOM, ABSALOM!   New York: Random House 1936. Also 300 signed. U.K.: Chatto & Windus (1937). Cream cloth, stamped in red and black. Top edges red. Glassine d/w.

THE UNVANQUISHED.   New York: Random House (1938). U.K.: Chatto & Windus 1938.

THE WILD PALMS.   New York: Random House (1939). Tan cloth. Earliest copies have the spine stamped in gold and green; later stamped in brown and green. U.K.: Chatto & Windus 1939.

THE HAMLET.   New York: Random House 1940. The earliest dust wrapper has adverts for other books on the back, but reviews of the present book were added later. U.K.: Chatto & Windus 1940.

GO DOWN, MOSES.   New York: Random House (1942). Black cloth. Top edges red. Also issued in various cloths, with top edges plain – these are regarded as less desirable. U.K.: Chatto & Windus 1942.

INTRUDER IN THE DUST.   New York: Random House (1948). U.K.: Chatto & Windus 1949.

KNIGHT'S GAMBIT.   New York: Random House (1949). U.K.: Chatto & Windus 1951.

COLLECTED STORIES.   New York: Random House (1950). Blue and black printed title-page. Top edges blue. U.K. Chatto & Windus 1951.

REQUIEM FOR A NUN.   New York: Random House (1951). Copies with top edges grey are thought to be of the earliest issue. U.K.: Chatto & Windus 1953.

A FABLE.   New York: Random House (1954). Maroon cloth. Top edges grey. U.K.: Chatto & Windus 1954.

FAULKNER'S COUNTRY.   London: Chatto and Windus 1955.

THE TOWN.   New York: Random House (1957). Red cloth. Top edges grey, endpapers grey. Dust wrapper flap has date code 5/57. Various bindings used later. U.K.: Chatto & Windus 1958.

NEW ORLEANS SKETCHES.   Rutgers University Press 1958. U.K.: Sidgwick & Jackson 1959.

THE COLLECTED STORIES.   London: Chatto & Windus 1958. 3 vols.

THE MANSION. New York: Random House (1959). U.K.: Chatto & Windus 1960.

THE REIVERS. New York: Random House (1962). Red cloth. Top edges red. Copies with the blind stamp of the Book of the Month Club on the back, are not so desirable. U.K.: Chatto & Windus 1962.

SELECTED SHORT STORIES. New York: Random House 1962.

EARLY PROSE AND POETRY. New York: Little Brown 1962. U.K.: Cape 1962.

ESSAYS, SPEECHES, AND PUBLIC LETTERS. New York: Random House 1966. U.K.: Chatto & Windus 1966.

FIELDING, Henry (1707–1754)

Wrote numerous plays, poetry, and other pieces, before publishing the novels on which his reputation rests. The novels listed below are not extremely rare, but are important enough to justify values in the range of £1000–£2000. An important minor work was the parody AN APOLOGY FOR THE LIFE OF MRS SHAMELA ANDREWS, published pseudonymously in 1741. The piece was an expression of contempt for Richardson's PAMELA, which had met with great popular success. It is somewhat scarcer than the major novels.

For some of his publications (his farces, in particular) he used the pseudonym 'Scriblerus Secundus'. His first farce was set in literary London, and was in two parts. It was THE AUTHOR'S FARCE; AND THE PLEASURES OF THE TOWN. As Acted at the Theatre in the Hay-Market. Written by Scriblerus Secundus . . . Printed for J. Roberts 1730. 8vo. His major works were:

THE HISTORY OF THE ADVENTURES OF JOSEPH ANDREWS. A. Millar 1742. 2 vols. 12mo. The Second Edition of 1742 was 'Revised and Corrected with Alterations and Additions by the Author' (2 vols).

THE HISTORY OF TOM JONES, A Foundling. A. Millar 1749. 6 vols. 12mo. The first issue has cancels (see Rothschild), an errata leaf in vol 1, and a misprinted title in Vol 5.
There is a case for calling the second issue a second edition, there having been extensive re-setting of the type to eliminate the errata. That aside, the second and third editions were published in the same year, and are worth several hundred pounds apiece.

AMELIA.   A. Millar 1752. 4 vols. 12mo. Press figure on p. 109 (usually) or
p. 108 (sometimes). Copies are rarely seen with a leaf of advertisements in
Volume II, page 262 – 'The Universal-Register-Office'.

MISCELLANIES.   Printed for the Author, 1743. 3 vols.
  Includes the first printing of JONATHAN WILD, A JOURNEY FROM
THIS WORLD TO THE NEXT, and numerous poems and other pieces.

THE LIFE OF MR. JONATHAN WILD THE GREAT.   'A New Edition,
with considerable corrections and additions'. A. Millar 1754. 12mo.
  The first separate edition. It originally appeared within MISCELLANIES.

THE WORKS.   A. Millar 1762. 4 vols. 4to.
  The First Collected Edition.

FIRBANK, Ronald (1886–1926)

Firbank financed the publication of most of his works. It was not until
Brentano's took on PRANCING NIGGER (entitled SORROW IN SUN-
LIGHT in the U.K.) that a publisher undertook the costs. They were
however, published by sound and established firms and, probably because of
this, they are not exceptionally scarce, despite being done in fairly small
numbers (usually 500 copies). Those in wrappers tend to be the hardest to
find. And those in cloth are certainly scarce in the dust wrappers.

ODETTE d'ANTREVERNES & A STUDY IN TEMPERAMENT.   Elkin
Mathews 1905. Crown 8vo. 48pp. Green wrappers, also rose wrappers. 500
copies. Also 10 copies on Japanese vellum.

VAINGLORY.   Grant Richards 1915. Black cloth, d/w. 500 copies. U.S.:
Brentano's (1925). Black cloth, d/w.

ODETTE.   Grant Richards 1916. Wrappers.

INCLINATIONS.   Grant Richards 1916. Black cloth, d/w.

CAPRICE.   Grant Richards 1917. Black cloth, d/w. 500 copies. Also 2 copies
on vellum.

VALMOUTH.   Grant Richards 1919. Black cloth, d/w. 500 copies.

THE PRINCESS ZOUBAROFF.   Grant Richards 1920. Black cloth, d/w.

SANTAL.   Grant Richards 1921. 300 copies. Wrappers.

THE FLOWER BENEATH THE FOOT. Grant Richards 1923. Black cloth, d/w. 1000 copies.

PRANCING NIGGER. New York: Brentano's (1924). Black cloth, d/w.

SORROW IN SUNLIGHT. Brentano's (U.K.) (1925). Black cloth, d/w. The U.K. edition of PRANCING NIGGER.

CONCERNING THE ECCENTRICITIES OF CARDINAL PIRELLI. Grant Richards 1926. Black cloth, d/w.

THE ARTIFICIAL PRINCESS. Duckworth 1934.

FIVE NOVELS. Duckworth 1949.
The five novels had all previously appeared separately.

FITZGERALD, Edward (1809–1883)

Fitzgerald is well known only for his free translation of the RUBÁIYÁT OF OMAR KHAYYÁM, but he did publish a few other works which are claiming the interest of collectors. Briefly, these include translations of the Persian allegory SALAMAN AND ABSAL, 1856, and of the AGAMEMNON (1865), and the anonymous POLONIUS, 1852, and EUPHRANOR, 1851.

THE RUBÁIYÁT was published at Fitzgerald's expense by the bookseller Bernard Quaritch, who reputedly placed them in his 'penny box' from which Rossetti and Swinburne obtained a few copies. According to the latter, they returned for more copies the next day, only to find that their interest had driven the price up to twopence. Soon afterwards (according to Swinburne), copies were selling at thirty shillings. Today, he would be lucky to get much change out of £10,000.

The four editions which appeared during Fitzgerald's lifetime were revised by the translator, and are consequently of some interest to collectors. The first edition contains 75 quatrains, the second contains 110, the third and fourth each contain 101. The fourth edition became the standard text and the basis for countless further editions.

RUBÁIYÁT OF OMAR KHAYYÁM. Translated into English Verse. Bernard Quaritch 1859. 4to. Brown wrappers. About 250 copies printed. Second Edition 1868, Third Edition 1872, Fourth Edition 1879. U.S.: no publisher, place or date (Columbus, Ohio 1870). 'Second Edition' at foot of title-page. This first American Edition was a piracy. About 100 copies were probably printed, for distribution among the admirers of the work in Columbus. Second U.S. Edition: Boston: Osgood 1878. 'First American From the Third London Edition' appears on the title-page.

The translator's name does not appear on the title-page in any of the editions listed above. After the first edition, according to the title-pages, the work was not translated, but 'Rendered into English Verse'. The pirated American edition is very much rarer than the Quaritch first edition, but is far less valuable.

FITZGERALD, F. Scott (1896–1940)

Many stories by Fitzgerald first appeared in periodicals like Vanity Fair, Saturday Evening Post, and The Smart Set, before being collected into volume form. His first novel, THIS SIDE OF PARADISE, was a great success and made him a celebrity. Subsequent volumes were then published in quite large numbers. Despite this, his first editions in general, and especially the early ones, are hard to come by – demand greatly exceeding the supply.

THIS SIDE OF PARADISE. New York: Scribners 1920. Green cloth. 'Published April, 1920' & Scribners seal on verso title. U.K.: Collins (1921).

FLAPPERS AND PHILOSOPHERS. New York: Scribners 1920. U.K.: Collins 1922.

THE BEAUTIFUL AND DAMNED. New York: Scribners 1922. Green cloth. 'Published March, 1922' on verso title. First issue has no ads at end; the d/w has the title printed in solid black. U.K.: Collins 1922.

TALES OF THE JAZZ AGE. New York: Scribners 1922. First printing: 'and' on line 6, p. 232; Second printing: 'and' has become 'an'. U.K.: Collins 1923.

THE VEGETABLE. New York: Scribners 1923. U.K.: 1923.

THE GREAT GATSBY. New York: Scribners 1925. Error on p. 205, line 9 – 'sick in tired'. The second state has the misprint 'sickantired' on page 205. First state d/w has list of works by Fitzgerald and Lardner on the flaps, and an erroneous lower-case 'j' on the back. U.K.: Chatto & Windus 1925.

ALL THE SAD YOUNG MEN. New York: Scribners 1926. The first printing has the publisher's seal on the verso title-page.

JOHN JACKSON'S ARCADY. New York: Baker 1928.

TENDER IS THE NIGHT. New York: Scribners 1934. Green cloth. Publisher's seal & 'A' on verso title. U.K.: Chatto & Windus 1934.

A 'restructured version' was published by Scribners in 1951, and in the U.K. by Grey Walls Press in 1953.

TAPS AT REVEILLE. New York: Scribners 1935. Second state has pp. 349–352 cancelled.

THE LAST TYCOON. New York: Scribners 1941. U.K.: Grey Walls Press 1949.

THE CRACK-UP. (No place): New Directions (1945). Red brown and black title-page, colophon on p. 348. Later printings have title-page in black only, and no colophon. New Directions 'British Empire' issue: identical with the U.S. issue but with a label on p. 2 saying the book is 'distributed through the British Empire'. U.K.: Grey Walls Press 1947.
The appeal of the Grey Walls Press edition is somewhat diminished by the earlier appearance of the British Empire issue, but it nevertheless stands as the first edition from a U.K. publisher.

THE STORIES. Intro by Cowley. New York: Scribners 1951.

BORROWED TIME. (short stories). London: Grey Walls Press 1951.

AFTERNOON OF AN AUTHOR. New York: Scribners 1957. U.K.: Bodley Head 1958.
Princeton University Press published a private edition in 1957.

THE PAT HOBBY STORIES. New York: Scribners (1962).

THE LETTERS. New York: Scribners (1963). U.K.: Bodley Head 1964.

THE APPRENTICE FICTION. U.S.: Rutgers U.P. 1965.

IN HIS OWN TIME. Kent State U.P. 1971.

DEAR SCOTT / DEAR MAX. New York: Scribners 1971. U.K.: Cassell 1973.

AS EVER, SCOTT FITZ. New York: Lippincott 1972. U.K.: Woburn 1973.

THE BASIL AND JOSEPHINE STORIES. New York: Scribners 1973.

BITS OF PARADISE. New York: Scribners 1974. U.K.: Bodley Head 1973.

THE NOTEBOOKS. New York: Harcourt, etc. (1978).

THE PRICE WAS HIGH.   New York: Harcourt Brace 1979. U.K.: Quartet 1979.

THE CORRESPONDENCE.   New York: Random House 1980.

FLEMING, Ian (1908–1964)

The surge of interest in Fleming over the last two decades has almost certainly been due to the highly successful Bond films. The high prices achieved by his first novel CASINO ROYALE are astonishing (£500–£1000, sometimes more). His other early novels have got above £100. None of them are actually rare, and that includes CASINO ROYALE, of which 4750 copies of the first edition were printed. It has all been a case of a quickly escalating demand exceeding supply. An additional factor has doubtless been that the books were not valued in the first place, and many will have been treated badly by those who bought them merely to read. With Fleming, of course, we are in a corner of the market where condition is absolutely crucial. To achieve the sort of prices mentioned above, both the books and the dust wrappers must be absolutely fine.

Fleming's first appearance in print is the piece 'Foreign News' in THE KEMSLEY MANUAL OF JOURNALISM, published by Cassell in 1950. It is a rather unattractive largish volume and even now is often seen languishing in some dark corner of a bookshop.

The Bond novels are not very interesting bibliographically and identification of the first editions is straightforward. They were all published in England by Cape, who employed the standard legend 'First Published in. . . .' on the verso title. In the absence of any indication of a subsequent impression, the books can be taken as first editions. They were all published in black cloth.

There are two points to look out for. The dust wrapper of CASINO ROYALE must carry only the price at the bottom on the front flap. And DR. NO may have the figure of a woman on the front cover, or it may not – both versions are equally first editions.

CASINO ROYALE.   Cape 1953. U.S.: Macmillan 1954.

LIVE AND LET DIE.   Cape 1954. U.S.: Macmillan 1955.

MOONRAKER.   Cape 1955. U.S.: Macmillan 1955.

DIAMONDS ARE FOREVER.   Cape 1956. U.S.: Macmillan 1956.

FROM RUSSIA, WITH LOVE.   Cape 1957. U.S.: Macmillan 1957.

THE DIAMOND SMUGGLERS.   Cape 1957. U.S.: Macmillan 1958.

DR. NO.   Cape 1958. U.S.: Macmillan 1958.

GOLDFINGER.   Cape 1959. U.S.: Macmillan 1959.

FOR YOUR EYES ONLY.   Cape 1960. U.S.: Viking 1960.

THUNDERBALL.   Cape 1961. U.S.: Viking 1961.

THE SPY WHO LOVED ME.   Cape 1962. U.S.: Viking 1962.

ON HER MAJESTY'S SECRET SERVICE.   Cape 1963. Also, 250 copies signed. U.S.: NAL 1963.

THRILLING CITIES.   Cape 1963. U.S.: NAL 1964.

YOU ONLY LIVE TWICE.   Cape 1964. U.S.: NAL 1964.

CHITTY-CHITTY-BANG-BANG.   Adventure Number I. Cape 1964. 4to.; Adventure Number 2. Cape 1964. 4to.; Adventure Number 3. Cape 1965. 4to.; U.S.: all three by Random House 1964.

THE MAN WITH THE GOLDEN GUN.   Cape 1965. U.S.: NAL 1965.

IAN FLEMING INTRODUCES JAMAICA.   Deutsch 1965. U.S.: Hawthorne 1965.

OCTOPUSSY AND THE LIVING DAYLIGHTS.   Cape 1966. U.S.: NAL 1966.

FORD, Ford Madox (Ford Hermann Madox Hueffer 1873–1939)

He changed his name to Ford Madox Ford in 1919. Prior to that his books were published under the name of Hueffer or the pseudonym Daniel Chaucer. From 1908 to 1909 he was editor of THE ENGLISH REVIEW, in which some of his work was published. During his term as editor, THE NATURE OF A CRIME, on which he collaborated with Conrad, was serialized. It was not published in book form until 1924. All his books up to the first World War are now scarce, and these are listed below. The list ends with his masterpiece THE GOOD SOLDIER which is worth something like £2000 in the very scarce dust wrapper (and considerably less without it).

THE BROWN OWL. By Ford H. Heuffer. T. Fisher Unwin 1892 (1891). Tan cloth. U.S.: Putnam 1892.

THE SHIFTING OF THE FIRE. By H. Ford Hueffer. T. Fisher Unwin 1892.

THE INHERITORS. By Conrad & Hueffer. New York: McClure, Phillips 1901 Dec. yellow cloth. U.K.: Heinemann 1901. Dec. yellow cloth.

ROMANCE. By Conrad & Hueffer. Smith, Elder 1903. White-lettered blue cloth. U.S.: McClure Phillips 1904 (May). Blue cloth, gilt.

THE BENEFACTOR. Brown, Langham & Co 1905. Black-lettered tan cloth.

THE FIFTH QUEEN. Alston Rivers 1906. Red cloth, gilt.

PRIVY SEAL. Alston Rivers 1907.

AN ENGLISH GIRL. Methuen 1907.

THE FIFTH QUEEN CROWNED. Eveleigh Nash 1908.

MR. APOLLO. Methuen 1908.

THE 'HALF-MOON'. Eveleigh Nash 1909.

A CALL. Chatto & Windus 1910.

THE PORTRAIT. Methuen 1910.

THE SIMPLE LIFE LIMITED. By Daniel Chaucer (pseud.). John Lane 1911.

LADIES WHOSE BRIGHT EYES. Constable 1911.

THE PANEL. Constable 1912.

THE NEW HUMPTY-DUMPTY. By Daniel Chaucer (pseud.). John Lane 1912.

MR. FLEIGHT. Howard Latimer 1913.

THE YOUNG LOVELL. Chatto & Windus 1913.

THE GOOD SOLDIER.   John Lane 1915.

FORSTER, E. M. (1879–1970)

There has been a strong surge of interest in Forster since his death, triggered
by the publicity which attended the posthumous publication of MAURICE
and the highly successful film versions of his novels. The Hogarth Press,
publisher of several Forster books, was at Richmond, Surrey until 1924,
when it moved to London.

WHERE ANGELS FEAR TO TREAD.   Edinburgh: Blackwood 1905. Blue
cloth, gold lettering on spine, ruby endpapers. Adverts at end – these vary,
but the earliest do not mention WHERE ANGELS FEAR TO TREAD. 1050
copies were printed. U.S.: Knopf 1920. Black cloth, d/w.
   No bibliography of Forster mentions a dust wrapper for the U.K. edition,
and I have not seen nor heard of one in recent times. However, I am certain
I had one in stock many years ago.

THE LONGEST JOURNEY.   Blackwood 1907. Green cloth, blue d/w.
U.S.: Knopf 1922.

A ROOM WITH A VIEW.   Arnold 1908. Dark red cloth, d/w. U.S.: Putnam
1911.

HOWARD'S END.   Arnold 1910. Dark red cloth, d/w. U.S.: Putnam 1910.

THE CELESTIAL OMNIBUS.   Sidgwick & Jackson 1911. U.S.: Knopf 1923.

THE STORY OF THE SIREN.   Hogarth Press 1920. 16pp. Marbled wrappers, with paper label. The label on the first issue divides the title thus THE
STORY/OF THE SIREN. There are two other versions of the label. In all,
500 copies were printed.

THE GOVERNMENT OF EGYPT.   Labour Research Dept. (1920).
Includes 'Notes on Egypt' by Forster. Wrappers with paper label.

ALEXANDRIA.   Alexandria: Whitehead Morris 1922. Boards, without d/
w. Folding map in pocket at end. New Revised Edition: Whitehead Morris
1938. Again issued in boards and without a d/w. There were 250 signed by
the author for the Royal Archaeological Society of Alexandria.
   Apparently many copies of the original edition were lost in a warehouse
fire.

PHAROS AND PHARILLON.   Hogarth Press 1923. Patterned boards with blue cloth spine, paper label (no dust wrapper). 900 copies printed. U.S.: Knopf 1923. Orange cloth.

A PASSAGE TO INDIA.   Arnold 1924. Red cloth. Also 200 signed. U.S.: Harcourt Brace 1924.

ANONYMITY.   Hogarth Press 1925. Boards or wrappers.

ASPECTS OF THE NOVEL.   Arnold 1927. U.S.: Harcourt Brace 1927.

THE ETERNAL MOMENT and Other Stories.   Sidgwick & Jackson 1928. The first binding was maroon cloth stamped in gold, and had a dust wrapper bearing the price 5s. A later binding was stamped in black. U.S.: Harcourt Brace 1928.

A LETTER TO MADAN BLANCHARD.   Hogarth Press 1931. Wrappers. U.S.: Harcourt Brace 1932.

GOLDSWORTHY LOWES DICKINSON.   Arnold 1934. U.S.: Harcourt Brace 1934.

ABINGER HARVEST.   Arnold (1936). First issue includes 'A Flood in the Office', later removed (pp. 277–281). U.S.: Harcourt Brace 1936.

WHAT I BELIEVE.   Hogarth Press 1939. Wrappers.

READING AS USUAL.   Tottenham Public Libraries 1939. Wrappers. Scarce.

ENGLAND'S PLEASANT LAND.   Hogarth Press 1940.

NORDIC TWILIGHT.   Macmillan 1940. Wrappers.

VIRGINIA WOOLF.   C.U.P. 1942. Wrappers. U.S.: Harcourt Brace 1942.

TOLSTOY'S 'WAR AND PEACE'.   B.B.C. (1943). Wrappers.

THE DEVELOPMENT OF ENGLISH PROSE.   Glasgow: Jackson 1945. Wrappers.

COLLECTED SHORT STORIES.   Sidgwick & Jackson (1947).

THE COLLECTED TALES.   New York: Knopf 1947.
   The U.S. edition of COLLECTED SHORT STORIES.

TWO CHEERS FOR DEMOCRACY.   Arnold 1951. U.S.: Harcourt Brace 1951.

BILLY BUDD. (libretto, with E. Crozier). Boosey & Hawkes 1951. Wrappers.

THE HILL OF DEVI. Arnold 1953. U.S.: Harcourt Brace 1953.

BATTERSEA RISE. New York: Harcourt Brace 1955. Patterned boards.
An advance chapter of MARIANNE THORNTON, issued by the publishers as a New Year greeting gift.

MARIANNE THORNTON. Arnold 1956. Also 200 signed in slipcase. U.S.: Harcourt Brace 1956.

MAURICE. Arnold 1971. U.S.: Norton 1971.

ALBERGO EMPEDOCLE AND OTHER WRITINGS. New York: Liveright (1971).

THE LIFE TO COME. Arnold 1972. U.S.: Norton 1973.

SELECTED LETTERS. Collins 1983–84. 2 vols. U.S.: Harvard U.P. 1983–84.

FOWLES, John (b. 1926)

None of his works is positively rare, but demand has been very strong for some time now. The books from about 1974 on are very common, and the checklist ends at that point.

THE COLLECTOR. Cape 1963. Apparently, the first d/w had no extracts from reviews on the front flap. U.S.: Little Brown 1963.
The so-called first d/w is not unknown on second impressions of the book.

THE ARISTOS. New York: Little Brown 1964. U.K.: Cape 1965. Revised for the Pan paperback edition of 1968, and for the Cape hardback edition of 1977.

THE MAGUS. Cape 1966. U.S.: Little Brown 1966. Revised Edition: Cape 1977.

THE FRENCH LIEUTENANT'S WOMAN. Cape 1969. U.S.: Little Brown 1969.

MY RECOLLECTIONS OF KAFKA. University of Manitoba Press 1970. Limited Edition of 25 copies. Wrappers.

POEMS. New York: Ecco Press 1973.

CINDERELLA. (trans.). Cape 1974. 4to. U.S.: Little Brown 1975.

THE EBONY TOWER. Cape 1974. U.S.: Little Brown 1974.

SHIPWRECK. Cape 1974. U.S.: Little Brown 1975.

FROST, Robert Lee (1874–1963)

The following checklist ends with the publication of the COLLECTED POEMS in 1930. All the scarce and important first editions to that date are included. A number of publications followed, including many limited editions. These, unlike the earlier books, are not difficult to obtain and are mercifully free of bibiliographical complexity.

[TWILIGHT] FIVE POEMS. n.d. (1894). (20pp) Brown pebbled leather, gilt stamped 'Twilight'.
  Extremely rare.

A BOY'S WILL. David Nutt 1913. First Binding: Brown pebbled cloth, gilt. Uncut edges. 5 × 7½ins. Second Binding: Edges trimmed, bound in cream vellum cloth, red-stamped and red ruled border. Third binding: stiff cream wrappers, black-stamped, without ruled border, decorative flowers with 8 petals. Fourth binding: similar to the third binding, but the flowers have only 4 petals.
  All the variants are rare. The first U.S. edition was published in New York in 1915. In this, the last line of p. 14 has the misprint 'Aind'.

NORTH OF BOSTON. David Nutt. n.d. (1914). First Issue (Binding A): Nutt title page; bound in green buckram with the front cover having a blind ruled border all round; only the top edges trimmed. Second issue (Binding B): Henry Holt title-page tipped-in; bound in the same green buckram but with the blind rule at top and bottom only; all edges trimmed.
  There are further variants – 3 in green cloth, and one in blue cloth.

MOUNTAIN INTERVAL. New York: Henry Holt (1916). Blue cloth. First state: lines 6 and 7 of page 88 are repeated; on page 63, the 6th line from the bottom has the misprint 'Come' instead of 'Gone'; there is a portrait frontispiece. Second state: the errors are corrected and the portrait removed.

SELECTED POEMS. New York: Henry Holt 1923. Green cloth, gilt dec.

NEW HAMPSHIRE. New York: Henry Holt 1923. Green boards. Also, 350 signed.

WEST-RUNNING BROOK. New York: Henry Holt (1928). Green boards. The earliest copies did not contain the legend 'First Edition' as did later copies. There was also a special issue of 1000 signed copies.

A WAY OUT. New York: Harbor Press 1929. Salmon boards. Limited to 485 signed.

THE LOVELY SHALL BE CHOOSERS. New York: Random House 1929. Pamphlet in brown wrappers. Sold only in a set of 12 pamphlets of contemporary poets.

THE COW'S IN THE CORN. Gaylordsville: Slide Mountain Press 1929. Decorated boards. Limited to 91 signed.

COLLECTED POEMS. New York: Random House (1930). There was a First Trade Edition and an edition of 1000 signed.

G

GASKELL, Mrs E. C. (1810–1865)

CRANFORD. (by the author of 'Mary Barton', 'Ruth', etc.) Chapman & Hall 1853. Fcap. 8vo. Green cloth.

THE LIFE OF CHARLOTTE BRONTE. Smith, Elder 1857. 2 vols. Fcap 8vo. Dark brown cloth. Portrait frontispiece in volume one, view of Haworth as frontispiece in volume two.

GAY, John (1685–1732)

His most famous work, The Beggar's Opera, is worth around £500. His rarest work is his first, the poem WINE, of which only a handful of copies have survived.

WINE, A Poem. Keble 1708.

RURAL SPORTS. J. Tonson 1713.

THE FAN. A Poem. J. Tonson 1714. 32pp. Folio.

THE SHEPHERD'S WEEK. In Six Pastorals. Ferd. Burleigh 1714. 8vo. Frontis & 6 plates included in pagination.

THE WHAT D'YE CALL IT. Tonson (1715). 8vo. The second edition (same sheets with cancel title) in same year, also not dated.

TRIVIA. Bernard Lintot (1716). 8vo. There were 2000 copies on ordinary paper, and 250 on fine paper. Second edition same year, also not dated.

TWO EPISTLES. Bernard Lintot (1717). 8vo.

POEMS ON SEVERAL OCCASIONS. Tonson & Lintot 1720. 2 vols. 4to. Frontispiece & 2 plates. Second Edition: 1731. 2 vols. 12mo.

THE BEGGAR'S OPERA. John Watts 1728. First issue has three bars of music on p. 53; text ends on p. 59. 16 pp. engraved music. Second Edition, same year.

POLLY: an Opera. Being the second part of the Beggar's Opera. For the author 1729. 4to. 16 engraved ff of music at end.

FABLES. Printed by J. Tonson & J. Watts 1727 (First Series) & 1738. (Second Series). 2 vols.
    The edition by John Stockdale, 1793 in 2 vols, includes 12 plates engraved by William Blake, and is worth around £300.

ACHILLES, An Opera. J. Watts 1733. 8vo.

THE DISTRESS'D WIFE. Thomas Astley 1743. 8vo.

GISSING, George Robert (1857–1903)

Gissing was largely neglected by collectors until well into the second half of the twentieth century. It is no wonder therefore that many of his first editions are rare. His first book, WORKERS IN THE DAWN, has the reputation of being one of the rarest of all nineteenth century novels. This is hardly surprising, since there were only 277 copies in the first place, and they sold very slowly. It may be that a goodish number of copies met with a summary fate at some point, and were lost to collectors forever. In his bibliography of Trollope, Michael Sadleir acknowledges this novel's reputation for rarity, speaking of it in the same breath as those two other great rarities, Hardy's DESPERATE REMEDIES and Trollope's THE MACDERMOTS OF BALLYCLORAN. And yet, in his book on XIX Century Fiction, he rates WORKERS IN THE DAWN as only the fifth rarest of Gissing's novels. Some may dispute his judgment in this respect, but I merely infer from his conclusions that all of Gissing's early works are extremely rare, and there is plenty of evidence for that.

At a time when there is an ongoing revival of interest in this author, at least partly stimulated by Michael Collie's excellent bibliography, I think it appropriate to give a full summary of all his major works.

WORKERS IN THE DAWN. Remington & Co. 1880. 3 vols. Olive green cloth. Only 277 copies were printed.
  One of the rarest first editions in the whole of 19th Century fiction. It was published at Gissing's expense, in mid–1880, and by March of the following year, only 49 copies had been sold. No other edition was published during the author's lifetime. There are some surviving copies of an aborted American edition by Bowling Green Press (around 1930) but the first published American Edition came from Doubleday, Doran in 1935, in 2 vols.

THE UNCLASSED. Chapman and Hall 1884. 3 vols. Blue-green cloth. Second Edition (revised and shortened): Lawrence & Bullen 1895. One vol. Maroon cloth. U.S. (shortened version) R. F. Fenno & Company of New York (1896). One vol. Brown cloth, and also in wrappers.

ISABEL CLARENDON. Chapman and Hall 1886. 2 vols. Green cloth.

DEMOS / A STORY OF ENGLISH SOCIALISM. (Anon). Smith, Elder 1886. 3 vols. Brown cloth, also green cloth. Second Edition: Smith, Elder 1886. One vol. Brown cloth. In this, the author's name appears on the title-page. U.S.: Harper's Franklin Square Library series 1886. One vol.
  Gissing's first commercially successful book, though he gained little from it, having sold the copyright to Smith, Elder for £100.

THYRZA. Smith, Elder 1887. 3 vols. Reddish brown cloth. 500 copies were printed. Second Edition: 1891. One vol.

A LIFE'S MORNING. Smith, Elder 1888. 3 vols. Brick brown cloth. 500 copies were printed. Second Edition: 1889. One vol. U.S.: Lippincott 1888.

THE NETHER WORLD. Smith, Elder 1889. 3 vols. Blue cloth. 500 copies were printed. Second Edition: 1889. One vol. U.S.: Harper 1889.

THE EMANCIPATED. Richard Bentley & Son 1890. 3 vols. Brown cloth spine, patterned paper boards. Second Edition: Lawrence & Bullen 1893. One vol. U.S.: Way and Williams of Chicago 1895.

NEW GRUB STREET. Smith, Elder 1891. 3 vols. Blue-green cloth (simulated leather). Reissued in the same year, with 'Second Edition' on the title-page. One Volume Edition: Smith, Elder 1891.

DENZIL QUARRIER. Lawrence & Bullen 1892. Green cloth, also brown cloth. U.S.: Macmillan 1892 (later).

BORN IN EXILE. Black 1892. 3 vols. Purplish-brown cloth. 500 copies were printed. Reissued in 1893 in one volume.

THE ODD WOMEN. Lawrence & Bullen 1893. 3 vols. Maroon cloth. 750 copies were printed, of which 354 remained unbound at the end of 1894. Second Edition: 1894. One vol.

IN THE YEAR OF JUBILEE. Lawrence & Bullen 1894. 3 vols. Blue cloth. Second Edition: 1895. One vol. Copies are known which are erroneously dated 1894. Copies giving 'A. H. Bullen' as publisher were issued later (i.e. after the firm of Lawrence & Bullen was dissolved.). U.S.: Appleton 1895.

EVE'S RANSOM. New York: Appleton 1895. Green cloth. U.K.: Lawrence & Bullen 1895. Maroon cloth. 1000 copies printed from American plates, and issued almost simultaneously.

THE PAYING GUEST. London, Paris & Melbourne: Cassell 1895. Yellow cloth. A volume in Cassell's Pocket Library (as indicated on the front cover). Also issued in fawn wrappers. U.S.: Dodd, Mead 1895.

SLEEPING FIRES. T. Fisher Unwin 1895. Buff cloth. A volume in The Autonym Library. Also issued (slightly later) in rose pink or salmon wrappers. U.S.: Appleton 1896.

THE WHIRLPOOL. Lawrence & Bullen 1897. Maroon cloth.

HUMAN ODDS AND ENDS. Lawrence & Bullen 1898. Purple-brown cloth.

CHARLES DICKENS. Blackie & Son 1898. Maroon cloth. The Victorian Era Series. U.S.: Dodd, Mead 1898.

THE TOWN TRAVELLER. Methuen 1898. Red cloth. U.S.: Frederick A. Stokes (1898). Green cloth.

THE CROWN OF LIFE. Methuen 1899. Red cloth. Simultaneously issued in Canada. U.S.: Stokes 1899.

OUR FRIEND THE CHARLATAN. Chapman & Hall 1901. Blue cloth. Also, in green paper boards. U.S.: Henry Holt 1901.

BY THE IONIAN SEA. Chapman & Hall 1901. White cloth. Issued later in red cloth, also green cloth. U.S.: Scribner's Sons 1905.

THE PRIVATE PAPERS OF HENRY RYECROFT.   First appeared serialized in the Fortnightly Review, May 1902–February 1903. Book: Constable 1903 (January). Green cloth. 500 copies of the English sheets were issued in America by Dutton.

WILL WARBURTON.   Constable 1905. Red cloth.

VERANILDA.   Constable 1904. Red cloth.

THE HOUSE OF COBWEBS.   Constable 1906. Blue cloth.

CRITICAL STUDIES OF THE WORKS OF CHARLES DICKENS. New York: Greenberg 1924.
    Published later in the U.K. as THE IMMORTAL DICKENS (see below).

SINS OF THE FATHERS AND OTHER TALES.   Chicago: Pascal Corvici (1924). Limited to 550 copies. Quarter fawn cloth, decorative paper boards, paper label on spine.

THE IMMORTAL DICKENS.   Cecil Palmer (1925). Maroon cloth, paper label on the spine.

A VICTIM OF CIRCUMSTANCES.   Constable 1927. Blue cloth.

LETTERS OF GEORGE GISSING TO MEMBERS OF HIS FAMILY. Constable 1927. Green cloth.

BROWNIE . . . together with six other stories.   New York: Columbia University Press 1931. Quarter fawn cloth, decorative paper boards. Limited to 500 copies.

GEORGE GISSING AND H. G. WELLS, Their Friendship and Correspondence.   Hart-Davis 1961. Maroon cloth, d/w.

THE LETTERS OF GEORGE GISSING TO EDUARD BERTZ.   Constable (1961). Black cloth, d/w.

GEORGE GISSING'S COMMONPLACE BOOK.   New York Public Library 1962. Grey wrappers.

THE LETTERS OF GEORGE GISSING TO GABRIELLE FLEURY. New York Public Library 1964. Pink wrappers.

NOTES ON SOCIAL DEMOCRACY.   Enitharmon Press 1968. Pink wrappers. Limited to 400 copies.

MY FIRST REHEARSAL AND MY CLERICAL RIVAL. Enitharmon Press 1970. Green boards, paper label on spine. Limited to 350 copies.

ESSAYS AND FICTION. Baltimore and London: John Hopkins Press (1970). Green cloth with silver flecks.

GODWIN, William (1756–1836)

The following book is regarded as one of the earliest and best expositions of socialist and anarchist doctrine. (See Printing and the Mind of Man, 243.)

AN ENQUIRY CONCERNING POLITICAL JUSTICE, and its influence on general virtue and happiness. Printed for G.G.J. And J. Robinson 1793. 2 vols. 4to.

GOLDING, William (1911–1993)

His first book is extremely scarce and extremely valuable – well over £1000. His second, a modern classic, fetches over £500, as does the scarce pamphlet THE LADDER AND THE TREE. The rest are not in the same league.

POEMS. By W.G. Golding. Macmillan 1934. 'Contemporary Poets' series. 20 × 13cms. 34pp. Wrappers.

LORD OF THE FLIES. Faber (1954). Red cloth. U.S.: Coward McCann (1955).

THE INHERITORS. Faber (1955). U.S.: Harcourt Brace (1962).

PINCHER MARTIN. Faber (1956).

THE TWO DEATHS OF CHRISTOPHER MARTIN. New York: Harcourt Brace 1957.
   The American edition of PINCHER MARTIN.

THE BRASS BUTTERFLY. Faber (1958). U.S.: NAL 1962.

FREE FALL. Faber (1959). U.S.: Harcourt Brace (1960).

THE LADDER AND THE TREE. Marlborough College Press 1961. 16pp. Wrappers.

THE SPIRE. Faber (1964). U.S.: Harcourt Brace (1964).

THE HOT GATES.   Faber (1965). U.S.: Harcourt Brace (1965).

THE PYRAMID.   Faber (1967). U.S.: Harcourt Brace (1967).

THE SCORPION GOD.   Faber (1971). U.S.: Harcourt Brace (1972).

DARKNESS VISIBLE.   Faber (1979). U.S.: Farrar Straus 1979.

RITES OF PASSAGE.   Faber (1980). U.S.: Farrar Straus 1980.

A MOVING TARGET.   Faber (1982). U.S.: Farrar Straus 1982.

THE PAPER MEN.   Faber (1984). U.S.: Farrar Straus 1984.

THE NOBEL LECTURE.   Sixth Chamber Press 1984. Wrappers. 500 copies. Also 50 specials, signed by the author, bound in goatskin and issued in a slipcase.
   Ordinary copies are frequently found signed by the author.

AN EGYPTIAN JOURNAL.   Faber (1985).

CLOSE QUARTERS.   Faber (1987).

FIRE DOWN BELOW.   Faber (1989).

GOLDSMITH, Oliver (c. 1730–1774)

AN HISTORY OF THE EARTH AND ANIMATED NATURE, one of his most popular works in the bookshops, went through numerous editions, but the first is not common. This however, is considered to be one of his hack works, of which he produced many. His real claim to fame is the play SHE STOOPS TO CONQUER, followed closely by a work of fiction THE VICAR OF WAKEFIELD. These two are major collector's items and each has a current value in excess of £1000. Below, is his first full-length work, followed by his most significant publications.

AN ENQUIRY INTO THE PRESENT STATE OF POLITE LEARNING IN EUROPE.   (anonymous). R. & J. Dodsley 1759.

THE CITIZEN OF THE WORLD: or, Letters from a Chinese Philosopher, Residing in London, to his Friends in the East.   Printed for J. Newbery, 1762. 2 vols. Sm. 8vo. Second issue: has the imprint 'Printed for the Author; and sold by J. Newbery and W. Bristow . . . (etc) 1762'.
   This work originally appeared in 'The Public Ledger' from Jan. 24, 1760. The Chinese Philosopher was the 'Lien Chi Altangi' (i.e. Goldsmith).

THE TRAVELLER: or, A Prospect of Society. A Poem . . . By Oliver Goldsmith. Newbery 1765.   4to. List of books at end.

THE VICAR OF WAKEFIELD: A Tale. Supposed to be written by Himself.
(i.e. anonymous). Salisbury: Printed by B. Collins, For F. Newbery . . . 1766.
2 vols. Sm. 8vo.
　　There are numerous points – 20 called for by Williams. Newbery published
　　second and third editions in the same year.

THE GOOD NATUR'D MAN.   W. Griffin 1768. The first issue has a 3½
line errata, and does not have 'Epi' at the foot of the last leaf.

THE DESERTED VILLAGE.   W. Griffin 1770. Large and small paper
editions.

SHE STOOPS TO CONQUER: or, The Mistakes of a Night.   A Comedy.
As it is Acted at the Theatre-Royal in Covent Garden. Printed for F. Newbery
1773. 8vo.
　　There are many issue points and variants. Briefly, early issues have 'Price
　　One Shilling and Sixpence' on the title-page, pp. 73–80 are not included in
　　the pagination, p. 65 is misnumbered 56, 'Diggory . . . Mr. Saunders' is
　　lacking in the Dramatis Personae, and 'Scene' is printed as a catchword at
　　the foot of p. viii.

AN HISTORY OF THE EARTH AND ANIMATED NATURE.   for J.
Nourse 1774. 8 vols.
　　Published posthumously and at first, anonymously.

GRAHAME, Kenneth (1859–1932)

Apart from his masterpiece WIND IN THE WILLOWS, Grahame's works
have never been very popular with the general public, nor until recently
with collectors. At present, however, there is keen interest in all his first
editions, and they are steadily increasing in value. They have a very long
way to go if they are ever to catch up with WIND IN THE WILLOWS.
The first edition of that is valued at around £500 in fine condition. In the
very rare dust wrapper, over £1000 would be required. It seems a shame
that the first edition was not illustrated (apart from a frontispiece), but time
has made up for the dull start – there are many later editions which are
beautifully illustrated, and many of these are popular with collectors.

One Kenneth Grahame item which was not written by him, but which
cannot be ignored, is the play by A. A. Milne based on WIND IN THE
WILLOWS but called TOAD OF TOAD HALL. The book of the play was
first published by Methuen in 1929 but more importantly, there was a special

issue of 200 numbered copies, signed by both Milne and Kenneth Grahame. This excellent Grahame item is currently selling for in excess of £300.

PAGAN PAPERS. John Lane & Elkin Mathews 1894 (1893). Beardsley frontispiece. Limited to 450 copies.

THE GOLDEN AGE. John Lane 1895. Not illustrated. Edition illustrated by Maxfield Parrish: John Lane 1900. Edition illustrated by E. H. Shepard: Bodley Head 1928. Also a special issue signed by Grahame & Shepard.

DREAM DAYS. John Lane 1898. Not illustrated. Edition illustrated by Max-field Parish: John Lane 1902. Illustrated by Shepard: Bodley Head 1930. Also a special issue signed by author & artist.

THE HEADSWOMAN. John Lane 1898.
This appeared originally in the Yellow Book, October 1894.

WIND IN THE WILLOWS. Methuen 1908. Frontispiece by Graham Robertson, but not otherwise illustrated. Cloth and d/w. First Illustrated Edition: Methuen 1913, with illustrations by Paul Bransom. First illustrated by Ernest Shepard: Methuen 1931. First Illustrated by Arthur Rackham: New York: Limited Editions Club 1940. Trade Edition: Heritage Press 1940.
In the first 'Shepard' edition, the illustrations were in black and white only. In various subsequent editions, Shepard's illustrations were coloured and augmented. The edition from Scribners of New York in 1953 contains additional drawings by Shepard. In Methuen's 1959 edition, 8 coloured plates were added, and their 1971 edition was in full colour. The Rackham version was published in the U.K. by Methuen in 1950, but this edition lacked some of the coloured plates in the American edition.

GRAVES, Robert (1895–1985)

So far, the death of Graves has not resulted in any slackening of interest in his works. He undoubtedly remains one of the most popular writers of the 20th century. A long-lived and prolific author, he produced books across the whole range of English literature. The poetry however is the crux of his work, and the early volumes of poetry are the crucial ingredients of a satisfactory collection. But his prose cannot be ignored. Bibliographically speaking, it is the prose work GOODBYE TO ALL THAT which is his most celebrated work and provides the most notorious rarity. Details are given below. The first issue would be a highlight in any collection of modern literature. As for the early volumes of poetry, they are all moderately scarce and perhaps very scarce in fine condition. One or two are very scarce in any condition. His first book, OVER THE BRAZIER, and his third, FAIRIES AND FUSILIERS, are both easier to get than the second and fourth. This is probably due simply to the number of copies printed in each case. In terms of value, OVER THE BRAZIER generally gets something close on £500, FAIRIES AND FUSILIERS rather less than that. Whereas GOLIATH AND DAVID is valued at close to £1000 and TREASURE BOX even more. The last two, be it noted, are significantly more valuable than the notorious first issue of GOODBYE TO ALL THAT.

As befits an author who has been consistently popular with collectors for more than half a century, I append an extensive list of his first editions.

OVER THE BRAZIER. The Poetry Bookshop 1916. Grey wrappers. Second Edition: (1920) Grey boards, blue d/w. Two pieces were omitted from this edition.

GOLIATH AND DAVID. No publisher or date. 10 leaves in blank dark red wrappers. Printed by Chiswick Press: Charles Whittingham & Co. (Printers note at end). 200 copies were printed.

FAIRIES AND FUSILIERS. Heinemann (1917). Red cloth, gilt lettered spine, d/w. 1000 copies. U.S.: Knopf 1918.

TREASURE BOX. No publisher or date (1919). 8 leaves in blank blue wrappers. Copies are also known in purple cloth with label, and in blue cloth with label and d/w. Printed at Chiswick Press. 200 copies.

COUNTRY SENTIMENT. Secker (1920). Blue boards with cobbled design, label on spine. 1000 copies. U.S.: Knopf 1920.

THE PIER GLASS. Secker (1921). Buff boards, label on spine, d/w. 500 copies. U.S.: Knopf 1921.

ON ENGLISH POETRY. New York: Knopf 1922. Cream boards. Misprints: 'that' for 'than that' on p. 33, and 'have' for 'how' on p. 145. U.K.: Heinemann (1922). Yellow cloth, d/w. Second state in buff boards with labels. Other variants known. Same misprints as U.S. edition.

WHIPPERGINNY. Heinemann (1923). Magenta boards, red labels, d/w. U.S.: Knopf 1923.

THE FEATHER BED. Hogarth Press 1923. Pink boards. Limited to 250 signed.

MOCK BEGGAR HALL. Hogarth Press 1924. Grey boards.

THE MEANING OF DREAMS. Cecil Palmer (1924). U.S.: Greenberg 1925.

POETIC UNREASON.   Cecil Palmer (1925).

JOHN KEMP'S WAGER.   Oxford: Blackwell / Shakespeare Head Press 1925. 750 copies. White boards. Also, 100 signed. U.S.: French 1925. 250 copies.

MY HEAD! MY HEAD!   Secker 1925. U.S.: Knopf 1925.

CONTEMPORARY TECHNIQUES IN POETRY.   Hogarth Press 1925. Blue boards.

WELCHMAN'S HOSE.   The Fleuron 1925. White boards.

THE AUGUSTAN BOOKS OF MODERN POETRY – ROBERT GRAVES.   Benn (1925). Pamphlet, front serving as title-page.

THE MARMOSITE'S MISCELLANY.   By John Doyle (pseud.). Hogarth Press 1925. Floral boards.

ANOTHER FUTURE OF POETRY.   Hogarth Press 1926. Blue Boards. 1000 copies (400 pulped).

THE ENGLISH BALLAD.   Benn 1927.

LARS PORSENA.   London: Kegan Paul / New York: Dutton. (1927). 15.3 × 10.4 cms. Boards, d/w. Revised Edition: Kegan Paul 1936.

IMPENETRABILITY.   Hogarth Press 1926. Boards. 1000 copies (400 pulped).

POEMS (1914–1926).   Heinemann 1927. U.S.: Doubleday, Doran 1929.

POEMS (1914–1927).   Heinemann 1927. 115 signed copies. White boards, parchment spine.

LAWRENCE AND THE ARABS.   Cape (1927). U.S. Edition entitled LAW-RENCE AND THE ARABIAN ADVENTURE: Doubleday 1928.

A SURVEY OF MODERNIST POETRY.   By Graves & Riding. Heinemann 1927. Cream boards, black cloth spine. U.S.: Doubleday, Doran 1928.

A PAMPHLET AGAINST ANTHOLOGIES.   By Graves & Riding. Cape (1928). Brown cloth, d/w. U.S.: Doubleday, Doran 1928.

MRS FISHER OR THE FUTURE OF HUMOUR.   Kegan Paul / New York: Dutton 1928. Boards, d/w.

GRAVES

THE SHOUT.   Elkin Mathews (1929). 530 signed. Boards, d/w.

GOODBYE TO ALL THAT.   Cape (1929). Salmon cloth, d/w. The second issue has a passage expurgated from p. 290, a poem by Sassoon replaced by asterisks on pp. 341–343, and an erratum slip inserted between pp. 398 & 399. U.S. (Expurgated): Cape & Smith (1930).   Revised Edition: Doubleday of New York and (a week later) Cassell of London 1957.
    The first issue is a notorious rarity, perhaps consisting of less than 100 copies. The second issue is not rare (5000 copies printed).

POEMS 1929.   Seizin Press 1929. 225 signed.

TEN POEMS MORE.   Paris: Hours Press 1930. 200 signed.

BUT IT STILL GOES ON.   Cape (1930). The first issue refers to 'The Child She Bare' on p. 157. In the second issue, there is no such reference and the leaf is a cancel. However, a copy is known in which the changed leaf is integral. U.S.: Cape & Harrison Smith (1931).

POEMS 1926–1930.   Heinemann 1931.

TO WHOM ELSE?   Majorca: The Seizin Press 1931. 200 signed.

NO DECENCY LEFT.   By Barbara Rich (pseud.). Cape (1932).

THE REAL DAVID COPPERFIELD.   Barker (1933). The U.S. edition (Harcourt Brace 1934) varies somewhat from the U.K. edition and is entitled DAVID COPPERFIELD By Charles Dickens, Condensed by Robert Graves.

POEMS 1930–1933.   Barker 1933. Grey boards, black cloth spine.

OLD SOLDIERS NEVER DIE.   By Private Frank Richards (Rewritten by Graves). Faber (1933). Sydney, Australia: Angus & Robertson 1933.

I, CLAUDIUS.   Barker (1934). Black cloth, d/w. Remainders were issued in orange cloth. U.S.: Smith & Haas 1934.

CLAUDIUS THE GOD.   Barker 1934. U.S.: Smith & Haas 1935.

OLD-SOLDIER SAHIB.   By Private Frank Richards (Rewritten by Graves). Faber (1936). U.S.: Smith & Haas (1936).

ANTIGUA, PENNY, PUCE.   Majorca: Seizin Press & London: Constable (1936).

COUNT BELISARIUS.   Cassell (1938). U.S.: Random House (1938).

— 142 —

COLLECTED POEMS.   Cassell (1938). Random House (1939).

NO MORE GHOSTS.   Faber (1940). Boards, d/w.

SERGEANT LAMB OF THE NINTH.   Methuen (1940). U.S.: Random House (1940).

THE LONG WEEKEND.   By Graves and Hodge. Faber (1940). U.S.: Macmillan 1941.

PROCEED, SERGEANT LAMB.   Methuen (1941). U.S.: Random House (1941).

WIFE TO MR. MILTON.   Cassell (1943). U.S.: Creative Age Press (1944).

THE READER OVER YOUR SHOULDER.   By Graves & Hodge. Cape (1943). U.S.: Macmillan 1943.

THE AUGUSTAN POETS – ROBERT GRAVES.   Eyre & Spottiswoode (1943). Red wrappers.

THE GOLDEN FLEECE.   Cassell (1944). U.S.: Creative Age (1945).

POEMS 1938–1945.   Cassell (1945). U.S.: Creative Age (1946).

KING JESUS.   New York: Creative Age (1946). U.K.: Cassell (1946).

COLLECTED POEMS (1914–1947).   Cassell (1948).

THE WHITE GODDESS.   Faber (1948). U.S.: Creative Age 1948.

WATCH THE NORTH WIND RISE.   New York: Creative Age 1949. Boards, black cloth spine.

SEVEN DAYS IN NEW CRETE.   Cassell (1949). The U.K. edition of WATCH THE NORTH WIND RISE.

THE COMMON ASPHODEL.   Hamilton (1949).

THE ISLANDS OF UNWISDOM.   New York: Doubleday 1949. U.K.: Cassell 1950, entitled THE ISLES OF UNWISDOM.

OCCUPATION: WRITER.   New York: Creative Age 1950. U.K.: Cassell 1951.

THE TRANSFORMATIONS OF LUCIUS ... THE GOLDEN ASS. Translated by Graves. Penguin (1950). Wrappers. Also issued in cloth. Limited

Issue: Penguin 1950 (but 1951). 2000 signed. Marbled boards, parchment spine. U.S.: Farrar Straus (1951).

POEMS AND SATIRES.   Cassell 1951.

POEMS 1953.   Cassell (1953). Also, 250 signed.

THE NAZARENE GOSPEL RESTORED.   By Graves & Podro. Cassell 1953. U.S.: Doubleday, Doran 1954.

THE CROSS AND THE SWORD.   By Galvan. Translated by Graves. Bloomington: Indiana U.P. (1954). U.K.: Gollancz 1956.

HOMER'S DAUGHTER.   Cassell (1955). U.S.: Doubleday, Doran 1955.

THE GREEK MYTHS.   Penguin (1955). 2 vols. Wrappers. U.S.: Penguin (Baltimore) (1955).

COLLECTED POEMS 1955.   New York: Doubleday 1955.

ADAM'S RIB.   Trianon Press (1955). Also, 276 signed. U.S.:: Yoselof (1958).

THE CROWNING PRIVILEGE.   Cassell (1955). U.S.: Doubleday, Doran 1956.

THE INFANT WITH THE GLOBE.   By Alarcon. Translated by Graves. Trianon Press (1955). U.S.: Yoselof (1955).

WINTER IN MAJORCA.   By Sand. Translated by Graves. Cassell (1956). Red cloth, d/w. Mallorca: Valldemosa Edition (1956). Yellow wrappers. Issued on the same day as the Cassell edition.

¡CATACROK!   Cassell (1956).

LUCAN / PHARSALIA/DRAMATIC EPISODES . . . (Trans.).   Penguin (1956). Wrappers.

THE TWELVE CAESARS. (Trans.).   Penguin (1957). Wrappers.

JESUS IN ROME.   Cassell (1957).

THEY HANGED MY SAINTLY BILLY.   Cassell (1957). U.S.: Doubleday 1957.

POEMS SELECTED BY HIMSELF.   Penguin (1957). Wrappers.

5 PENS IN HAND.   New York: Doubleday 1958.

THE POEMS OF ROBERT GRAVES. New York: Doubleday 1958. Wrappers (Anchor Books series).

STEPS. Cassell (1958).

COLLECTED POEMS 1959. Cassell (1959).

THE ANGER OF ACHILLES. (Trans.). New York: Doubleday 1959. U.K.: Cassell (1960).

FOOD FOR CENTAURS. New York: Doubleday 1960. Second Issue lacks edition notice on verso title.

GREEK GODS AND HEROES. New York: Doubleday 1960.

MYTHS OF ANCIENT GREECE. Cassell (1961). The U.K. edition of GREEK GODS AND HEROES (different illustrations).

THE PENNY FIDDLE. Cassell (1960). Boards.

MORE POEMS 1961. Cassell (1961).

COLLECTED POEMS 1961. New York: Doubleday 1961. A variant d/w has 'C.P.' above the price.

THE MORE DESERVING CASES. Marlborough College Press 1962. Limited Edition.

OXFORD ADDRESSES ON POETRY. Cassell (1962). U.S.: Doubleday 1962.

ORATIO CREWEIANA / MDCCCCLXII. (O.U.P. 1962). Pamphlet. 1400 copies.

THE BIG GREEN BOOK. New York: Crowell-Collier (1962). 28.6 × 19cms. No d/w. U.K.: Puffin (1978). Wrappers.

NEW POEMS 1962. Cassell (1962). U.S.: Doubleday 1963.

THE SIEGE AND FALL OF TROY. Cassell (1962). Boards. U.S.: Doubleday (1963).

NINE HUNDRED IRON CHARIOTS. Cambridge, Mass. 1963. Wrappers.

MAMMON. London School of Economics and Political Science 1964. Wrappers 500 copies.

HEBREW MYTHS / THE BOOK OF GENESIS.   By Graves & Patai. New York: Doubleday (1964). U.K.: Cassell (1964).

COLLECTED SHORT STORIES.   New York: Doubleday 1964. U.K.: Cassell (1965).

MAN DOES, WOMAN IS.   Cassell 1964. U.S.: Doubleday 1964.

EL FENOMENO DEL TURISMO.   Madrid 1964. Wrappers.

ORATIO CREWEIANA MDCCCCLXIV.   (O.U.P., 1964). Pamphlet.

ANN AT HIGHWOOD HALL.   Cassell (1964). U.S.: Doubleday (1964).

MAMMON AND THE BLACK GODDESS.   Cassell (1965). U.S.: Doubleday 1965.

MAJORCA OBSERVED.   By Graves & Hogarth. Cassell (1965). U.S.: Doubleday (1965).

LOVE RESPELT.   Cassell (1965). 250 signed. U.S.: Doubleday 1966.

COLLECTED POEMS 1965.   Cassell (1965).

SEVENTEEN POEMS MISSING FROM LOVE RESPELT.   Privately Printed 1966. 300 signed. Boards, d/w.

TWO WISE CHILDREN.   U.S.: Harlin Quist (1966).

POETIC CRAFT AND PRINCIPLE.   Cassell (1967).

COLOPHON TO LOVE RESPELT.   Privately Printed 1967. 350 signed. Boards, d/w.

SIXTEEN POEMS.   Oxford: College of Technology 1967. 75 copies. Cloth, no d/w.

THE RUBAIYYAT OF OMAR KHAYAAM.   Translation etc. by Graves & Hodges. Cassell (1967). U.S.: Doubleday 1968.

THE POOR BOY WHO FOLLOWED HIS STAR.   Cassell (1968). U.S.: Doubleday (1969).

GREEK MYTHS AND LEGENDS.   Cassell (1968). Cloth, no d/w.

POEMS 1965–1968.   Cassell (1968). U.S.: Doubleday 1969.

LOVE RESPELT AGAIN.   New York: Doubleday (1969).

THE CRANE BAG.   Cassell (1969).

ON POETRY.   New York: Doubleday 1969.

BEYOND GIVING.   Privately Printed 1969. 500 signed. Card covers, d/w.

POEMS ABOUT LOVE.   New York: Doubleday (1969). U.K.: Cassell (1969).

POEMS 1968–1970.   Cassell (1970). U.S.: Doubleday 1971.

THE GREEN-SAILED VESSEL.   Privately Printed 1971. 500 signed.

POEMS: ABRIDGED FOR DOLLS AND PRINCES.   (Cassell 1971).

DEYA, A PORTFOLIO.   By Graves & Hogarth. Motif Editions 1972. Loose leaves in portfolio. 75 signed.

DIFFICULT QUESTIONS, EASY ANSWERS.   Cassell (1972). U.S.: Doubleday 1973.

POEMS 1970–1972.   Cassell (1972). U.S.: Doubleday 1973.

TIMELESS MEETING.   Privately Printed 1973. 500 signed.

SONG OF SONGS.   New York: Potter (1973). U.K.: Collins 1973.

AT THE GATE.   Privately Printed 1974. 500 signed.

COLLECTED POEMS 1975.   Cassell (1975). U.S.: Doubleday 1977.

TWIN TO TWIN.   Sidcot: Gruffyground Press 1977. 25 copies. Wrappers.

ADVICE TO COLONEL VALENTINE.   Sidcott: Gruffyground Press 1979. 25 copies. Pamphlet.

POEMS.   New York: Limited Edition Club 1980.

AN ANCIENT CASTLE.   Owen (1980).

IN BROKEN IMAGES.   Hutchinson (1982).

TWO POEMS.   Mercator Press 1982. 45 copies. Wrappers.

ELEVEN SONGS. (Mallorca: New Seizin Press 1983). 100 copies. Wrappers.

BETWEEN MOON AND MOON. Hutchinson (1984).

GRAY, John (1866–1934)

SILVERPOINTS. Elkin Mathews & John Lane, 1893. Tall 8vo. Green cloth with gilt design by Charles Ricketts. 250 numbered copies.

One of the high-spots of 1890s book design, and worth in the region of £800 in fine condition.

GRAY, Thomas (1716–1771)

His first published poem appeared in GRATULATIO ACADEMIAE CAN-TABRIGIENSIS, published at Cambridge in 1736. This is rare. The famous poem which he wrote in a country churchyard is one which all collectors of English poetry would like in their collections. The first edition is worth well over a thousand pounds, indeed I have seen the second edition for as much.

ELEGY WROTE IN A COUNTRY CHURCH YARD. Dodsley 1751. 4to. 6 leaves. In the first issue, page 10, line 4, are the words 'some hidden'. Subsequently, these were replaced by 'kindred'.

There were four authorised editions in 1751, and many pirated editions. The Third Edition has an extra stanza. An amusing anonymous parody appeared shortly after the poem's first appearance, with the title AN ELEGY, written in Covent-Garden. An engraving on the title-page shows a man heading for the gallows at Tyburn. It was published by J. Ridley, undated but probably 1752.

DESIGNS BY MR. R. BENTLEY, For Six Poems by Mr. T. Gray. Dodsley 1753. Large 4to. 6 eng. plates, 12 engs. in text. Printed on rectos only. Half-title reads 'Drawings, &c' – changed to 'Designs, &c.' for the 2nd and 3rd editions of the same year.

ODES. By Mr. Gray. Printed at Strawberry-Hill, (Twickenham) for R. and J. Dodsley, 1757. 4to. 21pp.

The first book issued from Walpole's Private Press.

POEMS. Dodsley 1768.

In the same year there was a Dublin Edition from William Sleater, and a Glasgow Edition from Foulis (Fine paper & Ordinary paper issues).

GREVILLE, Fulke (First Baron Brooke 1554–1628)

Greville is well-known for his LIFE OF SIR PHILIP SYDNEY, published in 1652. With the Countess of Pembroke, he was instrumental in the preservation of Sydney's writings and their ultimate publication. He was also a poet and dramatist in his own right, and the definitive early edition of his best works, including his Caelica sonnets and plays, is:

CERTAINE LEARNED AND ELEGANT WORKES. Henry Seyle 1633. Folio. Nothing between title and p. 23 (probably due to suppression of A Treatise of Religion). Copies on large paper have a circular, as opposed to a unicorn, watermark.

GREEN, Henry (1905–1973)

A steady favourite with collectors, even his later first editions are getting respectable prices (£40 or thereabouts, and often more), but the rarest are the first two, and these are being priced in excess of £500.

BLINDNESS. Dent 1926. Dark blue cloth gilt, d/w. U.S.: Dutton 1926.

LIVING. Dent 1929. Maroon cloth gilt, d/w. U.S.: Dutton 1929.

PARTY GOING. Hogarth Press 1939. Blue cloth, d/w. 1200 copies. Toronto, Canada: Longman 1939. U.S.: Viking 1951.

PACK MY BAG. Hogarth Press 1940. 1500 copies. First binding: red cloth gilt, pink d/w, priced at 7/6d. Second binding (from c. 1943): issued cheaper with a new d/w as number 3 in the Hogarth Crown Library series. Later binding: mid-blue cloth, also metallic-blue cloth. Toronto, Canada: Macmillan 1940.

CAUGHT. Hogarth Press 1943. Red cloth gilt, d/w. 2000 copies. Toronto, Canada: Macmillan 1943.

LOVING. Hogarth Press 1945. Blue cloth, d/w. Toronto, Canada: Macmillan 1945.

BACK. Hogarth Press 1946. Grey cloth, d/w. 5000 copies. Toronto, Canada: Oxford 1946.

CONCLUDING. Hogarth Press 1948. Blue cloth gilt, d/w. 5000 copies. U.S.: Viking 1950.

NOTHING. Hogarth Press 1950. Pink cloth gilt, d/w. U.S.: Viking 1950.

DOTING. Hogarth Press 1952. Blue cloth gilt, d/w. U.S.: Viking 1952.

GREENE, Graham (1904–1991)

Along with Evelyn Waugh, Greene has been the most popular of the
collected 'literary' authors during the last decade or so. Several of his first
editions, in fine condition with dust wrappers, have reached prices well over
£1000. His post-war first editions are still common.

BABBLING APRIL: POEMS. Oxford: Blackwell 1925. Grey boards, d/w.
About 300 copies.

THE MAN WITHIN. Heinemann (1929). U.S.: Doubleday 1929.

THE NAME OF ACTION. Heinemann (1930). Issued first at 7s.6d and
later at 3s.6d. The first d/w has reviews of THE MAN WITHIN on the back
cover, later on the flap. U.S.: Doubleday 1931.

RUMOUR AT NIGHTFALL. Heinemann 1931. U.S.: Doubleday 1932.

STAMBOUL TRAIN. Heinemann 1932.

ORIENT EXPRESS. New York: Doubleday 1933.
   The American edition of STAMBOUL TRAIN.

IT'S A BATTLEFIELD. Heinemann 1934. U.S.: Doubleday 1934.

THE BEAR FELL FREE. Grayson Books 1935. Limited Edition of 285, of
which 250 were signed. Cloth, d/w.

ENGLAND MADE ME. Heinemann 1935. U.S.: Doubleday 1935.

THE BASEMENT ROOM. Cresset Press 1935.

A GUN FOR SALE. Heinemann 1936.

THIS GUN FOR HIRE. New York: Doubleday 1936.
   The U.S. edition of A GUN FOR SALE, and published a month before
   the London edition.

JOURNEY WITHOUT MAPS. Heinemann 1936. U.S.: Doubleday 1936.

BRIGHTON ROCK.   New York: Viking 1938 (June). U.K.: Heinemann 1938 (July).

THE CONFIDENTIAL AGENT.   Heinemann 1939. U.S.: Viking 1939.

TWENTY FOUR STORIES.   (By Greene, Laver & Warner). Cresset Press 1939.

THE LAWLESS ROADS.   London, New York, Toronto: Longman (1939). Gold-lettered red cloth, d/w. Later binding is blue-lettered red cloth, d/w.

ANOTHER MEXICO.   New York: Viking 1939.
   The U.S. edition of LAWLESS ROADS.

THE POWER AND THE GLORY.   Heinemann 1940.

THE LABYRINTHINE WAYS.   New York: Viking 1940.
   The U.S. edition of THE POWER AND THE GLORY.

BRITISH DRAMATISTS.   Collins 1942. Britain in Pictures series. Slim 4to. Boards, d/w.

THE MINISTRY OF FEAR.   Heinemann 1943. U.S.: Viking 1943.

THE LITTLE TRAIN.   (anon). Eyre & Spottiswoode 1946. U.S.: Lothrop 1958.

NINETEEN STORIES.   Heinemann 1947. U.S.: Viking 1949.

THE HEART OF THE MATTER.   Heinemann 1948. U.S.: Viking 1948. Ivory cloth spine, maroon boards.
   Some copies were specially issued for the friends of Viking Press, and these are of greater value than the trade issue.

WHY DO I WRITE?   By Bowen, Greene & Pritchett. Marshall 1948.

THE LITTLE FIRE ENGINE.   Parrish 1950. U.S. (THE LITTLE RED FIRE ENGINE): Lothrop 1952.

THE THIRD MAN.   New York: Viking 1950.
   The film screenplay by Greene and Carol Reed, was first published by Lorrimer in 1969.

THE THIRD MAN & THE FALLEN IDOL.   Heinemann 1950.

THE END OF THE AFFAIR.   Heinemann 1951. U.S.: Viking 1951.

THE LOST CHILDHOOD.   Eyre & Spottiswoode 1951.

THE LITTLE HORSE BUS.   Parrish 1952. U.S.: Lothrop 1954.

THE LITTLE STEAM ROLLER.   Parrish 1953. U.S.: Lothrop 1965.

THE LIVING ROOM.   Heinemann 1953. U.S.: Viking 1954.

LOSER TAKES ALL.   Heinemann 1955. U.S.: Viking 1957.

THE QUIET AMERICAN.   Heinemann 1955. U.S.: Viking 1956.

THE POTTING SHED.   New York: Viking 1957. U.K.: Heinemann 1958.

OUR MAN IN HAVANA.   Heinemann 1958. U.S.: Viking 1958.

THE COMPLAISANT LOVER.   Heinemann 1959. U.S.: Viking 1961.

IN SEARCH OF A CHARACTER.   Bodley Head 1961. U.S.: Viking 1961.

A BURNT-OUT CASE.   Heinemann 1961. U.S.: Viking 1961.

A SENSE OF REALITY.   Bodley Head 1963. U.S.: Viking 1963.

CARVING A STATUE.   Bodley Head 1964.

THE COMEDIANS.   Bodley Head 1966. U.S.: Viking 1966.

MAY WE BORROW YOUR HUSBAND?   Bodley Head 1967. Also a signed limited edition. U.S.: Viking 1967.

COLLECTED ESSAYS.   Bodley Head 1969. U.S.: Viking 1969.

TRAVELS WITH MY AUNT.   Bodley Head 1969. U.S.: Viking 1970.

A SORT OF LIFE.   Bodley Head 1971. U.S.: Simon & Schuster 1971.

THE PLEASURE DOME.   Secker & Warburg 1972. U.S.: Simon & Schuster 1972.

THE COLLECTED STORIES.   Bodley Head & Heinemann 1972. U.S.: Viking 1973.

THE HONORARY CONSUL.   Bodley Head 1973. U.S.: Viking 1973.

LORD ROCHESTER'S MONKEY.   Bodley Head 1974. U.S.: Viking 1974.

SHADES OF GREENE.   Bodley Head & Heinemann 1975.

THE RETURN OF A. J. RAFFLES.   Bodley Head 1975. Also 250 signed. U.S.: Simon & Schuster 1978.

THE HUMAN FACTOR.   Bodley Head 1978. U.S.: Simon & Schuster 1978.

DR FISHER OF GENEVA.   Bodley Head 1980. U.S.: Simon & Schuster 1980.

WAYS OF ESCAPE.   Bodley Head 1980. U.S.: Simon & Schuster 1981.

THE GREAT JOWETT.   Bodley Head 1981. Limited to 500 signed.

MONSIGNOR QUIXOTE.   Canada: Lester & Orpen 1982. U.K.: Bodley Head 1982. U.S.: Simon & Schuster 1982.

J'ACCUSE.   Bodley Head 1982. Wrappers. U.S.: Simon & Schuster 1982.

FOR WHOM THE BELL CHIMES & YES AND NO.   Bodley Head 1983. Limited to 775 signed.

GREENE, Robert (1558–1592)

A popular hack writer, celebrated for a probable reference to Shakespeare in an autobiographical piece:

GREENE'S GROATS-WORTH OF WITTE. 1592.
The relevant piece reads 'in his owne conceit the onely Shake-scene in a countrey'.

GROSSMITH, George & Weedon (1847–1912 & 1852–1919)

THE DIARY OF A NOBODY.   Bristol: Arrowsmith (1892). 3/6d series. Decorated brown cloth.

H

HAGGARD, H. Rider (1856–1925)

The first three books in the checklist were printed in modest numbers and are now very scarce in any condition. In anything like fine original condition, they are positively rare. With KING SOLOMON'S MINES, the number of copies printed begins to rise significantly, but many of his first editions remain stubbornly hard to come by in acceptable condition. The later ones had pictorial dust wrappers, but these are rarely seen nowadays.

CETYWAYO AND HIS NEIGHBOURS.   Trubnor 1882. Large crown 8vo. Green cloth. 750 copies were printed.

DAWN.   Hurst & Blackett 1884. 3 vols, light green cloth, gold lettered on spines with red & green decoration; fronts lettered in red with red & green decoration. 16pp publishers adverts at end. 500 copies printed. One Vol Edition: Maxwell 1887. U.S.: Lovell 1887.
  His first published novel.

THE WITCH'S HEAD.   Hurst & Blackett 1885. 3 vols. Dark greeny-grey cloth. 500 copies printed. One Vol Edition: Maxwell 1887. U.S.: Appleton 1885.

KING SOLOMON'S MINES.   Cassell 1885. Red cloth. Folded map. 8 leaves of publishers catalogue, dated 5G.8.85 (first issue, 1000 copies), or dated 5G.10.85 (second issue, 500 copies). A further 500 copies of the first printing were sent to Cassell's New York office for an American issue.

SHE.   New York: Harper Bros 1886. U.K.: Longmans, Green 1887. Blue cloth, bevelled edges.

JESS.   Smith, Elder 1887. Red cloth. (B.L. copy is green). U.S.: Harper 1887.

ALLAN QUARTERMAIN.   Longmans, Green 1887. Blue cloth, bevelled edges. Also 112 copies on large paper (crown 4to).

MAIWA'S REVENGE.   Longmans, Green 1888. Black cloth, also pale green-grey boards (no priority established).

MR MEESON'S WILL.   Spencer Blackett 1888. Red cloth. Griffith, Farran published an edition in the same year, as did Harper in New York.

COLONEL QUARITCH V.C. Longmans, Green 1888. 3 vols. Red cloth.

CLEOPATRA. Longmans, Green 1889. Blue cloth, bevelled edges. Also 50 copies on large paper.

ALLAN'S WIFE. Spencer Blackett 1889.

BEATRICE. Longmans, Green 1890.

THE WORLD'S DESIRE. Longmans, Green 1890.

ERIC BRIGHTEYES. Longmans, Green 1891.

NADA THE LILY. Longmans, Green 1892.

MONTEZUMA'S DAUGHTER. Longmans, Green 1893.

THE PEOPLE OF THE MIST. Longmans, Green 1894.

JOAN HASTE. Longmans, Green 1895.

HEART OF THE WORLD. Longmans, Green 1896.

THE WIZARD. Bristol & London: Arrowsmith/Simpkin 1896. Wrappers (104 × 164 mm) lettered on front 'One Shilling / Christmas 1896/ARROW-SMITH'S ANNUAL' etc. Some copies were issued in brown cloth, and some of these were designated 'Arrowsmith's Bristol Library' on the verso title.

DR. THERNE. Longmans, Green 1898. Some copies have rounded spines, some have flat spines.

SWALLOW. Longmans, Green 1899.

A FARMER'S YEAR. Longmans 1899. Blue cloth. Also Large Paper copies in blue boards with white spine – 300 were printed, but 200 were 'wasted'.

THE LAST BOER WAR. Kegan Paul etc. 1899. Grey wrappers, priced at one shilling on the front.
    Extracted from his earlier book CETAWAYO AND HIS WHITE NEIGH-
    BOURS. It was published in the U.S. as A HISTORY OF THE TRANS-
    VAAL, by New Amsterdam Book Company.

BLACK HEART AND WHITE HEART AND OTHER STORIES. Long-mans, Green 1900.

ELISSA. New York: Longmans, Green 1900.

The U.S. edition (version) of BLACK HEART AND WHITE HEART AND OTHER STORIES, but containing two stories, not three.

LYSBETH.   Longmans, Green 1901.

A WINTER PILGRIMAGE.   Longmans 1901.

RURAL ENGLAND.   Longmans, Green 1902. 2 vols. Blue cloth.

PEARL-MAIDEN.   Longmans, Green 1903.

STELLA FRAGELIUS.   New York: Longmans, Green 1903. U.K.: Longmans, Green 1904.

THE BRETHREN.   Cassell 1904.

AYESHA.   Ward Lock 1905.

A GARDENER'S YEAR.   Longmans, Green 1905.

THE POOR AND THE LAND.   Longmans, Green 1905. Red cloth. Also, red wrappers.

THE WAY OF THE SPIRIT.   Hutchinson 1906.

BENITA.   Cassell 1906.

THE SPIRIT OF BAMBATSE.   New York: Longmans 1906.
   U.S. edition of BENITA.

FAIR MARGARET.   Hutchinson 1907.

MARGARET.   New York: Longmans 1907.
   The U.S. edition of FAIR MARGARET.

THE GHOST KINGS.   Cassell 1908.

THE LADY OF THE HEAVENS.   New York: Frank Lovell 1909.
   The U.S. edition of THE GHOST KINGS.

THE YELLOW GOD.   New York: Cupples and Leon 1908. U.K.: Cassell 1909.

THE LADY OF BLOSSHOLME.   Hodder & Stoughton 1909. 15,190 copies printed. 775 have the imprint of both Hodder and Frowde (Toronto) at foot of title-page.

MORNING STAR.   Cassell 1910.

QUEEN SHEBA'S RING.   Evelyn Nash 1910. Colonial Edition has imprint of Bell & Sons.

REGENERATION.   Longmans, Green 1910.

RED EVE.   Hodder & Stoughton (1911). Red cloth, coloured illustration pasted on front.

THE MAHATMA AND THE HARE.   Longmans, Green 1911.

RURAL DENMARK.   Longmans, Green 1911.

MARIE.   Cassell 1912.

CHILD OF STORM.   Cassell 1913.

THE WANDERER'S NECKLACE.   Cassell 1914.

THE HOLY FLOWER.   Ward, Lock 1915.

ALLAN AND THE HOLY FLOWER.   New York: Longmans 1915.
   U.S. edition of THE HOLY FLOWER.

THE IVORY CHILD.   Cassell (1916).

FINISHED.   Ward, Lock 1917.

LOVE ETERNAL.   Cassell (1918).

MOON OF ISRAEL.   Murray 1918.

WHEN THE WORLD SHOOK.   Cassell (1919).

THE ANCIENT ALLAN.   Cassell (1920).

SMITH AND THE PHARAOHS AND OTHER TALES.   Arrowsmith (and) Simkin, etc. 1920. Front cover says '. . . Stories', title-page says '. . . Tales'.

SHE AND ALLAN.   Hutchinson (1921). Red cloth. 24pp. Catalogue of New Books for Spring 1921 at end.

THE VIRGIN OF THE SUN.   Cassell (1922).

WISDOM'S DAUGHTER.   Hutchinson (1923). Rec cloth. 40pp Announcements for Spring 1923 at end.

HEU-HEU. Hutchinson (1924). Red cloth. 48pp Catalogue of New Novels for Spring 1924 at end.

QUEEN OF THE DAWN. Hutchinson (1925). Greeny-grey cloth. 48pp New Books for Spring 1925 at end.

THE TREASURE OF THE LAKE. Hutchinson (1926). Blue cloth. 16pp Books for Autumn 1926 at end.

THE DAYS OF MY LIFE. Longmans, Green 1926. 2 vols. Red cloth.

ALLAN AND THE ICE GODS. Hutchinson (1927). Red cloth.

A NOTE ON RELIGION. Longmans, Green 1927. Blue wrappers.
A chapter from the earlier THE DAYS OF MY LIFE.

MARY OF MARION ISLE. Hutchinson (1929). Grey cloth. Some copies have 24pp Books for Autumn 1928 at end. Later binding (Cheap 3/6d edition) has double thin black line around front cover (rather than a single line).

MARION ISLE. New York: Doubleday 1929.
U.S. edition of MARY OF MARION ISLE.

BELSHAZZAR. Stanley Paul & Co. (1928) Ltd. (1930). Light brown cloth. 32pp Autumn Announcements for 1930 at end.

HALL, Radclyffe (1886–1943)

THE WELL OF LONELINESS. Cape 1928. Cloth, d/w. First state of the text has 'whip' for 'whips' in line 3 of page 50. U.S.: Covici 1928. Cloth and boards, & slipcase. 500 copies. Also in 1929, 225 signed, in 2 vols.
In the U.K., the book was declared obscene and officially destroyed, but many copies survived. In America, attempts to suppress it failed. The U.K. and U.S. first editions were issued simultaneously.

HAMMETT, Dashiell (1894–1961)

Hammett's five major works (the first five listed below) are very highly valued, none of them fetching less than £500. Much of the author's work appeared first in various issues of THE BLACK MASK magazine.

RED HARVEST. New York: Knopf 1929. Approx. 3000 copies printed. U.K.: Knopf/Cassell 1929.

THE DAIN CURSE.   New York: Knopf 1929. Misprint p. 260 line 19 – 'dopped' for 'dropped'. U.K.: Knopf/Cassell 1929 (1930). Some copies have skull and crossbones on front.

THE MALTESE FALCON.   New York: Knopf 1930. U.K.: Knopf/Cassell 1930.

THE GLASS KEY.   London: Knopf/Cassell 1931. U.S.: Knopf 1931.

THE THIN MAN.   New York: Knopf 1934. U.K.: Barker 1934.

SECRET AGENT X–9.   2 vols. Philadelphia (1934). No d/ws.

$106,000 BLOOD MONEY.   New York: Spivak 1943.

BLOOD MONEY.   World 1943.
    This is a new edition of $106,000 BLOOD MONEY.

THE ADVENTURES OF SAM SPADE.   New York: Spivak 1944.

THE CONTINENTAL OP.   New York: Spivak 1945.
    The 1974 edition by Random House contains new material.

THE RETURN OF THE CONTINENTAL OP.   New York: Spivak 1945.

HAMMETT HOMICIDES.   New York: Spivak 1946.

DEAD YELLOW WOMEN.   New York: Spivak 1947.

NIGHTMARE TOWN.   New York: Spivak 1948.

THE BIG KNOCK-OVER.   New York: Spivak 1948.
    A new edition of $106,000 BLOOD MONEY. The same title was used by Random House in 1966, for a volume subtitled 'Selected Stories and Short Novels'.

THE CREEPING SIAMESE.   New York: Spivak 1950.

WOMAN IN THE DARK.   New York: Spivak 1950.

A MAN NAMED THIN AND OTHER STORIES.   New York: Ferman 1952.

THE HAMMETT STORY OMNIBUS.   Cassell 1966.
    The U.K. edition of the 1966 Random House collection THE BIG KNOCK-OVER.

HARDY, Thomas (1840–1928)

Hardy's first novel is extremely rare and worth something in excess of £1000, perhaps a great deal more. Demand is strong for all the early novels, and they are all hard to come by nowadays and are usually priced in hundreds of pounds at least. The last few volumes of fiction and the poetry is readily obtainable. But his first volume of poetry, WESSEX POEMS, is rarely under £100 nowadays. The later poetry first editions, even in their dust wrappers, can frequently be obtained for less than £50.

Hardy himself was the author in all but name of the two biographical works THE EARLY LIFE OF THOMAS HARDY and THE LATER YEARS OF THOMAS HARDY, both supposedly by Florence Emily Hardy, and published by Macmillan in 1928 and 1930, respectively.

DESPERATE REMEDIES. A Novel. Tinsley Brothers 1871. 3 vols. Blue cloth, also red cloth. Remainder Issue: 3 vols in 1, in green cloth. 500 copies printed.

UNDER THE GREENWOOD TREE. Tinsley Brothers 1872. 2 vols. Green cloth.

A PAIR OF BLUE EYES. Tinsley Brothers 1873. 3 vols. Green cloth.

FAR FROM THE MADDING CROWD. Smith, Elder 1874. 2 vols. Green cloth. 750 copies. First issue: 'Sacrament' in first line, page 2, volume one.

THE HAND OF ETHELBERTA. Smith, Elder 1876. 2 vols. Brown cloth. In each volume, following the text, is a leaf of publisher's adverts.

THE RETURN OF THE NATIVE. Smith, Elder 1878. 3 vols. Brown cloth. A leaf of publisher's adverts at the end of vol II. Binding 'A' has triple blind frame on the back. Binding 'B' has double blind frame on back.

THE TRUMPET-MAJOR. Smith, Elder 1880. 3 vols. Red cloth with double blind frame on back; later binding (almost certainly) with triple blind frame on back (and other minor differences).

FELLOW-TOWNSMEN. New York: Harper 1880. Small 24mo. Half-Hour Series.
   One of the stories included later in 'Wessex Tales'.

A LAODICEAN. New York: Henry Holt 1881. Pictorial mustard cloth. U.K. (a week later): Sampson Low 1881. 3 vols. Grey cloth.

TWO ON A TOWER. Sampson Low etc. 1882. 3 vols. Green cloth.

THE ROMANTIC ADVENTURES OF A MILKMAID. New York: George Munro's Sons (1883). 90pp. Wrappers. 32 page Catalogue of Munro's publications bound in at the end. The date 'Dec. 15, 1883.' appears on the front wrapper. The book is no. 139 in the Seaside Library, Pocket Edition series.

THE MAYOR OF CASTERBRIDGE. Smith, Elder 1886. 2 vols. Plum cloth. Adverts at the end of each vol – one leaf in vol I, two leaves in vol II.

THE WOODLANDERS. London & New York: Macmillan 1887. 3 vols. Fine-grained smooth green cloth; later, a coarser grained green cloth. Leaf of adverts at end of volume I.

WESSEX TALES. London & New York: Macmillan 1888. 2 vols. Green cloth. 4pp. book adverts at end of volume II.

A GROUP OF NOBLE DAMES. Osgood, McIlvaine 1891. Light brown cloth, blocked in gold on the front and the spine, with brown lettering on the spine. Secondary binding does not have the gold blocking.

TESS OF THE D'URBERVILLES. James R. Osgood, McIlvaine 1891. 3 vols. Tan cloth.
   The edition of 1912 (Wessex Edition in maroon cloth), contains material inadvertently omitted from earlier editions and is therefore the First Definitive Edition.

LIFE'S LITTLE IRONIES. Osgood, McIlvaine 1894. Green cloth.
   Five further editions appeared in the same year.

JUDE THE OBSCURE. Osgood, McIlvaine 1896 (1895). Dark Green cloth. Volume VIII of the Wessex Novels. U.S.: Harpers 1896.

THE WELL-BELOVED. Osgood, McIlvaine (1897). Green cloth. Volume XVII of The Wessex Novels. Map at end. Issued later by Harpers.

WESSEX POEMS AND OTHER VERSES. With 30 illustrations by the author. London & New York: Harper & Brothers 1898. Green cloth. 500 copies printed. Copies for presentation were done in white buckram.

POEMS OF THE PAST AND THE PRESENT. London and New York: Harper & Brothers 1902 (1901). Green cloth. Presentation copies were bound in white buckram.

THE DYNASTS. Macmillan, 3 vols, dated 1903, 1906, and 1908. Green cloth. Second issue of volume I, dated 1904, has a cancel title page. The second volume was actually issued in 1905. First One-Volume Edition: 1910. A signed edition of 525 copies was issued in 1927.

TIME'S LAUGHINGSTOCKS AND OTHER VERSES.   Macmillan 1909.
Green cloth. 4pp. adverts of Hardy's works follow the text.

A CHANGED MAN . . . AND OTHER TALES.   Macmillan 1913. Dark
green cloth. Vol XVIII of The Wessex Novels. Issued later by Harpers.

SATIRES OF CIRCUMSTANCE, LYRICS AND REVERIES.   Macmillan
1914. Green cloth. Advert leaf at end.

SONG OF THE SOLDIERS.   Published in The Times, 9th September.
Reprinted at Hove by permission, 16th September 1914. 4pp. leaflet, pages 3
and 4 being blank. Four days earlier, Clement Shorter had 12 copies printed
for private circulation.
    The Hove leaflet was issued free to soldiers on active service abroad. In
    1915, another edition was produced at Hove. This was 8pp. in wrappers.

THE OXEN.   Published in The Times, 24th December 1915. Reprinted at
Hove, 28th December 1915. 4pp. in grey wrappers.
    This poem, 'printed for private circulation', was issued free to soldiers on
    active service abroad.

SELECTED POEMS.   Macmillan 1916.

MOMENTS OF VISION.   Macmillan 1917.

COLLECTED POEMS.   Macmillan 1919.

LATE LYRICS AND EARLIER.   Macmillan 1922.

THE FAMOUS TRAGEDY OF THE QUEEN OF CORNWALL.   Macmillan 1923.

HUMAN SHOWS FAR PHANTASIES.   Macmillan 1925.

LIFE AND ART.   U.S. 1925.

YULETIDE IN A YOUNGER WORLD.   Faber, Ariel Poem 1927. Wrappers. Also, limited edition of 350.

WINTER WORDS.   Macmillan 1928.

THE SHORT STORIES.   Macmillan 1928.

OUR EXPLOITS AT WEST POLEY.   O.U.P. 1952.

HARRIS, Joel Chandler (1848–1908)

Author of other works but associated mainly with the Uncle Remus stories, which were contained in a series of books from 1881 onwards. The first was:

UNCLE REMUS: HIS SONGS AND HIS SAYINGS.   New York: Appleton 1881. Pictorial cloth, usually blue, but variants are known. The first issue has 'presumptive' in the last line of page 9. This was subsequently changed to 'presumptuous'. At the back are 8pp. adverts. These should not mention the present volume. The U.K. edition, same year, was entitled UNCLE REMUS AND HIS LEGENDS OF THE OLD PLANTATION.

HAWTHORNE, Nathaniel (1804–1864)

His first novel FANSHAWE was published anonymously at his own expense. Subsequently, he tried to suppress it and is reputed to have destroyed many copies. It is now extremely rare and worth in excess of $10,000. Some of his early pieces were published in the periodical THE TOKEN.

FANSHAWE.   Boston: Marsh & Capen 1828. Qr. cloth, boards, labels.

TWICE-TOLD TALES.   Boston: American Stationers Co. / John B. Russell 1837. First issue: fifth story listed in Contents as at p. 78, not p. 77. New Edition, with extra tales: Munroe 1842. 2 vols.

PETER PARLEY'S UNIVERSAL HISTORY . . .   Boston: American Stationers Co. / John B. Russell 1837. 2 vols.

THE GENTLE BOY.   Boston: Weeks, Jordon / New York & London: Wiley & Putnam 1839. Brown wrappers.

GRANDFATHER'S CHAIR.   Boston: Peabody / New York: Wiley & Putnam 1841.

FAMOUS OLD PEOPLE.   Boston: Peabody 1841.

LIBERTY TREE.   Boston: Peabody 1841.

THE CELESTIAL RAILROAD.   Boston: Wilder 1843. Buff wrappers.

MOSSES FROM AN OLD MANSE.   New York: Wiley & Putnam 1846. 2 vols. Wrappers. Also issued as one vol in cloth. Verso title-pages give printer as 'R. Craighead's Power Press'. This is missing or changed in later impressions.

In the first issue of the wrappers, each vol has adverts on the back – vol 1 with 15 entries, vol 2 with 16 or 17.

THE SCARLET LETTER. Boston: Ticknor, Reed, & Fields 1850. 322pp. Brown cloth. 4pp adverts tipped-in at front, dated March 1st 1850. Misprint 'reduplicate' on p. 21, line 20. Later: less pages, 1849 ads and 1849 title-page. U.K.: Bohn's Cheap Series, Routledge's Railway Library, and Walker's, all 1851.

TRUE STORIES FROM HISTORY AND BIOGRAPHY. Boston: Ticknor, Reed, and Fields 1851. First issue: 'Cambridge: Printed by Bolles & Houghton' on verso title-page; and signature mark (a★) at foot of page (iii) is under and left of the 'a' in the final line.

THE HOUSE OF THE SEVEN GABLES. Boston: Ticknor, Reed, and Fields 1851. Adverts dated March 1851.

A WONDER BOOK FOR BOYS AND GIRLS. Boston: Ticknor, Reed, and Fields 1852. First issue has design at top of spine only, not entire spine.

THE SNOW-IMAGE AND OTHER TWICE-TOLD TALES. Boston: Ticknor, Reed, and Fields 1852. (Issued Dec. 1851, as was the London issue dated 1851).

THE BLITHEDALE ROMANCE. Boston: Ticknor, Reed, and Fields 1852. U.K.: THE BLITHEDALE ROMANCES. Chapman & Hall 1852. 2 vols. Slightly preceded the US edition and has some textual differences.

LIFE OF FRANKLIN PIERCE. Boston: Ticknor, Reed, and Fields 1852.

TANGLEWOOD TALES. Boston: Ticknor, Reed, and Fields 1853. First issue: imprint of stereotyper only (not printer) on verso title, and adverts dated 'August, 1853'.

A RILL FROM THE TOWN PUMP. Cash 1857. 12pp in grey wrappers. Extremely rare.

TRANSFORMATIONS. Smith, Elder 1860 (Feb.). 3 vols. The U.K. Edition of THE MARBLE FAUN. It preceded the U.S. edition.

THE MARBLE FAUN. Boston: Ticknor & Fields 1860 (April). 2 vols.

OUR OLD HOME. Boston: Ticknor & Fields 1863. First issue: publisher's list on leaf opposite p. 398.

PANSIE. John Camden Hotten. n.d. (1864).

HAZLITT, William (1778–1830)

The following is only a selection of his many works.

AN ESSAY ON THE PRINCIPLES OF HUMAN ACTION: being an Argument in Favour of the Natural Disinterestedness of the Human Mind. To which are Added, some Remarks on the System of Hartley and Helvetius. (Anonymous). for J. Johnson 1805.
His rare first book.

MEMOIRS OF THE LATE THOMAS HOLCROFT. Written by Himself . . . for Longman (etc) 1816. 3 vols. 12mo.

CHARACTERS OF SHAKESPEARE'S PLAYS. C. H. Reynell for R. Hunter and C. and J. Ollier 1817. Second Edition: for Taylor & Hessey 1818.

LECTURES ON THE ENGLISH POETS. for Taylor & Hessey 1818.

A VIEW OF THE ENGLISH STAGE; or, a Series of Dramatic Criticisms. London: 1818. Second Issue: title-page with imprint of John Warren 1821.

LECTURES ON THE ENGLISH COMIC WRITERS. for Taylor & Hessey 1819.

POLITICAL ESSAYS, WITH SKETCHES . . . Hone 1819.

TABLE-TALK; or, Original Essays. John Warren 1821. S4 is a cancel. Second Series: same publisher 1822.
Copies in the original boards were published with the cancellans as preliminary leaf [a]4 for the binder to transfer to S4. However, it is not unknown for a copy in the original boards to have the cancel leaf already at S4.

LIBER AMORIS; or, The New Pygmalion. John Hunt 1823.

THE SPIRIT OF THE AGE: or, Contemporary Portraits. (anon). H. Colbourn 1825.

THE PLAIN SPEAKER: Opinions on Books, Men, and Things. (anon). H. Colbourn 1826. 2 vols.

THE CHARACTER OF W. COBBETT, M.P. to which is added, several Interesting Particulars of Mr. Cobbett's Life and Writings. J. Watson 1835. 16pp.
The first separate edition.

LITERARY REMAINS. Saunders & Otley 1836. 2 vols.

HEMINGWAY, Ernest (1899–1961)

The story THE SNOWS OF KILIMANJARO on which the film was based, first appeared in the periodical Esquire, in August 1936. No book was published with this title. The story was included in the 1938 collection, THE FIFTH COLUMN . . .

THREE STORIES AND TEN POEMS. Paris: Privately Printed by Robert McAlmon, Contact Publishing Co. 1923. Limited to 300 copies. Grey-blue wrappers, black lettering.

IN OUR TIME. Paris: Three Mountains Press 1924. Limited to 170 copies. New York: Boni & Liveright 1925. U.K.: Cape 1926.

THE TORRENTS OF SPRING. New York: Scribners 1926. U.K.: Cape 1933. An edition was published in Paris in 1932. Of this, there was a large paper edition priced at 125 francs & a smaller edition at 10 francs. Both in wrappers.

THE SUN ALSO RISES. New York: Scribners 1926. Publisher's seal on verso title-page. Misprint on p. 181 line 26 – 'stoppped'. Error on earliest d/w – 'In Our Times' for 'In Our Time'.

FIESTA. Cape 1927.
The U.K. edition of THE SUN ALSO RISES.

MEN WITHOUT WOMEN. New York: Scribners 1927. U.K.: Cape 1928.

A FAREWELL TO ARMS. New York: Scribners 1929. Publisher's seal on verso title-page. Disclaimer on page (x) – 'None of these characters (etc)' denotes second printing. U.K.: Cape 1929. Misprint on p. 66 line 28 – 'seriosu' for 'serious'.

DEATH IN THE AFTERNOON. New York: Scribners 1932. U.K.: Cape 1932.

WINNER TAKE NOTHING. New York: Scribners 1933. U.K.: Cape 1934.

GREEN HILLS OF AFRICA. New York: Scribners 1935. U.K.: Cape 1936.

TO HAVE AND HAVE NOT. New York: Scribners 1937. U.K.: Cape 1937.

THE FIFTH COLUMN AND THE FIRST FORTY-NINE STORIES. New York: Scribners 1938. U.K.: Cape 1939.

FOR WHOM THE BELL TOLLS. New York: Scribners 1940. Earliest d/w does not have the photographer's name on the back. U.K.: Cape 1941.

ACROSS THE RIVER AND INTO THE TREES. Cape 1950. U.S. (3 days later): Scribners 1950. First issue d/w has yellow letters on spine; second issue has orange letters on spine.

THE OLD MAN AND THE SEA. New York: Scribners 1952. Earliest d/w has deep blue ink in Hemingway photograph – later, olive. U.K.: Cape 1952. First d/w printed on one side of the sheet only.

A MOVEABLE FEAST. New York: Scribners 1964. U.K.: Cape 1964.

BY-LINE. New York: Scribners 1967. U.K.: Collins 1968.

ISLANDS IN THE STREAM. New York: Scribners 1970. U.K.: Collins 1970.

EIGHTY-EIGHT POEMS. New York: Harcourt Brace 1980.

SELECTED LETTERS 1917–1961. New York & London: Granada 1981.

THE DANGEROUS SUMMER. New York: Scribners 1985. U.K.: Hamilton 1985.

ON WRITING. New York & London: Granada 1985.

THE GARDEN OF EDEN. Scribners 1986. U.K.: Hamilton 1987.

HENTY, G. A. (1832–1902)

Henty, the most popular of the boy's adventure writers operating in the late nineteenth and early twentieth centuries, is closely identified in the public mind with the publishers Blackie, and with their particular style of pictorial cloth binding. But Blackie does not figure at all in Henty's early period, and later on, the first editions are frequently the American ones.

The collecting of Henty, by both text-collectors and first edition collectors, has strengthened significantly in the last two or three decades. With the inevitable result that they have largely disappeared from the shelves of bookshops, and collecting them has become much more difficult. Later first editions fall generally in the price-range of £30 to £50, but the earliest are extremely difficult to get and very expensive. The first three or four books are all firmly established at prices of £1000 or more.

I believe the following list includes all the major novels. They were virtually all published in cloth, and occasionally in cloths of different colours. So far as I am aware, no priority has been established for particular colours. It is a popular myth that all the first editions had bevelled or 'olivine' edges and reprints did not. There is an element of truth in this, but it is not an infallible rule. Similarly, the idea that first editions were dated on the title-page and reprints were not, is only partially true. There is in fact, still a fair degree of uncertainty about Henty's publishing career. The loss of records at Blackie's in particular, and the unavailability of data from other publishers, has not helped. As both of Henty's principal bibliographers (Farmer & Dartt) have readily admitted, there is still some way to go, before all the uncertainties can be eliminated. In these circumstances, I give the following list with some apprehension and with the warning that it should not be regarded as definitive.

A SEARCH FOR A SECRET.   Tinsley Brothers 1867. 3 vols. Blue or green cloth. One vol edition, later same year.

THE MARCH TO MAGDALA.   Tinsley Brothers 1868. Blue cloth.

ALL BUT LOST.   Tinsley Brothers 1869. 3 vols. Blue cloth.

OUT ON THE PAMPAS.   Griffith & Farran 1871. Blue or brown cloth.

THE YOUNG FRANC-TIREURS.   Griffith & Farran 1872. Blue, red, or green cloth.

THE MARCH TO COOMASSIE.   Tinsley 1874. Blue cloth.

SEASIDE MAIDENS.   Tinsley 1880. Orange cloth.

THE YOUNG BUGLERS.   Griffith & Farran 1880. Adverts dated October 1879. Red or green cloth.

THE CORNET OF HORSE.   Sampson, Low & Marston 1881. Adverts dated January 1881. Red cloth.

IN TIMES OF PERIL.   Griffith & Farran 1881. Adverts dated October 1881. Red or blue cloth.

FACING DEATH.   Blackie 1882. Blue or brown cloth. Later issue dated 1883.

WINNING HIS SPURS.   Sampson, Low & Marston 1882. Red cloth.

FRIENDS THOUGH DIVIDED.   Griffith & Farran 1883. Adverts dated September 1883. Red, blue, brown or green cloth.

JACK ARCHER.   Sampson, Low & Marston 1883. Red cloth.

UNDER DRAKE'S FLAG.   Blackie 1883. Green or brown cloth.

BY SHEER PLUCK.   Blackie 1884. Adverts headed 'New Series for 1885'. Red cloth.

WITH CLIVE IN INDIA.   Blackie 1884. Red, brown or blue cloth.

THE YOUNG COLONISTS.   Routledge 1885. Blue/gold cloth.

TRUE TO THE OLD FLAG.   Blackie 1885. Blue, grey, red or green cloth.

IN FREEDOM'S CAUSE.   Blackie 1885. Blue, brown or red cloth.

ST. GEORGE FOR ENGLAND.   Blackie 1885. Brown, blue or green cloth.

THE LION OF THE NORTH.   Blackie 1886. Brown or green cloth.

THE DRAGON AND THE RAVEN.   Blackie 1886. Brown or green cloth.

FOR NAME AND FAME.   Blackie 1886. Brown or grey cloth.

THROUGH THE FRAY.   Blackie 1886. Brown or red cloth.

YARNS ON THE BEACH.   Blackie 1886. Brown or red cloth.

THE YOUNG CARTHAGINIAN.   Blackie 1887. Blue or green cloth.

THE BRAVEST OF THE BRAVE.   Blackie n.d. (1887). Red or blue cloth.

A FINAL RECKONING.   Blackie 1887. Blue or green cloth.

WITH WOLFE IN CANADA.   Blackie 1887. Green, blue or red cloth.

THE SOVEREIGN READER: SCENES FROM THE LIFE AND REIGN OF QUEEN VICTORIA.   Blackie 1887. Red or purple cloth.

IN THE REIGN OF TERROR.   Blackie 1888. Red, blue, grey or green cloth.

STURDY AND STRONG.   Blackie 1888. Red, blue or orange cloth.

ORANGE AND GREEN.   Blackie 1888. Red, blue or orange cloth.

BONNIE PRINCE CHARLIE.   Blackie 1888. Brown or red cloth.

FOR THE TEMPLE.   Blackie 1888. Brown, red or blue cloth.

GABRIEL ALLEN, M.P.   Spencer & Blackett, n.d. (1888). Red cloth.

CAPTAIN BAYLEY'S HEIR.   Blackie 1889. Red, brown or blue cloth.

THE CAT OF BUBASTES.   Blackie 1889. Blue, brown, grey or green cloth.

THE LION OF ST. MARK.   Blackie 1889. Red, blue or grey cloth.

THE CURSE OF CARNE'S HOLD.   Spencer & Blackett 1889. 2 vols. Blue cloth.

THE PLAGUE SHIP.   SCK Penny Library of Fiction 1889. Wrappers.

BY PIKE AND DYKE.   Blackie 1890. Brown or green cloth.

ONE OF THE 28TH.   Blackie 1890. Red, brown, green or blue cloth.

TALES OF DARING AND DANGER.   Blackie 1889 (but 1890). Blue or green cloth.

WITH LEE IN VIRGINIA.   Blackie 1890. Brown or blue cloth.

THE ART OF AUTHORSHIP.   Clarke 1890. Blue or brown cloth.

THOSE OTHER ANIMALS.   Henry & Co. n.d. (1891). Green cloth.

BY ENGLAND'S AID.   Blackie 1891. Blue or brown cloth.

BY RIGHT OF CONQUEST.   Blackie 1891. Green or brown cloth.

MAORI AND SETTLER.   Blackie 1891. Brown, blue, red or green cloth.

A CHAPTER OF ADVENTURES.   Blackie 1891. Blue or grey cloth.

A HIDDEN FOE.   Sampson, Low & Marston 1891. 2 vols. Grey cloth.

THE DASH FOR KHARTOUM.   New York: Scribner 1891. U.K.: Blackie 1892. Brown, red, grey or green cloth.

HELD FAST FOR ENGLAND. New York: Scribner 1891. U.K.: Blackie 1892. Red, grey or brown cloth.

REDSKIN AND COWBOY. New York: Scribner 1891. U.K.: Blackie 1892. Red, green or brown cloth.

THE RANCH IN THE VALLEY. SCK Penny Library of Fiction 1892. Wrappers.

BERIC THE BRITON. New York: Scribner 1891. U.K.: Blackie 1892. Blue or brown cloth.

CONDEMNED AS A NIHILIST. New York: Scribner 1892. U.K.: Blackie 1893. Brown or blue cloth.

IN GREEK WATERS. New York: Scribner 1892. U.K.: Blackie 1893. Grey, brown or green cloth.

TALES FROM HENTY. Blackie 1893. Red cloth.

RUJUB THE JUGGLER. Chatto 1893. 3 vols. Blue morocco cloth shot with bronze. One vol edition (first illustrated): Chatto 1893. U.S.: Hurst n.d. (1891 according to Dartt). One vol.

A TALE OF WATERLOO. New York: Worthington 1894. Tan cloth.

A JACOBITE EXILE. New York: Scribner 1893. U.K.: Blackie 1894. Brown, green, grey or blue cloth.

THROUGH THE SIKH WAR. New York: Scribner 1893. U.K.: Blackie 1894. Green cloth.

ST. BARTHOLOMEW'S EVE. New York: Scribner 1893. U.K.: Blackie 1894. Green, blue or red cloth.

DOROTHY'S DOUBLE. Chatto 1894. 3 vols. Blue cloth.

WHEN LONDON BURNED. New York: Scribner 1894. U.K.: Blackie 1895. Blue cloth.

A WOMAN OF THE COMMUNE. F. V. White 1895. Red cloth.

WULF THE SAXON. New York: Scribner 1894. U.K.: Blackie 1895. Green cloth.

IN THE HEART OF THE ROCKIES. New York: Scribner 1894. U.K.: Blackie 1895. Grey cloth.

A KNIGHT OF THE WHITE CROSS. New York: Scribner 1895. U.K.: Blackie 1896. Green cloth.

BEARS AND DACOITS. Blackie n.d. (1896). Green-brown cloth. Five children among flowered vine design on front.

SURLY JOE. Blackie n.d. (1896). Wrappers.

WHITE-FACED DICK. Blackie n.d. (1896). Limp orange cloth.

THROUGH RUSSIAN SNOWS. New York: Scribner 1895. U.K.: Blackie 1896. Grey cloth.

THE TIGER OF MYSORE. New York: Scribner 1895. U.K.: Blackie 1896. Blue cloth.

ON THE IRRAWADDY. New York: Scribner 1896. U.K.: Blackie 1897. Blue cloth.

AT AGINCOURT. New York: Scribner 1896. U.K.: Blackie 1897. Second Issue: adverts at end include quotes from reviews of the book. Green-grey cloth.

WITH COCHRANE THE DAUNTLESS. New York: Scribner 1896. U.K.: Blackie 1897. Blue cloth.

THE QUEEN'S CUP. Chatto 1897. 3 vols. Green or blue cloth. One vol edition later the same year.

AMONG MALAY PIRATES. New York: Hurst & Co. n.d. (1897). Grey-green cloth.
    Dartt gives this as 'possibly' the first edition. Several other American publishers issued the book without date.

WITH MOORE AT CARUNNA. New York: Scribner 1897. U.K.: Blackie 1898. Green or blue cloth.

COLONEL THORNDYKE'S SECRET. Chatto 1898. Pink cloth.

WITH FREDERICK THE GREAT. New York: Scribner 1897. U.K.: Blackie 1898. Red cloth. pp32 adverts headed either 'Books for Young People' or 'Illustrated Story-Books'.

UNDER WELLINGTON'S COMMAND. New York: Scribner 1898. U.K.: Blackie 1899. Blue cloth.

AT ABOUKIR AND ACRE.   New York: Scribner 1898. U.K.: Blackie 1899. Red cloth.

BOTH SIDES THE BORDER.   New York: Scribner 1898. U.K.: Blackie 1899. Blue cloth.

THE LOST HEIR.   Bowden 1899. Adverts. Green cloth.

THE GOLDEN CANON.   New York: Mershon 1899. Light brown cloth.
Also published in New York, undated, by Federal Book Co. decorated on the front with military engagements in ovals. The contents, in each case, include 'filler' stories, not by Henty. Several other variants were published in America.

ON THE SPANISH MAIN.   Chambers 1899. Red wrappers.

A ROVING COMMISSION.   New York: Scribner 1899. U.K.: Blackie 1900. Red cloth.

WON BY THE SWORD.   New York: Scribner 1899. U.K.: Blackie 1900. Blue cloth.

NO SURRENDER!   New York: Scribner 1899. U.K.: Blackie 1900. Red cloth.

DO YOUR DUTY.   Blackie n.d. (1900). Blue or green cloth.

THE SOLE SURVIVORS.   Chambers 1901. Red wrappers.

IN THE IRISH BRIGADE.   New York: Scribner 1900. U.K.: Blackie 1901. 32pp adverts. Green cloth.

OUT WITH GARIBALDI.   New York: Scribner 1900. U.K.: Blackie 1901. Blue cloth.

JOHN HAWKE'S FORTUNE.   Chapman & Hall Young People's Library 1901. Wrappers.

WITH BULLER IN NATAL.   New York: Scribner 1900. U.K.: Blackie 1901. Blue cloth.

QUEEN VICTORIA.   Blackie 1901. Purple cloth.

TO HERAT AND CABUL.   New York: Scribner 1901. U.K.: Blackie 1902. Blue cloth.

WITH ROBERTS TO PRETORIA. New York: Scribner 1901. U.K.: Blackie 1902. Red cloth.

AT THE POINT OF THE BAYONET. New York: Scribner 1901. U.K.: Blackie 1902. Green cloth.

IN THE HANDS OF THE CAVE DWELLERS. New York & London: Harper 1900. First Blackie Edition dated 1903, but issued in 1902.

AT DUTY'S CALL. London & Edinburgh: Chambers n.d. (1902). Red wrappers, also in cloth.

THE TREASURE OF THE INCAS. New York: Scribner 1902. U.K.: Blackie 1903. Green cloth.

WITH THE BRITISH LEGION. New York: Scribner 1902. U.K.: Blackie 1903. Blue or green cloth.

WITH KITCHENER IN THE SOUDAN. New York: Scribner 1902. U.K.: Blackie 1903. First Issue: 32pp catalogue at end, starts with 'With Buller in Natal'. In the second issue, the catalogue starts with 'With Roberts to Pretoria'. Red cloth.

THROUGH THREE CAMPAIGNS. New York: Scribner 1903. U.K.: Blackie 1904. Red cloth.

WITH THE ALLIES TO PEKIN. New York: Scribner 1903. U.K.: Blackie 1904. Green cloth.

BY CONDUCT AND COURAGE. New York: Scribner 1904. U.K.: Blackie 1905. pp. 1–381 or 11–384 (no priority established). Red cloth.

GALLANT DEEDS. Chambers 1905. White or grey cloth.

IN THE HANDS OF THE MALAYS. Blackie 1905. Red cloth.

A SOLDIER'S DAUGHTER. Blackie 1906. Red, blue or green cloth.

HOBBES, Thomas (1588–1679)

LEVIATHAN, or The Matter, Forme & Power of a Commonwealth Ecclesiasticall and Civill. Printed for Andrew Crooke, at the Green Dragon in St. Pauls Church-yard 1651. Folio. 'Head' woodcut on engraved title-page. pp. (viii), 396. Folding table.

HODGSON, William Hope (1877–1918)

Hodgson is so little known, he does not even merit an entry in the latest edition of The Oxford Companion to English Literature. However, he is of increasing interest to collectors, and his first editions (which are all rare) are mostly valued in three figures. Early reprints of his eight principal books came from Holden & Hardingham, and even these are collector's items (in view of the scarcity of the first editions).

THE BOATS OF THE 'GLEN CARRIG' . . . As told by John Winterstraw, Gent., to his Son James Winterstraw . . . Chapman & Hall 1907. Red cloth gilt.

THE HOUSE ON THE BORDERLAND. Chapman & Hall 1908. U.S. (THE HOUSE ON THE BORDERLAND AND OTHER NOVELS): Arkham House 1946.

THE GHOST PIRATES. Stanley Paul 1909.
An abridged copyright edition was put out a little earlier by the author.

THE NIGHT LAND. Eveleigh Nash 1912. Colonial Edition: George Bell 1912. Green wrappers.
There was an abridged edition in 1921.

POEMS, AND THE DREAM OF X. A. P. Watt 1912. Brown cloth, white lettering.
Extremely rare.

CARNACKI THE GHOST-FINDER. Eveleigh Nash 1913. U.S.: Sauk City: Mycroft & Moran 1947. This contains three stories previously unpublished.
In 1910, the author had printed for copyright purposes, a 14pp booklet in blue wrappers, entitled CARNAKI, THE GHOST FINDER, AND A POEM. The stories in this exceedingly rare booklet are greatly abridged.

CARGUNKA, AND POEMS AND ANECDOTES. A. P. Watt (London) & R. Harold Paget (New York) 1913. 84pp. Blue-grey wrappers. Issued to establish copyright.

MEN OF THE DEEP WATERS. Eveleigh Nash 1914. Red cloth gilt. Remaindered in light brown cloth, black lettering.

THE LUCK OF THE STRONG. Eveleigh Nash 1916.

CAPTAIN GAULT. Eveleigh Nash 1917. U.S.: McBride (New York) 1918.

THE CALLING OF THE SEA. Selwyn & Blount (1920). Grey-blue boards, paper label on spine. 500 copies printed.

THE VOICE OF THE OCEAN. Selwyn and Blount (1921). Grey-blue boards, paper label on spine. 500 copies printed.

DEEP WATERS. U.S.: Arkham House 1967.

OUT OF THE STORM. U.S.: Donald Grant 1975.

THE DREAM OF X. U.S.: Donald Grant 1977.

HORNE, Richard Hengist (The 'Farthing Poet') (1802–1884)

Horne contributed articles to Dickens' HOUSEHOLD WORDS and DAILY NEWS, wrote several tragedies (in blank verse) and some volumes of poetry. He was acquainted with Elizabeth Barrett Browning, whose letters to him were published in 1877, wrote an interesting volume on Australia, and adapted a number of plays. But he is now remembered only as the 'Farthing Poet' – a consequence of his publishing an allegorical epic and pricing it at a farthing, with the object of marking the 'public contempt' into which epic poetry had fallen. It was:

ORION: an Epic Poem. In three Books. J. Miller . . . 1843. 8vo.
Many reprints followed.

GALATEA SECUNDA, An Odaic Cantata . . . Melbourne 1867. Pamphlet.
A Wise forgery.

HOUSMAN, A. E. (1859–1936)

After a slow start, A SHROPSHIRE LAD became immensely popular during 1914–1918, and since then has become established as a firm favourite with both readers and collectors. It is one of the key books of modern poetry. The first edition is rare, as might be expected of an edition of only 500 copies, published a century ago. Listed below are his rare first publication, his second (SHROPSHIRE LAD) and four volumes which will be familiar to regular browsers in the bookshops.

INTRODUCTORY LECTURE. Printed at The University Press, Cambridge 1892. Pamphlet of 10 leaves. Private Reprint: same press 1933. 100 copies. First Published Edition: C.U.P. 1937. Blue boards. U.S.: Macmillan & C.U.P. 1937. Blue cloth.
Copies of the first edition were given to members of the Faculties to whom the lecture was delivered. Not many copies have survived.

A SHROPSHIRE LAD. Kegan Paul, Trench, Trubner & Co. Ltd. 1896. 12mo. White parchment spine with paper label lettered (usually) in red, pale blue boards, glazed d/w. Four versions of the paper label are known (priority uncertain). Of 500 copies printed, 150 were issued in America by John Lane with his imprint on a cancel title-page, dated 1897. Second Edition: Grant Richards 1898. Green buckram. 500 copies.
Rare, especially in the d/w. A price of £2000 would not be unreasonable.

LAST POEMS. Grant Richards 1922.

THE NAME AND NATURE OF POETRY. C.U.P. 1933.

MORE POEMS. Cape (1936).

THE COLLECTED POEMS. Cape (1939).

HUDSON, William Henry (1841–1922)

The demand for Hudson's first editions comes strongest from collectors of books on natural history and country life, but there is substantial interest among collectors of literature. His first book (listed below) is sometimes priced at around £1000, but is often far less. It is rare in fine condition with an unfaded binding. The later and pseudonymous FAN, is even rarer. He produced a number of leaflets and pamphlets, mainly published by the Society for the Protection of Birds. These are not in the checklist.

THE PURPLE LAND THAT ENGLAND LOST. Sampson Low, etc. 1885. 2 vols. Light blue cloth, later in purple cloth. First issue has adverts in vol 2 dated October.

A CRYSTAL AGE. (anonymous). T. Fisher Unwin 1887. 32pp adverts at end. Black cloth, also red cloth.

ARGENTINE ORNITHOLOGY. A Descriptive Catalogue ... By P. L. Sclater ... With Notes ... by W. H. Hudson. R. H. Porter 1888–89. 2 vols. Blue-grey boards. Also 200 signed.
The book contains 20 hand-coloured plates, and though not his rarest book, it is one of his most expensive at something close on £2000 for the signed copies.

A NATURALIST IN LA PLATA. Chapman & Hall 1892. Green cloth.

FAN, The Story of a Young Girl's Life. By Henry Harford (pseud). Chapman & Hall 1892. 3 vols. Green cloth.
Probably his rarest book. Decent copies can get about £5000.

IDLE DAYS IN PATAGONIA. Chapman & Hall 1893. Crimson buckram, publisher's device on back. 2 leaves of ads. Variants exist.

BIRDS IN A VILLAGE. Chapman & Hall 1893. Chocolate buckram.

BRITISH BIRDS. London & New York: Longmans, Green 1895. Green cloth.

NATURE IN DOWNLAND. London, New York & Bombay: Longmans, Green 1900. Green buckram.

BIRDS AND MAN. London, New York & Bombay: Longmans, Green 1901. Green cloth.

EL OMBU. Duckworth 1902. Green cloth.

HAMPSHIRE DAYS. London, New York & Bombay: Longmans, Green 1903. Green cloth.

GREEN MANSIONS. Duckworth 1904. Green cloth. First Issue has no publisher's design on back cover.

A LITTLE BOY LOST. Duckworth 1905. Yellow buckram.

THE LAND'S END. Hutchinson 1908. Blue cloth.

AFOOT IN ENGLAND. Hutchinson 1909. Green cloth.

A SHEPHERD'S LIFE. Methuen (1910). Green cloth. 32pp adverts dated April, 1910.

ADVENTURES AMONG BIRDS. Hutchinson 1913. Green cloth.

FAR AWAY AND LONG AGO. London & Toronto: Dent / New York: Dutton 1918. Green cloth.

THE BOOK OF A NATURALIST. London, New York, Toronto: Hodder & Stoughton (1919). Green cloth.

BIRDS IN TOWN AND VILLAGE. London & Toronto: Dent / New York: Dutton 1919. Green cloth.

DEAD MAN'S PLACK and AN OLD THORN. London & Toronto: Dent / New York: Dutton 1920. Green cloth.

A TRAVELLER IN LITTLE THINGS. London & Toronto: Dent 1921. Green cloth.

HUEFFER, Ford H. Madox
see under FORD MADOX FORD.

HUGHES, Thomas (1822–1896)

The perennial favourite TOM BROWN'S SCHOOLDAYS was his only work to achieve popularity. The sequel TOM BROWN AT OXFORD proved to be a disappointment and is hardly read at all nowadays. His one other novel, THE SCOURING OF THE WHITE HORSE, based on his own early life, was received moderately well, but has not stood the test of time. This last was, however, an attractive illustrated production and is welcomed into the libraries of those who collect Victorian illustrated books. All three, be it noted, were published anonymously. The price of a first edition of TOM BROWN'S SCHOOLDAYS varies greatly with the condition, but at its best is close on £1000.

TOM BROWN'S SCHOOLDAYS. By an Old Boy. Cambridge: Macmillan 1857. Blue cloth. First Illustrated: Macmillan 1869 (1868). Illustrations by Arthur Hughes and Sidney Prior Hall.
The first edition is rarely found in very good condition.

THE SCOURING OF THE WHITE HORSE; or, The Long Vacation Ramble of a London Clerk. Cambridge: Macmillan 1859. Illustrated by Richard Doyle. Gilt-decorated cloth (by Doyle). First issue: in the second paragraph of p. 60 the 'u' is missing from the word 'up'.
The loss of the attractive original binding makes rebound copies particularly unsatisfactory. However, the original gilt is rarely found in a clean bright state.

TOM BROWN AT OXFORD. By the author of 'Tom Brown's Schooldays'. Cambridge & London: Macmillan 1861. 3 vols. Blue cloth. Not illustrated.

HUXLEY, Aldous (1894–1963)

Huxley's first three publications are scarce. Today, his most famous book is BRAVE NEW WORLD. This is not scarce, but there is a strong demand for it, and it has a current value (fine in the d/w) in the region of £500. There was a signed limited issue of the work, and this is valued at over £1000. Most of his many works are fairly easy to obtain.

THE BURNING WHEEL. Oxford: Blackwell 1916. Yellow wrappers with paper label.

JONAH.   Oxford: Printed at the Holywell Press 1917. 16pp. Wrappers (same paper as text). About 50 copies printed – all signed, apparently.

THE DEFEAT OF YOUTH AND OTHER POEMS.   Oxford: Blackwell 1918. 52pp. Decorated stiff green wrappers, paper label – the front wrapper serving as title-page. Limited to 250 copies.

LEDA.   Chatto & Windus 1920. Red cloth, paper label on spine. Also, 160 signed, in canvas spine, grey boards. U.S.: Doran 1920.
   The first of his books to be published in America. In 1929, Doran published a new edition with illustrations by Eric Gill, not in earlier editions. There were 361 signed copies.

LIMBO.   Chatto & Windus 1920. Green cloth, paper label on spine, d/w. Top edges brown. 25 advance copies had top edges green. U.S.: Doran 1920.

CROME YELLOW.   Chatto & Windus 1921. Yellow cloth, paper label on spine, d/w. Top edges green. U.S.: Doran 1922.
   His first novel.

A VIRGIN HEART.   By De Gourmont. Translated by Huxley. New York: Nicholas L. Brown 1921. Pale blue cloth.

MORTAL COILS.   Chatto & Windus 1922. Pale blue cloth, paper label on spine, d/w. U.S.: Doran 1922.

ANTIC HAY.   Chatto & Windus 1923. Yellow cloth, paper label on spine, d/w. U.S.: Doran 1923.

ON THE MARGIN.   Chatto & Windus 1923. Greenish-blue cloth, paper label on spine, d/w. U.S.: Doran 1923.

LITTLE MEXICAN AND OTHER STORIES.   Chatto & Windus 1924. Red cloth, paper label on spine, d/w.

YOUNG ARCHIMEDES.   New York: Doran 1925.
   The U.S. edition of LITTLE MEXICAN.

ALONG THE ROAD.   Chatto & Windus 1925. Bluish-green canvas, paper label on spine, d/w. U.S.: Doran 1925.

SELECTED POEMS.   Oxford: Blackwell 1925. Decorated boards. No d/w. Also 100 signed. U.S.: Appleton 1925.

THOSE BARREN LEAVES.   Chatto & Windus 1925. Brown canvas, paper label on spine, d/w. U.S.: Doran 1925. 250 signed copies. First binding: smooth brown cloth.

ESSAYS NEW AND OLD.   At the Florence Press / Chatto & Windus 1926. Blue buckram spine, marbled boards. Limited to 650 signed. U.S.: Doran 1927.

JESTING PILATE.   Chatto & Windus 1926. Blue buckram, gilt, d/w. U.S.: Doran 1926.

TWO OR THREE GRACES.   Chatto & Windus 1926. Blue cloth, gilt, d/w. U.S.: Doran 1926.

PROPER STUDIES.   Chatto & Windus 1927. U.S.: Doubleday Doran 1928.

POINT COUNTER POINT.   Chatto & Windus 1928. U.S.: Doubleday Doran 1928.

ARABIA INFELIX.   New York: Fountain Press & London: Chatto 1929. Limited to 692 signed. Glassine d/w.

DO WHAT YOU WILL.   Chatto & Windus 1929. U.S.: Doubleday Doran 1929.

HOLY FACE.   The Fleuron Press 1929. Limited to 300 copies.

APENNINE.   U.S.: Slide Mountain Press 1930. Limited to 91 signed.

BRIEF CANDLES.   Chatto & Windus 1930. Doubleday Doran 1930.

VULGARITY IN LITERATURE.   Chatto & Windus Dolphin Books series 1930. Also 260 signed.
   Probably the commonest of his pre-war first editions.

THE CICADAS AND OTHER POEMS.   Chatto & Windus 1931. Also 160 signed. U.S.: Doubleday Doran 1931.

MUSIC AT NIGHT.   Chatto & Windus 1931. Also 1684 signed. U.S.: Doubleday Doran 1931.

THE WORLD OF LIGHT.   Chatto & Windus 1931. Also 160 signed. U.S.: Doubleday Doran 1931.

BRAVE NEW WORLD.   Chatto & Windus 1932. Also 324 signed. U.S.: Doubleday 1932. Also 250 signed.

ROTUNDA.   Chatto & Windus 1932.

T. H. HUXLEY AS A MAN OF LETTERS.   Macmillan 1932. 28pp.

TEXTS AND PRETEXTS.   Chatto & Windus 1932. U.S.: Harper 1933.

BEYOND THE MEXIQUE BAY.   Chatto & Windus 1934. Also 210 signed.
U.S.: Harper 1934.

EYELESS IN GAZA.   Chatto & Windus 1936. Also 200 signed. U.S.: Harper
1936.

THE OLIVE TREE.   Chatto & Windus 1936. U.S.: Harper 1937.

WHAT ARE YOU GOING TO DO ABOUT IT?   Chatto & Windus 1936.
35pp. Pamphlet. U.S.: Harper 1937.

ENDS AND MEANS.   Chatto & Windus 1937. Also 160 signed. U.S.:
Harper 1937.

AFTER MANY A SUMMER.   Chatto & Windus 1939. U.S.: Harper 1939.

GREY EMINENCE.   Chatto & Windus 1941. U.S.: Harper 1941.

THE ART OF SEEING.   Chatto & Windus 1942. U.S.: Harper 1942.

TIME MUST HAVE A STOP.   New York: Harper 1944. U.K.: Chatto &
Windus 1944.

THE PERENNIAL PHILOSOPHY.   Chatto & Windus 1945. U.S.: Harper
1945.

SCIENCE, LIBERTY AND PEACE.   Chatto & Windus 1946. U.S.: Harper
1946.

VERSES AND A COMEDY.   Chatto & Windus 1946.

APE AND ESSENCE.   New York: Harper 1948. U.K.: Chatto & Windus
1949.

THE GIOCONDA SMILE.   Chatto & Windus 1948. U.S.: Harper 1948.

THE PRISONS.   Trianon Press 1949. Limited to 1212 copies (212 signed).
U.S.: Zeitlin & Ver Brugge 1949. Limited to 212 signed only.

THEMES AND VARIATIONS.   Chatto & Windus 1950. U.S.: Harper 1950.

THE DEVILS OF LOUDUN.   Chatto & Windus 1952. U.S.: Harper 1952.

THE DOORS OF PERCEPTION.   Chatto & Windus 1954. U.S.: Harper
1954.

THE GENIUS AND THE GODDESS. Chatto & Windus 1955. U.S.: Harper 1955.

ADONIS AND THE ALPHABET. Chatto & Windus 1956.

TOMORROW AND TOMORROW AND TOMORROW. New York: Harper 1956.
The American edition of ADONIS AND THE ALPHABET.

HEAVEN AND HELL. Chatto & Windus 1956. U.S.: Harper 1956.

COLLECTED SHORT STORIES. Chatto & Windus 1957. U.S.: Harper 1957.

BRAVE NEW WORLD REVISITED. Chatto & Windus 1958. U.S.: Harper 1958.

COLLECTED ESSAYS. New York: Harper 1959.

ISLAND. Chatto & Windus 1961. U.S.: Harper 1961.

I

ISHERWOOD, Christopher (b. 1904)

The list below includes his principal literary works, but not his writings on Vedanta. As a boy at Repton, Isherwood contributed to the school magazine; but his first book publication was in the third volume of the anthology PUBLIC SCHOOL VERSE, edited by Gilkes, Hughes & Lyon, and published in 1923. His contribution, under the name C. W. B. Isherwood, was the poem 'Mapperley Plains'.

ALL THE CONSPIRATORS. Cape (1928). Sold less than 300 copies, and was remaindered. U.S.: New Directions 1958.

THE MEMORIAL. Hogarth Press 1932. Pink cloth lettered in blue. Later in blue cloth, also ochre cloth. U.S.: New Directions 1946.

MR NORRIS CHANGES TRAINS. Hogarth Press 1935.

THE LAST OF MR NORRIS. New York: Morrow 1935.

The American edition of MR NORRIS CHANGES TRAINS.

THE DOG BENEATH THE SKIN. By Isherwood & Auden. Faber 1935. U.S.: Random House 1935.

THE ASCENT OF F6. By Isherwood & Auden. Faber 1936. U.S.: Random House 1937.

SALLY BOWLES. Hogarth Press 1937.

ON THE FRONTIER. By Isherwood & Auden. Faber 1938. U.S.: Random House 1939.

LIONS AND SHADOWS. Hogarth Press 1938. Blue cloth lettered in black – later lettered in gilt. U.S.: New Directions 1948.

GOODBYE TO BERLIN. Hogarth Press 1939. U.S.: Random House 1939.

JOURNEY TO A WAR. By Isherwood & Auden. Faber (1939). U.S.: Random House 1939.

PRATER VIOLET. New York: Random House 1945. U.K.: Methuen 1946.

THE BERLIN STORIES. U.S.: New Directions 1946.
A collection of three novels previously published separately in the U.K.

THE CONDOR AND THE COWS. New York: Random House 1949. U.K.: Methuen 1949. Different photographs.

THE WORLD IN THE EVENING. New York: Random House 1954. U.K.: Methuen 1954.

DOWN THERE ON A VISIT. New York: Simon & Schuster 1962. U.K.: Methuen 1962.

A SINGLE MAN. New York: Simon & Schuster 1964. U.K.: Methuen 1964.

EXHUMATIONS. New York: Simon & Schuster 1966. U.K.: Methuen 1966.

A MEETING BY THE RIVER. New York: Simon & Schuster 1967. U.K.: Methuen 1967.

KATHLEEN AND FRANK. New York: Simon & Schuster 1971. U.K.: Methuen (1971).

FRANKENSTEIN: THE TRUE STORY. (screenplay). New York: Avon 1973.

THE BERLIN OF SALLY BOWLES. Hogarth Press 1975.
A collection of novels, all previously published separately, and collected earlier in the New Directions volume entitled THE BERLIN STORIES.

CHRISTOPHER AND HIS KIND. New York: Simon & Schuster 1977. U.K.: Eyre Methuen 1977.

OCTOBER. New York: Twelvetrees Press 1980. Leather. Limited Edition. U.K.: Methuen 1982. Wrappers. 1000 copies.

PEOPLE ONE OUGHT TO KNOW. New York: Doubleday 1982. U.K.: Macmillan 1982.

J

JAMES, Henry (1843–1916)

James's first published story appeared in the journal Continental Monthly, February 1864. All the major works are included in the checklist below. The spate of posthumous volumes, mainly non-fiction, has been excluded. His earliest novels – RODERICK HUDSON, THE AMERICAN, WATCH AND WARD, and THE EUROPEANS – sell nowadays for sums in the region of £1000.

A PASSIONATE PILGRIM, AND OTHER TALES. Boston: Osgood 1876 (1875). Green cloth, bevelled edges; with 'J. R. Osgood & Co.' on the spine (later 'Houghton, Osgood & Co.' and still later 'Houghton, Mifflin & Co.'). U.K.: Macmillan 1879. 3 vols.

TRANSATLANTIC SKETCHES. Boston: Osgood 1875. Later copies were issued (in 1883) with the imprint of Houghton, Mifflin on the spine.

RODERICK HUDSON. Boston: Osgood 1876. Green cloth, bevelled edges (and variants). Earliest binding with Osgood imprint on the spine (later, Houghton Mifflin).

THE AMERICAN. Boston: Osgood, 1877. The U.K. (unauthorized): Ward Lock 1877. Authorized U.K. Edition: Macmillan 1879. Dark blue cloth.

WATCH AND WARD. Boston: Houghton, Osgood 1878. Green cloth. Blank leaf after p. 219.
 Not published in the U.K. until the collected edition – Macmillan 1923.

FRENCH POETS AND NOVELISTS. Macmillan 1878.

THE EUROPEANS. Macmillan 1878. (Sept). 2 vols. Blue cloth.
 The U.S. Edition (one vol.) was issued in October 1878, but dated 1879.

DAISY MILLER: a Study. New York: Harper 1879. 32mo. Wrappers or green cloth. First issue has a list of only 79 titles in the Half Hour Series.

DAISY MILLER: a Study. AN INTERNATIONAL EPISODE. FOUR MEETINGS. Macmillan 1879. 2 vols. Blue cloth. 40pp Catalogue dated November 1878, at end.

AN INTERNATIONAL EPISODE. New York: Harper 1879. 32mo. Buff wrappers. No 91 in the Half Hour series.

HAWTHORNE. Macmillan 1879. U.S.: Harper 1880. First binding: red-stamped black cloth.

THE MADONNA OF THE FUTURE AND OTHER TALES. Macmillan 1879. 2 vols. Blue cloth.

THE DIARY OF A MAN OF FIFTY AND A BUNDLE OF LETTERS. New York: Harper, 1880. Half-Hour Series. Wrappers. Also flexible cloth.

CONFIDENCE. Chatto & Windus 1880 (1879). 2 vols. Olive-brown cloth. 32pp Catalogue dated December 1879. U.S.: Boston: Houghton, Osgood 1880.

WASHINGTON SQUARE. New York: Harper 1881 (1880). Pictorial olive-green cloth.

WASHINGTON SQUARE / THE PENSION BEAUREPAS / A BUNDLE OF LETTERS. Macmillan 1881. 2 vols. Dark blue-green cloth.

THE PORTRAIT OF A LADY. Macmillan 1881. 3 vols. Dark blue-green cloth. Catalogue at end (see below). U.S.: Houghton, Mifflin 1882. One vol. Green cloth gilt. Also light tan cloth. First issue has a full-stop after the Copyright date.
 Sadleir's copy of the U.K. edition had a 24pp catalogue dated April 1881, but Edel & Laurence apparently believe the catalogue dated December 1881 to be the earliest. Some copies have no catalogue.

DAISY MILLER; a Comedy. Privately Printed 1882. Wrappers. Published Edition: Boston: Osgood 1883.

THE SEIGE OF LONDON, THE PENSION BEAUREPAS, AND THE POINT OF VIEW. Boston: Osgood 1883.

PORTRAIT OF PLACES. Macmillan 1883. U.S.: (PORTRAITS . . .) Osgood 1884.

TALES OF THREE CITIES. Boston: Osgood 1884. U.K.: Macmillan 1884. Green cloth.

A LITTLE TOUR IN FRANCE. Boston: Osgood 1885.

STORIES REVIVED. Macmillan 1885. 3 vols. Dark blue-green cloth, chocolate endpapers (later blue & white patterned endpapers).

THE AUTHOR OF BELTRAFFIO / PANDORA [ornament]/GEORGINA'S REASONS / THE PATH OF DUTY / FOUR MEETINGS. Boston: Osgood 1885.

THE BOSTONIANS. Macmillan 1886. 3 vols. Dark blue-green cloth.

THE PRINCESS CASAMASSIMA. London & New York: Macmillan 1886. 3 vols. Dark blue-green cloth.

PARTIAL PORTRAITS. London & New York: Macmillan 1888.
   The U.K. Edition preceded the U.S. Edition.

THE ASPERN PAPERS / LOUISA PALLANT / THE MODERN WARNING. London & New York: Macmillan 1888. 2 vols. Blue cloth banded in gold.
   The U.K. Edition preceded the U.S. Edition.

THE REVERBERATOR. London & New York: Macmillan, 1888. 2 vols. Blue cloth, also green cloth.
   The U.K. Edition preceded the U.S. Edition.

LONDON LIFE / THE PATAGONIA / THE LIAR/MRS. TEMPERLEY. London & New York: Macmillan 1889. 2 vols. Blue cloth.
   The U.K. edition preceded the U.S. edition.

THE TRAGIC MUSE. Boston and New York: Houghton, Mifflin 1890. 2 vols. U.K.: Macmillan 1890. 3 vols. Blue cloth.

THE LESSON OF THE MASTER / THE MARRIAGES, THE PUPIL /

BROOKSMITH / THE SOLUTION, SIR EDMUND ORME. New York & London: Macmillan 1892.
The London edition came out two months after the New York edition.

THE PRIVATE LIFE. THE WHEEL OF TIME. LORD BEAUPRE. THE VISITS. COLLABORATION. OWEN WINGRAVE. Osgood McIlvaine 1893. Grey-blue cloth.

THE PRIVATE LIFE / LORD BEAUFRE / THE VISITS. New York: Harper 1893.

THE REAL THING AND OTHER TALES. New York & London: Macmillan 1893.
The U.S. edition preceded the U.K. edition (from American sheets) by 2 months.

THE WHEEL OF TIME / COLLABORATION / OWEN WINGRAVE. New York: Harper 1893.

PICTURE AND TEXT. New York: Harper 1893.

ESSAYS IN LONDON AND ELSEWHERE. New York: Harper 1893. U.K.: Osgood, McIlvaine 1893. Pale salmon cloth.

THEATRICALS / TWO COMEDIES / TENANTS DISENGAGED. Osgood, McIlvaine 1894.

'THE QUEST OF THE HOLY GRAIL' . . . first portion of a Series of Paintings . . . By Edwin A. Abbey . . . at the galleries, 9, Conduit St., W. (London) . . . January, 1895. An anonymous pamphlet of 7pp.

THEATRICALS / SECOND SERIES / THE ALBUM, THE REPROBATE. Osgood, McIlvaine 1895.   /

TERMINATIONS / THE DEATH OF THE LION / THE COXON FUND / THE MIDDLE YEARS / THE ALTAR OF THE DEAD. New York: Harper 1895. U.K.: Heinemann 1895. Second issue does not name the stories on the title page.

EMBARRASSMENTS. New York & London: Macmillan 1896. Blue cloth with four irises on the front. Later binding has 9 irises. Variant in red cloth. The U.K. edition has the title in red and black, and the four stories in the volume are named on the title page. A second issue has the title all in black and does not name the stories. There was a Colonial issue in red cloth.
The U.S. edition preceded the U.K. edition by 2 days.

THE OTHER HOUSE. New York & London: Macmillan 1896. 2 vols.

THE SPOILS OF POYNTON. Boston & New York: Houghton, Mifflin 1897. U.K.: Heinemann 1897. Blue cloth.

WHAT MAISIE KNEW. Chicago & New York: Herbert S. Stone & Co. 1897. U.K.: Heinemann 1898. Blue cloth.

IN THE CAGE. Duckworth 1898. Buff canvas, blocked & lettered in black.

THE TWO MAGICS. New York: Macmillan 1898. Crimson cloth.

THE AWKWARD AGE. Heinemann 1899. Blue cloth with blind pansy decoration. Secondary issues have blind tulip decoration. 32pp Catalogue at end, undated – earliest version has the last page carrying no reviews of the novels listed.

THE SOFT SIDE. Methuen 1900. Red Cloth. U.S.: Macmillan 1901. Maroon cloth.

THE SACRED FOUNT. New York: Scribners 1901. Biscuit cloth. U. K.: Methuen 1901.

THE WINGS OF THE DOVE. New York: Scribners 1902. 2 vols. Biscuit cloth. U.K.: Archibald Constable 1902. Blue cloth.

THE AMBASSADORS. Methuen 1903. Scarlet cloth. 40pp catalogue dated July 1903.

THE BETTER SORT. Methuen 1903. Red cloth. 40pp Catalogue dated February 1903.

WILLIAM WETMORE STORY AND HIS FRIENDS. Houghton, Mifflin 1903. 2 vols.

THE GOLDEN BOWL. New York: Scribners 1904. 2 vols. Pinkish-biscuit cloth. U.K.: Macmillan 1905.

THE QUESTION OF OUR SPEECH / THE LESSON OF BALZAC. Boston: Houghton, Mifflin 1905.

ENGLISH HOURS. Heinemann 1905. Grey cloth. Second binding: green buckram spine, green boards. U.S.: Boston. Houghton, Mifflin 1905.

THE AMERICAN SCENE. Chapman & Hall 1907. Maroon buckram. U.S.: New York 1907. Blue cloth.

VIEWS AND REVIEWS. Boston: The Ball Publishing Co. 1908. Green cloth.

ITALIAN HOURS. Boston & New York: Houghton, Mifflin 1909.

THE FINER GRAIN. Methuen 1910. Pinkish-brown cloth. 32pp Catalogue dated September 1910.

THE OUTCRY. Methuen 1911. Green cloth. 32pp Catalogue dated August 1911.

A SMALL BOY AND OTHERS. Macmillan 1913.

NOTES OF A SON AND BROTHER. Macmillan 1914.

NOTES ON NOVELISTS. New York: Scribner 1914. U.K.: Dent 1914.

THE IVORY TOWER. New York: Scribners 1917. U.K.: Collins (1917).

THE SENSE OF THE PAST. New York: Scribners 1917. U.K.: Collins 1917. Dark blue cloth, d/w.

THE MIDDLE YEARS. Collins 1917.

JAMES, M. R. (1862–1936)

James wrote many scholarly books, but he is best known for his ghost stories, which are avidly collected. These are listed below. The first is the most valuable at around £200. Another work worth noting is THE FIVE JARS – 'more or less a fairy tale'. This was published by Arnold (1922).

GHOST STORES OF AN ANTIQUARY. Arnold 1904. 4 plates by James McBryde. Fawn canvas, yapped edges. First issue has 16pp adverts at end, dated November 1904.

MORE GHOST STORIES. Arnold 1911.

A THIN GHOST. Arnold 1919.

A WARNING TO THE CURIOUS. Arnold 1925.

WAILING WELL. Stanford Dingley: Mill House Press 1928. Limited Edition of 157 copies. Small 4to.

COLLECTED GHOST STORIES. Arnold 1931.

JEFFERIES, Richard (1848–1887)

All Jefferies early publications (up to 1878 when he had his first commercial success with THE GAMEKEEPER) are scarce. After that, the first editions are fairly easily obtained. The major works (especially those in two or three volumes) are generally priced at something over £100.

A MEMOIR OF THE GODDARDS OF NORTH WILTS. Simmons & Botten (1873). Small 4to. Blue cloth.

REPORTING, EDITING, AND AUTHORSHIP. Practical Hints for Beginners. John Snow & Co. (1873).

JACK BRASS, EMPEROR OF ENGLAND. T. Pettit & Co. 1873. 12pp. Drab wrappers.

THE SCARLET SHAWL. Tinsley Brothers 1874. Red cloth (and later variants).

RESTLESS HUMAN HEARTS. Tinsley Brothers 1875. 3 vols. Scarlet cloth (later green cloth).

SUEZ-CIDE, or how Miss Britannia bought a dirty puddle. John Snow 1876. Magenta wrappers.

WORLD'S END. Tinsley Brothers 1877. 3 vols. Slate (or dove-grey) cloth.

THE GAMEKEEPER AT HOME. (anonymous). Smith, Elder 1878. Blue/green cloth (various shades). First illustrated Edition: Smith, Elder 1880. Green or drab pictorial cloth. 41 illustrations by Charles Whymper.

WILD LIFE IN A SOUTHERN COUNTY. By the Author of 'The Gamekeeper at Home' etc. (anon). Smith, Elder 1879. Dark brown or olive cloth.

THE AMATEUR POACHER. By the Author of 'The Gamekeeper at Home'. (anon). Smith, Elder 1879. Brown cloth.

ROUND ABOUT A GREAT ESTATE. Smith, Elder 1880. Blue cloth.

HODGE AND HIS MASTERS. Smith, Elder 1880. 2 vols. Dark brown cloth, pictorially blocked in black and gold (differing on each volume).

GREENE FERNE FARM. Smith, Elder 1880. Yellow or Olive-green cloth.

WOOD MAGIC. London, Paris & New York: Cassell, Peter, Galpin & Co. 1881. 2 vols. Pictorial dark green cloth. 8pp catalogue dated '5.81'. One-vol edition later the same year.

BEVIS. Sampson Low, etc. 1882. 3 vols. Brown cloth (later green cloth). Vols 2 & 3 published without half-titles. Not illustrated. 32pp catalogue dated December 1881 in some copies.

THE STORY OF MY HEART. Longmans, Green 1883. Sage Green cloth. 12pp catalogue dated April 1883. The second edition of 1891 contains important material in the preface.

NATURE NEAR LONDON. Chatto & Windus 1883. Pictorial cloth. No half title.

RED DEER. Longmans, Green 1884. Pictorial grey-green cloth, lettered in dark red. Second (First Illustrated) Edition: Longmans, Green 1892. Red cloth, lettered in silver.

THE LIFE OF THE FIELDS. Chatto & Windus 1884. Pictorial yellow cloth.

THE DEWY MORN. Richard Bentley 1884. 2 vols. Green cloth. No half-titles.

THE OPEN AIR. Chatto & Windus 1885. Pictorial yellow cloth.

AFTER LONDON, or Wild England. Cassell 1885. Ochre cloth. 8pp. catalogue dated '4.85' at end.

THE DOVE'S NEST and other tales. By Joseph Hatton & Richard Jefferies. Vizetelly 1886. Illustrated by various artists (including Caldecott). Cloth.

AMARYLLIS AT THE FAIR. Sampson Low, etc. 1887. Pictorial dark green cloth, bevelled edges.

FIELD AND HEDGEROW. Longmans, Green 1889. Also 200 copies on large paper.

THE TOILERS OF THE FIELD. Longmans, Green 1892. Also 105 on large paper.

JEFFERIES LAND, A HISTORY OF SWINDON AND ITS ENVIRONS. Simpkin, Marshall 1896. Also 50 large paper copies.

THE EARLY FICTION. Simpkin, Marshall 1896. 2 vols. Also 50 on large paper.

T.T.T. (short story). Arthur Young 1896. 100 copies.

THE HILLS AND THE VALE. Duckworth 1909.

THE NATURE DIARIES AND NOTEBOOKS. With an Essay . . . Grey Walls Press 1941. Also 105 on large paper. The edition of 1948 has additional material.

CHRONICLES OF THE HEDGES AND OTHER ESSAYS. Phoenix House 1948.

THE OLD HOUSE AT COATE. Lutterworth Press 1948.

BEAUTY IS IMMORTAL (FELISE OF THE DEWY MORN). Worthing Cavalcade 1948.

FIELD AND FARM. Phoenix House 1957.

LANDSCAPE AND LABOUR. Moonraker Press 1979.

BY THE BROOK. Stevens 1981. 170 copies, also 20 in leather & slipcase.

JEROME, Jerome K. (1859–1927)

Jerome's most famous work, THREE MEN IN A BOAT, is scarce in its original form (see below) and is currently valued at around £100. Some of his other works are scarcer, but of less value. Most of his works are very modestly priced.

ON THE STAGE – AND OFF. Field & Tuer 1885. 4 × 3 inches approx. A volume of humorous pieces about the theatre.

BARBARA. Lacy 1886.

THE IDLE THOUGHTS OF AN IDLE FELLOW. Field & Tuer (1886). '2/6' on yellow front cover. The first thousand copies comprise the first edition.

SUNSET. New York: Fitzgerald n.d. (1888).

FENNEL. French n.d. (1888).

WOODBARROW FARM. French n.d. (1888).

PLAYWRITING: A HANDBOOK FOR WOULD-BE DRAMATISTS. By 'A Dramatist' (probably Jerome). Stage Office 1888. Wrappers.

STAGE-LAND. Chatto & Windus 1889.

THREE MEN IN A BOAT. Bristol: Arrowsmith 1889. Green cloth, silhouette and black lettering on front, gilt lettered spine. Publisher's address at foot of title page is 'Quay Street' (Later '11 Quay Street'). Adverts on front paste-down are headed 'J. W. Arrowsmith, Bristol' (later '11 Quay Street, Bristol').

TOLD AFTER SUPPER. Leadenhall Press 1891.

THE DIARY OF A PILGRIMAGE. Bristol: Arrowsmith 1891. Three-and-Sixpenny-Series.

K. By McK (probably Jerome). Bristol: Arrowsmith 1892.

NOVEL NOTES. Leadenhall Press 1893.

JOHN INGERFIELD. McClure 1894.

THE PRUDE'S PROGRESS. French 1895.

SKETCHES IN LAVENDER, BLUE AND GREEN. Longman 1897. Blue cloth, gilt.

THE SECOND THOUGHTS OF AN IDLE FELLOW. Hurst & Blackett 1898.

THREE MEN ON THE BUMMELL. Bristol: Arrowsmith 1900.

THE OBSERVATIONS OF HENRY. Bristol: Arrowsmith 1901.

MISS HOBBS. French 1902.

PAUL KLEVER. Hutchinson 1902.

TEA-TABLE TALK. Hutchinson 1903.

TOMMY AND CO. Hutchinson 1904.

AMERICAN WIVES AND OTHERS. U.S.A.: Stokes 1904.

IDLE IDEAS IN 1905. Hurst & Blackett 1905.

THE PASSING OF THE THIRD FLOOR BACK. (novel). Hurst & Blackett 1907.
   The play of the same name, was published in 1910 (same publishers).

THE ANGEL AND THE AUTHOR. Hurst & Blackett 1908.

THEY AND I. Hutchinson 1909.

FANNY AND THE SERVANT PROBLEM.   Lacy 1909.

THE MASTER OF MRS CHILVERS.   T. Fisher Unwin 1911.

ROBINA IN SEARCH OF A HUSBAND.   Lacy 1914.

MALVINA OF BRITTANY.   Cassell 1916.

ALL ROADS LEAD TO CALVARY.   Hutchinson 1919.

ANTHONY JOHN.   Cassell 1923.

A MISCELLANY OF SENSE AND NONSENSE.   Bristol: Arrowsmith 1923.

THE CELEBRITY.   Hodder & Stoughton 1926.

MY LIFE AND TIMES.   Hodder & Stoughton 1926.

THE SOUL OF NICHOLAS SYNDERS.   Hodder & Stoughton 1927.

JOHNSON, Lionel (1867–1902)

Johnson's first book, POEMS, is one of the most important of the nineties period. The first issue, of which there were only 25 copies, has a current value of about £4000. After those first copies were printed, the first and last gatherings were revised and reset, and the initial capitals were changed throughout the book. What is generally known as the second issue (strictly speaking, a second edition) was then printed and put into a different binding.

POEMS.   Elkin Mathews (London) and Copeland & Day (Boston) 1895. First issue: 25 copies, signed by the author. Brown buckram. Second issue (or edition): 750 copies in blue-grey boards.

JOHNSON, Samuel (1709–1784)

In his early days, while living in Birmingham, Johnson contributed some essays to the Birmingham Journal, and made a translation of Lobo's VOYAGE TO ABYSSINIA. After moving (with Garrick) to London, he became a regular contributor to The Gentleman's Magazine and, in the midst of much hack-work, published his poem LONDON. Six years later came the important biography AN ACCOUNT OF THE LIFE OF MR RICHARD SAVAGE. Work on his epoch-making A DICTIONARY OF THE ENG-LISH LANGUAGE began in 1746 with the backing of several publishers and the help of six assistants. The Plan for the work was issued in 1747 and work upon it continued until it was finally published in 1755. A copy in a good binding of the period would today be priced at something like £5000.

His novel, now familiar under the title RASSELAS, originally appeared as THE PRINCE OF ABYSSINIA (q.v.). The following checklist includes the most important of his many publications.

VOYAGE TO ABYSSINIA.   By Lobo. Bettesworth & Hitch 1735.
Translated by Johnson, but no mention is made of this within the volume.

LONDON.   R. Dodsley 1738.

AN ACCOUNT OF THE LIFE OF MR RICHARD SAVAGE.   J. Roberts 1744. First issue has no errata on the last leaf, and does not have the word 'not' on line 9 of p.77.
A landmark in the development of biography. The text was later included in THE LIVES OF THE ENGLISH POETS.

THE VANITY OF HUMAN WISHES, an imitation of the Tenth Satire of Juvenal.   R. Dodsley 1749.
The first of his works to appear under his name.

IRENE: A Tragedy.   for R. Dodsley 1749.
This play was written in part while he was still a schoolboy.

THE RAMBLER.   There were 208 issues of this fortnightly journal, published from March 20, 1750 to March 14, 1752. They were afterwards published in 2 thick folio volumes, and reprinted many times.

A DICTIONARY OF THE ENGLISH LANGUAGE.   Printed by W. Strahan, For J. and P. Knapton; T. and T. Longman; C. Hitch and L. Hawes; A. Millar; and R. and J. Dodsley. 1775. 2 vols, thick folio.

THE PRINCE OF ABYSSINIA.   R. and J. Dodsley and W. Johnston 1759. 2 vols. 12mo. Second edition same year.
Apparently written in a week to defray the cost of his mother's funeral. The work is now better known as RASSELAS.

THE IDLER.   A series of papers written for the Universal Chronicle: or, Weekly Gazette, published from April 15, 1758 to April 5, 1760. The First Collected Edition was published by J. Newbery, 1761, in 2 vols, small 8vo.

THE FALSE ALARM.   T. Cadell 1770.
The first of his political pamphlets. Though done anonymously, it was immediately recognised as Johnson's work.

A JOURNEY TO THE WESTERN ISLANDS OF SCOTLAND. for W. Strahan; and T. Cadell, 1775. The first issue has a 12-line errata, the second has a 6-line errata.

THE LIVES OF THE MOST EMINENT ENGLISH POETS. Unauthorised Dublin Edition: Whitestone, Williams . . . 1779–81. 3 volumes. First London Edition: C. Bathurst, etc. 1781. 4 vols. Leaf of adverts at the end of the last volume. Copies are known with a leaf of four extra labels for the spines.

Originally written (and published) as Prefaces to a series of poetical works, they were afterwards collected and published together under the now familiar title.

AN ACCOUNT OF THE LIFE OF DR. SAMUEL JOHNSON, from his Birth to his Eleventh Year, written by Himself. To which are added . . . (etc). Richard Phillips 1805. Sm.8vo.

According to the Preface, the manuscript was saved from the flames by Francis Barber, Johnson's black servant. 32 pages had been torn out and destroyed by Johnson.

LETTERS TO AND FROM THE LATE SAMUEL JOHNSON, LL. D. To which are added some Poems never before printed. Published from the original MSS. in her possession by Hester Lynch Piozzi. London: for A. Strahan; and T. Cadell 1788. 2 vols. Errata slip at the end (rarely). Dublin Edition same year.

JONSON, Ben (c. 1572–1637)

Jonson took a close interest in the printing of his collected WORKES and introduced many changes during the process. As a result there are numerous 'points' and 'states' affecting almost every page. The first volume was published during his lifetime, but the second volume, though started in 1631 (and initially overseen by Jonson) was not completed until three years after his death. The publisher Meighen, however, obtained the author's manuscripts of his later poems, plays and essays, and incorporated them into the volume. The result is one of the most important publications in seventeenth century literature, with a value in the region of £4000. Copies of the second and third folio editions can occasionally be had for about £400.

THE WORKES OF BENJAMIN JONSON . . . Imprinted at London by Will Stansby . . . 1616. (and) . . . the second Volume . . . Printed for Richard Meighen, 1640 (i.e. 1631–40). Small folios. Second Folio Edition: Richard Bishop, sold by Andrew Crooke 1640. Third Folio Edition, 'With Additions': Thomas Hodgkin for H. Herringham 1692.

JOYCE, James (1882–1941)

An exceedingly rare early publication by Joyce is his contribution to TWO ESSAYS issued by Gerrard Bros. of Dublin in 1901. The two essays were 'A Forgotten Aspect of the University Question' by F. J. C. Skeffington, and 'The Day of the Rabblement' by James A. Joyce. Also very rare, are the three stories Joyce contributed to 'The Irish Homestead' (an agricultural magazine) in 1904. These appeared under the pseudonym 'Stephen Dedalus'.

CHAMBER MUSIC. Elkin Mathews (1907). 500 copies. U.S. (Unauthorized): Cornhill Co. 1918. Authorized U.S. edition: Huebsch 1918 (later).

DUBLINERS. Grant Richards 1914. Red cloth, d/w. 1250 sets of sheets printed, of which 504 were used for the U.S. edition by Huebsch 1916.

A PORTRAIT OF THE ARTIST AS A YOUNG MAN. New York: Huebsch 1916. Blue cloth, d/w. U.K.: Egoist 1917. Green cloth, d/w. American sheets, 750 copies. Second U.K. Edition: Egoist 1918. 1000 copies.

EXILES. Grant Richards 1918. Half cloth & boards. U.S.: Huebsch 1918.

ULYSSES. Paris: The Shakespeare Press 1922 (February). Small 4to. Wrappers. 1000 numbered copies (100 signed). First Unlimited Edition (being the 4th edition): The Shakespeare Press 1924 (January). U.K. (being the 2nd edition): Egoist Press 1922 (October). 2000 numbered copies. (500 were detained by the New York Post Authorities). Second U.K. Edition (being the 3rd edition): Egoist Press 1923 (January). 500 numbered copies (499 were seized by the Customs Authorities, Folkestone). 3rd U.K. Edition: Bodley Head 1936 (October). Limited to 1000 numbered copies (100 signed). First Unlimited U.K. Edition: The Bodley Head 1937 (September). U.S.: The Shakespeare Press of Paris produced an unauthorized edition for America in 1929. First Authorized U.S. Edition: Random House 1934 (January). First Printing 100 copies, Second Printing 10,300 copies.
    In 1919, modified extracts from Chapters II, III, VI and X appeared in Harriet Shaw Weaver's literary periodical 'Egoist'. In March of the same year, the New York periodical 'Little Review' began serializing the work. Some episodes were confiscated before the project was stopped completely, following a court case in February 1921.

POMES PENYEACH. Paris: Shakespeare & Co. 1927. Also, 100 signed. U.S.: Sylvia Beach 1931. 50 copies. U.K.: Obelisk Press 1932. Printed in France. New Edition: Faber 1933.

ANNA LIVIA PLURABELLE. New York: Crosby Gaige 1928. Limited to 800 signed & 50 not signed. U.K.: Faber 1930. Criterion Miscellany series. Wrappers.

TALES TOLD OF SHEM AND SHAUN. Paris: Black Sun Press 1929. Limited to 650 (100 signed). Wrappers, slipcase.

TWO TALES OF SHEM AND SHAUN. Faber (1932). Boards, d/w. Extracted from TALES TOLD OF SHEM AND SHAUN.

HAVETH CHILDERS EVERYWHERE. U.S.: Fountain Press 1930. Limited to 685 (100 signed). Printed in France. U.K.: Faber 1931. Cloth, also wrappers.

THE MIME OF MICK NICK AND THE MAGGIES. Netherlands: Servire Press 1934. 1000 copies, also 29 signed. Wrappers & slipcase.

COLLECTED POEMS. New York: Black Sun Press 1936. Limited to 800 (50 signed). Unlimited Edition: Viking 1937.

STORIELLA AS SHE IS SYUNG. Corvinus Press (1937). 175 copies, of which 25 were signed by the author. Orange vellum, slipcase.

FINNEGANS WAKE. Faber 1939. Also, 425 signed (115 for U.K. & 310 for U.S.). U.S.: Viking 1939. Trade edition, also the aforementioned 310 signed.

STEPHEN HERO. Cape (1944). U.S.: New Directions 1944.

THE ESSENTIAL JAMES JOYCE. Cape 1948.

THE LETTERS. Faber 1957 (Vol I) and 1966 (Vols 2 & 3).

THE CRITICAL WRITINGS. Faber 1959.

THE CAT AND THE DEVIL. Faber 1965.

GIACOMO JOYCE. New York: Viking 1968. U.K.: Faber 1968.

K

KEATS, John (1795–1821)

The collector of Keats' first editions has little to aim for and a lot to pay. Only three volumes were published during the author's lifetime, and though some new material was published posthumously, those first three books contain all the essential poetry. The first book, POEMS, is extremely rare. It did not sell well and, though Keats had his supporters, the critical response was negative. It is now worth in the region of £10,000.

ENDYMION and LAMIA are not so very rare, but they are landmarks in English Poetry. A copy of either would be a bargain at £2000, and a price of £5000 would be nearer the mark.

The letters of Keats are of great importance. They are not merely correspondence, but works of art in their own right. As T. S. Eliot said (in THE USE OF POETRY AND THE USE OF CRITICISM) Keats' letters are 'certainly the most notable and most important ever written by any English poet'.

POEMS.   Printed for C. & J. Ollier 1817. Boards with paper label on the spine. Tipped-in title-page, with a vignette portrait of Spenser.
   The discovery of a copy with an integral title-page, without the portrait, would be a major bibliographical event.

ENDYMION.   Printed for Taylor & Hessey 1818. Boards with paper label on the spine. Errata slip between pages x and xi. The first issue has a single line of errata and 2 leaves of adverts at the end, the second issue has 5 lines of errata and 5 leaves of adverts. Some copies were issued c.1835 in gilt-lettered black cloth. These have no Errata slip, the errata being printed on page xi.

LAMIA, ISABELLA, THE EVE OF ST. AGNES, AND OTHER POEMS. Printed for Taylor & Hessey 1820. 12mo. Boards with paper label on the spine.

POETICAL WORKS.   William Smith 1841. First Collected Edition. Green cloth. Another edition was issued by Moxon in 1851.

LIFE, LETTERS, AND LITERARY REMAINS.   Edited by Richard Monckton Milnes. Moxon 1848. 2 vols. Frontispiece in each volume. Errata slip in volume 1. Purple cloth.

LETTERS TO FANNY BRAWNE.   Introduction & Notes by Harry Buxton Forman. Printed for Private Circulation 1878. 50 copies. Blue cloth. Trade Edition: Reeves & Turner 1878. U.S.: Scribner, Armstrong 1878.

THE POETICAL WORKS AND OTHER WRITINGS.   Edited by Harry Buxton Forman. Reeves & Turner 1883. 4 vols. Red cloth.
   Contains previously unpublished poems and letters.

POETRY AND PROSE.   Edited by H. Buxton Forman. Reeves & Turner 1890. White cloth.

Contains previously unpublished material.

KEROUAC, Jack (1922–1969)

His first three books (the U.S. editions) are now fetching two or three hundred dollars. The small limited issues of DOCTOR SAX and MEXICO CITY BLUES are in much the same league. His first book was published in a surprisingly large number of copies, which is probably why it is not as rare as one might expect it to be. The long period between his first book and his second, was spent writing works which failed (at the time) to interest publishers. His fortunes changed dramatically after publication of ON THE ROAD. A number of broadsides are excluded from the following list.

THE TOWN AND THE CITY. By John Kerouac. New York: Harcourt Brace (1950). Red cloth, d/w. 10,500 printed. U.K.: Eyre & Spottiswoode (1951).

ON THE ROAD. New York: Viking 1957. Black cloth, d/w. U.K.: Deutsch 1958.
Some Review Copies of the New York edition were sent out in an extra white dust wrapper, bearing the legend 'This is a copy of the first edition'. These copies are greatly prized today. Signet Books issued a paperback edition in 1958.

THE SUBTERRANEANS. U.S.: Grove Press (1958). Also, 100 numbered U.K.: Deutsch 1962.

THE DHARMA BUMS. New York: Viking 1958. U.K.: Deutsch 1959.

MEXICO CITY BLUES. U.S.: Grove Press (1959). Grey cloth, d/w. Also 26 signed, lettered A-Z, and 4 numbered. Also in wrappers – an Evergreen Paperback.

HYMN – GOD PRAY FOR ME. Privately Printed 1959.

DOCTOR SAX: FAUST PART THREE. U.S.: Grove Press (1959). Wrappers. Also 26 signed & lettered A-Z, and 4 numbered. U.K.: Evergreen 1961. Wrappers. U.K. Hardback: Deutsch 1970.

MAGGIE CASSIDY. U.S.: Avon 1959. Wrappers. U.K.: Panther 1960. Wrappers.

EXCERPTS FROM 'VISIONS OF CODY'. U.S.: New Directions 1959. 750 signed. U.K.: Deutsch 1973.

TRISTESSA.   U.S.: Avon 1960. Wrappers. U.K.: World Distributors 1963. Wrappers.

RIMBAUD.   U.S.: City Lights 1960.

BOOK OF DREAMS.   U.S.: City Lights 1960. Wrappers.

THE SCRIPTURE OF THE GOLDEN ETERNITY.   U.S.: Totem-Corinth 1960.

LONESOME TRAVELLER.   New York: McGraw Hill 1960. U.K.: Deutsch 1962.

PULL MY DAISY.   U.S.: Grove Press 1961. Wrappers. U.K.: Evergreen 1961. Wrappers.

BIG SUR.   New York: Farrar Straus 1962. U.K.: Deutsch 1963.

POEM.   Privately Printed 1962.

VISIONS OF GERARD.   New York: Farrar Straus 1963. U.K.: Deutsch 1964.
   The U.K. edition includes the novel TRISTESSA.

DESOLATION ANGELS.   U.S.: Coward McCann 1965. U.K.: Deutsch 1966.

SATORI IN PARIS.   U.S.: Grove Press 1966. U.K.: Deutsch 1967.

HUGO WEBER.   U.S.: Portents 1967.

SOMEDAY YOU'LL BE LYING.   Privately Printed 1968.

VANITY OF DULUOZ.   U.S.: Coward McCann 1968. U.K.: Deutsch 1969.

A LAST HAIKU.   Privately Printed 1969.

PIC.   U.S.: Grove Press 1971. U.K.: Deutsch 1973.
   The U.K. edition includes the novel THE SUBTERRANEANS.

SCATTERED POEMS.   U.S.: City Lights 1971. Wrappers.

TRIP, TRAP.   Grey Fox Press 1973. Wrappers.

OLD ANGEL MIDNIGHT.   Brighton: Unicorn Press 1976. Wrappers. U.S.: Midnight Press 1985. Wrappers.

TAKE CARE OF MY GHOST. U.S.: Ghost Press 1977. Wrappers.

HEAVEN AND OTHER POEMS. Grey Fox Press 1977.

BABY DRIVER. U.S.: St. Martin's 1981. U.K.: Deutsch 1982.

SAN FRANCISCO BLUES. U.S.: Beat Books 1983. Wrappers.

TWO STORIES. U.S.: Pacific Red Car 1984. Wrappers. 100 copies.

THE GREAT WESTERN BUS RIDE. U.S.: Pacific Red Car 1984. Wrappers. 100 copies.

CELINE AND OTHER TALES. U.S.: Pacific Red Car 1985. Wrappers. 100 copies.

THE VISION OF THE HOODED WHITE ANGELS. U.S.: Pacific Red Car 1985. Wrappers. 100 copies.

HOME AT CHRISTMAS. U.S.: Pacific Red Car, n.d. (1986). Wrappers.

KINGSLEY, Charles (1819–1875)

Though Kingsley wrote one of the most famous children's books of all time, THE WATER BABIES, his first editions in general are not widely collected and are not expensive. Even that one very famous book is not tremendously expensive, averaging only around £200. It is not especially rare, but is often found rubbed with the gilt dull. A really fine, bright copy would be fairly unusual.

He wrote two other books which are well-known, and these are given below.

WESTWARD HO! Macmillan 1855. 3 vols.

THE WATER BABIES. A Fairy-Tale for a Land-Baby. London & Cambridge: Macmillan 1863. Gilt-lettered dark green cloth, decorated with a gold fish and water baby. Quarto (approximately 16 × 21½cms). Frontispiece and one other full-page illustration by J. Noel Paton, plus vignette chapter-heads. The rare First Issue, of 200 copies, has a leaf bearing a verse entitled 'L'Envoi'.

HEREWARD THE WAKE. Macmillan 1866. 2 vols.

KIPLING, Rudyard (1881–1923)

The Indian Railway Library booklets – some of Kipling's earliest first editions – can be puzzling. They went through many editions (and issues) and need to be carefully examined. I believe I have given just sufficient information below, for the first issues/editions to be safely identified.

Kipling has not always received the blessing of the literary critics. Even now, his status in English literature is a little uncertain. But he is a perennial favourite with readers and collectors, and for this reason I have treated his works at some length. Of his many books, some are rare, but most are not, and for the average collector of modest means, collecting Kipling is a feasible proposition. In the list below, I have included all the major items but have excluded many minor pieces and limited editions.

SCHOOLBOY LYRICS. Lahore. Printed at the 'Civil & Military Gazette' Press 1881. Small 12mo. 46pp. First issued in plain white, then lettered brown wrappers (about 25 copies in each case).

ECHOES. By Two Writers. No imprint or date (1884). Small 12mo. 72pp. in brown wrappers.
The two writers were Kipling and his sister.

QUARTETTE, The Christmas Annual of the Civil & Military Gazette. By Four Anglo-Indian Writers. Lahore: The Civil & Military Gazette Press 1885. Grey wrappers.
The writers were Kipling, his father, mother & sister.

DEPARTMENTAL DITTIES AND OTHER VERSES. The Civil and Military Gazette Press (Lahore 1886). Oblong brown wrappers with an envelope-style flap. Second Edition: Calcutta: Thacker, Spink and Co. 12mo. Grey boards, blue or red lettering. Contains 5 new poems. First U.K. (i.e. 9th edition): Thacker & Co. 1897. Blue cloth. Also 150 copies on handmade paper and 30 copies on vellum paper.

PLAIN TALES FROM THE HILLS. Calcutta & London. Thacker 1888. Citron Indian cloth. First Issue has 24pp adverts at the end, dated 'Calcutta December 1887'. The Second Issue has 32pp adverts with the same date. Copies with page number '192' printed at the inner corner rather than the outer, are thought to be the first to be bound up. Some of the Indian sheets were bound up in London and issued with adverts dated 2000/9/87. First U.K. Edition (with 'Third Edition' on the title-page): Macmillan 1890. Blue cloth. 62pp adverts dated February 1890.
The first issue of the first edition is extremely rare. Only a few copies are known.

SOLDIERS THREE. Allahabad: Printed At The 'Pioneer' Press 1888.

Green-grey illustrated wrappers. U.K.: Sampson Low 1888. Illustrated grey-green wrappers. 'No. 1 Indian Railway Library'.

THE STORY OF THE GADSBYS.   Allahabad: Wheeler & Co. n.d. (1888). Grey-green illustrated wrappers. 'No. 2 Indian Railway Library' 8pp adverts at the end. Later issues have only 2pp adverts at the end, and 'Mayo School of Art, Lahore' on the front. U.K.: Wheeler . . . Allahabad (&) Sampson, Low . . . London. n.d. (1888) Green-grey wrappers. 2pp adverts.

IN BLACK & WHITE.   Allahabad: Wheeler & Co. (1888). Illustrated cream wrappers. 'No. 3 Indian Railway Library'. U.K.: Wheeler . . . Allahabad (&) Sampson, Low . . . London. n.d. (1888). Grey-green wrappers.

UNDER THE DEODARS.   Allahabad: Wheeler & Co. n.d. (1888). Illustrated green wrappers. 'No. 4 Indian Railway Library'. There are several issues, and the issue points are complicated. The first issue meets the following description in all respects. The title page reads: Under the Deodars. / By / Rudyard Kipling. / [line followed by 7 lines of verse] / 'The City of Dreadful Night' / [line] / Published By / Messrs. A. H. Wheeler & Co., / Allahabad. There are viii pages of prelims in the following sequence: 2 pp adverts; title-page; verso title-page reading 'Reprinted in chief from The Week's News'; Preface; Contents. The text (106pp) is followed by 8pp adverts (the last not numbered). There should not be an inserted advert for the Standard Life Office. The wrappers are green, not grey-green, and are not shaded on the front. U.K.: Wheeler . . . Allahabad . . . (&) . . . Sampson, Low . . . London. n.d. (1888). Illustrated green-grey wrappers.

THE PHANTOM RICKSHAW AND OTHER TALES.   Allahabad: Wheeler & Co. n.d. (1888). Illustrated green-grey wrappers. 'Indian Railway Library No. 5'. Later issues have 'Mayo School of Art, Lahore' on the front wrapper. U.K.: Wheeler . . . Allahabad . . . (&) . . . Sampson, Low . . . London. n.d. Illustrated green-grey wrappers.

WEE WILLIE WINKIE AND OTHER CHILD STORIES.   Allahabad: Wheeler & Co. n.d. (1888). Illustrated green-grey wrappers. 'Indian Railway Library No. 6'. Second issue has 'Mayo School of Art, Lahore' on front wrapper. Third issue has 96pp instead of 104. U.K.: Wheeler . . . Allahabad . . . (&) Sampson, Low . . . London. n.d. Illustrated green-grey wrappers.

THE COURTING OF DINAH SHADD AND OTHER STORIES.   New York: Harper 1890. 12mo. Blue wrappers.

THE CITY OF DREADFUL NIGHT AND OTHER SKETCHES.   Allahabad: Wheeler & Co. 1890. Brown cloth. There is reason to believe that the edition was cancelled and only 3 copies survived.

THE CITY OF DREADFUL NIGHT AND OTHER PLACES.   Allahabad:

Wheeler & Co. 1891. Illustrated green-grey wrappers. Indian Railway Library, No. 14. U.K.: Wheeler . . . Allahabad . . . (&) Sampson, Low . . . London. n.d. (1891). Illustrated green-grey wrappers. There should be an apology slip pasted to the title-page.

AMERICAN NOTES. By Rudyard Kipling . . . and THE BOTTLE IMP by Robert Louis Stevenson. New York: M. J. Ivers & Co. n.d. (1891). Blue wrappers with Colgate advert on back. The rare first issue gives the publisher's address at the foot of the title-page as '86 Nassau Street'.

THE SMITH ADMINISTRATION. Allahabad: Wheeler & Co. 1891. Plain grey wrappers.

LETTERS OF MARQUE. Allahabad: Wheeler & Co. 1891. Red and blue cloth (diagonally divided). Suppressed by Kipling. 100 copies survived.

THE LIGHT THAT FAILED. Philadelphia: Lippincott. n.d. (1891). Wrappers. First U.K. Edition: MacMillan 1891. 12mo. Blue cloth. A pirated edition was published by Rand, McNally & Co. (Chicago & New York) in 1891.

MY OWN PEOPLE. New York: Hurst & Co. n.d. (1891). Cream wrappers, giving the title as MINE OWN PEOPLE. Pirated. First authorized edition: New York: United States Book Company 1891. Red cloth.

LIFE'S HANDICAP. Macmillan 1891. Blue cloth.

THE NAULAHKA. By Kipling and Wolcott Balestier. Heinemann 1892. Red cloth.

BARRACK-ROOM BALLADS AND OTHER VERSES. Methuen 1892. Red cloth. An Indian edition was published in Calcutta in the same year. A pirated edition without imprint exists.

MANY INVENTIONS. MacMillan 1893. Blue cloth.

PICTURESQUE BRATTLEBORO. Northampton, Mass.: Picturesque Publishing Co. (1894). Green cloth, silver decoration.

THE JUNGLE BOOK. MacMillan 1894. Blue cloth.

THE SECOND JUNGLE BOOK. Macmillan 1895. Blue cloth.

OUT OF INDIA. New York: G. W. Dillingham 1895. Blue cloth.

THE SEVEN SEAS. Methuen 1896. Maroon buckram.

SOLDIER TALES. Macmillan 1896. Blue cloth.

CAPTAINS COURAGEOUS.   Macmillan 1897. Blue cloth.

WHITE HORSES.   Printed for Private Circulation. London 1897. Lilac wrappers.
  A Wise Forgery.

AN ALMANAC OF TWELVE SPORTS.   By William Nicholson. Words by Kipling. Heinemann 1898. Folio. Illustrated boards.

THE DAY'S WORK.   Macmillan 1898. Blue cloth.

A FLEET IN BEING.   Macmillan 1898. Blue wrappers, also in cloth.

BLACK JACK.   F. Tennyson Neely 1899. Red cloth.

STALKY & CO.   Macmillan 1899. Red cloth, elephant's head on front.

THE BRUSHWOOD BOY.   New York: Doubleday 1899. Red cloth. (First Separate Edition). U.K.: Macmillan 1907.

FROM SEA TO SEA.   New York: Doubleday & McClure 1899. 2 vols. Cloth. U.K.: Macmillan 1900. 2 vols. Red cloth, elephant's head on front.

THE WHITE MAN'S BURDEN.   Printed for Private Circulation. London 1899. Lilac wrappers.
  A Wise Forgery.

KIM   Macmillan 1901. Red cloth, elephant's head on front.

JUST SO STORIES FOR LITTLE CHILDREN.   Macmillan 1901. Red cloth.

THE FIVE NATIONS.   Methuen 1903. Red buckram.

TRAFFICS AND DISCOVERIES.   Macmillan 1904. Red cloth, elephant's head on front.

THEY.   Macmillan 1905. White cloth.

PUCK OF POOK'S HILL.   Macmillan 1906. Red cloth, elephant's head on front.

COLLECTED VERSE.   New York: Doubleday 1907. U.K. (with minor variations): Hodder 1912. Quarter canvas, blue boards. Also 500 on handmade paper in white vellum, and also 100 Signed by Kipling, in brown morocco.

WITH THE NIGHT MAIL.   New York: Doubleday 1909. (First Separate

Edition). Macmillan issued the piece in plain wrappers, in the same year, to establish U.K. copyright.

ACTIONS AND REACTIONS. Macmillan 1909. Red cloth, elephant's head on front.

ABAFT THE FUNNEL. New York: B. W. Dodge 1909. Blue cloth, lettered in gold. There was a later, cheaper issue, lettered in red. Pirated (both issues). First Authorized Edition: New York: Doubleday 1909 (later). Grey cloth, also green cloth.
   The book has the reputation, in the U.K. at least, of being scarce, but this is not my impression.

REWARDS AND FAIRIES. Macmillan 1910. Red cloth, elephant's head on front.

THE DEAD KING. Hodder 1910. Purple cloth, also in purple wrappers.

A HISTORY OF ENGLAND. By C. R. L. Fletcher & R. Kipling. Oxford: Clarendon Press (and) London: Henry Frowde and Hodder & Stoughton. Blue cloth. Also, a Schools Issue in red cloth.

SONGS FROM BOOKS. New York: Doubleday 1912. Green cloth. U.K.: Macmillan 1913. Red cloth. Containing many additional poems.

A SONG OF THE ENGLISH. Illustrated by W. Heath Robinson, Hodder, n.d. (1913). 4to. There was an ordinary issue in cloth and also an Edition de Luxe of 50 copies signed by Kipling, in pigskin. 13 coloured plates. This is the First Separate Edition and the First Illustrated Edition. The text had previously been included in THE SEVEN SEAS (1896).

FRANCE AT WAR. Macmillan 1915. White wrappers with a tricolor on front.

THE FRINGES OF THE FLEET. Macmillan 1915. White wrappers with White Ensign on front.

SEA WARFARE. Macmillan 1916. Blue cloth. U.S. (simultaneously): Doubleday. Red cloth.

A DIVERSITY OF CREATURES. Macmillan 1917. Red cloth, elephant's head on front.

THE EYES OF ASIA. New York: Doubleday 1918. Brown buckram, paper labels.

TWENTY POEMS. Methuen n.d. (1918). 38pp in blue wrappers.

THE YEARS BETWEEN. Methuen. n.d. (1919). Maroon buckram.

RUDYARD KIPLING'S VERSE INCLUSIVE EDITION. Hodder 1919. 3 vols. Red cloth. Also, 100 copies signed by Kipling, in full vellum. The one volume edition on India Paper was issued in 1922.

LETTERS OF TRAVEL. Macmillan 1920. Red cloth, elephant's head on front.

THE KING'S PILGRIMAGE. Hodder 1922. Purple cloth.

INDEPENDENCE. Macmillan 1923. Red cloth, also in blue wrappers.

LAND AND SEA TALES FOR SCOUTS AND GUIDES. Macmillan 1923. Red cloth. The American Edition is entitled LAND AND SEA TALES FOR BOYS AND GIRLS

L

LAMB, Lady Caroline (1785–1828)

GLENARVON. printed for Henry Colburn 1816. 3 vols. Large 12mo. Wrappers.
This thinly disguised romance of Byron appeared in three editions in 1816. The author's Preface first appeared in the second edition.

LAMB, Charles (1775–1834)

Four of Lamb's sonnets appeared in Coleridge's POEMS ON VARIOUS SUBJECTS, first published in 1796. They are signed merely 'C. L.' but the author is acknowledged in full by Coleridge, in his Preface. In the 'Second Edition' of Coleridge's POEMS (1797), some of Lamb's poems are added, along with some by Charles Lloyd. (See under Coleridge for full details of those two publications.) His famous Essays of Elia first appeared in the London Magazine and were published separately in 1823. The Last Essays of Elia were published in 1833. Both series were published by Moxon in two volumes in 1835. In the meantime however, both series had been published in Philadelphia in 1828 (by Carey, Lea & Carey). Apart from the aforementioned, his earliest and best-known publications were:

BLANK VERSE.   By Lamb & Charles Lloyd. Printed by T. Bensley; for John and Arthur Arch 1798. Small 8vo.
   A very important volume in the field of English poetry, and worth about £1000.

A TALE OF ROSAMUND GRAY AND OLD BLIND MARGARET.
Birmingham: Pearson 1798. First London Issue: Lee & Hurst 1798. Small 8vo.
   His earliest book of any length, and a rare one.

JOHN WOODVIL,   a Tragedy . . . To which are added Fragments of Burton. for G. & J. Robinson 1802.

TALES FROM SHAKESPEARE,   designed for the Use of Young Persons. By Charles & Mary Lamb. Thomas Hodgkins 1807. 2 vols. 12mo.

THE ADVENTURES OF ULYSSES.   T. Davison for The Juvenile Library 1808. 12mo.

SPECIMENS OF ENGLISH DRAMATIC POETS.   Longman 1808.
   The work which established his reputation as a literary critic.

WORKS.   C. & J. Olliver 1818. 2 vols.
   Lamb wrote many more works after this very early collection. Moxon published many collections after the author's death.

THE LETTERS . . . with a Sketch of his Life by Thomas Noon Talfourd. Moxon 1837. 2 vols.

FINAL MEMORIALS . . . chiefly Letters not before Published.   Moxon 1848. 2 vols.

LANGLAND, William (14th century)

   It was thought at one time that Langland wrote RICHARD THE REDE-LESS, but nowadays the only work ascribed to him is:

THE VISION OF PIERCE PLOWMAN.   Printed by Robert Crowley 1505 (1550). The first issue was misdated 1505. The second issue has the correct date of 1550. The Second Edition, also dated 1550, has additional matter, namely 'certayne notes and cotations in the mergyne'.

LARKIN, Philip (1922–1985)

Larkin is currently one of the most keenly collected poets of modern times. His early works are already scarce and the dust wrappers of his first three publications are astonishingly difficult to come by. The first editions of those three books, in the elusive dust wrappers, are already being priced in the region of £500 and sometimes much higher.

THE NORTH SHIP. Fortune Press 1945. Black cloth, maroon d/w. In 1965, about 500 unauthorized copies in maroon cloth were produced, but were eventually recalled on Larkin's insistence. The Faber edition of 1966 includes an extra poem and has a new introduction.

JILL. Fortune Press 1946. Cloth, d/w. Revised Edition: Faber 1964. U.S. (revised version): St Martin's Press 1964.

A GIRL IN WINTER. Faber 1947. Mottled blue-green cloth, d/w. U.S.: St Martin's 1957.

XX POEMS. Belfast: Privately Printed for the author. 1951. 100 copies. Wrappers.

THE FANTASY POETS NO. 21. Fantasy Press 1954. 300 copies approx.

THE LESS DECEIVED. Marvell Press 1955. U.S.: St Martin's 1960.

THE WHITSUN WEDDINGS. Faber 1964. U.S.: Random House 1964.

ALL WHAT JAZZ. Faber 1970. U.S.: St Martin's 1970.

THE EXPLOSION. Poem of the Month Club 1970. Broadside. 1000 signed copies only.

HIGH WINDOWS. Faber 1974. U.S.: Farrar Straus 1974.

REQUIRED WRITING. Faber 1983. Paperback original. U.S.: Farrar Straus 1983.

COLLECTED POEMS. Faber 1989.

LAWRENCE, D. H. (1885–1930)

Hardly any of Lawrence's first editions can be obtained for under £50, and quite a few are running into hundreds of pounds. Decent dust wrappers are very difficult to get. Secker's dust wrappers in particular seem to have deteriorated rapidly. THE WHITE PEACOCK is extremely scarce in fine condition in a decent dust wrapper. It is virtually impossible to get even the second issue for under $600. The U.K. edition is equally hard to come by.

THE WHITE PEACOCK. New York: Duffield 1911. Blue cloth, d/w. The first issue has an integral title-page, later becoming a cancel. The copyright date is given as 1910 in the first issue, subsequently 1911. U.K.: Heinemann 1911. Dark blue-green cloth, d/w. In the first issue, pp.227–230 are tipped in. On the earliest binding, Heinemann's windmill device appears on the back cover. There are several variants.

THE TRESPASSER. Duckworth 1912. Dark blue cloth. Copies are known in green cloth, and these are probably of later issue. U.S.: Kennerley 1912.

LOVE POEMS AND OTHERS. Duckworth 1913. U.S.: Kennerley 1913.

SONS AND LOVERS. Duckworth 1913. Blue cloth, d/w. (two versions of uncertain priority). Two states of the title-page – dated cancel leaf or integral leaf with dated printer's imprint. U.S.: Kennerley 1913. Purple cloth, d/w.
  According to Jacob Schwartz about six copies are known with an undated integral title-page.

THE PRUSSIAN OFFICER AND OTHER STORIES. Duckworth (1914). Blue cloth. 20pp or 24pp adverts. Copies known in red cloth. Later issues have only 16pp adverts. U.S.: Huebsch 1916.

THE WIDOWING OF MRS HOLROYD. New York: Kennerley 1914. U.K.: Duckworth 1914. From American sheets. (500 copies).

THE RAINBOW. Methuen (1915). Blue-green cloth, d/w. Adverts dated Autumn 1914. There are variants (Colonial Library Issue) in red or brown cloth, or wrappers. 2500 copies were printed. U.S.: Huebsch 1916.
  Court action about five weeks after publication of the Methuen edition, resulted in destruction of an unknown number of copies.

TWILIGHT IN ITALY. Duckworth (1916). Dark blue cloth. Copies are known in a lighter blue cloth. U.S.: Huebsch 1916.

AMORES. Duckworth (1916). First issue has adverts. U.S.: Huebsch 1916.

LOOK! WE HAVE COME THROUGH! Chatto 1917.

NEW POEMS. Secker 1918. Grey wrappers. (500 copies). U.S.: Huebsch 1920.

BAY. A Book of Poems. Beaumont Press 1919. Limited edition, including

30 on Japanese vellum with hand-coloured illustrations, signed by the author and artist (Anne Estelle Rice).

THE LOST GIRL. Secker 1920. Brown cloth, d/w. Three issues. In the first and third, pp. 256 & 268 are integral, in the second they are cancels. In the first, p. 256, line 15 reads 'she was taken to her room'. In the second and third, this is changed to 'she let be'. On p. 268, the first issue reading 'whether she noticed anything in the bedrooms, in the beds' is changed in the second and third issues to 'whether she noticed anything'. U.S.: Seltzer 1921.

TOUCH AND GO. London 1920. Flexible orange boards, paper labels, d/w. U.S.: Seltzer 1920. Orange boards, d/w.

WOMEN IN LOVE. Privately Printed. (1250 copies), issued in New York and London (American sheets) 1920. Secker issued 50 signed copies in London (1922) with an inserted colophon. Trade Edition: Secker 1921. Brown cloth, d/w. The earliest copies have 'come round to the flat' on p. 61, line 31, and 'dark, soft fluffy hair' on p. 63, line 19. The 'Second Impression' incorporates changes occasioned by Philip Heseltine's accusation of libel.

TORTOISES. New York: Seltzer 1921. Pictorial boards, d/w.

MOVEMENTS IN EUROPEAN HISTORY. By Lawrence H. Davison (pseud.). O.U.P. 1921. Brown cloth (no d/w). Second issue: light blue cloth.

SEA AND SARDINIA. New York: Seltzer 1921. Cloth spine, boards. U.K.: Secker 1923.

AARON'S ROD. New York: Seltzer 1922. U.K.: Secker 1922 (later).

FANTASIA OF THE UNCONSCIOUS. New York: Seltzer 1922. Blue ribbed cloth. U.K.: Secker 1923. 1000 copies. Purple cloth.

ENGLAND, MY ENGLAND. New York: Seltzer 1922. U.K.: Secker 1924.

PSYCHOANALYSIS AND THE UNCONSCIOUS. New York 1921. Grey boards, d/w. U.K.: Secker 1923.

STUDIES IN CLASSIC AMERICAN LITERATURE. New York 1923. Appeared 10 months before the U.K. edition.

THE LADYBIRD. THE FOX. THE CAPTAIN'S DOLL. Secker 1923.

THE CAPTAIN'S DOLL. New York: Seltzer 1923. The U.S. edition of THE LADYBIRD ... (etc).

KANGAROO. Secker 1923. U.S.: Seltzer 1923.

BIRDS BEASTS AND FLOWERS. New York: Seltzer 1923. U.K.: Secker 1923. First Illustrated Edition: Cresset Press 1930. 500 copies. Sm. folio. Vellum spine, marbled boards.

THE BOY IN THE BUSH. By D. H. L. & M. L. Skinner. Secker 1924. U.S.: Seltzer 1924.

ST. MAWR & THE PRINCESS. Secker 1925. In the first issue, the 'Contents' gives the start of the text as page 9 (later corrected to page 7). In the American edition, same year, THE PRINCESS was omitted, making it the First Separate Edition of ST. MAWR.

REFLECTIONS ON THE DEATH OF A PORCUPINE and Other Essays. Philadelphia: Centaur Press 1925. Edition of 925 copies. Of these, 475 were distributed in the U.K. by Simpkin, Marshall, Hamilton, Kent & Co. (from March 1926, according to the English Catalogue of Books). The U.K. issue has a slip tipped in, naming the distributors. Patterned boards & slipcase.

THE PLUMED SERPENT. Secker 1926. U.S.: Knopf 1926.

DAVID; a Play. Secker 1926. 500 copies. U.S.: Knopf 1926.

GLAD GHOSTS. Benn 1926. 500 copies. Wrappers.

SUN. Archer 1926. 100 copies. Expurgated. Wrappers. Unexpurgated: Paris: Black Sun Press 1928. Limited Edition.

MORNINGS IN MEXICO. Secker 1927. (1000 copies). U.S.: Knopf 1927.

THE WOMAN WHO RODE AWAY. Secker 1928. U.S.: Knopf 1928.

LADY CHATTERLEY'S LOVER. Privately Printed, Florence 1928. Limited to 1000 copies signed by the author. Mulberry boards, plain (purely protective) d/w. A 'Second Edition' (being a cheap paper issue of the first edition) was issued in wrappers. There were 200 copies of this. A Privately Printed edition was published in France, 1929. U.K. (Expurgated): Secker 1932. Unexpurgated: Penguin 1960. Wrappers. U.S. (Expurgated): Knopf 1932. Unexpurgated: Grove Press 1959.
   The original Florence edition is the one to have, of course. It now sells for about £2000.

SEX LOCKED OUT. By the Author of 'Lady Chatterley's Lover'. 1928. 12pp. Pamphlet.
   Privately Printed, and apparently issued without authority. It was reprinted from The Sunday Dispatch, now extinct.

THE WOMAN WHO RODE AWAY and Other Stories.   Secker 1928.

RAWDON'S ROOF.   Elkin Mathews, Woburn Books 1928. Limited Edition of 530 signed. Boards & d/w.

THE COLLECTED POEMS.   Secker 1928. 2 vols. Brown cloth. Also, 100 signed, in quarter parchment, boards.

THE PAINTINGS.   Mandrake Press 1929. 4to. 500 copies. Three-quarter brown morocco, slipcase.

PANSIES.   Secker 1929. Patterned boards, d/w. Also, 250 signed.
   There were several other limited issues/editions in the same year.

PORNOGRAPHY AND OBSCENITY.   Faber 1929. Orange wrappers.

THE ESCAPED COCK.   Paris: Black Sun Press 1929. 500 copies, including 50 signed.

NETTLES.   Faber 1930. Orange wrappers.

A PROPOS OF LADY CHATTERLEY'S LOVER.   Mandrake Press 1930.

THE VIRGIN AND THE GYPSY.   Florence: Orioli 1930. Limited Edition. U.K.: Secker 1930. U.S.: Knopf 1930.

LOVE AMONG THE HAYSTACKS.   Nonesuch Press 1930. 1600 copies. Quarter linen, yellow buckram, d/w.

THE TRIUMPH OF THE MACHINE.   Faber, Ariel Poems (1930). Wrappers.

ASSORTED ARTICLES.   Secker 1930. Red cloth. U.S.: Knopf 1930.

THE MAN WHO DIED.   Secker 1931. Green buckram. Large 8vo. 2000 copies.

THE ESCAPED COCK.   U.S.: Knopf 1931.
   The U.S. edition of THE MAN WHO DIED.

APOCALYPSE.   Florence: Orioli 1931. Limited Edition. U.K.: Secker 1932.

LAST POEMS.   Florence: Orioli 1932. Limited Edition. U.K.: Secker 1933.

THE LETTERS.   (ed. Huxley). Heinemann 1932. Also 525 copies in full parchment.

ETRUSCAN PLACES.   Secker 1932.

THE LOVELY LADY.   Secker 1932 (1933). U.S.: Viking 1933.

THE SHIP OF DEATH.   Secker 1933. Boards, d/w.

THE PLAYS.   Secker 1933.

THE TALES.   Secker 1934.

A MODERN LOVER.   Secker 1934.

A COLLIER'S FRIDAY NIGHT.   Secker 1934.

PORNOGRAPHY AND SO ON.   Faber 1936.

PHOENIX, THE POSTHUMOUS PAPERS.   Heinemann 1936.

POEMS.   Heinemann 1939. 2 vols.

FIRE AND OTHER POEMS.   San Francisco. Book Club of California 1940.

SEX, LITERATURE AND CENSORSHIP.   Heinemann 1955.

THE COMPLETE POEMS.   Heinemann 1957. 3 vols.

THE COMPLETE PLAYS.   Heinemann 1965.

LETTERS TO MARTIN SECKER.   Privately Printed 1970. Limited to 500 copies.

THE LETTERS.   C.U.P. 1979 (Vol I) & 1981 (Vol II).

MR NOON.   C.U.P. 1984.

LAWRENCE, T. E. (1888–1935)

The first two publications listed below are scarce, but apart from those, none of Lawrence's conventionally published first editions are particularly rare. The most difficult to get hold of, as might be expected, are those works published in severely limited editions, and of course, the privately issued copies of SEVEN PILLARS OF WISDOM. The latter were spasmodically produced and marketed by the author, and issued in various states of completion. The process is summarized under the relevant entry below.

THE WILDERNESS OF ZIN. By C. Leonard Woolley & T. E. Lawrence. Palestine Exploration Fund 1915. (The date 1914 appears on the title page, and 1914–1915 on the front cover and spine). Grey boards, blue buckram spine.

A BRIEF RECORD OF THE ADVANCE OF THE EGYPTIAN EXPEDITIONARY FORCE. Cairo: The Palestine News 1919. Cloth spine, wrappers. (Lawrence's contributions are unsigned). U.K.: H.M.S.O. 1919. Buckram spine, grey boards.

SEVEN PILLARS OF WISDOM. 8 copies were printed by The Oxford Times 1922. Two of these were used for the issuing of single leaves. A proof of the 8 introductory chapters was circulated in 1924. 100 proof copies of 7 chapters were issued to subscribers in 1925. The 'Cranwell' Edition of 169 complete and 32 incomplete copies was distributed to subscribers in 1926. Also in 1926, in New York, Doubleday issued a Copyright Edition of 22 copies. In 1935, Cape issued a Limited Edition of 750 copies, an unlimited 'first trade edition', and a privately issued edition of 60 copies. Also in 1935, Doubleday issued an edition of 750 copies, and an unlimited edition.

THE FOREST GIANT. By Adrien Le Corbeau. Translated by J. H. Ross (i.e. Lawrence). Cape 1924. U.S.: Harper 1924.

REVOLT IN THE DESERT. Cape 1927. Also a Limited Edition of 315 copies. U.S.: George H. Doran Company 1927. Also a Limited Edition of 250 copies.
    An abridged version of SEVEN PILLARS OF WISDOM. Doubleday, Doran issued an undated edition in 1928.

THE ODYSSEY OF HOMER. Translated by T. E. Shaw (i.e. Lawrence). Sir Emery Walker, Wilfred Merton & Bruce Rogers 1932. Edition of 530 copies. U.S.: Oxford University Press, New York 1932. Also a Limited Edition of 34 copies, U.K. Trade Edition: O.U.P. 1935.

LETTERS FROM T. E. SHAW TO BRUCE ROGERS. U.S.: Privately Printed at The Press of William Edwin Rudge (1933). 200 copies.

MORE LETTERS FROM T. E. SHAW TO BRUCE ROGERS. U.S.: Privately Printed (1936). 300 copies.

THE MINT. By 352087 A/C Ross. (i.e. Lawrence). New York: Doubleday, Doran 1936. 'Copyright Edition' of 50 copies. Same publisher: 1000 copies in 1955. U.K.: Cape 1955. Limited De Luxe issue of 2000 copies. Ordinary issue expurgated.

CRUSADER CASTLES. Golden Cockerel Press 1936. 2 vols. 1000 numbered copies. U.S.: Doubleday, Doran 1937.

AN ESSAY ON FLECKER.   Corvinus Press 1937. Limited to 30 copies.
U.S. 'Copyright' Edition: Doubleday 1937. 56 copies.

THE DIARY OF T. E. LAWRENCE MCMXI.   Corvinus Press 1937. 203
copies.

TWO ARABIC FOLK TALES.   Corvinus Press 1937. 31 copies.

THE LETTERS OF T. E. LAWRENCE.   Cape 1938. Incorrect initials on
page 496 are corrected in the second state.

T. E. LAWRENCE TO HIS BIOGRAPHER, ROBERT GRAVES.   (2nd
vol: TO . . . LIDDELL HART). New York: Doubleday, Doran 1938. 2 vols
in dust wrappers & slipcase. Limited to 1000 signed copies (i.e. first vol signed
by Graves, the 2nd by Hart). 500 copies were for America & 500 for the U.K.
Trade Edition: Faber (1939). Second Edition (combining the two volumes into
one, not signed): Cassell & Doubleday & Co. 1963.

SECRET DESPATCHES FROM ARABIA.   Golden Cockerel Press 1939.
1000 copies.

ORIENTAL ASSEMBLY.   Williams & Norgate 1939. U.S.: Dutton 1940.

MEN IN PRINT.   Golden Cockerel Press (1940). Limited to 500 copies.
Also 30 specials.

THE ESSENTIAL T. E. LAWRENCE.   Cape 1951.

THE HOME LETTERS OF T. E. LAWRENCE AND HIS BROTHERS.
Oxford: Blackwell 1954. U.S.: Macmillan 1954.

EVOLUTION OF A REVOLT.   Pennsylvania State U.P. 1968.

LEAR, Edward (1812–1888)

All of Lear's early works, be they 'nonsense', travel, or natural history, are
collectors items of the first order, and mostly enormously expensive. His first
book PARROTS is valued in tens of thousands of pounds. His GLEANINGS
is valued at £10,000 or more. The rest are mostly in the hundreds of
pounds, sometimes exceeding £1000. These prices faithfully reflect the
combination of genuine scarcity and enormous demand. Only the later
'nonsense' books, letters, and odds and ends are less than £100.

ILLUSTRATIONS OF THE FAMILY PSITTACIDAE, OR PARROTS.
Ackerman & Lear 1832. 12 folios. 42 plates, hand-coloured. 175 copies.

VIEWS IN ROME AND ITS ENVIRONS.   Maclean 1841. 25 plates. Folio.
Green leather spine, green cloth.

ILLUSTRATED EXCURSIONS IN ITALY.   Maclean 1846. 2 vols. 30 plates
(vol 1) & 25 plates (vol 2).

GLEANINGS FROM THE MENAGERIE AND AVIARY AT KNOWSLEY
HALL, KNOWSLEY.   Privately printed. Knowsley 1846. Folio. Half green
morocco.

A BOOK OF NONSENSE.   By Derry Down Derry (i.e. Lear). Thomas
Maclean 1846 (February 10th). 2 vols. Oblong wrappers. Containing 72 limer-
icks lithographed on rectos only. In later copies, the plates are rearranged, ten
being transferred from volume 1 to volume 2. Enlarged (Third) Edition: By
Edward Lear. Routledge 1861. Illustrations engraved on wood by Dalziel
(who also printed and bound the book).
    The first edition is a very rare book, valued at several thousand pounds.
(£8000 has been achieved at auction).

JOURNALS OF A LANDSCAPE PAINTER IN ALBANIA.   Bentley 1851.
Map & 20 plates. Large 8vo. Blue cloth.

JOURNALS OF A LANDSCAPE PAINTER IN SOUTHERN CAL-
ABRIA.   Bentley 1852. 2 maps & 20 plates.

VIEWS IN THE SEVEN IONIAN ISLANDS.   Privately Published by Lear
1863. 20 plates. Folio.

JOURNAL OF A LANDSCAPE PAINTER IN CORSICA.   Robert John
Bush 1870. 41 plates (wood engravings). Reddish brown cloth.

NONSENSE SONGS, STORIES, BOTANY & ALPHABETS.   Robert John
Bush 1871.
    Contains 'The Owl and the Pussycat', 'The Jumblies', etc. It was also
published in Boston, in the same year.

MORE NONSENSE, PICTURES, RHYMES, BOTANY, ETC.   Robert
John Bush 1872.

TORTOISES, TERRAPINS AND TURTLES DRAWN FROM LIFE.   By
Lear & Sowerby. Southeran & Baer 1872. Folio. Red cloth.

LAUGHABLE LYRICS.   Robert John Bush 1877.

THREE POEMS BY TENNYSON.   With 24 illustrations by Lear. U.K. &
U.S.: Bousson, Valadon & Co., and Scribner & Welford 1889. Limited to 100
signed by Tennyson. Folio.

NONSENSE SONGS AND STORIES. Warne 1895.

LETTERS. T. Fisher Unwin 1907.

LATER LETTERS. T. Fisher Unwin 1911.

QUEERY LEARY NONSENSE. Mills & Boon 1911.

THE LEAR COLOURED BIRD BOOK FOR CHILDREN. Mills & Boon 1912.

EDWARD LEAR'S NONSENSE OMNIBUS. Warne 1943.

THE COMPLETE NONSENSE. Faber 1947.

THE COLLECTED NONSENSE SONGS. Grey Walls Press 1947.

A NONSENSE ALPHABET. H.M.S.O. 1952.

TEAPOTS AND QUAILS. Murray 1953. Slim 4to.

EDWARD LEAR'S INDIAN JOURNAL. Jarrolds 1953.

ABC. Constable Young Books 1965.

LE FANU, J. Sheridan (1814–1873)

The rarest of Le Fanu's major works appears to be the collection of stories entitled GHOST STORIES AND TALES OF MYSTERY. A very good copy should be worth well over £1000, which is more or less what his major novels are getting, excepting THE FORTUNES ... which is not especially rare.

THE COCK AND ANCHOR. (anonymous). Dublin: William Curry Jun. & Co. 1845. 3 vols. A small format edition (Fcap 8vo, 3 vols) was issued by Curry with the same date (but later). This has minor differences in the type setting and collates in eights instead of twelves. The Irish sheets were issued with a new title-page by Longman/Parry dated 1847. First illustrated Edition: 'By Sheridan Le Fanu'. Downey & Co. (1895). Frontis., pictorial title, 8 plates, & illustrations in the text, by Brinsley Le Fanu. One vol. Brown cloth, blocked in black & gold.

SIR HENRY ASHWOODE: THE FORGER. (anonymous). Parry & Co. 1851. 3 vols, Fcap 8vo.

A new edition of THE COCK AND ANCHOR, from the sheets of the 1845 small format Curry edition, with new titles.

THE FORTUNES OF COLONEL TORLOGH O'BRIEN. (anonymous). Originally published as 10/11 parts in pink wrappers, from April 1846. Book: Dublin & London: James McGlashan & William S. Orr 1847. 22 plates by Phiz. Pictorial green cloth & variants.

GHOST STORIES AND TALES OF MYSTERY. (anonymous). Dublin & London: James McGlashan & William S. Orr 1851. 4 plates by Phiz. Red cloth, variant decorations.

THE HOUSE BY THE CHURCH-YARD. Tinsley 1863. 3 vols.
A bibliographically complicated book, with a number of variant issues of the first edition, stemming from the fact that Le Fanu had the book printed (and some sheets bound) in Ireland, before it was taken over by Tinsley. Basically, there is an All Irish First Issue, a First Issue with English Prelims, a Second Issue (with 'Second Edition' on the title-page), a Third Issue (with 'Third Edition' on the title-page, and a Remainder Issue – all in 3 vols and all using the original sheets printed in Ireland. Bindings are green or blue cloth of various kinds.

WYLDER'S HAND. Bentley 1864. 3 vols. Grey-purple cloth.

UNCLE SILAS. Bentley 1864. 3 vols. Claret cloth. First Illustrated Edition: Bentley 1865. One volume, green cloth.

GUY DEVERELL. Bentley 1865. 3 vols. Carmine cloth.

THE PRELUDE. By John Figwood Esq. Dublin: G. Herbert 1865. Wrappers.

ALL IN THE DARK. Bentley 1866. 2 vols. Claret cloth.

THE TENANTS OF MALORY. Tinsley 1867. 3 vols. Scarlet cloth.

THE BEAUTIFUL POEM OF SHAMUS O'BRIEN. (Anonymous). Manchester: John Heywood 1867. Orange wrappers.

A LOST NAME. Bentley 1868. 3 vols. Scarlet cloth. Secondary binding: red-brown cloth without imprint.

HAUNTED LIVES. Tinsley 1868. 3 vols. Dark green cloth.

THE WYVERN MYSTERY. Tinsley 1869. 3 vols. Dark maroon cloth.

CHECKMATE.   Hurst & Blackett 1871. 3 vols. Green cloth. 16pp Catalogue dated January 1871.

THE ROSE AND THE KEY.   Chapman & Hall 1871. 3 vols. Brown cloth.

CHRONICLES OF GOLDEN FRIARS.   Bentley 1871. 3 vols. Violet cloth. Illustrated Edition: A CHRONICLE OF GOLDEN FRIARS. Downey & Co. 1896. Blue cloth.

IN A GLASS DARKLY.   Bentley 1872. 3 vols. Claret cloth.

WILLING TO DIE.   Hurst & Blackett 1873. 3 vols. Brown cloth.

MORLEY COURT.   Chapman & Hall 1873.
   A slightly revised version of THE COCK AND ANCHOR.

THE PURCELL PAPERS.   Bentley 1880. 3 vols. Blue cloth, bevelled boards (and three variants).

THE WATCHER, AND OTHER WEIRD STORIES.   Downey (1894). White-flecked grey linen, blocked in black and silver. Frontis., pictorial title, & illustrations in the text by Brinsley Le Fanu.
   A collection of previously published stories.

THE EVIL GUEST.   Downey (1895). Dark green cloth blocked in black & gold. Frontis., pictorial title, & illustrations in the text.
   A previously published story, with some minor changes.

THE POEMS OF JOSEPH SHERIDAN LE FANU.   Downey & Co. 1896. Olive green cloth, blocked and lettered in gold on front and spine, with publisher's blind monogram on the back. Remaindered in a plainer binding.

MADAM CROWL'S GHOST.   Bell 1923.
   A story from CHRONICLES OF GOLDEN FRIARS.

A STRANGE ADVENTURE IN THE LIFE OF MISS MAURA MILDMAY.   Home & Van Thal 1947.

BORRHOMEO THE ASTROLOGER.   Edinburgh: Tragara Press 1985. Wrappers.

LEWIS, C. S. (1898–1963)

By far the rarest and most valuable of Lewis's first editions are the two early volumes of pseudonymous poetry (the first two items in the list below). The three science fiction novels (Ransom Trilogy) are scarce and cannot normally be had for less than £50 apiece. The seven volumes of the Narnia stories, though published only in the 1950s, are not easy to obtain in fine condition, and their prices are rising rapidly. The first in the series – THE LION, THE WITCH AND THE WARDROBE – is already around £100. The following checklist gives only his rarest and most popular publications.

SPIRITS IN BONDAGE. By Clive Hamilton (pseud.). Heinemann 1919.

DYMER. By Clive Hamilton (pseud.). Dent 1926. Blue patterned cloth gilt.

THE PILGRIM'S REGRESS. Dent 1933.

THE ALLEGORY OF LOVE. O.U.P. 1936. U.S.: O.U.P 1936.

OUT OF THE SILENT PLANET. Bodley Head 1938. U.S.: Macmillan 1943.

REHABILITATIONS. O.U.P. 1939.

THE PERSONAL HERESY. By Lewis & Tillyard. O.U.P. 1939.

A PREFACE TO 'PARADISE LOST'. O.U.P. 1942.

THE SCREWTAPE LETTERS. Bles 1942. U.S.: Saunders 1942.

PERELANDRA. Bodley Head 1943. U.S.: Macmillan 1944.

THAT HIDEOUS STRENGTH. Bodley Head 1945. U.S.: Macmillan 1946.

THE LION, THE WITCH AND THE WARDROBE. Bles 1950. U.S.: Macmillan 1950.

PRINCE CASPIAN. Bles 1951. U.S.: Macmillan 1951.

THE VOYAGE OF THE DAWN TREADER. Bles 1952. U.S.: Macmillan 1952.

THE SILVER CHAIR. Bles 1953. U.S.: Macmillan 1953..

THE HORSE AND HIS BOY. Bles 1954. U.S.: Macmillan 1954.

THE MAGICIAN'S NEPHEW. Bles 1955. U.S.: Macmillan 1955.

THE LAST BATTLE. Bles 1956. U.S.: Macmillan 1956.

A GRIEF OBSERVED. By N. W. Clerk (pseud). Faber 1961. U.S.: Seabury 1963.

LEWIS, Matthew Gregory (1775–1818)

THE MONK: a Romance. (anonymous). Printed for J. Bell . . . 1796. 3 vols. 12mo.

LEWIS, Wyndham (1882–1957)

His earliest publications were stories contributed to The English Review, 1909. He was founder and editor of the Vorticist movement journal BLAST. Of this, there were only two issues, published by John Lane in 1914 and 1915. There were also two other Lewis journals – THE TYRO, 2 issues by The Egoist Press 1921 & 1922; and THE ENEMY, 3 volumes by The Arthur Press, the first two in 1927, the third in 1929. (Of Volume 2, there were also 150 signed by Lewis). The Arthur Press, be it noted, was Lewis's own imprint, used for the publication of THE ENEMY, and also for the first edition of THE APES OF GOD, and the pamphlet SATIRE AND FICTION. The three journals were all reprinted by Frank Cass during 1968 and 1970.

TIMON OF ATHENS. Benmar & Co. (1913). A portfolio of 16 loose plates.

THE IDEAL GIANT. Privately Printed for the London Office of the Little Review (1917). Cloth spine, illustrated boards. Wire-stitched and strung on silk thread in a portfolio.

TARR. First appeared in The Egoist magazine, April 1916 to November 1917. Book: New York: Knopf 1918 (June). Red cloth. Later, blue cloth. U.K.: The Egoist Press 1918 (July). 1000 copies.

THE CALIPH'S DESIGN. The Egoist Press 1919. Boards. No d/w.

FIFTEEN DRAWINGS. The Ovid Press 1920.

THE ART OF BEING RULED. Chatto & Windus 1926.

THE LION AND THE FOX. Grant Richards 1927.

TIME AND WESTERN MAN. Chatto & Windus 1927.

THE WILD BODY.   Chatto & Windus 1927. Orange or red cloth, d/w. Also, 85 signed in quarter cloth, boards & d/w.

THE CHILDERMASS: SECTION 1.   Chatto & Windus 1928. Also, 231 signed.

PALEFACE.   Chatto & Windus 1929.

THE APES OF GOD.   The Arthur Press 1930. Limited to 750 signed. Trade Edition: Nash & Grayson 1931.

HITLER.   Chatto & Windus 1931.

THE DIABOLICAL PRINCIPLE AND THE DITHYRAMBIC SPECTATOR.   Chatto & Windus 1931. First binding: gold-stamped cloth.

DOOM OF YOUTH.   New York: Robert McBride 1932. U.K.: Chatto & Windus 1932.

FILIBUSTERS IN BARBARY.   Grayson 1932.

ENEMY OF THE STARS.   Harmsworth 1932.

SNOOTY BARONET.   Cassell 1932.

THIRTY PERSONALITIES AND A SELF-PORTRAIT.   Harmsworth 1932. Portfolio containing 31 loose plates. There were 200 signed sets only.

THE OLD GANG AND THE NEW GANG.   Harmsworth 1933.

ONE WAY SONG.   Faber 1933. Also, 40 signed copies.
   His only volume of poetry.

MEN WITHOUT ART.   Cassell 1934.

LEFT WINGS OVER EUROPE.   Cape 1936.

COUNT YOUR DEAD: THEY ARE ALIVE!   Lovat Dickson 1937. Yellow cloth.

THE REVENGE FOR LOVE.   Cassell 1937.

BLASTING AND BOMBADIERING.   Eyre & Spottiswoode 1937. (2000 copies). Orange cloth, stamped in black.

THE MYSTERIOUS MR BULL.   Robert Hale 1938.

THE JEWS, ARE THEY HUMAN? Allen & Unwin 1939.

WYNDHAM LEWIS THE ARTIST, FROM 'BLAST' TO BURLINGTON HOUSE. Laidlaw & Laidlaw 1939.

THE HITLER CULT. Dent 1939.

AMERICA, I PRESUME. New York: Howell & Soskin 1940.

ANGLOSAXONY: A LEAGUE THAT WORKS. Canada: Ryerson 1941.

THE VULGAR STREAK. Robert Hale 1941.

AMERICA AND COSMIC MAN. Nicholson & Watson 1948. U.S.: Doubleday 1949.

RUDE ASSIGNMENT. Hutchinson 1950 (2500 copies).

ROTTING HILL. Methuen 1951.

THE WRITER AND THE ABSOLUTE. Methuen 1952.

SELF CONDEMNED. Methuen 1954.

THE DEMON OF PROGRESS IN THE ARTS. Methuen 1954.

THE HUMAN AGE. Methuen 1955.

THE RED PRIEST. Methuen 1963.

THE LETTERS. Metheun 1963.

A SOLDIER OF HUMOUR AND SELECTED WRITINGS. New York: New American Library 1966. Wrappers.

WYNDHAM LEWIS: AN ANTHOLOGY OF HIS PROSE. Methuen 1969.

WYNDHAM LEWIS ON ART. Thames & Hudson 1969.

UNLUCKY FOR PRINGLE. Unpublished and Other Stories. Vision Press 1973.

THE ROARING QUEEN. Secker & Warburg 1973. Also, 130 signed by Mrs Wyndham Lewis.

ENEMY SALVOES: SELECTED LITERARY CRITICISM. Vision Press 1976.

THE CODE OF A HERDSMAN. Wyndham Lewis Society 1977. Pamphlet.

IMAGINARY LETTERS. Wyndham Lewis Society 1977. Pamphlet.

MRS DUKES' MILLIONS. Toronto, Canada: The Coach House Press 1977.

LONDON, Jack (1876–1916)

London's early success ensured that his works were mostly published in large numbers, and consequently none are very rare. His masterpiece THE CALL OF THE WILD, without the dust jacket, gets around $500 dollars. A few of his works get more than that. His plays are particularly hard to find. However, for the earlier works, jackets are at a premium, and their presence makes a huge difference. Broadly, the publications before 1904 are the scarcest and most valuable. The first issue of THE SEA WOLF is particularly scarce and particularly valuable ($2000–$3000). THE CRUISE OF THE DAZZLER seems difficult to find in very good condition. The U.K. editions are all worth a lot less than the U.S. firsts.

Below are his earliest and best known works.

THE SON OF THE WOLF. New York: Houghton Mifflin 1900. There were three trial bindings before it was issued in grey cloth stamped in silver. The first issue does not have a blank leaf after page (252). U.K.: A. P. Watt & Son (1900).
His first book.

THE GOD OF HIS FATHERS & OTHER STORIES. New York: McClure, Philips 1901.

CHILDREN OF THE FROST. New York & London: Macmillan 1902.

A DAUGHTER OF THE SNOWS. Philadelphia: Lippincott 1902 (October). U.K.: Isbister 1904.

THE CRUISE OF THE DAZZLER. New York: Century Co. 1902 (October). U.K.: Hodder & Stoughton 1906.

THE KEMPTON-WACE LETTERS. (By London & Anna Strunsky). New York & London: Macmillan 1903. Green cloth.

THE CALL OF THE WILD.   New York & London: Macmillan 1903 (July).

THE PEOPLE OF THE ABYSS.   New York & London: Macmillan 1903 (October).

THE SEA-WOLF.   New York: Macmillan 1904. Integral title-page (later a cancel) with copyright notices on verso, dated 1904 only (later dated 1903 and 1904). U.K.: Macmillan 1904.

THE FAITH OF MEN AND OTHER STORIES.   New York & London: Macmillan 1904.

WHITE FANG.   New York: Macmillan 1906 (October). The first issue has an integral title-page, the second issue has the title-page tipped in. U.K.: Macmillan 1906.

REVOLUTION AND OTHER ESSAYS.   New York: Macmillan 1910 (March). Maroon cloth. 'The Macmillan Company' on the spine. Adverts at end. Variant binding: brown cloth; on spine 'Macmillan'; no adverts.

THE JACKET.   Mills & Boon 1915. The U.K. edition of THE STAR ROVER.

ISLAND TALES.   Mills & Boon 1920. The U.K. edition of ON THE MAKALOA MAT.

LONGFELLOW, Henry Wadsworth. (1807–1882)

Longfellow's earliest publications were text books and language books (he was a teacher of modern languages). From about the 1840s, however, he became a popular poet in both America and England, eventually becoming perhaps the most popular poet of the age, apart from Tennyson. 15,000 copies of MILES STANDISH were sold on the first day of publication. Today, he is best known (perhaps only known) as the author of the ever-popular 'Hiawatha'.

ELEMENTS OF FRENCH GRAMMAR.   By M. Lhomond. Translated . . . By an Instructer. Portland: Colman / Brunswick: Griffin's Press 1830. Cloth. 5 errata slips, the earliest printing of these in smaller type.

FRENCH EXERCISES . . .   By M. Lhomond . . . By an Instructer. Portland: Colman / Brunswick: Griffin's Press 1830. Brown cloth. 2 Errata slips. (Also issued bound with the Grammar).

MANUEL DE PROVERBS DRAMATIQUES.   Portland: Colman / Brunswick: Griffin's Press 1830. Cloth. First issue has paper label on cover reading 'Tome I' (but no other volume was issued) and 'Diette' in the half-title (and other points).

NOVELAS ESPANOLAS . . .   Brunswick: Griffin / Portland: Colman 1830. Cloth spine, marbled boards. Second & Later issues have pp. 9–10 pasted in on stub.

LE MINISTRE DE WAKEFIELD . . .   Par M. Hennequin. Boston: Gray et Brown 1831. Brown boards, paper label.

SYLLABUS DE LA GRAMMAIRE ITALIENNE.   Boston: Gray et Brown 1832. Red cloth, also black cloth. Earliest issue has 'La traite' for 'Le traite' in the 'advertisement' (p. iii, line 13). Later, the reprinted leaf pasted in on stub.

OUTRE-MER . . . NO. I.   Boston: Hilliard, Gray 1833. Marbled wrappers. First issue does not have quote from Mandeville on cover.

OUTRE-MER . . . NO. II.   Boston: Lilly, Wait 1834. Grey wrappers.

VOICES OF THE NIGHT.   Cambridge: John Owen 1839. First Issue: p. 78, line 10 reads 'His, Hector's Arm . . .'.

HYPERION.   New York: Colman 1839. 2 vols. Brown boards, also cloth.

BALLADS AND OTHER POEMS.   Cambridge: John Owen 1842. Yellow boards. First issue: small 't' in 'teacher', p. 88, last line, and quotation marks at end of first line, page 34.

POEMS ON SLAVERY.   Cambridge: John Owen 1842. Wrappers. No blank fly-leaves (2nd edition has 2 at front and 2 at end).

THE SPANISH STUDENT.   Cambridge: John Owen 1843. Boards, paper label.

THE POETS AND POETRY OF EUROPE.   Philadelphia: Carey & Hart 1845. Cloth, also morocco. Imprint of Metcalf & Company on p.[iv].

POEMS.   Illus Huntington. Philadelphia: Carey & Hart 1845. Cloth, also morocco.

THE BELFRY OF BRUGES.   Cambridge: John Owen 1846. Wrappers. First issue: dated 1845 on front wrapper.

EVANGELINE.   Boston: Ticknor 1847. Brown boards (yellow boards, later). First issue: on p. 61, line 1 – the 'ng' of long is dropped or missing.

KAVANAGH. Boston: Ticknor, etc. 1849. Brown cloth. First Issue: the word 'end' is not at bottom of p. 188, and last line of p. 173 has 'At the sight of him' (later 'to Cecilia').

THE SEASIDE AND THE FIRESIDE. Boston: Ticknor, etc. 1850. Brown cloth, also boards. First issue: publisher's list dated 'October 1st, 1849'.

THE SONG OF HIAWATHA. Boston: Ticknor, etc. 1855. Brown cloth, later issues red cloth. First Issue, misprints: p. 96, 'dove' for 'dive'; p. 32, line 11 reads 'In the Moon . . . etc.'.

THE COURTSHIP OF MILES STANDISH. London: W. Kent 1858. Wrappers. Also issued in cloth (the text of the wrappered edition 'leaded-out' and thus 100 pages longer). U.S.: Boston: Ticknor & Fields 1858. Brown cloth, also purple cloth.
    The London edition came out about a month before the Boston edition.

TALES OF A WAYSIDE INN. Boston: Ticknor & Fields 1863. Cloth. First issue: imprint at bottom of p. 225.

NOEL. Privately Printed. Cambridge: 1864. Pamphlet. 50 copies.

HOUSEHOLD POEMS. Boston: Ticknor & Fields 1865. Blue wrappers, also cloth.

FLOWER-DE-LUCE. Boston: Ticknor & Fields 1867. Cloth.

THE NEW ENGLAND TRAGEDIES. Privately Printed 1868. Half green morocco. 10 copies. Published Edition: Boston: Ticknor & Fields 1868. Cloth.

FOR THE COMPANION, MAIDEN AND WEATHERCOCK. 12mo broadside. No place or date (c. 1870).

THE DIVINE TRAGEDY. Boston: Osgood 1871. Cloth. Also (few days later) a large-paper edition.

FAIR FOR OUR DUMB ANIMALS. Boston: 1871. Pamphlet.

EXCELSIOR. New York: Excelsior Life 1872. Cloth.

THREE BOOKS OF SONGS. Boston: Osgood 1872. Cloth.

CHRISTUS. Boston: Osgood 1872. 3 vols. Cloth.

AFTERMATH. Boston: Osgood 1873. Cloth.

THE HANGING OF THE CRANE. Boston: Osgood 1874. Pamphlet

(Copyright issue, only a few copies known). Regular Edition of 1875 was preceded by the U.K. Edition: Routledge 1874.

THE MASQUE OF PANDORA.   Boston: Osgood 1875. Cloth.

KERAMOS AND OTHER POEMS.   Boston: Houghton, Osgood 1878. 12mo, cloth.

THE EARLY POEMS.   London: Pickering 1878. Cloth.

BAYARD TAYLOR.   [Cambridge: 1879]. 12mo. 2 leaves.

FROM MY ARM-CHAIR.   1879. 12mo. 2 leaves.

ULTIMA THULE.   Boston: Houghton, Mifflin 1880. Cloth.

MICHAEL ANGELO.   Boston: Houghton, Mifflin 1884.

LOWRY, Malcolm (1909–1957)

Lowry only came into vogue with collectors some little while after his death. By then, his first two books had begun to disappear. And now, in the 1990s, they are rather scarce in the dust wrappers. The first, being significantly scarcer than the second, has a current value in the region of £3000. The second gets more like £500.

ULTRAMARINE.   Cape (1933). 1500 copies (about half were pulped). Revised Ed.: Philadelphia: Lippincott 1962; London: Cape 1963.

UNDER THE VOLCANO.   New York: Reynal & Hitchcock 1947. Grey cloth. U.K.: Cape 1947.

HEAR US O LORD FROM HEAVEN THY DWELLING PLACE.   Philadelphia: Lippincott 1961. U.K.: Cape 1962.

LETTERS BETWEEN MALCOLM LOWRY AND JONATHAN CAPE ABOUT 'UNDER THE VOLCANO'.   Cape 1962.

SELECTED POEMS.   San Francisco: City Lights 1962.

LUNAR CAUSTIC.   Appeared in Paris Review 29, Winter/Spring 1963. Wrappers. Book: New York: Grossman 1968. U.K.: Cape 1968.

SELECTED LETTERS.   Philadelphia: Lippincott 1965: U.K.: Cape 1967.

DARK AS THE GRAVE WHEREIN MY FRIEND IS LAID. New York:
New American Library 1968. U.K.: Cape 1969.

OCTOBER FERRY TO GABRIOLA. New York: World 1970. U.K.: Cape
1971.

PSALMS AND SONGS. New York: New American Library 1975.

LYTTON, Sir Edward Bulwer (1803–1873)

Some of his many publications were issued anonymously. He also used the
pseudonym Owen Meredith. Perhaps his best known work is:

THE LAST DAYS OF POMPEII. (anon). Bentley 1834. 3 vols. Errata slips
in vols II & III.
The first 729 copies were sold unbound in quires. Issued thereafter in
publisher's binding.

M

MACDIARMID, Hugh (C. M. Grieve 1892–1978)

His adopted pseudonym appears variously as M'Diarmid, Mc'Diarmid, and
MacDiarmid. Some of his works were published under his real name.

ANNALS OF THE FIVE SENSES. Montrose: Published by the Author
1923. New Edition: Edinburgh: Porpoise Press 1930.

SANGSCHAW. Edinburgh: Blackwood 1925.
His first volume of verse.

PENNY WHEEP. Edinburgh: Blackwood 1926. Blue cloth. Also boards.

A DRUNK MAN LOOKS AT THE THISTLE. Edinburgh: Blackwood
1926.

CONTEMPORARY SCOTTISH STUDIES. L. Parsons 1926.

THE PRESENT CONDITION OF SCOTTISH ARTS AND AFFAIRS. Pamphlet. No publisher (P.E.N. Club) or date (1927?).

THE PRESENT POSITION OF SCOTTISH MUSIC. Montrose: Published by the Author. 1927. Pamphlet.

THE LUCKY BAG. Edinburgh: Porpoise Press 1927.

ALBYN, OR SCOTLAND AND THE FUTURE. K. Paul 1927.

THE SCOTTISH ASSOCIATION OF APRIL FOOLS. Aberdeen U.P. 1928. Pamphlet.

TO CIRCUMJACK CENCRASTUS. Edinburgh: Blackwood 1930. Wrappers. Also cloth.

FIRST HYMN TO LENIN AND OTHER POEMS. Unicorn Press 1931.

SECOND HYMN TO LENIN. Thakeham: Valda Trevlyn (1932). Pamphlet.

TARRAS. Edinburgh: Free Man 1932. Pamphlet.

SCOTS UNBOUND AND OTHER POEMS. Stirling: Mackay 1932.

FIVE BITS OF MILLER. London: Published by the Author. 1934. Pamphlet.

STONY LIMITS AND OTHER POEMS. Gollancz 1934.

SELECTED POEMS. Macmillan 1934. Glasgow: W. Maclellan (1944).

AT THE SIGN OF THE THISTLE. S. Nott (1934).

SCOTTISH SCENE. By MacDiarmid & Gibbon. Jarrolds 1934.

SCOTLAND IN 1980. Montrose: Published by the Author (1935).

SECOND HYMN TO LENIN AND OTHER POEMS. Nott 1935.

SCOTTISH ECCENTRICS. Routledge 1936.

CHARLES DOUGHTY AND THE NEED FOR HEROIC POETRY. (St Andrews 1936) Pamphlet.

DIREADH. (Dunfermline: Voice of Scotland 1938). Pamphlet.

THE ISLANDS OF SCOTLAND. Batsford 1939.

LUCKY POET.   Methuen 1943.

CORNISH HEROIC SONG FOR VALDA TREVLYN.   Glasgow: Caledonian Press (1943). Pamphlet.

FIDELITY IN SMALL THINGS.   Pamphlet. No publisher (J. W. Sault) or date.

POEMS OF THE EAST-WEST SYNTHESIS.   Glasgow: Caledonian Press 1946. Pamphlet.

SPEAKING FOR SCOTLAND.   Baltimore: Contemporary Poetry 1946.

A KIST OF WHISTLES.   Glasgow: Maclellan (1947).

CUNNINGHAME GRAHAM.   Glasgow: Caledonian Press (1952).

IN MEMORIUM JAMES JOYCE.   Glasgow: Maclellan 1955.

FRANCIS GEORGE SCOTT.   Edinburgh: M. Macdonald 1955.

STONY LIMITS & SCOTS UNBOUND & OTHER POEMS.   Edinburgh: Castle Wynd Printers 1956.

THREE HYMNS TO LENIN.   Edinburgh: Castle Wynd Printers 1957.

THE BATTLE CONTINUES.   Edinburgh: Castle Wynd Printers 1957.

BURNS TODAY AND TOMORROW.   Edinburgh: Castle Wynd Printers 1959.

THE KIND OF POETRY I WANT.   Edinburgh: K. D. Duval 1961.

DAVID HUME.   Edinburgh: Paperback Bookshop (1962). Pamphlet.

THE MAN OF (ALMOST) INDEPENDENT MIND.   Edinburgh: Giles Gordon 1962. Pamphlet.

BRACKEN HILLS IN AUTUMN.   Edinburgh: C. H. Hamilton 1962. Pamphlet.

THE UGLY BIRDS WITHOUT WINGS.   Edinburgh: Allan Donaldson 1962. Pamphlet.

COLLECTED POEMS.   New York: Macmillan / Edinburgh: Oliver & Boyd 1962.

MACDONALD, George (1824–1905)

Interest in MacDonald has been growing apace for some time now, and a recent bibliography by Ben Shaberman was greatly welcomed by collectors. The books for children have long been favourites, but interest has only recently spread to the rather melodramatic novels and the poetry. As a whole, his books are not easy to find in original bindings and in good condition. But the first four are particularly difficult. Two early volumes of translation are essential to the specialist and very rare. The first, privately published in 1851, was TWELVE OF THE SPIRITUAL SONGS OF NOVALIS. The second was EXOTICS, published by Strahan in the same year.

WITHIN AND WITHOUT: a Dramatic Poem. Longman 1855. Olive-brown cloth, framed in blind on front and back, gold lettering on spine. 24pp Publishers' catalogue dated March 1856 at end.

POEMS. Longman 1857.

PHANTASTES; a Faerie Romance. Smith, Elder 1858. Green cloth blocked in gold on the spine. The Second edition was the First Illustrated: Chatto & Windus 1894. Blue cloth, decoratively blocked in gold on the front and the spine. Illustrations by John Bell.
    The author's son Greville objected to the illustrations. He is reputed to have bought up all the copies he could obtain and to have destroyed them. Both the first edition and the illustrated second edition are rare, especially in fine condition.

DAVID ELGINBROD. Hurst & Blackett 1863. 3 vols. Red cloth. U.S.: Boston: Loring (1863). Lavender cloth.
    His rare first novel, currently valued at £500–£600

ADELA CATHCART. Hurst & Blackett 1864. 3 vols.

THE PORTENT. Smith, Elder 1864.

ALEC FORBES OF HOWGLEN. Hurst & Blackett 1865. 3 vols.

DEALINGS WITH THE FAIRIES. Strahan 1867. Illustrations by Arthur Hughes. Small square 8vo. Blue or green cloth with elaborate decoration in gold and black.

THE DISCIPLE AND OTHER POEMS. Strahan 1867.

ANNALS OF A QUIET NEIGHBOURHOOD. Hurst & Blackett 1867. 3 vols.

UNSPOKEN SERMONS. Strahan 1867; Second Series: Longmans 1885; Third Series: Longmans 1889.

GUILD COURT. Hurst & Blackett 1868. 3 vols.

ROBERT FALCONER. Hurst & Blackett 1868. 3 vols.

THE SEABOARD PARISH. Tinsley 1868. 3 vols.

ENGLAND'S ANTIPHON. Macmillan (1868).

THE MIRACLES OF OUR LORD. Strahan 1870.

AT THE BACK OF THE NORTH WIND. Strahan 1871. With 76 wood-engraved illustrations in the text, by Arthur Hughes. There are variant bindings. The traditional first binding is a bright blue cloth with elaborate gold-blocking. On the front is a picture of Nanny looking through a window in the moon, and a decorative rustic frame (three sided) in gold, with another frame in black. There is a similar binding, less elaborately blocked (lacking the gold rustic frame, for example). And another in magenta cloth and yet another in green cloth. Bindings which bear the name of Daldy. Isbister & Co. on the spine are later, the firm having only come into existence during 1874. U.S.: George Routledge, n.d. Decorative cloth binding similar to the U.K. edition.

RANALD BANNERMAN'S BOYHOOD. Strahan 1871. Illustrated by Arthur Hughes. Orange-red cloth, blocked in black and gold.

WORKS OF FANCY AND IMAGINATION. Strahan 1871. 10 vols. 16mo. Green cloth.

THE PRINCESS AND THE GOBLIN. Strahan 1872. Illustrated with wood-engravings in the text by Arthur Hughes. Brown cloth blocked in gold and black – Princess surrounded by goblins, on the front; Princess at foot of stairs, on the spine. Also known in green cloth.

WILFRED CUMBERMEDE. Hurst & Blackett 1872. 3 vols.

THE VICAR'S DAUGHTER. Tinsley 1872. 3 vols.

GUTTA PERCHA WILLIE. King 1873. Blue cloth.

THE WISE WOMAN. Strahan 1875. Blue cloth.

MALCOLM. King 1875. 3 vols.

ST GEORGE AND ST MICHAEL. King 1876. 3 vols.

THOMAS WINGFOLD. Hurst & Blackett 1876. 3 vols.

THE MARQUIS OF LOSSIE. Hurst & Blackett 1877. 3 vols.

PAUL FABER.   Hurst & Blackett 1879. 3 vols.

SIR GIBBIE.   Hurst & Blackett 1879. 3 vols.

A BOOK OF STRIFE.   Privately Printed 1880. New Edition: Longman 1889. Narrow 12mo. Red cloth.

MARY MARSTON.   Sampson, Low 1881. 3 vols.

WARLOCK O'GLEN WARLOCK.   Boston: Lothrop 1881.

ORTS.   Sampson Low 1882.

CASTLE WARLOCK.   Sampson, Low 1882. 3 vols.
    The U.K. Edition of WARLOCK O'GLEN WARLOCK.

WEIGHED AND WANTING.   Sampson, Low 1882. 3 vols.

THE GIFTS OF THE CHILD CHRIST.   Sampson Low 1882. 2 vols.

A THREEFOLD CORD: Poems by Three Friends.   Edited by George MacDonald. Privately Printed (1883).
    The authors were MacDonald, his brother, & G. E. Matheson.

THE PRINCESS AND THE CURDIE.   Chatto & Windus 1883. Illustrated with a frontispiece and 10 lithographed plates by James Allen. Pale green cloth, blocked in red, brown & gold.

DONAL GRANT.   Kegan Paul 1883. 3 vols. Scarlet cloth.

THE TRAGEDIE OF HAMLET . . . a study with the text . . . Longmans 1885.

WHAT'S MINE'S MINE.   Kegan Paul 1886. 3 vols.

CROSS PURPOSE AND THE SHADOWS.   Blackie 1886.

HOME AGAIN.   Kegan Paul 1887.

THE ELECT LADY.   Kegan Paul 1888. Scarlet cloth, bevelled edges. Frontispiece.

THERE AND BACK.   Kegan Paul 1891. 3 vols.

A ROUGH SHAKING.   Blackie 1891. Brown or red cloth.

THE FLIGHT OF THE SHADOW.   Kegan Paul 1891.

THE HOPE OF THE GOSPEL. Ward, Lock 1892.

HEATHER AND SNOW. Chatto & Windus 1893. 2 vols.

THE LIGHT PRINCESS AND OTHER FAIRY TALES. New York: Putnam (1893).

A DISH OF ORTS. Sampson Low 1893.
  An enlarged edition of ORTS.

POETICAL WORKS. Chatto & Windus 1893. 2 vols.

LILITH. Chatto & Windus 1895. Gold-lettered black cloth.

SALTED WITH FIRE. Hurst & Blackett 1897.

FAR ABOVE RUBIES. New York: Dodd, Mead 1899.

FAIRY TALES. Fifield 1904. Issued in 5 parts and also in one volume.

MACHEN, Arthur (1863–1947)

Several of Machen's works are rare, but the rarest of all is a poem entitled ELEUSINIA, issued in wrappers. He had 100 copies printed c.1880 (when he was still in his teens) but very few copies appear to have survived (in fact, only two copies are recorded). Machen was fashionable during the 1920s, and again briefly during the 1960s, but he is now a minor cult figure with a small but very keen band of followers. Some of his earliest works were translations. These are not included in the list below. Briefly, they are THE HEPTAMERON (1886), THE FORTUNATE LOVERS (1887), FANTASTIC TALES (1890), MEMOIRS OF CASANOVA (1894).

THE ANATOMY OF TOBACCO. By Leolinus Siluriensis (pseud). George Redway 1884. Parchment boards.
  Rare, and worth perhaps £150.

THE CHRONICLES OF CLEMENDY. Carbonnek 1888. Privately Printed. 250 copies.

THE GREAT GOD PAN AND THE INMOST LIGHT. John Lane 1894. Cloth, with Beardsley decoration.

THE THREE IMPOSTORS. John Lane 1895.

HIEROGLYPHICS. Grant Richards 1902.

DR. STIGGINS.   Griffiths 1906.

THE HOUSE OF SOULS.   Grant Richards 1906.

THE HILL OF DREAMS.   Grant Richards 1907. Red buckram, with 'E. Grant Richards' at foot of spine. There were also 150 signed.

THE BOWMEN AND OTHER LEGENDS OF THE WAR.   Simpkin, Marshall 1915. Sm.8vo. Illustrated boards.
   The second edition, same year, has extra stories and a silhouette of the author as frontispiece.

THE GREAT RETURN.   Faith Press 1915.

THE TERROR.   Duckworth 1917.

WAR AND THE CHRISTIAN FAITH.   Skeffington 1918.

THE SECRET GLORY.   Secker 1922.

FAR OFF THINGS.   Secker 1922.

THINGS NEAR AND FAR.   Secker (1923). Also, 100 Large Paper copies, signed. Boards, paper label.

THE SHINING PYRAMID.   Chicago: Covici-McGee 1923. Black cloth, d/w. Only 875 copies were printed.
   Not published in London until 1925

STRANGE ROADS & WITH THE GODS IN SPRING.   Classics Press 1923.

DOG AND DUCK.   New York: Knopf 1924. U.K.: Cape 1924.

THE LONDON ADVENTURE.   Secker 1924.

THE GLORIOUS MYSTERY.   Chicago: Covici-McGee 1924.

PRECIOUS BALMS.   Spurr & Swift 1924.

ORNAMENTS IN JADE.   New York: Knopf 1924. Limited to 1000 copies, all signed by the author.

THE SHINING PYRAMID.   Secker 1925.

THE CANNING WONDER.   Chatto 1925.

DREADS AND DROLLS. Secker 1926.

NOTES AND QUERIES. Spurr & Swift 1926.

THE GREEN ROUND. Benn 1933.

THE COSY ROOM AND OTHER STORIES. Rich & Cowan 1936.

THE CHILDREN OF THE POOL AND OTHER STORIES. Hutchinson 1936.

HOLY TERRORS. Penguin 1946. Wrappers.

TALES OF HORROR AND THE SUPERNATURAL. New York: Knopf 1948. U.K.: Richards Press 1949.

MACNEICE, Louis (1907–1963)

BLIND FIREWORKS; poems. Gollancz 1929. First binding: Cream canvas boards, d/w.
His first book

ROUNDABOUT WAY. By Louis Malone (pseud). Putnam 1932. Cloth, d/w.
His second book and his only novel.

MANSFIELD, Katherine (1888–1923)

Writers whose forte is the short story, never become really big names in the world of literature. But collectors, possibly influenced by her connections with D. H. Lawrence, have been keen on Mansfield's work pretty well from the start. Today, she remains as popular as ever, and her scarcest works are not cheap. From a collector's point of view, she is an attractive proposition in that she produced a small body of work – which holds out the promise of a completed collection within a short lifetime. And at the same time, her publications have some bibliographical interest and present some challenges.

Her first appearances in print were in the periodical New Age, to which she contributed a number of stories during 1910.

THE OPEN WINDOW. Locke, Ellis. October 1910-September 1911. 2 vols. White cloth spines, blue paper boards.
Her contribution to this anthology (her first appearance in a book) was 'A Fairy Story' by 'Katherina Mansfield'. The book in that collective form has

a current value of about £200, but the separate issue for December 1910 (in which the story appears) in stiff wrappers turns up occasionally and tends to be priced at £50 or so.

IN A GERMAN PENSION.   Stephen Swift 1911 (December). Green cloth, d/w. Second Edition: Constable (1926). U.S.: Knopf 1926.
A fine copy in a fine d/w would probably be priced in the region of £1000.

PRELUDE.   Hogarth Press 1918. Wrappers – some copies have a design by J. D. Fergusson on the front and the back, some have a design only on the front, and some do not have the design at all.
The variant states of the wrappers do not affect the value greatly – all are in the area of £1000.

JE NE PARLE PAS FRANCAIS.   Hampstead: The Heron Press 1919. Wrappers. About 100 copies.
The Heron Press was the imprint of the author and her husband John Middleton Murry.

BLISS AND OTHER STORIES.   Constable (1920). Red cloth. Page 13 numbered '3'.

THE GARDEN PARTY AND OTHER STORIES.   Constable (1922). Misprint 'sposition' on last line of p. 103. Blue cloth, lettered in blue. There were only 25 copies thus. Later copies have the lettering in ochre. New Edition (different contents): Printed in Italy at Verona Press and published in London dated 1939, though actually published in 1947.

THE DOVES' NEST AND OTHER STORIES.   Constable (1923). Blue-grey, cloth, lettered on the spine in blue. The second issue has 'First published June, 1923' on the verso title.

POEMS.   Constable 1923. U.S.: Knopf 1924. Enlarged Edition: Constable 1930.

SOMETHING CHILDISH AND OTHER STORIES.   Constable 1924. Grey cloth. The second issue has 'First published, 1924' on the verso title.

THE LITTLE GIRL AND OTHER STORIES.   New York: Knopf 1924.
The U.S. edition of SOMETHING CHILDISH . . .

THE JOURNAL.   Constable 1927. Revised & Enlarged Edition: Constable 1954.

THE LETTERS.   Constable 1928. 2 vols.

THE ALOE.   Constable 1930. U.S.: Knopf 1930.

Revised version of PRELUDE.

NOVELS AND NOVELISTS.   Constable 1930.

TO STANISLAW WYSPIANSKI.   Privately Printed 1938. 100 copies.

THE SCRAPBOOK.   Constable 1939.

THE COLLECTED STORIES.   Constable 1946.

LETTERS TO JOHN MIDDLETON MURRY   1913–1922. Constable 1951.

LETTERS AND JOURNALS.   Allen Lane 1977.

THE UREWERA NOTEBOOK.   O.U.P. 1978.

THE COLLECTED LETTERS.   O.U.P. 1984 & 1987. 2 vols.

THE CRITICAL WRITINGS.   Macmillan 1986.

MARRYAT, Captain F. (1792–1848)

His first novel was THE NAVAL OFFICER, Colburn 1829, in 3 vols. His three best-known novels are:

MR MIDSHIPMAN EASY.   (by the author of 'Japhet in Search of a Father', 'Peter Simple', 'Jacob Faithful', etc.). Saunders & Otley 1836. 3 vols. Half-cloth boards, labels.

MASTERMAN READY,   or the Wreck of the Pacific. Written for Young People. Longman etc. 1841 (vol I) & 1842 (vols II & III). 3 vols. Sm. 8vo. Vol I in navy blue cloth, vols II & III in dark slate cloth, all three vols with pictorial blind blocking on front and back, and gold lettered on the spine. The first issue of volume I does not have 'VOL. I' on the spine. Some copies have publishers catalogue at end of volume one.

CHILDREN OF THE NEW FOREST.   H. Hurst n.d. (1847). 2 vols. Sm.8vo. Dark green cloth. 4 plates in each volume. Some copies have stab-holes in the inner margins, having been bound from sheets of an aborted part issue.
   Sadleir records a copy of volume one with 8 plates, in a binding of dark green morocco cloth, rather than pebble-grain cloth. This appears to be an earlier issue. The sheets for four part issues were printed, but apparently only Part I was published.

MARVELL, Andrew (1621–1678)

Known in his own time principally as a satirist, he is now most highly regarded as a lyric poet. This later reputation is due to the posthumous publication of his poems under the title MISCELLANEOUS POEMS, which contains the first printing of most of his work in the field. His satires were published as POEMS ON AFFAIRS OF STATE in 1689–1697, but there is some doubt about his authorship of some of the pieces.

MISCELLANEOUS POEMS . . . Printed for Robert Boulter M.DC.LXXXI (i.e. 1681). Folio, in fours. Portrait. In most copies, S1 and X1 are cancels.
The Preface is signed by 'Mary Marvell' who in fact was his housekeeper Mary Palmer. She posed as his widow in order to inherit his money. It was she who discovered the poems among his papers, and caused them to be published. The cancel leaves found in most copies replace 13 leaves which were suppressed because they bore poems in praise of Cromwell.

MATURIN, Rev. C. R. (1782–1824)

The following checklist includes all the Gothic fiction for which he is celebrated – MELMOTH THE WANDERER being the key book. None are easy to obtain nowadays. There is little demand for his volumes of sermons.

FATAL REVENGE. Longman 1807. 3 vols. Boards, labels.

THE WILD IRISH BOY. By the author of 'Montorio'. Longman 1808. 3 vols. Boards, labels.

THE MILESIAN CHIEF. By the author of 'Montorio' and 'The Wild Irish Boy'. Colburn 1812. 4 vols. Boards, labels.

BERTRAM. Murray 1816.

MANUEL. By the author of 'Bertram'. Murray 1817.

WOMEN. By the author of 'Bertram' etc. Edinburgh: Constable 1818. 3 vols. Boards, labels.

FREDOLFO. Edinburgh: Constable 1819.

MELMOTH THE WANDERER. By the author of 'Bertram'. Edinburgh: Constable 1820. 4 vols. Boards, labels.

THE ALBIGENSES. Hurst, Robinson & Co. 1824. 4 vols. Boards, labels.

MAURIER, George Du (1834–1896)

Not widely collected, but the following three books have their fans.

PETER IBBETSON. New York & London: Harper Brothers (1891). Verso title states 'Copyright 1891'. Green cloth. U.K.: Osgood, McIlvaine 1892. 2 vols. Square demy 8vo. Buff linen, blocked in black & brown (later blocked in black only).

TRILBY. Osgood, McIlvaine 1894. 3 vols. Pictorial buff canvas.

THE MARTIAN. Harper 1898. Square cr. 8vo. Pictorial blue cloth. Also, a Large Paper Edition of 250 copies in green buckram with vellum spine.

MELVILLE, Herman (1819–1891)

During his lifetime, Melville was more popular in Great Britain than in his native land. And it was in Great Britain that most of his books were first published. His first book, the fictional NARRATIVE OF A FOUR MONTH'S RESIDENCE, was the most popular. The book for which he is now famous, MOBY DICK, was received rather coolly by the public. Indeed, it was not until well into the Twentieth century that Melville's popularity in general and his great literary reputation were firmly established.

His first editions are now expensive to collect. His first book is usually priced in excess of $2000 and THE WHALE (i.e. the London edition of MOBY DICK) is one of the few nineteenth century works of fiction capable of getting $15,000 or £10,000. Some of his works, it will be noted, were published in wrappers and also in cloth. Copies in wrappers are generally the more expensive – not because they have priority, but because their survival rate has not been so good.

The following checklist covers all the important publications.

NARRATIVE OF A FOUR MONTHS' RESIDENCE . . . (etc). Murray 1846. Issued in two parts, in wrappers, and also with the two parts bound in carmine cloth. The first issue has the word 'Pomarea' in the first line of page 19. This was later changed to 'Pomare'. Publishers' catalogue dated March 1846 (earliest state). U.S.: entitled TYPEE (q.v.).

TYPEE. New York: Wiley & Putnam 1846. Two parts in thick wrappers, also in one volume, blue or brown cloth. The first American edition of NARRATIVE . . .

OMOO. Murray 1847. Two vols in wrappers, also one volume in red cloth.

U.S.: Harper 1847. Two vols in wrappers, or one volume in blue watered muslin.

MARDI: and A Voyage Thither. Bentley 1849. 3 vols. Green cloth. U.S.: Harper 1849. 2 vols. Wrappers, also brown or green muslin.

REDBURN: HIS FIRST VOYAGE. Bentley 1849. 2 vols. Blue cloth. Remainder issue has 'T. C. Newby' on spine. U.S.: Harper 1849. Purple-brown muslin.

WHITE JACKET. Bentley 1850. 2 vols. Blue cloth. U.S.: Harper 1850. Brown, also blue-grey cloth, also as 2 parts in yellow wrappers.
   The U.K. Edition was expurgated.

THE WHALE. Bentley 1851. 3 vols. Cream cloth spine, blue cloth. U.S.: entitled MOBY DICK (q.v.).

MOBY DICK. New York: Harper 1851. Blue, black, brown, or scarlet cloth, with Harper's circular device on the front and back.
   The U.K. edition, under the title THE WHALE, appeared earlier, but the U.S. edition has additional passages.

PIERRE. New York: Harper 1852. Grey cloth, also wrappers. U.K.: Sampson, Low 1852. American sheets with cancel title. Blue cloth.

ISRAEL POTTER. New York: Putnam 1855. 12mo. Purple-brown or green cloth. In the first printing, Chapter XIV was erroneously headed Chapter XVI. U.K.: Routledge 1855.

THE PIAZZA TALES. New York: Dix & Edwards 1856. Blue cloth. First copies had yellow endpapers, later copies, blue endpapers. U.K.: Sampson, Low 1856. American sheets with cancel title-page.

THE CONFIDENCE-MAN. New York: Dix, Edwards 1857. Green, also purple-brown cloth. U.K.: Longman 1857. Yellow-brown cloth. In the first issue 'Roberts' is not included in the publishers name at the foot of the front free endpaper (below adverts).

BATTLE-PIECES AND ASPECTS OF THE WAR. New York: Harper 1866. Blue cloth.

CLAREL: A Poem and Pilgrimage in the Holy Land. New York: Putnam's Sons 1876. 2 vols. Red cloth.
   About 220 copies were pulped, after poor sales.

JOHN MARR AND OTHER SAILORS. (anonymous). New York: De Vinne Press 1888. Yellow wrappers. 25 copies.

TIMOLEON. (anonymous). New York: Caxton Press 1891. Buff wrappers.

MILNE, A. A. (1882–1956)

Milne wrote many books in various fields, but the majority have been
overshadowed by his phenomenally successful quartet of children's stories –
the Christopher Robin/Winnie the Pooh books. Of these, there have been
many spin-offs, all keenly collected, as much for their illustrations as for
their texts. Outside the quartet, there are two Milne books which are much
in demand, and these are included below.

WHEN WE WERE VERY YOUNG. Methuen (1924). Illustrated by Ernest
Shepard. Blue cloth, gilt decs., d.w. Also, 100 signed by author and artist, in
half maroon cloth and grey boards, d/w.
   In 1974, Methuen issued an edition of 300 copies, signed by Christopher
Milne.

GALLERY OF CHILDREN. Illustrated by Saida. Stanley Paul 1925. 4to.
Trade edition, also an edition of 500 signed by Milne.
   The illustrator 'Saida' was in fact Willebeek le Mair. The signed edition is
currently selling for around £500.

WINNIE-THE-POOH. Methuen (1926). Illustrated by Ernest Shepard.
Dark green cloth, gilt decs., d/w. There were also copies in green leather, red
leather, and blue leather. Also 350 signed by author and artist, and a further
20 specials, similarly signed.
   In 1976, Methuen issued an edition of 300 signed by Christopher Milne.

NOW WE ARE SIX. Methuen (1927). Illustrated by Ernest Shepard. Red
cloth, gilt decs., d/w. Also issued in red leather, green leather, and blue leather.
Also, 200 signed by author and artist, and 20 specials.

THE HOUSE AT POOH CORNER. Methuen (1928). Illustrated by Ernest
Shepard. Salmon cloth, gilt decs., d/w. Also issued in red leather, blue leather,
and green leather. Also, 350 signed by author and artist, and 20 specials.

TOAD OF TOAD HALL. Methuen (1929). Blue cloth, paper label. Also
edition of 200 signed by Milne and Kenneth Grahame.
   A play, based of course on Grahame's WIND IN THE WILLOWS. The
trade edition creates little excitement, but the signed edition is a gem, and
currently gets close on £500.

MILTON, John (1608–1674)

Milton was a prolific pamphleteer in political and religious causes, and the author of several major prose works, all of which are important and valuable; but demand is greatest for the volumes of poetry. His first appearance in print was in one of the great books of English Literature – the second folio Shakespeare, to which he contributed an epitaph.

Two of his best known works, COMUS and LYCIDAS were originally published under other titles – see the first two items in the select checklist below.

A MASKE PRESENTED AT LUDLOW CASTLE. Humphrey Robinson 1634.
Better known as COMUS.

JUSTA EDOUARDO KING NAUFRAGO, AB AMICIS MOERENTIBUS AMORIS/Obsequies to the Memorie of Mr Edward King. Printed by Thomas Buck and R. Daniel, Cambridge 1638.
Better known as LYCIDAS.

AREOPAGITICA; a Speech of Mr. John Milton for the Liberty of Unlicenc'd Printing, To the Parlament of England. Printed in the Yeare, 1644. Sm.4to.
His famous and much quoted piece in defence of a free press.

POEMS ... both English and Latin, compos'd at several times. Printed by his true Copies ... was Printed by Ruth Raworth for Humphrey Moseley 1645. 8vo. Engraved portrait. Separate title-pages for 'Comus' and 'Latin Poems'. What is probably the earliest issue has an imprint including 'Paul's Church-yard', rather than 'S. Paul's church-yard'. Second Edition: 1673.
    A very important collector's item. It includes all his poetry to that date, much of it here printed for the first time.

THE TENURE OF KINGS AND MAGISTRATES by 'J.M.' Printed by Matthew Simmons 1649. Small 4to.
    Milton's defence of the execution of King Charles I, published only two weeks after the event. One of the most important political tracts in English history. After the short title given above, comes 'Proving, that it is Lawfull, and hath been held so through all Ages, for Any, who have the Power, to call to account a Tyrant, or wicked King, and after due Conviction, to Depose, and put him to Death; if the ordinary Magistrate have neglected, or deni'd to doe it. And that they, who of late, so much blame Deposing, are the Men that did it themselves.'

PARADISE LOST. A POEM written in Ten Books. By John Milton. Printed, and are to be sold by Peter Parker ... 1667. Also (see below): PARADISE LOST. A POEM in Ten Books. The Author J. M. London,

Printed, and are to be sold by Peter Parker . . . Robert Boulter . . . and Mathias Walker . . . 1668. Small 4to. Second Edition: 'Revised and Augmented by the same Author'. Printed by S. Simmons, and are to be sold by T. Helder . . . 1669. Small 4to. First Illustrated Edition: 'Adorn'd with Sculptures', namely a portrait and 12 plates. Miles Flesher for Jacob Tonson 1688. Folio (the first thus).

The first edition of this, Milton's most celebrated work, is a bibliographical puzzle. Even now, more than three centuries after it was first published, scholars are not fully agreed on all points. Essentially there are eight different title-page states (variously dated, the earliest date being 1667) and variable contents. One version of the title-page gives the author as 'J.M.', others give his full name. The traditional view is that the two versions dated 1667 are the earliest, but this is disputed. One authority (Amory) has it that the 1667 title-pages were used for remainders of the first issue (the 1668 title-pages having been exhausted). A good case has been made (see Quaritch 1091) for the 1668 'J.M.' issue, to be regarded as the First Issue with the First Authorised state of the title-page. (This is the second version given above.) In terms of content, the traditional fifth issue, dated 1669, is the most complete. It contains the Preface and the Arguments, and was 'Printed by S. Simmons, and are to be sold by T. Helder'.

There is no disputing the fact that the printing was done by the stationer Samuel Simmons, who got the text licensed and registered for copyright on August 20, 1667. It may be that the printing was begun earlier, possibly in late Spring. And it is probable that the Preface and preliminaries which include the 'arguments' for each canto, were printed much later (probably in May 1668). Exactly why and when different versions of the title-pages were set, and how and when they were used, remains a matter for conjecture.

PARADISE REGAIN'D. A Poem. In IV Books. To which is added Sampson Agonistes . . . J. M. for John Starkey 1671. The earliest printing has 11 lines missing after line 537 of 'Samson Agonistes'. The correct reading 'loth' on p.67 indicates a later issue.

PARADISUS AMISSA. Impensis Thomae Dring. C LXXVI (in fact, 1676). Sm.4to.
This is the first Latin version of Paradise Lost, Book One.

HISTORY OF BRITAIN. 1670. Second edition: 1677.

THE WORKS. 1697. Folio.
A COMPLETE COLLECTION in 3 quarto volumes, was published in Amsterdam in 1698.

MITCHELL, Margaret (1900–1949).

Margaret Mitchell published just one novel – GONE WITH THE WIND.
This is a book which was probably 'read to death' as often as not, and
certainly not carefully preserved as a potentially valuable collectors item.
Very fine copies in dust wrappers are thus hard to come by. In a first issue
dust wrapper, it currently gets prices in the range of $2000-$3000. In the
second issue dust wrapper, the price drops to well under $1000. And the first
U.K. edition sells for a paltry few hundred pounds.

GONE WITH THE WIND. New York: Macmillan 1936. Grey cloth, d/w.
The legend 'Published May, 1936' appears on the verso title-page, and of
course there should be no mention of subsequent printings. Two issues of the
dust wrapper are known. The first has the present book included in the second
column of publications listed on the back. On the second issue, the title
appears at the top of the first column. U.K. (and Canada): Macmillan 1936.

MITFORD, Mary Russell (1787–1855)

Well-known only for the single book OUR VILLAGE, a minor classic of
English Literature, she published a number of volumes of poetry and some
other works of prose. These are possibly under-rated at present, but there is
a stir of interest in her work. OUR VILLAGE is very scarce in first edition
form, yet copies are available occasionally for prices in the region of £150.
Her first book of poems, which is even scarcer, gets about the same.

POEMS. Valpy & Longman 1810. Boards. Second Edition 'With Considerable Additions': Valpy & Rivington 1811.

CHRISTINA . . . A Poem. Valpy & Rivington 1811.

NARRATIVE POEMS ON THE FEMALE CHARACTER IN THE VARI-
OUS RELATIONS OF LIFE. Valpy & Rivington 1813. Volume I (all
published). In some copies, p.332 is blank; in others, it carries adverts. Boards,
label.

OUR VILLAGE: Sketches of Rural Character and Scenery. G. & W. B.
Whittaker. 5 vols, dated 1824, 1826, 1828, 1830, 1832. Boards, labels.

DRAMATIC SCENES: Sonnets and other Poems. Geo B. Whittaker 1827.
Boards, label.

FOSCARI. Whittaker 1826. 80pp issued without covers, or perhaps in
wrappers.

FOSCARI AND JULIAN.   Whittaker 1827. Boards, label.

AMERICAN STORIES.   First Series. Whittaker, Treacher 1831. 3 vols. 12mo. Steel eng. frontis & title in each vol.

AMERICAN STORIES.   Second Series. Whittaker, Treacher 1832. 3 vols. 12mo. Steel eng. frontis. & title in each vol.

LIGHTS AND SHADOWS OF AMERICAN LIFE. (Edited by Mary Russell Mitford).   Colburn & Bentley 1832. 3 vols. Boards, labels.

CHARLES THE FIRST.   John Duncombe 1834.

BELFORD REGIS.   Bentley 1835. 3 vols. Boards, labels.

SADAK AND KALASRADE . . . A Romantic Opera in Two Acts.   Printed for the Proprietors of the Lyceum Opera House 1835. 32pp unbound, or perhaps in wrappers.

COUNTRY STORIES.   Saunders & Otley 1837. Half-cloth boards, label.

ATHERTON AND OTHER TALES.   Hurst & Blackett 1854. 3 vols.

DRAMATIC WORKS.   Hurst & Blackett 1854. 2 vols.

MOORE, Marianne (1887–1972)

She was editor of the distinguished periodical THE DIAL from 1925 to 1929. Her earliest works are scarce and priced in hundreds of dollars. The earliest are:

POEMS.   Egoist Press 1921. Wrappers, paper label.

MARRIAGE.   New York: Munro Wheeler 1923. Manikin Number Three. Wrappers.

OBSERVATIONS.   New York: Dial Press 1924.

SELECTED POEMS.   Faber 1935. Cloth, d/w. The earliest copies bound have untrimmed fore-edges and bottom edges. U.S.: Macmillan 1935.
   The U.K. edition only, has an Introduction by T. S. Eliot.

THE PANGOLIN AND OTHER VERSE.   Brendin Publishing Co. 1936. Decorated boards, paper label, without d/w. 120 copies.

WHAT ARE YEARS. New York: Macmillan 1941. Cloth, d/w.

NEVERTHELESS. New York: Macmillan 1944.

A FACE. Cummington, Mass.: Cummington Press for the New Colophon 1949. Pamphlet.

MORRIS, William (1834–1896)

Morris, with others, founded the OXFORD AND CAMBRIDGE MAGAZINE in 1856. It lasted for about a year, during which time there were 12 issues. They contain some of Morris's earliest work, and are very scarce.

His own works, including translations, are listed below. Works by other authors, published at Morris's Kelmscott Press, are not included. The Kelmscott Press productions are generally the most expensive. The majority of his other works, some of them not at all common, are comparatively modestly priced (under £100), but interest is continually growing.

THE DEFENCE OF GUENEVERE, AND OTHER POEMS. Bell & Daldy 1858. Cloth. There was a new edition in 1875, of which 25 copies were on large paper. The Kelmscott Press Edition was done in 1892, limited to 300 copies, of which 10 were printed on vellum.

SIR GALAHAD: A Christmas Mystery. Bell & Daldy 1858. Pamphlet.
A Wise Forgery.

THE LIFE AND DEATH OF JASON. Bell & Daldy 1867. Cloth. There were (also) 25 copies on large paper. Another edition was published by Ellis & White (in 1869) of which some were on large paper.

THE EARTHLY PARADISE. F. S. Ellis, in four parts, 1868 (parts 1 & 2 together) & 1870 (parts 1, 2, 3 & 4). There were (also) 25 copies on large paper. A Popular Edition was issued in 10 parts in 1872. There were new editions in 1880 (4 vols), 1886 (5 vols) and 1890 (one vol, white cloth.). Kelmscott Press Edition: 1896–97. 6 vols.

THE GOD OF THE POOR. Printed At The Office of Justice, London (and) Printed by the Twentieth-Century Press, London 1868. Red wrappers.
A Wise Forgery.

GRETTIS SAGA. (The Story of Grettir the Strong). Trans. Morris & Magnusson. F. S. Ellis 1869. Navy blue cloth, paper label. Also, 25 copies on large paper.

VOLSUNGA SAGA (The Story of Volsungs and Niblungs). Trans. Morris & Magnusson. F. S. Ellis 1870. Decorative binding. Also, 25 on large paper.

LOVE IS ENOUGH. Ellis & White 1873. (1872). Square crown 8vo. Navy blue cloth.

THREE NORTHERN LOVE STORIES AND OTHER TALES. Trans. Morris & Magnusson. Ellis & White 1873 (1872). Cloth. Also, some large paper copies.

THE STORY OF SIGURD THE VOLSUNG, AND THE FALL OF THE NIBLUNGS. Ellis & White 1877 (1876). Also, 25 copies on large paper. Kelmscott Press 1898.

THE AENEIDS OF VIRGIL, Done into English Verse. Ellis & White 1876. Navy blue cloth. Also, 25 copies on large paper, in 2 vols.

THE TWO SIDES OF THE RIVER. HAPLESS LOVE AND THE FIRST FORAY OF ARISTOMENES. London 1876 (1890). Green wrappers.
   A Wise/Forman Forgery

HOPES AND FEARS FOR ART. Ellis & White 1882. Navy blue cloth, paper label. There were some large paper copies.

THE VOICE OF TOIL: ALL FOR THE CAUSE. TWO CHANTS FOR SOCIALISTS. Reprinted from 'Justice', the Organ of the Social Democratic Federation. (1884). Yellow wrappers.
   A Wise/Forman Forgery.

SOCIALISTS AT PLAY. South Place Institute, June 11, 1885. Wrappers.
   A Wise/Forman Forgery.

PILGRIMS OF HOPE. Appeared in The Commonweal (journal of The Socialist League) March 1885-July 1886. Privately Printed by H. Buxton Forman 1886.

THE ODYSSEY OF HOMER, Done into English Verse. Reeves & Turner 1887. 2 vols. Small 4to. Half parchment.

THE AIMS OF ART. The Commonweal 1887.

THE TABLES TURNED. The Commonweal 1887.

SIGNS OF CHANGE. Reeves & Turner 1888. Cloth.

TRUE AND FALSE SOCIETY. The Socialist League 1888. Pamphlet.

A DREAM OF JOHN BALL, AND A KING'S LESSON. Appeared in The Commonweal, 1887–88. Book: Reeves & Turner 1888. Small 4to. Cloth. Also, on large paper, in half vellum. Kelmscott Press edition: 1892. Vellum, with green strings. 300 copies, plus 11 on vellum.

A TALE OF THE HOUSE OF THE WOLFINGS AND ALL THE KINDREDS OF THE MARK. Reeves & Turner 1889. 8vo. Also, 100 copies on large paper, 4to. in red cloth with white label on front.

THE ROOTS OF THE MOUNTAINS. Reeves & Turner 1890. 8vo. Also, 250 copies on large paper, 4to. in decorative covers.

NEWS FROM NOWHERE. Appeared in The Commonweal 1890. Book: Reeves & Turner 1891. Also, 250 copies on large paper, 4to. in half vellum, blue boards, white label on front. Kelmscott Press: 1892 (1893). 300 copies, plus 10 on vellum. U.S.: Boston: Roberts Bros. 1890. Unauthorized.

THE STORY OF THE GLITTERING PLAIN. Printed at the Kelmscott Press, and published by Reeves & Turner (1891). Small 4to. White vellum, leather strings. 200 copies. plus 6 on vellum. Second Edition: Printed at Kelmscott Press, published by Reeves & Turner 1894. With 23 woodcuts by Walter Crane.
   The first book printed at Kelmscott.

POEMS BY THE WAY. Reeves & Turner 1891 (March). 16mo. Also, 100 copies on large paper. Kelmscott Edition: 1891 (September). 300 copies, plus 13 on vellum. Small 4to. bound in vellum, green strings.

THE SOCIALIST IDEAL OF ART. Reprinted from The New Review, January 1891. Pamphlet.
   A Wise/Forman Forgery.

THE ORDER OF CHIVALRY & L'ORDENE DE CHEVALERIE. Kelmscott Press 1892 (1893).

GOTHIC ARCHITECTURE. Kelmscott Press 1893. Parchment spine, blue boards.

A TALE OF KING FLORUS AND THE FAIR JEHANE. Kelmscott Press 1893.

ON THE FRIENDSHIP OF AMIS AND AMILIE. Kelmscott Press 1894.

THE TALE OF THE EMPEROR COUSTANS AND OF OVER SEA. Kelmscott Press 1894.

THE WOOD BEYOND THE WORLD. Kelmscott Press 1894.

A TALE OF BEOWULF. Trans Morris & Wyatt. Kelmscott Press 1895.

CHILD CHRISTOPHER AND GOLDILIND THE FAIR. Kelmscott Press 1895.

OLD FRENCH ROMANCES. Kelmscott Press 1896.

THE WELL AT THE WORLD'S END. Kelmscott Press 1896.

THE WATER OF THE WONDROUS ISLES. Kelmscott Press 1897.

THE STORY OF THE SUNDERING FLOOD. Kelmscott Press 1897.

LOVE IS ENOUGH. Kelmscott Press 1897 (1898).

A NOTE BY WILLIAM MORRIS ON HIS AIMS IN FOUNDING THE KELMSCOTT PRESS. 1898.

N

NABOKOV, Vladimir (1899–1977)

Some of Nabokov's works were first published in Russian. The list below is of his earliest publications in the English language, up to LOLITA, the work which made him a celebrity.

CAMERA OBSCURA. By V. Sirin (i.e. Nabokov). John Long (1936).

DESPAIR. By V. Nabokoff-Sirin. Long (1937). Revised Edition: New York: Putnam (1966) & London: Weidenfeld (1966).

LAUGHTER IN THE DARK. Indianapolis: Bobbs Merrill (1938). First binding: green cloth. U.K.: Weidenfeld (1961).
A revised version of CAMERA OBSCURA, and his first American publication.

THE REAL LIFE OF SEBASTIAN KNIGHT. Norfolk, Conn.: New Directions (1941). Woven red burlap, d/w. Later binding: smooth red cloth. Variant d/ws (priority unknown): one has 'Nabokov', the other 'Nabokoff'. U.K.: Editions Poetry (1945).

NIKOLAI GOGOL. Norfolk, Conn.: New Directions (1944). Brown-lettered tan cloth. 5 titles listed on verso half-title. Price on d/w is $1.50. Variant (later): Blue stamped tan cloth; 14 titles listed; Price $2.00. U.K.: Editions Poetry (1947).

BEND SINISTER. New York: Holt (1947). U.K.: Weidenfeld (1960).

NINE STORIES. New York: New Directions (1947). An issue of Direction Two, devoted to Nabokov.

CONCLUSIVE EVIDENCE. New York: Harper (1951). 'A-A' on verso title.

SPEAK, MEMORY. Gollancz 1952. Blue-green cloth, d/w. Second issue: in blue cloth. Daily Mail device on spine and flap of d/w.
   The U.K. edition of CONCLUSIVE EVIDENCE. Revised Edition: Weidenfeld 1967.

LOLITA. Paris: Olympia Press (1955). 2 vols. 'Francs:900' on back cover. U.S.: Putnam (1958). One vol. U.K.: Weidenfeld (1959). One vol. Screenplay: McGraw-Hill 1974.
   The American Book Club Edition is so identified on the flap of the dust wrapper. Clipped, it cannot be distinguished from the standard first edition.

NESBIT, Edith (1858–1924)

From her large output, for both adults and children, I have selected for listing, her rare first substantial appearance in a book, and her best-known books for children. Of the latter, the most in demand (and the most expensive) are her classic THE RAILWAY CHILDREN and the physically attractive volume THE STORY OF THE FIVE REBELLIOUS DOLLS (each now fetching well in excess of £100). However many of her earlier and less well-known works are very much scarcer than these.

SPRING SONGS AND SKETCHES. With illustrations after Clausen, Addison, and others. Griffith Farran n.d. (1886). Sm. square 4to. Pictorial wrappers, with a separate dust wrapper decorated with an ornate initial letter. All edges gilt.
   Nesbit was editor of this children's anthology, and contributed five poems. It is rare, especially in the dust wrapper and in anything like fine condition. I have not seen a copy for sale recently, but its value must surely be two or three hundred pounds at least.

THE STORY OF THE TREASURE SEEKERS. Fisher Unwin 1899. Pictorial cloth gilt.

THE WOULDBEGOODS. Fisher Unwin 1901. Pictorial cloth gilt.

FIVE CHILDREN AND IT. Fisher Unwin 1902. Pictorial cloth gilt.

THE PHOENIX AND THE CARPET. George Newnes n.d. (1904). Pictorial cloth gilt.

THE STORY OF THE FIVE REBELLIOUS DOLLS. Ernest Nister 1904. 4to.

THE NEW TREASURE SEEKERS. Fisher Unwin 1904. Pictorial cloth gilt.

THE STORY OF THE AMULET. Fisher Unwin 1906. Pictorial cloth gilt.

THE RAILWAY CHILDREN. Wells, Gardner, Darton 1906. Pictorial cloth gilt.

THE ENCHANTED CASTLE. Fisher Unwin 1907. Pictorial cloth gilt.

O

ORCZY Baroness (Mrs Montague Barstow 1865–1947)

Most of her works can be obtained very cheaply in first edition form. Only her first novel and the famous SCARLET PIMPERNEL have any real value – £50 or so. However, there is a growing band of enthusiasts seeking her Scarlet Pimpernel stories in particular. Interest may soon spread to her other works.

THE EMPEROR'S CANDLESTICKS. Pearson 1899.
Her first novel. Apparently, less than 100 copies were sold, and this is probably why it is now hard to find. It was republished by Greening in 1905.

THE SCARLET PIMPERNEL.   Greening 1905.
Reprinted many times in that same year and subsequently.

ORWELL, George (1903–1950)

There was a surge of interest in Orwell during the 1970s and 1980s, perhaps
arising from the approach of 1984 and the attendant publicity when the year
duly arrived. The dust has now settled a little and it is doubtful if prices for
his first editions will continue to rise so rapidly. But critical and biographical
assessments have established him as an important and interesting author,
whose works will continue to be studied and collected. An impending
bibliography (by Gillian Fraser) expected in late 1994 or early 1995, may
act as a new stimulus to collectors, if one is needed.

Meanwhile, Orwell's first four books are all very scarce in the dust wrappers
and fetching prices not far from £1000. The later book INSIDE THE
WHALE is also very scarce, for the reasons mentioned below, and HOMAGE
TO CATALONIA is not seen too often. At present, it is difficult to judge
how much of their apparent scarcity is due to the strength of current
demand. But pre-war first editions in dust wrappers seem in general to be
uncommon, even for authors not in fashion; so those of Orwell are probably
genuinely scarce.

All his works of substance are included in the following list.

DOWN AND OUT IN PARIS AND LONDON.   Gollancz 1933. Black
cloth, d/w. 1500 copies were printed. U.S.: Harper 1933.

BURMESE DAYS.   New York: Harper 1934. U.K.: Gollancz 1935.

A CLERGYMAN'S DAUGHTER.   Gollancz 1935. U.S.: Harper 1936.

KEEP THE ASPIDISTRA FLYING.   Gollancz 1936. U.S.: Harcourt Brace
1956

THE ROAD TO WIGAN PIER.   Gollancz 1937. Issued in two forms –
blue cloth gilt with yellow d/w, and in limp orange cloth (Left Book Club
issue). There were 1750 copies of the cloth issue, and over 40,000 of the limp
cloth issue.
   Naturally, the blue cloth issue is the scarcer of the two. In fact, it is literally
scarce, whereas the limp orange cloth issue is positively common – of all
Orwell's works, only THE ENGLISH PEOPLE is more frequently seen.
The book was subsequently issued in two more forms. The first, arising
presumably from an inadequate supply of the original hardback, consisted of
Left Book Club sheets bound up in blue cloth (hardback). There were 200

copies done thus. It is often described as the second issue of the 'Public' Edition (i.e. the hardback first edition), but it is more accurately described as a new issue of the Left Book Club Edition. It differs from the original issue in that it does not contain the Preface by Victor Gollancz. The other new issue, however, known as the Supplementary Issue, also consisted of L.B.C. sheets in limp orange cloth. It differs from the original L.B.C. issue in that it contains only Part I of the work (and 32 plates), and is consequently slimmer (150pp). Both of these later issues came out in May of 1937 – some two months after the original publication date. The book was not published in America until 1958 – by Harcourt Brace.

HOMAGE TO CATALONIA.   Secker & Warburg 1938. Green cloth, d/w. 1500 copies printed. U.S.: Harcourt Brace 1952.

COMING UP FOR AIR.   Gollancz 1939. U.S.: Harcourt Brace (1950).

INSIDE THE WHALE.   Gollancz 1940. Black cloth gilt, yellow d/w.
One of the scarcest of Orwell's works. 1000 copies were printed, but an unknown number were destroyed by enemy action during the war.

THE LION AND THE UNICORN.   Secker & Warburg, Searchlight Books No. I. 1941. Wrappers. Also issued in cloth with d/w.

ANIMAL FARM.   Secker & Warburg 1945. Illustrated Edition: Halas & Bachelor 1954. U.S.: Harcourt Brace (1946). Black cloth, d/w. (Book Club issue in green cloth).

JAMES BURNHAM AND THE MANAGERIAL REVOLUTION.   Socialist Book Centre 1946. 8pp in red wrappers. 3,000 copies printed.

CRITICAL ESSAYS.   Secker & Warburg 1946. Red cloth, d/w. 3028 copies printed.

DICKENS, DALI AND OTHERS.   New York: Reynal 1946. The American edition of CRITICAL ESSAYS.

THE ENGLISH PEOPLE   Collins. Britain in Pictures series no.100. 1947. Slim 4to., thin boards & d/w.
The most common of Orwell's works. There were 26,000 copies.

NINETEEN EIGHTY-FOUR.   Secker & Warburg 1949. Issued in a red (maroon) d/w and also in a green d/w. The red d/w appears to be the scarcer of the two. U.S.: Harcourt Brace (1949). Published in Canada (Toronto) by Reginald Saunders & Co., same year.

SHOOTING AN ELEPHANT.   Secker & Warburg 1950. Pale green cloth, d/w. U.S.: Harcourt Brace 1950.

SUCH, SUCH WERE THE JOYS. New York: Harcourt Brace (1953). Green cloth, d/w. Published in the U.K., with differences, as ENGLAND, YOUR ENGLAND.

ENGLAND, YOUR ENGLAND. Secker & Warburg 1953. Green cloth, d/w.

COLLECTED ESSAYS, JOURNALISM AND LETTERS. Secker & Warburg 1968. 4 vols. U.S.: Harcourt Brace 1968.

P

PEACOCK, Thomas Love (1785–1866)

Peacock's novels are most frequently seen in the popular illustrated editions in decorated cloth, which came out at the end of the 19th century. The anonymous first editions of these books (which were not illustrated) are keenly collected and fetch substantial prices (a few hundred pounds each). His poetry is not well known. His first volume of poetry PALMYRA AND OTHER POEMS, published in 1806, is very rare. His other early volumes – THE GENIUS OF THE THAMES, 1810; THE PHILOSOPHY OF MELANCHOLY, 1812; and SIR PROTEUS: A Satirical Ballad, 1814; are very scarce. His early poetry is not however, very highly regarded by the critics. His best work in this genre is considered to be RHODODAPHNE, in some respects a precursor of Keats' LAMIA. The early novels were all issued in boards.

HEADLONG HALL. T. Hookham 1816. 12mo.
The Second Edition, published in the same year, was revised.

MELINCOURT. T. Hookham 1817. 3 vols.

NIGHTMARE ABBEY. By the Author of Headlong Hall. T. Hookham, Jun., & Baldwin, Craddock & Joy 1818. 12mo.

RHODODAPHNE: or the Thessalian Spell. A Poem. T. Hookham 1818. Fcap 8vo. U.S.: Philadelphia: Carey & Son 1818.

MAID MARIAN. By the Author of Headlong Hall. Hookham & Longman 1822. 12mo.

THE MISFORTUNES OF ELPHIN. By the Author of Headlong Hall. T. Hookham 1829.

CROTCHET CASTLE. By the Author of Headlong Hall. T. Hookham 1831. 12mo. Boards. Remaindered in half red cloth, paper label.

GRYLL GRANGE. Parker, Son, and Bourn 1861. 8vo. Cloth.

CALIDORE AND MISCELLANEA. Ed. Richard Garnett. 1891.

PEAKE, Mervyn (1911–1968)

Peake's earliest work – the first in the checklist – is very scarce. It is thought that many copies (perhaps even most copies) were destroyed by enemy action during the war. It appears so infrequently on the market that it is a difficult book to put a value on. Which is no doubt why theoretical values I have seen placed upon it, range from a few hundred pounds to four-figure sums. Personally, if I had a fine copy in the dust wrapper, I would seriously consider putting a four-figure price on it. However, the possibility may never arise, because some commentators take the view that there never was a dust wrapper. (I can supply no evidence either way.) At all events, the book is so scarce, the second edition (which certainly did have a dust wrapper) has filled the vacuum and taken on the status of an important collector's item. It is frequently priced well in excess of £100. Indeed, some dealers appear to take the view that for practical purposes it may be regarded as the first edition.

CAPTAIN SLAUGHTERBOARD DROPS ANCHOR. Country Life 1939. 48pp. Cloth spine, boards. Second Edition: Eyre & Spottiswoode 1945. U.S.: Macmillan 1967.

SHAPES AND SOUNDS. Chatto & Windus 1941.

RHYMES WITHOUT REASON. Eyre & Spottiswoode 1944.

THE CRAFT OF THE LEAD PENCIL. Wingate 1946.

TITUS GROAN. Eyre & Spottiswoode 1946. The second impression is identified on the flap of the dust wrapper, near the price, and also carries extracts from reviews. U.S.: Reynal & Hitchcock 1946.
Words cannot adequately convey the subtle difference between the cloth of the first impression and that of the second. Essentially, the first is somewhat finer in texture and brighter in hue. But the two need to be seen side by side for the difference to be fully appreciated.

LETTERS FROM A LOST UNCLE FROM POLAR REGIONS. Eyre & Spottiswoode 1948.

THE DRAWINGS. Grey Walls Press 1949. Another (Different) Edition: Davis-Poynter 1974.

THE GLASSBLOWERS. Eyre & Spottiswoode 1950.

GORMENGHAST. Eyre & Spottiswoode 1950. U.S.: Weybright & Talley 1967.

MR PYE. Heinemann 1953.

TITUS ALONE. Eyre & Spottiswoode 1959. Revised Edition: Eyre & Spottiswoode 1970. U.S.: Weybright & Talley 1967.

THE RHYME OF THE FLYING BOMB. Dent 1962.

POEMS AND DRAWINGS. Keepsake Press 1965. Wrappers. Limited to 150.

A REVERIE OF BONE. Rota 1967. Limited to 300.

SELECTED POEMS. Faber 1972.

A BOOK OF NONSENSE. Owen 1972. U.S.: Dufour 1975.

PEPYS, Samuel (1633–1703)

The famous diary was written by Pepys in a form of shorthand. His manuscript, in six leather-bound volumes, is now in the Pepys Library at Magdalene College, Cambridge. It was the publication of John Evelyn's Diary in 1818 which sparked off an interest in that of his friend Pepys. Lord Grenville then transcribed a few pages, but John Smith, an undergraduate of St. John's College, set about transcribing the complete work. He suppressed the 'objectionable' passages, but filled 54 notebooks with his transcription. The book was published as MEMOIRS . . .

MEMOIRES RELATING TO THE STATE OF THE ROYAL NAVY OF ENGLAND, for Ten Years, determin'd December 1688 . . . Printed Anno MDCXC (i.e. 1690). 8vo. Portrait and folding table.
The only work published during his lifetime. The issue with the imprint as above is thought to have been privately distributed by Pepys.

(DIARY) MEMOIRS ... Edited by Lord Braybrooke. Colburn 1825. 2 vols. 4to.
A small selection from John Smith's notebooks. Second edition: 1828. 5 vols. 8vo. Third Edition: 1848–9.

New Edition: 1875–9. 6 vols.
This edition was based on a new transcription by the Rev. Mynors Bright. It was reprinted, with some revision and new footnotes by H. B. Wheatley, in 10 vols, in 1893–9. Neither of these editions is complete.

First Complete Edition: Bell and Hyman (London) and The University of California Press 1970–83. 11 vols.
Edited by Prof. William Matthews and Robert Latham (Pepys Librarian).

PLATH, Sylvia (1932–1963)

Her first separate publication, A WINTER SHIP, appears to be valued very highly indeed – at $1000 according to one authority (Ahearn's Collected Books). For what is no more than a leaflet published just over 30 years ago, that is an astonishing value by any standards. However, her first published piece, a story which appeared in Mademoiselle magazine while she was still at Smith College, would probably not get anything remotely like $1000. Scarce it may be, but contributions to periodicals are rarely that popular with collectors. A number of very small limited editions issued after 1969, are not included in the list below. The first three items are scarce. The next, ARIEL, was a successful publication and drew her to the attention of readers and collectors alike, and the books which followed are consequently not too hard to get.

A WINTER SHIP. (anonymous). Edinburgh: Tragara Press 1960. Leaflet.

THE COLOSSUS AND OTHER POEMS. Heinemann 1960. U.S.: Knopf 1962

THE BELL JAR. By Victoria Lucas (pseud.). Heinemann 1963. U.S.: Harper 1971.
It was issued under the name of Sylvia Plath by Faber in 1966.

ARIEL. Faber 1965. U.S.: Harper 1966

UNCOLLECTED POEMS. Turret Books 1965. Wrappers. Limited to 150.

THE COLOSSUS. Heinemann 1967.
A reissue of THE COLOSSUS AND OTHER POEMS.

THREE WOMEN. Turret Books 1968. Limited to 150.

THE ART OF SYLVIA PLATH. ed. Newman. Faber 1970. U.S.: Indiana
University 1970.
Includes previously unpublished material.

CROSSING THE WATER. Faber 1971. U.S.: Harper 1971.

WINTER TREES. Faber 1971. U.S.: Harper 1972

LETTERS HOME. New York: Harper 1975. U.K.: Faber 1976.

THE BED BOOK. Faber 1976. U.S.: Harper 1976

JOHNNY PANIC AND THE BIBLE OF DREAMS AND OTHER
WRITINGS. Faber 1977.

JOHNNY PANIC AND THE BIBLE OF DREAMS: SHORT STORIES,
PROSE AND DIARY EXCERPTS. New York: Harper 1979.

COLLECTED POEMS. Faber 1981. U.S.: Harper 1981

POE, Edgar Allan (1809–1849)

The first editions of Poe are among the rarest and most desirable in the
whole of American literature. All are valued in thousands of dollars, some
having fetched $50,000 or more in recent auctions. The U.K. editions,
where they exist, are valued in hundreds of pounds at least.

TAMERLANE AND OTHER POEMS. By a Bostonian. Boston: Calvin F.
S. Thomas . . . Printer 1827. Yellow wrappers.
A legendary rarity. It is believed that only 40 or 50 copies were printed.

AL AARAAF, TAMERLANE, AND MINOR POEMS. Baltimore: Hatch &
Dunning 1829. Blue or tan boards. 500 copies printed, the earliest dated 1820
in error.

POEMS. Second Edition. New York: Elam Bliss 1831. 12mo. Green boards.
About 500 copies printed.
A revised reprint of the poems included in the 1829 Baltimore book –
hence 'Second Edition'.

THE NARRATIVE OF ARTHUR GORDON PYM OF NANTUCKET.
(anon). New York: Harper 1838. Blue or grey cloth, paper label on spine.
U.K.: Wiley & Putnam 1838.

THE CONCHOLOGIST'S FIRST BOOK. Philadelphia: for the author, by Haswell, Barrington, and Haswell 1839. 12mo. Brown boards. The earliest copies have the plates coloured.
   Second edition 1840, has 10 extra pages. Third edition 1845 (same publisher).

TALES OF THE GROTESQUE AND ARABESQUE. Philadelphia: Lea and Blanchard 1840. 2 vols. Cloth, paper label on spine. 750 sets. First issue has 4 pp. of personal and editorial opinions & p.213 of Vol 2 is numbered 231.

THE PROSE ROMANCES. Uniform Serial Edition. No.1 . . . Murders in the Rue Morgue, and the Man That Was Used Up. Philadelphia: William H. Graham 1843. 40pp. Wrappers.
   No other numbers were issued.

TALES. New York: Wiley & Putnam 1845. Wrappers. First state has slugs of T. B. Smith and H. Ludwig on the verso title, and 12pp. ads at end. U.K.: Wiley & Putnam 1845. Cancel title-page. Green cloth. Some copies are dated 1846.
   Issued with 'The Raven' in one volume cloth, 1845 (probably remainders).

THE RAVEN AND OTHER POEMS. New York: Wiley & Putnam 1845. Wrappers. The first issue has 'T. B. Smith, Stereotyper' on the verso title. U.K.: Wiley & Putnam 1846. Cancel title-page. Green cloth.
   Issued with 'Tales' in one volume cloth, 1845 (probably remainders).

MESMORISM. London: Short & Co. 1846. 16pp. Pamphlet.

EUREKA. New York: Putnam 1848. Boards. 500 copies printed.

COLLECTED WORKS. New York: J. S. Redfield 1850–56. 4 vols, the first three dated 1850, the fourth dated 1856. The first collected edition.

POLIDORI, John William (1795–1821)

Polidori's celebrated Gothic romance was published anonymously. It is rare, and currently worth about £300.

THE VAMPIRE; A Tale. Printed for Sherwood, Neely and Jones 1819. Drab wrappers.

POPE, Alexander (1688–1744)

Pope published a great many works. The following list is merely a selection of the most interesting items, including his most important work THE RAPE OF THE LOCK. This appeared first in an anthology, before being expanded for separate publication. Both items are listed below.

AN ESSAY ON CRITICISM. Printed for W. Lewis ... and Sold by W. Taylor ... T. Osborn ... and J. Graves ... 1711. 4to.
His first book.

MISCELLANEOUS POEMS AND TRANSLATIONS. By Several Hands. Printed by John Watts and published by Bernard Lintott of Fleet Street, May 1712.
The earliest version of THE RAPE OF THE LOCK appeared anonymously in this collection.

WINDSOR FOREST. for Bernard Lintott 1713. Folio.

THE RAPE OF THE LOCK. for Bernard Lintott, March 1714. Illustrated with six copper engravings by Claude Du Bosc and Louis Du Guernier. Wrappers.
The original version of the poem, which appeared in MISCELLANEOUS POEMS AND TRANSLATIONS (q.v.) was expanded by 360 lines for this first separate edition. A copy fetched $10,000 in auction in 1990, but this (I believe) was exceptional.

A KEY TO THE LOCK. Or, a Treatise proving, beyond all Contradiction, the dangerous Tendency of a late Poem, entituled, The Rape of the Lock, to Government and religion. By Esdras Barnivelt, Apoth. (pseudonym). for J. Roberts 1715.

THE TEMPLE OF FAME: A Vision. for Bernard Lintott 1715.

COURT POEMS. for J. Roberts 1706 (1716).
The volume includes 'The Basset-Table. An Eclogue', anonymous but by Pope; and anonymous works by Lady Montagu and John Gay.

WORKS. W. Bowyer for Bernard Lintott 1717. 4to. also folio (simultaneously). Engraved portrait by Vertue. Title in red and black. The first issue does not have 'Tonson' in the imprint.
The first collected edition of Pope's verse. A second volume was published in 1735. Like volume I, this was printed simultaneously in both 4to and folio, but according to Rothschild, the 4to was published a 'day or two' after the folio.

WORKS. With his last Corrections, Additions, and Improvements; as they

were delivered to the Editor a little before his Death: Together with the Commentaries and Notes of Mr. Warburton. Printed for J. and P. Knapton, H. Lintot, J. and R. Tonson, and S. Draper 1751. 9 vols.
The first complete collection.

ELOISA TO ABELARD. for Lintott 1720. Frontispiece.
The Second Edition of the work, being the First Separate Edition.

THE DUNCIAD, VARIORVM. With the Prolegomena of Scriblerus. for A. Dod 1729. 4to.
This is the first complete edition of the first three books, less complete versions having appeared in 1728.

THE NEW DUNCIAD: as it was Found in the Year 1741. With the Illustrations of Scriblerus, and Notes Variorum. Printed for T. Cooper . . . 1742. 4to.
This is the first edition of Book IV.

OF FALSE TASTE. An Epistle to . . . Burlington. L. Gilliver 1731. Folio.
This, the Third Edition of the espistle, is the first with the amended title, and the first to contain Pope's Prefatory Letter.

OF THE USE OF RICHES: An Epistle . . . J. Wright, 1732. 22pp Folio.
The first issue has a line of errata on the last leaf and an uncorrected text. In the second issue, the text is corrected.

FIRST SATIRE OF THE SECOND BOOK OF HORACE. Imitated in a Dialogue between Alexander Pope of Twickenham in Com. Midd. Esq. on the one Part, and his Learned Council on the other. Printed by L. G. and sold by A. Dodd . . . 1733. Folio. There are five issues. In the rare first issue: there is no comma after the word 'Pope' on the title page, but there is after 'Virturi' (the reverse is the case in the other four issues); there is no mention of a price at the foot of the title-page; page 9, line 2 has the word 'Laureate'; the catchword on page 13 is 'In.' (a misprint, in fact).
There are further points, but the foregoing should be more than enough for identification purposes.

AN EPISTLE TO THE RIGHT HONOURABLE RICHARD LORD VISCT. COBHAM. for Lawton Gilliver 1733. Folio.

AN EPISTLE FROM MR. POPE, to Dr. Arbuthnot. J. Wright for Lawton Gilliver 1734. Folio.

OF THE CHARACTERS OF WOMEN: An Epistle to a Lady. J. Wright, for Lawton Gilliver at Horner's Head against St. Dunstan's Church in Flettstreet, 1735. Folio. The first issue of the first edition has the imprint thus. In subsequent issues 'Flettstreet' becomes 'Fleetstreet'.

HORACE HIS ODE TO VENUS. Lib. IV. Ode I. Imitated by Mr. Pope. J. Wright 1737. 10pp Folio.

THE SECOND EPISTLE OF THE SECOND BOOK OF HORACE IMITATED. for R. Dodsley 1737. Folio. The copy described by Wise has the note on page 12 incorrectly numbered 16 (and no number 15). Other copies have the note correctly numbered 15 (and no note 16).

ONE THOUSAND SEVEN HUNDRED AND THIRTY EIGHT: A Dialogue, something like Horace. for T. Cooper. (1738). Folio. The work is in two parts. First Issue: '(Price ONE SHILLING)' below Cooper's imprint for Part I, measuring $3\frac{1}{2}$ inches, including brackets. In Part II, the setting is '(Price One Shilling)'. Second issue: the setting is uniform in both parts (as per First Issue, Part II) and measures less than $2\frac{1}{2}$ inches.

THE UNIVERSAL PRAYER. By the Author of the Essay on Man. for R. Dodsley, 1738. 4to. The first issue does not have the signature B at the foot of page 5.

LETTERS OF THE LATE ALEXANDER POPE, ESQ., to a Lady. Never before published. for S. Dodsley, 1769. Small 8vo.

POUND, Ezra (1885–1972)

Pound's status as a major figure in English literature is slightly clouded by the events of his later life and perhaps by the sheer complexity of his poetry. It is difficult to see in his work, a single piece that could ever catch the public imagination and make him a household name. (There is no apparent equivalent of Eliot's 'Practical Cats', for example, or indeed 'The Waste-Land'). But his importance is not really in doubt. His influence on other literary figures in the early years of the 20th century, was considerable, and his sequence of Cantos is a monumental achievement which may gain wider recognition in due course. Meanwhile, some collectors seem to have no doubt about the value of his first editions. I see that a recent price guide (Ahearn's COLLECTED BOOKS) values his first publication at a staggering $50,000. Well, it is certainly rare.

Omitted from the list below are most of the pieces published in Italy (in Italian) during the Second World War and after, some translations, and many of the later selections, collections, and limited editions. All Pound's early works are now scarce to say the least. Most of them in fact, were published in smallish numbers.

A LUME SPENTO. (Venice 1908). On verso title: 'Published A. Antonini Cannaregio, 923 – Venice (Italy) . . . In the City of Aldus MCMVIII'. Green wrappers. 150 copies printed. Misprints: the word 'is' omitted in the dedication; 'manuscnipt' on p. 10. and 'immortalily' on p. 24.

A QUINZAINE FOR THIS YULE.   Pollock & Co. (1908). Pamphlet. 100 copies printed. Misprints: 'earth-hoards' on pp. 17/18; and 'Weston St. Llewmy' on p. 21. Second Issue: Imprint at end reads 'Printed for Elkin Mathews . . .' and misprints are corrected. There were 100 copies of the second issue.

PERSONAE.   Elkin Mathews 1909. Drab boards (later, light brown boards). On the earliest copies, the gilt lettering (5 lines) on the spine measures 2 cms., later only 1½ cms. approx. Altogether, 1000 sets of sheets were printed, of which half (or less) were used in 1913 for PERSONAE & EXULTATIONS (q.v.).

EXULTATIONS.   Elkin Mathews 1909. Red boards. 1000 sets of sheets printed, of which half (or less) were used in 1913 for PERSONAE & EXULTATIONS (q.v.).

THE SPIRIT OF ROMANCE.   Dent (1910). Olive brown cloth (later, olive green cloth), grey d/w. 1250 sets of sheets printed, of which 300 were used (with cancel title-page) for the American issue: Dent & Dutton (1910). Olive cloth.

PROVENCA.   Boston: Small, Maynard (1910). Tan boards & d/w. The boards lettered in dark brown, the d/w in dark brown and green. Probably 200 copies. A second impression was issued (probably 1917) with the tan boards and the d/w lettered in green.

CANZONI.   Elkin Mathews 1911. Grey cloth (later, brown boards). 1000 sets of sheets printed but some (perhaps half) were used later for the composite volume CANZONI & RIPOSTES

RIPOSTES.   Swift 1912. Grey cloth and d/w. Number printed unknown, but up to 500 sets of sheets were used later for CANZONI & RIPOSTES (q.v.), some were used for the American issue, and 400 were used for the Elkin Mathews issue of 1915. U.S.: Boston: Small, Maynard 1913. Red boards. Cancel title. New Edition/Issue: Elkin Mathews 1915. Wrappers. Cancel title. 400 copies.

PERSONAE & EXULTATIONS.   Elkin Mathews 1913. Drab boards. 500 copies (or less).
   A composite volume, made up from the two separately published volumes with the original title-pages removed, and new preliminary matter inserted. Apparently scarcer than the individual volumes.

CANZONI & RIPOSTES.   Elkin Mathews 1913. Brown boards. Not more than 500 copies.

Made up from the sheets of the earlier separate publications of the two works.

CATHAY. Elkin Mathews 1915. Tan wrappers. 1000 copies.

GAUDIER-BRZESKA. John Lane 1916. U.S. issue: John Lane 1916. 200 copies.

LUSTRA. Elkin Mathews (1916). Unabridged Text: 200 numbered copies. Abridged: about 800 copies, not numbered.

LUSTRA with Earlier Poems. New York 1917. For Private Circulation. 60 copies. Blue cloth. New York: Knopf 1917. Yellow boards, d/w.

CERTAIN NOBLE PLAYS OF JAPAN. Ireland: Cuala Press 1916. Boards, linen spine. Limited to 350 copies.

'NOH' OR ACCOMPLISHMENT. By Fennellosa & Pound. Macmillan 1916 (1917). U.S.: Knopf 1917.

DIALOGUES OF FONTENELLE. (Trans.). Egoist 1917. Wrappers. 500 copies.
    Unsold copies were issued in 1939 by Laidlaw.

PAVANNES AND DIVISIONS. New York: Knopf 1918.

THE FOURTH CANTO. Ovid Press 1919. 40 numbered copies. Single sheet of Japanese Vellum folded twice.

QUIA PAUPER AMAVI. Egoist (1919). Green boards, cloth spine. 500 copies. Also, 100 signed.

INSTIGATIONS. New York: Boni & Liveright 1920. (800 copies).

HUGH SELWYN MAUBERLEY. Ovid Press 1920. Boards, cloth spine. Limited to 200 copies.

UMBRA. Elkin Mathews 1920. Boards, canvas spine. Also, 100 signed.

POEMS 1918–21. New York: Boni & Liveright (1921). Boards, imitation vellum spine.

THE NATURAL PHILOSOPHY OF LOVE. Trans. New York: Boni & Liveright (1922). U.K.: Casanova Society 1926. Boards, cloth spine.

INDISCRETIONS. Paris: Three Mountains Press 1923. Boards, cloth spine. 300 copies.

THE CALL OF THE ROAD. New York: Boni & Liveright (1923).

ANTHEIL AND THE TREATISE ON HARMONY. Paris: Three Mountains Press 1924. Wrappers. 400 copies. There were 40 special copies, sold unsigned. Unsold copies were issued later with the label of Contact Editions on the title-page. U.S.: Chicago: Pascal Covici 1927.

A DRAFT OF XVI. CANTOS. Paris: Three Mountains Press 1925. Three quarter white vellum, decorated boards (later, red vellum). 90 copies.

PERSONAE. New York: Boni & Liveright 1926.

TA HIO. Trans. Seattle: University of Washington Book Store 1928. Wrappers, glassine envelope. 575 copies. U.K.: Nott (1936). Boards.

A DRAFT OF THE CANTOS 17–27. Rodker 1928. Limited to 101 copies.

SELECTED POEMS. ed. T. S. Eliot. Faber & Gwyer (1928). Also, 100 signed.

A DRAFT OF XXX CANTOS. Paris: Hours Press 1930. Limited to 212 copies. U.S.: Farrar & Rinehart (1933). U.K.: Faber (1933).

IMAGINARY LETTERS. Paris: Black Sun Press 1930. Limited to 375 copies.

HOW TO READ. Harmsworth (1931).

PROLEGOMENA I / EZRA POUND / HOW / TO READ / FOLLOWED BY / THE SPIRIT OF ROMANCE / PART I. France: Le Beausset (1932). Wrappers. Some copies were sold in America with the label of Bruce Humphries on the title-page.

ABC OF ECONOMICS. Faber (1933). 300 sets of sheets were imported into the U.S. and issued by New Directions with a cancel title (1940).

ABC OF READING. Routledge 1934. U.S.: Yale U.P. 1934.

MAKE IT NEW. Faber (1934). U.S.: Yale U.P. 1935.

ELEVEN NEW CANTOS XXXI-XLI. New York: Farrar & Rinehart (1934).

A DRAFT OF CANTOS XXXI-XLI Faber (1935). The U.K. edition of ELEVEN NEW CANTOS.

HOMAGE TO SEXTUS PROPERTIUS. Faber (1934).

ALFRED VENISON'S POEMS. By the Poet of Tichfield Street. Nott (1935). Wrappers.

SOCIAL CREDIT. Nott (1935). Wrappers.

JEFFERSON AND/OR MUSSOLINI. Nott (1935). Also, 30 signed. U.S.: Liveright/Nott (1936).

POLITE ESSAYS. Faber (1937). U.S.: New Directions (1940).

THE FIFTH DECAD OF CANTOS. Faber (1937). U.S.: Farrar & Rinehart (1937). (331 copies). Second issue of 419 copies with cancel title: New Directions (1940).

CONFUCIUS DIGEST OF THE ANALECTS. Milan: (G. Scheiwiller) XV (1937). Wrappers. 245 copies.

GUIDE TO KULCHUR. Faber (1938). U.S.: New Directions 1938.

WHAT IS MONEY FOR. Greater Britain Publications (1939). Pamphlet.

CANTOS LII-LXXI. Faber (1940). U.S.: New Directions (1940). The first 500 copies have an envelope containing a pamphlet pasted in at the end.

A SELECTION OF POEMS. Faber (1940). Boards, d/w.

THE PISAN CANTOS. New York: New Directions (1948). U.K.: Faber (1949).

THE CANTOS. New York: New Directions (1948). This is the first Collected Edition. On verso title: 'Printed from the plates of the original editions'.

SELECTED POEMS. (New York: New Directions). The New Classics Series (1949). A second impression was issued in 1950, but not identified as such.

SEVENTY CANTOS. Faber (1950). The First U.K. Collected Edition.

PATRIA MIA. Chicago: Seymour (1950). U.K.: Owen (1962).

THE LETTERS 1907–1941. New York: Harcourt Brace (1950). U.K.: Faber (1951).

CONFUCIAN ANALECTS. Reprinted . . . Hudson Review. New York: Square $ Series (1951). Wrappers. U.K.: Owen (1956).

THE TRANSLATIONS. Faber (1953). U.S.: New Directions (1953). Black cloth, d/w.

LITERARY ESSAYS. Faber (1954). U.S.: New Directions (1954).

THE CLASSIC ANTHOLOGY DEFINED BY CONFUCIUS. U.S.: Harvard U.P. 1954. U.K.: Faber (1955).

SECTION: ROCK-DRILL. Milano: (Vanni Scheiwiller) 1955. Grey boards, cellophane d/w. U.S.: New Directions (1956). U.K.: Faber (1957).

SOPHOKLES WOMEN OF TRACHIS. Spearman (1956). U.S.: New Directions (1957).

PAVANNES AND DIVAGATIONS. Norfolk, Conn.: New Directions (1958). U.K.: Owen (1960).

DIPTYCH ROME-LONDON . . . Limited Edition of 200 signed. Printed at Officina Bodoni 1957. Brown boards, box. 125 copies for the United States (New Directions), 50 for the U.K. (Faber), and 25 for Italy (Vanni Scheiwiller).
The three publishers issued the book with their own title-pages.

THRONES. Milano (Scheiwiller) 1959. (New York): New Directions (1959). U.K.: Faber (1960).

IMPACT. Chicago: Henry Regnery 1960.

EP TO LU. Indiana University Press 1963. Brown boards, acetate d/w.

A LUME SPENTO AND OTHER EARLY POEMS. (New York): New Directions (1965). Dec. boards, cloth spine, acetate d/w. U.K.: Faber (1966).

LETTERS TO JAMES JOYCE. (New York) New Directions (1967). U.K.: Faber (1969).

SELECTED CANTOS. Faber (1967). U.S.: New Directions (1970).

DRAFTS & FRAGMENTS OF CANTOS CX-CXVII. (New York) New Directions (1969). U.K.: Faber (1970).

SELECTED PROSE 1909–1965. Faber (1973). U.S.: New Directions (1973).

DK / SOME LETTERS. (Montreal, Canada): D C Books (1975). Wrappers. 2,000 copies.

POWYS, John Cowper (1872–1963)

The list below omits the series of Little Blue Books issued by Haldeman-Julius from Kansas in 1923 (being first separate editions of essays from SUSPENDED JUDGMENTS), and omits the numerous posthumously-published paperbacks, mainly from Village Press. An extremely rare ephemeral item which preceded Powys's first published book, is a 12 page pamphlet carrying the poem CORINTH, which was recited at Sherborne Preparatory School on Commemoration Day, June 1891. The only lettering on the front is 'ENGLISH VERSE'. Page 3 is headed 'CORINTH', and the author's name is at the end of the text (p. 11). The imprint (p. 12) is 'Oxford, Horace Hart, Printer to the University'. The only copy I have ever heard of is (or was) in the Bissell collection.

ODES AND OTHER POEMS. William Rider & Son, Limited 1896. Light green cloth, the front decorated with a design of gold webbing and fleurs-de-lis.

POEMS. William Rider & Son, Limited 1899. White boards, the front decorated with a design of gold webbing and fleurs-de-lis.

THE WAR AND CULTURE. New York: G. Arnold Shaw 1914. Red cloth, also in red wrappers.

THE MENACE OF GERMAN CULTURE. Rider 1915.
The U.K. edition of THE WAR AND CULTURE.

VISIONS AND REVISIONS. New York: G. Arnold Shaw 1915. White cloth spine, blue boards. U.K.: MacDonald (1955).

WOOD AND STONE. New York: G. Arnold Shaw 1915. Blue cloth. The gold stamping on the spine varies, but no priority has been definitely established. U.K.: Heinemann (1917). Grey cloth.

CONFESSIONS OF TWO BROTHERS. By J. C. & Llewellyn (sic.) Powys. Rochester, N.Y.: The Manas Press 1916. Blue cloth, paper labels.

WOLFS-BANE RHYMES. New York: G. Arnold Shaw 1916. Blue boards, paper labels. The first issue (100 copies) has a beetle design on the label.

ONE HUNDRED BEST BOOKS. New York: G. Arnold Shaw 1916. White cloth spine, brown boards.

RODMOOR. New York: G. Arnold Shaw 1916. Green cloth.

SUSPENDED JUDGMENTS. New York: G. Arnold Shaw 1916. Dark blue spine, light blue boards, d/w.

MANDRAGORA. New York: G. Arnold Shaw 1917. Blue cloth, paper label on spine.

THE COMPLEX VISION. New York: Dodd, Mead 1920. Green cloth. Later copies have errata tipped in at p.xx.

SAMPHIRE. New York: Seltzer 1922. Black boards, paper labels.

PSYCHOANALYSIS AND MORALITY. San Francisco: Jessica Colbert 1923. Brown cloth spine, brown-grey boards. Limited to 500 copies. About 200 copies were issued, about 200 were destroyed by fire, and some (50–75 copies) were purchased by Random House and issued c. 1925 (Second Issue). These latter, bound in imitation vellum spine, grey boards, were signed by the author on the front endpaper.

DUCDAME. New York: Doubleday 1925 (February 13th). Black cloth with blind-stamped coat of arms on the front, red-lettered spine. 3607 copies printed, plus 250 in Canada. U.K.: Grant Richards 1925 (August). Black cloth, stamped and lettered in black. One copy is known with a Heinemann imprint on a cancel title-page.

THE RELIGION OF A SCEPTIC. New York: Dodd, Mead 1925. Dark blue cloth spine, blue cloth sides. 1000 copies.

WOLF SOLENT. New York: Simon & Schuster 1929. 2 vols. Black cloth, d/ws & box. U.K.: Cape (1929). One vol.

THE MEANING OF CULTURE. New York: Norton (1929). Black cloth, red label. 'First Edition' on verso title. U.K.: Cape 1930.
   Norton issued an edition in red cloth, in 1939.

THE OWL, THE DUCK, AND – MISS ROWE! MISS ROWE! Chicago: Black Archer Press 1930. Limited to 250 signed.

IN DEFENCE OF SENSUALITY. New York: Simon & Schuster (1930). Red cloth, black label. U.K.: Gollancz 1930.

DEBATE! IS MODERN MARRIAGE A FAILURE? By Bertrand Russell & J. C. Powys. New York: The Discussion Guild (1930). Blue cloth.

DOROTHY M. RICHARDSON. Joiner & Steele 1931. Also a limited edition of 60 signed.

A GLASTONBURY ROMANCE. New York: Simon & Schuster 1932. Also 204 signed. U.K.: John Lane Bodley Head (1933).

A PHILOSOPHY OF SOLITUDE. New York: Simon & Schuster 1933.

WEYMOUTH SANDS. New York: Simon & Schuster 1934. Top edges stained red (earliest issue only). U.K.: first issued as JOBBER SKALD (q.v.). Issued as WEYMOUTH SANDS by Macdonald (1963).

AUTOBIOGRAPHY. New York: Simon & Schuster 1934. U.K.: John Lane Bodley Head (1934).

THE ART OF HAPPINESS. New York: Simon & Schuster 1935. U.K.: John Lane Bodley Head (1935).

JOBBER SKALD. John Lane Bodley Head (1935).
    The U.K. edition of WEYMOUTH SANDS.

MAIDEN CASTLE. New York: Simon & Schuster 1936. U.K.: Cassell (1937).

MORWYN. Cassell (1937). Blue cloth with blue-lettered gold panel on spine.
    Morwyn is Welsh for 'maid'.

ENJOYMENT OF LITERATURE. New York: Simon & Schuster 1938. Yellow-green buckram. 8000 copies printed.

THE PLEASURES OF LITERATURE. Cassell (1938).
    The U.K. edition (version) of ENJOYMENT OF LITERATURE, with an additional essay and some minor changes.

OWEN GLENDOWER. New York: Simon & Schuster (1940). 2 vols. Black cloth, no d/ws, in a box. U.K.: John Lane Bodley Head (1941). One vol.

MORTAL STRIFE. Cape (1942).

THE ART OF GROWING OLD. Cape (1944).

DOSTOIEVSKY. John Lane Bodley Head (1946).

OBSTINATE CYMRIC. Carmarthen: Druid Press (1947).

RABELAIS. Bodley Head (1948). U.S.: 500 copies were imported and issued in America by the Philosophical Library, New York in 1951.

PORIUS. Macdonald (1951). Also, 200 signed.

THE INMATES. Macdonald (1952).

IN SPITE OF. Macdonald (1953).

ATLANTIS.   Macdonald (1954).

LUCIFER.   Macdonald (1956). Limited to 560 signed.

THE BRAZEN HEAD.   Macdonald (1956).

UP AND OUT.   Macdonald (1957).

LETTERS TO LOUIS WILKINSON.   Macdonald 1958.

HOMER AND THE AETHER.   Macdonald (1959).

ALL OR NOTHING.   Macdonald (1960).

SELECTED POEMS.   Macdonald (1964).

LETTERS TO NICHOLAS ROSS.   Rota 1971.

R

RANSOME, Arthur (1884–1967)

The books in Ransome's Swallows and Amazons series are currently in vogue, and these are all listed below. The first two in the series were not originally illustrated by the author, though he did illustrate later editions. From the third book in the series, he illustrated all the first editions. The first of the series, with the essential illustrated dust wrapper is currently being priced in excess of £50. The remainder are somewhat cheaper. There is far less interest in his many other works, with one or two exceptions. The exceptions include RACUNDRA'S FIRST CRUISE, and three of his earlier books for children. These are included in the checklist.

THE ABC OF PHYSICAL CULTURE.   Drane 1904.
His first book. Scarce, but there is little demand for it.

HIGHWAYS AND BYWAYS IN FAIRYLAND.   Rivers, Pinafore Library 1906.

OLD PETER'S RUSSIAN TALES.   Jack 1916. Illustrations by Mitrokhin.

ALADDIN AND HIS WONDERFUL LAMP. Nisbet 1919. Illustrated by Mackenzie.

RACUNDRA'S FIRST CRUISE. Allen & Unwin 1923.
A non-fiction sailing book. Regarded as a precurser to the Swallows and Amazons series, and popular now, as it was on first publication.

SWALLOWS AND AMAZONS. Cape 1930. New Edition: illustrated by Clifford Webb. Cape 1931. New Edition: illustrated by Ransome. Cape 1938.

SWALLOWDALE. Illustrated by Webb. Cape 1931. New Edition: illustrated by Ransome. Cape 1936.

PETER DUCK. Cape 1932.

WINTER HOLIDAY. Cape 1933.

COOT CLUB. Cape 1934.

PIGEON POST. Cape 1936.

WE DIDN'T MEAN TO GO TO SEA. Cape 1937.

SECRET WATER. Cape 1939.

THE BIG SIX. Cape 1940.

MISSEE LEE. Cape 1941.

THE PICTS AND MARTYRS. Cape 1943.

GREAT NORTHERN. Cape 1947.

READE, Charles (1814–1884)

Not an author in favour with collectors at present, nor I fancy with readers. But the author of one classic worth mentioning:

THE CLOISTER AND THE HEARTH. Trubner 1861. 4 vols. Grey-green cloth. Second edition (with textual differences): Trubner 1861. 4 vols.
It is a measure of the popularity of the work at the time, that a third edition, again in 4 vols, was issued in the same year.

RICHARDSON, Samuel (1689–1761)

Richardson, a successful printer, published some of his own books, though not the first edition of his most famous work PAMELA. In 1733, he wrote and published THE APPRENTICE'S VADE MECUM, a book on moral conduct and, six years later, his own moralistic version of AESOP'S FABLES. Around this time, he began writing what were called 'familiar letters' dealing with the practical and moral problems of everyday life. In these lay the foundations of the epistolary novel PAMELA. The letters were actually published in 1741 as LETTERS ... TO AND FOR PARTICULAR FRIENDS.

PAMELA inspired a rash of spurious continuations, 'anti-Pamelas', and parodies, which form an interesting field for collectors. One of the quickest off the mark, and one which played a part in causing Richardson to write his sequel, was John Kelly's anonymous PAMELA'S CONDUCT IN HIGH LIFE. It was Printed for Ward and Chandler ... et al 1741 (May), and was in one volume, 12mo. A second volume came out in September. The rare first edition of the first volume is not identified as Volume I on the title-page.

PAMELA: or, Virtue Rewarded. In a Series of Familiar Letters from a Beautiful Young Damsel, to her Parents. Now first Published in order to cultivate the Principles of Virtue and Religion in the Minds of the Youth of Both Sexes ... London: Printed for C. Rivington ... and J. Osborn 1741 (November 1740). 2 vols. 12mo. The continuation, or sequel, was in 2 vols dated 1742 (December 1741).

The first two volumes were a commercial success and were rapidly reprinted while the sequel was being written. Amid the general acclaim (and derision) which greeted the first two volumes however, there was some protestation at the impropriety of the work, which the author evidently took to heart; for he made extensive revisions for the second edition. (He was in fact a compulsive reviser of all his works.) Sets of the four volumes in mixed editions are quite often encountered, and the collector must decide what is acceptable to him. He will take account of the fact that a set of the four volumes, each in true first edition form, in a good contemporary binding, might well cost something in the region of £5000.

CLARISSA: or, The History of a Young Lady. Published by the author 1747 (2 vols) and 1748 (5 vols). 12mo. Folding leaf of music in volume 2.

THE HISTORY OF SIR CHARLES GRANDISON. In a Series of Letters published from the Originals, by the Editor of Pamela and Clarissa. Published by the author 1753–54. 7 vols. 12mo. Second Edition: 1754. 6 vols. 8vo.

The last of his three novels. The more expensive 'large paper' second edition, incorporating revisions made while the 12mo edition was in the press, was published simultaneously with the latter.

A COLLECTION OF THE MORAL AND INSTRUCTIVE SENTI-
MENTS, MAXIMS, CAUTIONS AND REFLECTIONS, CONTAINED
IN THE HISTORIES OF PAMELA, CLARISSA, AND SIR CHARLES
GRANDISON. Published by the author 1755. 12mo.
   This, according to Richardson, contains the pith of all his works.

THE CORRESPONDENCE... Selected from the original Manuscripts... Richard Phillips 1804. 6 vols. 8vo. Edited, with a 'Biographical
Account of the Author' by Anna Laetitia Barbauld.

ROSENBERG, Isaac (1890–1918)

His first three books are very scarce. The first is worth several thousand
pounds and the next two get several hundred pounds apiece. Even his fourth,
being the first from a commercial publisher, is not easy to find. The subsequent two collections however are comparatively common.

NIGHT AND DAY. Privately Printed 1915. Wrappers.

YOUTH: a Play. Privately Printed. I. Narodiczky 1915. Tan wrappers.

MOSES: A PLAY. Privately Printed 1916.

POEMS. Heinemann 1922.

COLLECTED WORKS. Chatto & Windus 1937. New & Much Enlarged
Edition: Chatto & Windus 1979 & O.U.P. (U.S.A.) 1979.

COLLECTED POEMS. Chatto & Windus 1949. U.S.: Schocken 1949.

ROSSETTI, Christina Georgina (1830–1894)

Some of her early poems were contributed to the journal The Germ, 1850,
under the pseudonym 'Ellen Alleyn'. (See under D. G. Rossetti for more
details of The Germ.)

VERSES DEDICATED TO HER MOTHER. Privately printed at G. Polidori's 1847. Sm.8vo. Cancel leaf at pp. 55–6.
   Her first book. A rare and valuable item, worth something near £1000.

GOBLIN MARKET and Other Poems. Cambridge: Macmillan 1862. Two
designs by D. G. Rossetti. Gilt and blind decorated dark blue cloth. 16pp
undated adverts at end (first state). First 'Housman' Edition: Macmillan 1893.
With illustrations by Laurence Housman (12 full-page, etc).

THE PRINCE'S PROGRESS and Other Poems. Macmillan 1866. Fcap 8vo. Green buckram gilt.

COMMONPLACE and other Short Stories Macmillan 1870.

SING-SONG; a nursery rhyme book. Illustrations (and cover design) by Arthur Hughes. Macmillan 1872. Pictorial red cloth gilt.

SPEAKING LIKENESSES ... with pictures thereof by Arthur Hughes. Macmillan 1874. Pictorial blue cloth gilt, and black-printed dust wrapper.
    The dust wrapper is of course very rare indeed. There was a copy in the stock of Deighton Bell of Cambridge, a few years ago.

A PAGEANT and Other Poems. Macmillan 1881. Fcap 8vo. Gilt decorated dark blue cloth.

TIME FLIES: a reading diary. S.P.C.K. 1885. Reprinted by SPCK in 1897. U.S.: Boston: Roberts Bros 1886.

THE FACE OF THE DEEP. A Devotional Commentary on the Apocalypse. SPCK 1892. Cloth gilt.

NEW POEMS. Edited by W. M. Rossetti. Macmillan 1896. Fcap 8vo. Gilt decorated dark blue cloth. Second binding: dark green buckram. Errata leaf.

ROSSETTI, Dante Gabriel (1828–1882)

Some of Rossetti's early work (e.g. The Blessed Damozel) appeared in The Germ. This short-lived journal, the organ of the Pre-Raphaelite movement, was edited by W. M. Rossetti. First published January 1st 1850, there were only two issues before the name was changed to Art and Poetry. There were then only two further issues, the last on April 30th 1850. Subsequently, Rossetti was a contributor to the Oxford and Cambridge Magazine, founded by William Morris in 1856, when the latter was at Exeter College. There were four issues. A celebrated work in which Rossetti had a hand (as contributor and part editor) was Gilchrist's Life of William Blake, first published in 2 vols in 1863.

SIR HUGH THE HERON. By Gabriel Rossetti, Junior. G. Polidori's Private Press 1843. 4to. Wrappers.
Rossetti was only 15 when this rare and valuable item was printed.

SISTER HELEN; a ballad. Printed for Private Circulation. Oxford 1857. Pamphlet.
    A Forgery.

THE EARLY ITALIAN POETS FROM CIULLO D'ALCAMO TO DANTE ALIGHIERI . . . TOGETHER WITH DANTE'S VITA NUOVA. Translated by D. G. Rossetti. Smith, Elder 1861. Cloth.
> A revised version of the second part was published by Ellis & White in 1874.

POEMS. F. S. Ellis. 1870. Navy blue cloth. Also green buckram. Also 24 copies on large paper.
> For the third edition of 1881, some pieces were left out and some new ones brought in. In America, the original edition was pirated (Boston 1870) but in 1882, a complete edition was published by Roberts of Boston, incorporating all the pieces in the original edition plus the new ones introduced in 1881.

BALLADS AND SONNETS. Ellis & White 1881. Green buckram gilt. Also, 24 copies on large paper.

VERSES. Privately Printed. London 1881. Pink wrappers.
> A Forgery.

THE COLLECTED WORKS OF DANTE GABRIEL ROSSETTI. Ed. W. M. Rossetti. Ellis & Scrutton 1886. 2 vols. Dark green buckram. Also, a large paper issue of 25 copies, in 4 vols, grey paper spine, blue boards.
> The first collective edition of Rossetti's prose and poetry.

POETICAL WORKS OF DANTE GABRIEL ROSSETTI. Preface by W. M. Rossetti. 1891. Cloth. Also, some copies on large paper.

SONNETS AND LYRICAL POEMS. Hammersmith: Kelmscott Press 1894. Vellum. Edition of 316 copies.

HAND AND SOUL. reprinted from The Germ. Hammersmith: Kelmscott Press 1895. Sm.8vo. Vellum. Edition of 525 copies.

S

SAKI (pseud. H. H. Munro 1870–1916)

Munro's first published work was a story which appeared under his initials in the magazine St. Paul's, in February 1889. His first published book was a scholarly work, and was not a great success. With his second however, one of the more successful parodies of Lewis Carroll's 'Alice', he found his forte, and went on to produce a small body of work in the humourous/curious vein which finds favour with today's collectors. None of his publications are rare, but demand is growing steadily and prices are rising.

THE RISE OF THE RUSSIAN EMPIRE.   Grant Richards 1900.

THE WESTMINSTER ALICE.   Westminster Gazette (1902). 44pp. Illustrated blue wrappers with 'Westminster Popular No. 18' at top right of front wrapper. New Edition: Westminster Gazette 1902. 68pp. Illustrated red cloth.

REGINALD.   Methuen 1904. Red cloth.

REGINALD IN RUSSIA.   Methuen 1911. Blue cloth.

THE CHRONICLES OF CLOVIS.   John Lane 1911. Pictorial cloth.

THE UNBEARABLE BASSINGTON.   John Lane 1912. Green cloth. 22pp adverts.

WHEN WILLIAM CAME.   John Lane 1913.

BEASTS AND SUPERBEASTS.   John Lane 1914.

THE TOYS OF PEACE.   John Lane, Bodley Head 1919.

THE SQUARE EGG AND OTHER SKETCHES.   John Lane, Bodley Head 1924. d/w.

THE COLLECTED SHORT STORIES.   John Lane, Bodley Head 1930. d/w.

THE COLLECTED NOVELS AND PLAYS.   John Lane, Bodley Head 1933. d/w.

THE BODLEY HEAD SAKI.   1975. Reprinted stories.

SAKI, A LIFE OF HECTOR HUGH MUNRO.   By A. J. Langguth. Hamish Hamilton 1981.
    Contains six previously uncollected stories.

SAPPER (pseudonym of Cyril McNeile 1888–1937)

The first edition of the first Bull-Dog Drummond adventure was:

BULL-DOG DRUMMOND. The adventures of a Demobilised Officer who found Peace dull. By 'Sapper'. Hodder & Stoughton (1920). 320pp. Pale blue cloth, lettered in black.

SASSOON, Siegfried (1886–1967)

Sassoon (encouraged by his mother) began writing poetry as a young man, and had a number of poetry pamphlets privately printed in very small editions, before the first world war. These are all very rare. His earliest volume of any substance was the pseudonymous THE DAFFODIL MURDERER of 1913. Further pamphlets were issued during and after the war and these, like the earlier ones, are all hard to come by. His poetry was not popular at the time of publication, the more romantic poems of Rupert Brooke being preferred. But from 1920, his reputation grew steadily and by the end of the decade, he was established as a significant poet. His first editions from that point on, are consequently rather common. The checklist below is highly selective, but includes his earliest volumes and his most famous ones.

THE DAFFODIL MURDERER. Being the Chantry Prize Poem By Saul Kain. (i.e. Sassoon). John Richmond Ltd. 1913. Yellow wrappers with red lettering. 1000 copies printed.
　　John Richmond Ltd was an imprint of T. W. H. Crosland, who wrote the preface signed 'William Gilbert'. Despite the fairly large number of copies issued, it is quite a scarce booklet.

THE OLD HUNTSMAN. Heinemann 1917. Boards and d/w. U.S.: Dutton 1917.
　　A volume of (anti-) war poems. His first book by a commercial publisher.

COUNTER-ATTACK and Other Poems. Heinemann 1918. Wrappers. U.S.: Dutton 1918.

THE WAR POEMS. Heinemann 1919.

MEMOIRS OF A FOX-HUNTING MAN. (anonymous). Faber & Gwyer 1928.
　　In 1929, Faber brought out an edition illustrated by William Nicholson. Some copies of this edition exist with a frontispiece portrait of Sassoon which was suppressed before publication (and removed from the list of

illustrations). According to Keynes, there were only two or three advance copies in this form and none were issued for review or sale. However, this appears to have been an underestimate.

MEMOIRS OF AN INFANTRY OFFICER. Faber 1930. Also a signed edition of 750 copies.
This, the second book of a highly successful trilogy, had a first edition of 20,000 copies. It is consequently one of Sassoon's commonest first editions.

POEMS BY PINCHBECK LYRE. (i.e. Sassoon). Duckworth 1931. Boards, tissue d/w. 1000 copies printed.

SHERSTON'S PROGRESS. Faber 1936.
The third volume of the 'Memoirs' trilogy, and a common first edition.

SAYERS, Dorothy L. (1893–1957)

The list below gives her first two books, and her first five volumes of detective fiction. These are all very scarce, but demand is such that the detective fiction gets the higher prices. Her first book was a volume of poetry entitled OP.1. This, and the following work, have a current value of £100–£200, whereas her first two volumes of detective fiction are generally priced at close on £1000.

OP.1. Oxford: Blackwell 1916. Wrappers.

CATHOLIC TALES AND CHRISTIAN SONGS. (Oxford 1918).

WHOSE BODY? New York: Boni & Liveright (1923). First Issue does not have 'Inc.' after the publishers name on the title-page. U.K.: T. Fisher Unwin 1923.
Her first novel.

CLOUDS OF WITNESS. Unwin 1926. U.S.: Dial Press 1927.

UNNATURAL DEATH. Benn 1927.

THE DAWSON PEDIGREE. New York: Dial Press 1928.
The U.S. edition of UNNATURAL DEATH.

LORD PETER VIEWS THE BODY. Gollancz 1928. U.S.: Brewer 1929.

SCOTT, Sir Walter (1771–1832)

Scott's bibliographers, notably Worthington, Ruff, Van Antwerp and Todd, have recorded numerous issue points and states. But despite all their efforts, unrecorded variants and volumes in mixed state seem to occur with alarming frequency; and I have come to the conclusion that we are still a long way from having a definitive bibliography of this author. For this reason, in the checklist below, I have quoted the recorded issue points rather sparingly.

Scott published his first novel anonymously, apparently fearing that such a work might damage his reputation. His fear proved to be unfounded. WAVERLEY was a great success. All the same, he continued (like Jane Austen) to publish his novels anonymously, even when everyone knew the author's identity – using the legend 'by the author of WAVERLEY, ETC.' on his title-pages.

An early work of Scott's which is not in any of the bibliographies (his second book, in fact) is RULES AND REGULATIONS OF THE ROYAL EDINBURGH LIGHT DRAGOONS 1798. This was published (Edinburgh, 1799) as a 12mo in sixes. Scott was secretary of the committee which oversaw the creation of the work and though his precise involvement is not known, it is fairly certain that he drafted the text as well as writing the Preface. It is a rare book and worth in the region of £1000.

Scott was a prolific writer. In the checklist below, I have had to exclude many volumes of secondary interest. I believe I have included the most important and the most interesting. The original bindings were mostly typical of the period, being paper-covered boards with paper labels.

THE LAY OF THE LAST MINSTREL, a poem.   Edinburgh: for Longman 1805. 4to.

BALLADS AND LYRICAL PIECES.   Edinburgh. Printed by James Ballantyne and Co. for Longman, Hurst, Rees, and Orme. London; and Archibald Constable and Co., Edinburgh, 1806. 8vo. Second Edition same year, with a new poem added.

MARMION; a Tale of Flodden Field.   Edinburgh: for Constable 1808. 4to.

THE VISION OF DON RODERICK; a poem.   Edinburgh, Printed by James Ballantyne and Co. for John Ballantyne . . . and Longman (etc) . . . London 1811. 4to. Also 50 copies in 8vo for private distribution. Printed on a variety of stocks (various watermarks). First impression, first state has 'swell' in the second line of the poem. In the second state this becomes 'rise' and the book is mispaginated. An unrecorded variant includes the Dublin agent John Cumming in the imprint.

ROKEBY; a poem. Edinburgh: for Ballantyne . . . Longman (etc). 1813. 4to. Adverts at end.

THE BRIDAL OF TRIERMAIN, or the Vale of St John. Edinburgh. Ballantyne 1813.

WAVERLEY; or 'Tis Sixty Years Since. (anon). Edinburgh: Ballantyne for Archibald Constable . . . and Longman (etc). 1814. 3 vols. 12mo. 1000 copies printed.
> His first novel and a landmark in English Literature. Demand for the book was great and Second and Third Editions followed rapidly (same year) – 2000 and 1000 copies, respectively. The Third Edition incorporates minor corrections and revisions and a new Preface.

THE BORDER ANTIQUITIES OF ENGLAND AND SCOTLAND. London, printed for Longman . . . Constable and Co., Edinburgh, 1814–17. 2 vols. 4to. Engraved frontispiece and titles and 91 engravings.
> The work was also (originally) issued in parts with a 125pp introduction by Scott. There was a special royal quarto issue of the second edition, in which both volumes are dated 1814. The original plates were used for many subsequent impressions for at least the next quarter of a century – a process which generated numerous states and variants.

THE LORD OF THE ISLES, a poem. Edinburgh. for Constable . . . and Longman (etc). 1815. 4to. First impression has 4 cancels and 'hunters' u spears and bows' on p. 56. The corrected reading is 'hunters, spears, and bows'.
> According to Ruff, the corrected reading is peculiar to the second impression on Large Paper, but it does in fact occur in other variants. In July 1815, a suite of six engraved plates after Richard Westall, illustrating the poem, was produced and bound into later editions (that same year). However, some copies of the Large Paper First Edition may have been issued with these (according to Ruff). In any case, copies extra-illustrated with these plates appear occasionally. The Large Paper Edition was (in accordance with the apparent policy of Ballantyne) printed immediately after the ordinary copies (thus they are second impressions of the first edition). The evidence of when they were issued in relation to the small copies, is inconclusive. There were in any case only 50 such copies, Royal 4to (sometimes incorrectly described as Folio).

THE FIELD OF WATERLOO; a poem. Edinburgh. Ballantyne for Constable . . . Longman (etc). 1815. 8vo. Drab wrappers.

GUY MANNERING. Edinburgh. Ballantyne for Longman (etc) 1815. 3 vols. 12mo. 2000 copies printed.
> His second novel.

THE ANTIQUARY. Edinburgh. Ballantyne for Constable (etc). 1816. 3 vols. 12mo. Press-figure '1' on p. 75 of first volume.

PAUL'S LETTERS TO HIS KINSFOLK. Edinburgh. Ballantyne for Constable (etc). 1816. 8vo.
An anonymous account of a visit to the field of Waterloo, after the battle. There were two further editions, and another published in Philadelphia by Moses Thomas, in the same year.

TALES OF MY LANDLORD . . . by Jebediah Cleishbotham (pseud). Edinburgh for Blackwood & Murray 1816. 4 vols. 12mo. Also, Second Series (HEART OF MIDLOTHIAN): for Constable 1818. 4 vols. 12mo. Also, Third Series: for Constable . . . Longman (etc). 1819. 4 vols. 12mo.
The Third Series includes the Gothic masterpiece THE BRIDE OF LAMMERMOOR.

HAROLD THE DAUNTLESS; a poem. Edinburgh: Ballantyne . . . 1817.
His last long poem.

ROB ROY. Edinburgh: for Constable & Longman (etc). 1818. 3 vols. 8vo.

IVANHOE; a romance. Edinburgh, for Constable . . . Hurst, Robinson 1820 (December 1819). 3 vols. 8vo.

THE ABBOT. Edinburgh, for Longman (etc). 1820. 3 vols. 12mo.

THE MONASTERY. Edinburgh: for Longman . . . John Ballantyne, Bookseller to the King. 1820. 3 vols. 12mo.

MISCELLANEOUS POEMS. Edinburgh, for Constable (etc). 1820. 8vo.

KENILWORTH: A ROMANCE. Edinburgh, for Constable (etc) 1821. 3 vols. 8vo.

THE PIRATE. Edinburgh, for Constable (etc) 1822. 3 vols. 12mo.

THE FORTUNES OF NIGEL. Edinburgh, for Constable (etc) 1822. 3 vols. 8vo.

THE POETRY contained in the Novels, Tales, and Romances, of The Author of Waverley. Edinburgh, for Constable (etc) 1822. Engraved title.

HALIDON HILL. Edinburgh, for Constable (etc) 1822. Wrappers. 8pp Catalogue at end.

PEVERIL OF THE PEAK. Edinburgh, for Constable (etc) 1822 (January 1823). 4 vols. 8vo. Worthington gives Q7 as a cancel in the first state, but copies exist with the first state setting and Q7 integral.

QUENTIN DURWARD. Edinburgh, for Constable (etc) 1823. 3 vols. 8vo.

ST RONAN'S WELL. Edinburgh, for Constable (etc) 1824 (December 1823). 3 vols. 8vo. Blue boards, drab paper spines, labels. Secondary binding: Blue boards, red linen spine, labels.

RED GAUNTLET. A Tale of the Eighteenth Century. Edinburgh, for Constable (etc) 1824. 3 vols. 8vo.

TALES OF THE CRUSADERS. Edinburgh, for Constable (etc) 1825. 4 vols. 8vo.
Incorporates THE BETROTHED and THE TALISMAN.

WOODSTOCK; or, The Cavalier. Edinburgh, for Constable (etc) 1826. 3 vols. 8vo. L4 in Vol III is a cancel.

PROVINCIAL ANTIQUITIES AND PICTURESQUE SCENERY OF SCOTLAND, with descriptive illustrations by Sir Walter Scott, Bart. London, Published by John and Arthur Arch; and by William Blackwood, Edinburgh, 1826. 2 vols. 4to. Engraved Titles and 50 engraved plates (various artists).
Originally planned as 12 part issues by the publishers Rodwell & Martin, 10 parts were issued, 1819–1826. The remaining sheets were then sold to Arch and Blackwood, who brought the book out in four different states – the above ordinary issue, a Large Paper issue, a Large Paper issue with India proofs, and a Large Paper issue with India proofs and preliminary etchings.

THE LIFE OF NAPOLEON BUONAPARTE. Edinburgh. Ballantyne for Longman (etc) 1827. 9 vols. 8vo. The book contains many cancels (125 according to Ruff). All the variants are not recorded.

CHRONICLES OF THE CANONGATE. Edinburgh, for Cadell, Simpkin and Marshall 1827. 2 vols. 8vo. Also, Second Series: same publishers 1828. 3 vols. 8vo.
In this work, for the first time in a novel, Scott acknowledges his authorship by signing the introduction. A number of cancels have been identified and allocated priority in the bibliographies, but mysterious variants exist.

TALES OF A GRANDFATHER, being Stories taken from Scottish History. Edinburgh, for Cadell (etc) 1828 (December 1827). 3 vols. 12mo in half sheets. Dark blue quarter roan, marbled boards. Also, Second Series: 1829 (December 1828). 3 vols. 12mo in half sheets. Quarter green roan, drab boards. Also, Third Series 1830 (December 1829). 3 vols. 12mo in half sheets. Dark blue quarter roan, marbled boards. Also, Fourth Series, being Stories taken from the History of France: 1831 (December 1830). 3 vols. 16mo in half sheets (sic). Quarter green roan, drab boards.
According to Van Antwerp in his book A COLLECTOR'S COMMENT ON HIS FIRST EDITIONS OF THE WORKS OF SIR WALTER SCOTT, the fourth series is the rarest of the four. That was in 1932, but is probably still true.

ANNE OF GEIERSTEIN. Edinburgh, for Cadell & Simpkin and Marshall 1829. 3 vols. 12mo (although A-M in Vol I is in eights). L12D in Vol II a cancel.

THE WAVERLEY NOVELS. Magnum Opus Edition. Edinburgh: Ballantyne for Cadell . . . 1829–33. 48 vols. Royal 18mo & fcap 16mo.
The first complete collected edition of the novels.

THE POETICAL WORKS. (Edited by Lockhart). Edinburgh, for Cadell & Wittaker 1833–34. 12 vols. 8vo. Engraved frontispieces and vignette titles after Turner (first appearance of these designs).
The set was designed as a continuation of the Magnum Opus edition of the novels. Revisions and some new material are incorporated.

SHAKESPEARE, William (1564–1616)

The earliest surviving editions of individual plays date in the main from the 1590s and early 1600s. All copies from this period are very rare and valuable. Any new copy which came to light would need scholarly investigation, before any precise value (literary or monetary) could be placed upon it. Unlike the individual plays, which were generally pirated, the poems were in the main published with the author's authority. Like the plays, the earliest editions date from the 1590s and early 1600s, and these too are rare and extremely valuable.

The checklist below gives only the first collected edition of the poems, followed by the earliest editions of the collected plays. The first edition of the latter was published posthumously, but was scrupulously put together by two of Shakespeare's stage partners, John Heminge and Henry Condell. Their claim was to have used 'true original copies'.

The optimistic book hunter who hopes to stumble upon early editions of either the plays or the poems, is almost certain to be disappointed. But some later works of interest may be encountered. These include the First Illustrated Edition of the plays, which appeared in 1709–10 in seven volumes (both small and large paper editions). It was edited by Nicholas Rowe who contributed a biography of Shakespeare, divided and numbered the acts and scenes, indicated entrances and exits, and added the lists of dramatis personae for the first time. The second 'Rowe' edition of 1714 was in nine volumes. Another important later edition was edited by Lewis Theobald who in 1726 published an important early critical work entitled SHAKESPEARE RESTORED. His edition of the plays, with numerous corrections and alterations (largely accepted as valid by modern scholars) appeared in 1733–34 in seven volumes. It was reprinted several times. The First American Edition of the plays was published by Bioren and Madan of Philadelphia, in 1795–96.

The first separately printed edition of Shakespeare's life was SHAKESPEAR, WHOSE MONUMENT WAS LATELY ERECTED IN WESTMINSTER ABBEY AT THE EXPENSE OF THE PUBLICK. It was published anonymously in 1743.

POEMS: written by Wil. Shake-speare. Gent. Printed at London by Tho. Cotes, and are to be Sold by John Benson, dwelling in St. Dunstans Churchyard 1640. Dated and undated title-pages. Portrait frontispiece of the author, by William Marshall. Small 8vo.
The first collected edition of the poems.

MR WILLIAM SHAKESPEARE'S COMEDIES, HISTORIES, AND TRAGEDIES (compiled by Heminges and Condell). Printed by Isaac Jaggard and E. Blount 1623. Folio. Engraved portrait of the author by Droeshout on the title-page, and a leaf of verses by Ben Jonson preceding the title.

Second Edition: Printed by Thomas Cotes for Robert Allot 1632. Folio.
This edition incorporates some dubious corrections.

Third Edition: First issue: printed for Philip Chetwinde 1663. Folio. Blank space on the title where the portrait should be. Second issue: printed for P.C. 1664. Folio. Has the portrait on title-page with verses beneath.
The second issue has seven additional plays which, with one exception (Pericles), are now regarded as spurious. Most of the stock was burnt in a fire, making the 3rd edition rarer than the first.

Fourth Edition: First issue: printed for H. Herringham, E. Brewster, R. Chiswell and R. Bentley . . . 1665. Folio. Second issue: printed for H. Herringham, and 'are to be sold by Joseph Knight and Francis Saunders' . . . 1685. Folio.
This edition has the spelling modernized.

SHELLEY, Mary Wollstonecraft (1797–1851)

Mary Shelley is of course famous for one work – 'Frankenstein' – a rare and valuable collector's item in first edition form. Today, it would be difficult to obtain a copy in the original boards for less than £10,000. But she did write other books, and these are also keenly sought by collectors, and very hard to come by. Her first little book, heading the list below, is not well known, and indeed there is perhaps still some doubt about her authorship of it.

MOUNSEER NONGTONGPAW. (Anon. Verses after a song by Dibdin). Edward Baldwin. Juvenile Library series 1808. 16mo. Frontispiece & 11 plates by Mulready.

Edward Baldwin was a pseudonym of William Godwin. There are several early reprints – each of some value.

FRANKENSTEIN; OR, THE MODERN PROMETHEUS. (anon.). Printed for Lackington, Hughes, Harding, Mayor, & Jones 1818. 3 vols. Boards. Second Edition: Whitaker 1823. 2 vols. Third Edition (Revised, with a new introduction by the author): Colburn & Bentley 1831. Volume IX of the Standard Novels series. One vol. U.S.: Philadelphia: Carey Lea & Blanchard 1833.

VALPERGA. Printed for G. & W. B. Whittaker 1823. 3 vols. Boards. Small 8vos. No half-titles.

THE LAST MAN. Henry Colburn 1826. 3 vols. Boards, paper labels on spines. No half-titles.

THE FORTUNES OF PERKIN WARBECK. Henry Colburn and Richard Bentley 1830. 3 vols. Boards, cloth spines bearing paper labels.

LODORE. Richard Bentley 1835. 3 vols. Boards.

FALKNER. Saunders and Ottley 1837. 3 vols. Boards. Small 8vos.

RAMBLES IN GERMANY AND ITALY IN 1840, 1842, and 1843. 'By Mrs Shelley'. Edward Moxon 1844. 2 vols. Claret cloth with paper labels.

SHELLEY, Percy Bysshe (1792–1822)

Pretty well everything published in the author's lifetime is rare and expensive. The choicest items go for five-figure sums, many others for a few thousand pounds. Pirated editions and early reprints run to hundreds of pounds. For the average collector, even the first authorized collected edition of his Poetical Works (1839) is not cheap at £200–£300, though the one volume edition of the following year can generally be had for £50 or so.

I have included a number of ephemeral pieces in the checklist. These are particularly rare, many of them known only in a handful of copies. It is perhaps worth mentioning that none of these are Wise/Forman productions. The only Shelley piece which falls into that category (so far as I know) is POEMS AND SONNETS, edited by Charles Alfred Seymour, 'Printed for Private Circulation', Philadelphia 1887.

ZASTROZZI. By P. B. S. Printed for G. Wilkie & J. Robinson 1810. Boards, paper label on spine.

ORIGINAL POETRY: By Victor & Cazire. Printed by C. & W. Phillips, for the authors; and Sold by J. J. Stockdale 1810. Boards.

The authors were Shelley and his sister Elizabeth. The book is extremely rare, only a few copies having come to light. It was reprinted by John Lane in 1898.

POSTHUMOUS FRAGMENTS OF MARGARET NICHOLSON. Edited by John Fitzvictor (i.e. Shelley). Oxford: Printed and Sold by J. Munday 1810. Demy 4to. Plain wrappers.

A great rarity – only a few copies are known. There is a facsimile reprint, with several points of variance, the simplest point to check being that the words 'baleful streams' appear as 'hateful streams' on page 8 of the facsimile.

ST. IRVYNE; OR, THE ROSICRUCIAN. By 'A Gentleman of the University of Oxford'. (i.e. Shelley). J. J. Stockdale 1811. Boards.

Remaining sheets of the first edition were used for a new edition in 1822. This has a new title-page dated 1822, but beware of faked 1811 title-pages tipped-in. However, even the 1822 edition is now scarce.

THE NECESSITY OF ATHEISM. Worthing. n.d. (1811). Pamphlet of 8 leaves.

Only a few copies are known. Shelley was expelled from Oxford for circulating this pamphlet, which was written jointly with his friend T. J. Hogg.

AN ADDRESS TO THE IRISH PEOPLE. Dublin 1812. 22pp. Wrappers.

DECLARATION OF RIGHTS. (1812). Single leaf.

Only a few copies known.

THE DEVIL'S WALK. (1812). Single leaf.

Only a few copies known.

A LETTER TO LORD ELLENBOROUGH. (1812). 23pp.

The only known copy is in the Bodleian Library, Oxford.

PROPOSALS TO FORM AN ASSOCIATION. Dublin: Printed by J. Eton. (1812). 18pp. Wrappers.

Only a few copies known.

QUEEN MAB. Printed by P. B. Shelley. 1813. Boards. Handmade paper, water-marked 1812. First 'Published' Edition: W. Clark 1821. Grey boards. U.S.: William Baldwin & Co. 1821.

The author mutilated many (?) copies of the original edition by removing the title-page, along with the dedication and imprint. Thus unmutilated copies are at a premium. The work was the subject of much piracy. A number of pirated editions were issued by the Carlile family from 1822 onwards.

A VINDICATION OF NATURAL DIET. Printed for J. Callow . . . By Smith and Davy 1813. 43pp. Plain wrappers.

A REFUTATION OF DEISM. for Schulz & Dean. 1814. Plain boards.

ALASTOR. for Baldwin, Cradock and Joy . . . and Carpenter and Son . . . By S. Hamilton 1816. Boards, paper label on spine.

THE REVOLT OF ISLAM. for C. & J. Ollier . . . By B. M'Millan 1817. Boards, paper label on spine. Copies dated 1817 constitute the first issue. For later issues, the date was corrected to 1818.

A PROPOSAL FOR PUTTING REFORM TO THE VOTE. Printed for C. & J. Ollier . . . By C. H. Reynell 1817. 15pp. Wrappers.

LAON AND CYTHNA. for Sherwood, Neely & Jones . . . and C. & J. Ollier . . . By B. M'Millan 1818. Boards, paper label.

ROSALIND AND HELEN . . . with other poems. C. & J. Ollier 1819. Plain wrappers.

THE CENCI. Italy: for C. & J. Ollier 1819. (i.e. Printed in Italy for Ollier of London). Boards, paper label on spine. (250 copies). Second Edition: London: for Ollier 1821. Wrappers, paper label on front.
   This was the only work of Shelley to be reprinted in his life-time, other than the unauthorized QUEEN MAB.

PROMETHEUS UNBOUND. C. and J. Ollier 1820. Boards, paper labels. The first issue has 'Misellaneous' in the table of contents. In later issues, this was corrected to 'Miscellaneous'.

OEDIPUS TYRANNUS. Published for the Author, By J. Johnson . . . and sold by All Booksellers 1820. A 39pp unbound booklet.
   Very rare – only a few copies are known.

EPIPSYCHIDION. C. & J. Ollier 1821. Wrappers.

ADONAIS. Pisa: 1821. 25pp. Blue wrappers. U.K.: Cambridge: W. Metcalfe 1829.

HELLAS. Charles and James Ollier 1822. Wrappers, paper label on the front.

POSTHUMOUS POEMS. for John and Henry Hunt 1824. Boards, paper label on spine.

THE MASQUE OF ANARCHY. Edward Moxon 1832. Boards, paper label on spine lettered vertically SHELLEY'S MASQUE.

THE POETICAL WORKS. Edited by Mrs Shelley. 1839. 4 vols. Reprinted in a single volume in 1840 – purple cloth, but variants are known.
There were editions in 3 vols in 1847 and 1857.

LETTERS. Introductory Essay by Robert Browning. Edward Moxon 1852. Claret cloth.

SHELLEY, Percy Bysshe & Mary

HISTORY OF A SIX WEEKS' TOUR THROUGH A PART OF FRANCE, SWITZERLAND, GERMANY, AND HOLLAND. T. Hookham, jun. & C. & J. Ollier 1817. Boards, paper label on the spine, lettered vertically.

SHENSTONE, William (1714–1763)

Shenstone assisted Percy on his RELIQUES, and acted as adviser to the Birmingham printer, Baskerville. He published his first substantial work, POEMS UPON VARIOUS OCCASIONS in 1737, while still at Oxford. His other works of note are:

THE JUDGMENT OF HERCULES (Anon). for R. Dodsley, and Sold by T. Cooper 1741.

THE SCHOOL-MISTRESS: A Poem. In imitation of Spencer. Printed for R. Dodsley, and Sold by T. Cooper . . . 1742.
The first draft of this poem, in 12 stanzas, appeared in POEMS UPON VARIOUS OCCASIONS, 1737. In the first edition of 1742, there are 28 stanzas. Two stanzas were removed from later editions.

THE WORKS IN VERSE AND PROSE. Dodsley 1764–69. 3 vols. 8vo.
The first collected edition.

SITWELL, Edith (1887–1964)

THE MOTHER AND OTHER POEMS. Printed for the author, Oxford 1915. 500 copies printed, but about 200 were pulped c. 1925.
Her rare first book.

FACADE. Kensington: Favil Press. 150 signed copies. Brick-patterned red boards.
The poems going under this title were read by the author to Walton's music,

at a private gathering in January 1922. Typed copies of the 16 poems read were handed out. Nine of them, along with five others were included in the first published edition (as above). The definitive edition, revised and increased to 21 poems, was not published until 1951.

SMOLLETT, Tobias (1721–1771)

Smollett's first literary effort was the tragic play THE REGICIDE. It was never performed in his lifetime, but was eventually published in 1749 by Osborn & Miller. Before that, however, after a spell in the navy, he had some small success with a poem entitled THE TEARS OF SCOTLAND (his first publication, 1746), and two satiric poems on London life – ADVICE (1746) and REPROOF (1747). His first major commercial success was his COMPLETE HISTORY (1757–58), which provoked much controversy. This followed hard on the heels of his naval farce THE REPRISAL, which Garrick successfully put on at Covent Garden. (It was published in 1757). Today, however, it is his novels that are most highly regarded – a comparatively modern view, for they were not much admired during the 19th Century. His most significant first editions are:

THE ADVENTURES OF RODERICK RANDOM.   (anon.). for J. Osborn 1748. 2 vols.
His first novel.

THE ADVENTURES OF PEREGRINE PICKLE. (anon.). London: Printed for the Author, and sold by D. Wilson 1751. 4 vols. Sm. 8vo.
Much material was suppressed for the second and subsequent editions. A Revised Edition was published in 1758.

A FAITHFUL NARRATIVE OF THE BASE AND INHUMAN ARTS THAT WERE LATELY PRACTISED UPON THE BRAIN OF HABBAK-KUK HILDING.   By Drawcansir Alexander (pseudonym). 1752. Pamphlet.
A scurrilous work which attacked Fielding. Though Smollett did show much animosity towards Fielding (which was returned) it is not absolutely certain that Smollett was the author of the pamphlet. At all events, it is rare.

THE ADVENTURES OF FERDINAND COUNT FATHOM.   (anon.) By the Author of Roderick Random. for W. Johnston 1753. 2 vols. Sm. 8vo.

A COMPLETE HISTORY OF ENGLAND.   1757–8. 4 vols. Second edition: 1758–60. 11 vols. A CONTINUATION OF THE COMPLETE HISTORY. 1760–1. 4 vols. Another volume was added in 1765.

THE ADVENTURES OF SIR LAUNCELOT GREAVES.   1762. 2 vols.

Appeared earlier in Smollett's periodical The British Magazine, vols I & II, 1760–1.

TRAVELS THROUGH FRANCE AND ITALY.   for R. Baldwin 1766. 2 vols. 8vo.
This work caused Sterne, author of the SENTIMENTAL JOURNEY, to give Smollett the nickname 'Smelfungus'.

THE HISTORY AND ADVENTURES OF AN ATOM.   for Robinson and Roberts 1749 (i.e. 1769). 2 vols. Sm. 8vo. Copies of the second issue are correctly dated. Dublin Edition (pirated): for P. & W. Wilson, etc. 1769. 2 vols.
This work is regularly catalogued as by Smollett, but it is not absolutely certain that he was the author.

THE EXPEDITION OF HUMPHRY CLINKER.   for W. Johnston and B. Collins 1671 (1771). 3 vols. Sm. 8vo. Vol 1 is misdated 1671 only in the first issue.
This, his last work, is considered to be his masterpiece. A few months after it was published, he died at his home in Italy. The pre-dating of the work was not confined to the first edition. The Third Edition of 1783 was pre-dated 1683.

PLAYS AND POEMS, with Memoirs . . .   for Evans & Baldwin 1777.   Sm. 8vo.
The First Collected Edition.

MISCELLANEOUS WORKS.   Edinburgh: David Ramsey 1790. 6 vols. New Edition with Memoirs by R. Anderson: Edinburgh 1796. 6 vols.
Reprinted with enlarged memoir in 1800.

LETTERS HITHERTO UNPUBLISHED.   Dumbarton 1859.

SOMERVILLE & ROSS (Edith Somerville 1861–1949 & Violet Martin 1865–1915)

For their first collaboration, both adopted pseudonyms. Edith changed hers for the second edition. Thereafter, all their books appeared under the now familiar pseudonyms of Somerville & Ross. After Violet Martin's death in 1915, Edith wrote another 13 books.

AN IRISH COUSIN.   By Geilles Herring & Martin Ross (pseuds.). Bentley 1889. 2 vols. Black cloth. (500 copies).
For the second edition, Miss Somerville changed her pseudonym to 'Viva Graham'.

NABOTH'S VINEYARD. Spencer Blackett 1891. Red cloth. Standard Library series.
   Later issued undated by Griffith Farran & Co.

IN THE VINE COUNTRY. Allen 1893. Primary binding: Pictorial green cloth, blocked in black, gold-lettered; very dark grey endpapers. Catalogue at end dated January 1893.

THROUGH CONNEMARA IN A GOVERNESS CART. Allen 1893. Pictorial green cloth. Also, in pictorial scarlet cloth.

THE REAL CHARLOTTE. Ward & Downey 1894. 3 vols. Scarlet bubble-grain cloth, lettered in gold; fawn flowered endpapers. Secondary Binding: Violet or brown cloth, blocked in black, lettered in gold, white endpapers.

BEGGARS ON HORSEBACK. Blackwood 1895. Unglazed blue cloth, grey-blue endpapers, catalogue at end, dated '6/95'. Secondary binding: Slightly glazed darker blue cloth, greenish-grey endpapers, no catalogue.

THE SILVER FOX. Lawrence & Bullen 1898. Scarlet cloth.

SOME EXPERIENCES OF AN IRISH R. M. Longman 1899. Sage-green cloth, pictorially blocked, lettered in red and black, spine lettered in gold, black endpapers.

A ST PATRICK DAY'S HUNT. Longman 1902. 4to. Pictorial boards.

SLIPPER'S ABC OF FOX HUNTING. Longman 1903. 4to. Pictorial boards.

ALL ON THE IRISH SHORE. Longman 1903. Pictorial grey cloth.

SOME IRISH YESTERDAYS. Longman 1906.

FURTHER EXPERIENCES OF AN IRISH R. M. Longman 1908. Green cloth with band of white across front board and spine, d/w.

DAN RUSSELL THE FOX. Methuen 1911. Decorated brown cloth.

IN MR KNOX'S COUNTRY. Longman 1915. White-flecked green cloth.

IRISH MEMORIES. Longman 1917. Green half-cloth boards, label.

MOUNT MUSIC. Longman 1919. Green cloth.

STRAY-AWAYS. Longman 1920.

AN ENTHUSIAST.   Longman 1921. Green cloth, d/w.

WHEEL-TRACKS.   Longman 1923. Brown half-cloth boards, label.

THE BIG HOUSE OF INVER.   Heinemann 1925. Navy-blue cloth, d/w.

FRENCH LEAVE.   Heinemann 1928. Red cloth, d/w.

SARAH'S YOUTH.   Longman 1938. Green cloth.

SOMERVILLE, William (1675–1742)

His most famous work is the poem THE CHACE. The first edition is worth £100–£200. His three other first editions get about the same.

OCCASIONAL POEMS, TRANSLATIONS, FABLES, TALES ETC. Lintot 1798. 8vo.

THE CHACE. A POEM.   G. Hawkins, sold by T. Cooper 1735. 4to. Frontis. Page of Errata.
An 8vo edition was issued in the same year.

HOBBINOL, OR THE RURAL GAMES.   A Burlesque Poem in Blank Verse. for J. Stagg 1740. 4to.

FIELD SPORTS: a poem.   for J. Stagg 1742. Folio.

SPENSER, Edmund (c. 1552–1599)

As a young man at Cambridge, Spenser contributed some translations of Petrarch and Du Bellay to van der Noodt's THEATRE FOR WORLD-LINGS, published in English, 1569. This was his first appearance in print, and it is an extremely rare book, only a few copies being known (11, I believe). His major publications are given below. The first, THE SHEPHEARDES CALENDAR, is another extremely rare first edition, only seven copies being known. The seventh came to light at a provincial sale and was purchased for a few pounds, as recently as 1980. It made just over £40,000 at Christie's.

THE SHEPHEARDES CALENDAR.   Printed by Hugh Singleton 1579. Second Edition 1581. Third Edition 1586.
The 'Glosses' – Preface, arguments and verbal commentary – by 'E. K.' were probably written by Spenser's friend Edward Kirke.

THE FAERIE QUEENE.   Books I to III. William Ponsonbie 1590. The first issue has extra sonnets (8pp) at the end, and some Welsh words left as blank spaces. Books IV-VI were published, along with 'Fowre Hymnes', in 1596. The First Folio Edition was published in 1609. The First Collected Edition in 1611 (see below).

The work was originally intended to consist of 12 books, but only six were published, apart from a fragment of Book 7 which was first included in the 1609 Folio Edition.

COMPLAINTS, Containing Sundrie Small Poems of the Worlds Vanitie. William Ponsonbie 1591.

A volume of juvenilia and minor verse, published on the strength of the success of 'The Faerie Queen, I-III'.

DAPHNAIDA.   William Ponsonbie 1591.

COLIN CLOUTS COME HOME AGAINE.   William Ponsonbie 1595. Sm. 4to. First issue has 'worthylie' on line 24, leaf C. Also published under the imprint 'T. C. for William Ponsonbie' (T. C. being Thomas Creede).

'Complaints' by Colin Clout appear as Eclogues I & XII in the earlier SHEPHEARDES CALENDER.

EPITHALAMION & AMORETTI.   1595.

PROTHALAMION.   1596.

VIEW OF THE PRESENT STATE OF IRELAND.   1596.

THE FAERIE QUEEN: THE SHEPHEARDS CALENDAR: Together with Other Works . . .   H. L. for Mathew Lownes 1611. Folio.

The First Collected Edition.

STEINBECK, John (1902–1968)

The first issue of Steinbeck's first book is rare, and in the dust wrapper has a value of several thousand dollars. The second issue, put out by Corvici Friede after the critical success of TORTILLA FLAT, is relatively common and is valued at considerably less (more like $400, in fact). In general, the pre-war first editions are all scarce in fine condition with the dust wrappers.

CUP OF GOLD.   New York: McBride 1929. First issue in yellow cloth, top edges blue, pictorial d/w. 2476 copies sold. U.K.: Heinmann 1937. Blue cloth, pictorial d/w.

Sheets of the first printing were issued by Covici Friede of New York in their edition (i.e. the second issue) of 1936.

THE PASTURES OF HEAVEN. New York: Brewer, Warren & Putnam 1932. Green cloth, top edges black. Later copies have Ballou imprint on spine and (eventually) Ballou dust wrapper. U.K.: Allan 1933. Green cloth, black lettering on spine.
His first U.K. publication.

TO A GOD UNKNOWN. New York: Ballou 1933. U.K.: Heinemann 1935.

TORTILLA FLAT. New York: Covici Friede (1935). Tan cloth, blue letters. U.K.: Heinemann 1935. Blue cloth, gilt.

IN DUBIOUS BATTLE. New York: Covici Friede 1936. Top edges red. Also, 99 signed. U.K.: Heinemann 1936.

OF MICE AND MEN. New York: Covici Friede 1937. First issue has the digits of the page number '88' separated by a bullet (later removed); and p. 9 line 20–21 reads 'and only moved because the heavy hands were pendula,'. Dramatized version: same publisher, same year. U.K.: Heinemann 1937.

THE RED PONY. New York: Viking 1937. 699 signed copies. Trade/ Enlarged edition: Viking 1945.

THE LONG VALLEY. New York: Viking 1938. U.K.: Heinemann 1939.

THE GRAPES OF WRATH. New York: Viking 1939. The first edition dust wrapper is identified as such on the flap. U.K.: Heinemann 1939.

SEA OF CORTEZ. By Steinbeck & Ricketts. New York: Viking 1941. Green cloth, top edges orange. New Edition (The Log From the Sea of Cortez): Viking 1951. Maroon cloth, and variants.

THE MOON IS DOWN. New York: Viking 1942. First issue has no printer's name on verso title. U.K.: Heinemann 1942. Terra-cotta cloth.

BOMBS AWAY. New York: Viking 1942.

CANNERY ROW. New York: Viking 1945. Light buff cloth. Second issue in yellow cloth. U.K.: Heinemann 1945. Various shades of yellow/orange cloth.

THE WAYWARD BUS. New York: Viking 1947. Dark reddish orange cloth with lighter blind-stamped bus. U.K.: Heinemann 1947. Red cloth.

THE PEARL. New York: Viking 1947. U.K.: Heinemann 1948.

A RUSSIAN JOURNAL. New York: Viking 1948. U.K.: Heinemann 1949.

BURNING BRIGHT.   New York: Viking 1950. U.K.: Heinemann 1951.

EAST OF EDEN.   New York: Viking 1952. U.K.: Heinemann 1952.

SWEET THURSDAY.   New York: Viking 1954. U.K.: Heinemann 1954.

THE SHORT REIGN OF PIPPIN IV.   New York: Viking 1957. U.K.: Heinemann 1957.

ONCE THERE WAS A WAR.   New York: Viking 1958. U.K.: Heinemann 1959.

THE WINTER OF OUR DISCONTENT.   New York: Viking 1961. U.K.: Heinemann 1961.

TRAVELS WITH CHARLIE IN SEARCH OF AMERICA.   New York: Viking 1962. U.K.: Heinemann 1962.

AMERICA AND AMERICANS.   New York: Viking 1966. U.K.: Heinemann 1966.

THE ACTS OF KING ARTHUR AND HIS NOBLE KNIGHTS.   New York: Farrar Straus 1976. U.K.: Heinemann 1977.

STERNE, Laurence (1713–1768)

Sterne's two major books were enormously influential. The highly original TRISTRAM SHANDY marked the beginning of the 'stream of consciousness' brand of writing. A SENTIMENTAL JOURNEY was a masterpiece of parody. Both inspired many imitators and forgers. The first editions each fetch prices in the area of £1000 to £5000, depending on the usual factors.

THE LIFE AND OPINIONS OF TRISTRAM SHANDY, GENTLE-MAN.   Frontispiece by Ravanet. (York) and London: R. and J. Dodsley 1760–67. 9 vols. Sm. 8vo
The first two volumes were initially rejected by Dodsley. Sterne re-wrote them and they were then published in York, with half the edition being issued in London. The work made him a celebrity, and a second edition (1760) was quickly produced to meet the demand. The next four volumes came out in 1761, volumes VII and VIII in 1765, and the last in 1767. Another volume, a forgery, appeared after Sterne's death.

A SENTIMENTAL JOURNEY THROUGH FRANCE AND ITALY.   By Mr. Yorick. (pseud.). London: Printed for T. Becket and P. A. De Hondt . . . 1768. 2 vols. Sm. 8vo. Advert leaf (rare). Also, 135 copies on large paper.

There are variants, and copies are often found in mixed states. It was pirated by Miller & White 1774. 12mo. The work was continued by 'Eugenius' in 1769. Sterne's friend Hall-Stevenson has been suspected of writing it, but modern scholars have discounted him. The true author remains unknown.

THE SERMONS OF MR. YORICK.   for R. and J. Dodsley n.d. (1760–69). 7 vols. Sm. 8vo.
When the first volume came out, the mere title was regarded in some quarters as scandalous.

LETTERS TO HIS MOST INTIMATE FRIENDS.   For T. Beckett 1775. 3 vols. Sm. 8vo.

LETTERS TO HIS FRIENDS, ON VARIOUS OCCASIONS.   To which is added, his History of a Watch Coat ... Kearsley, Johnson 1775. Sm. 8vo.
William Combe is thought to have 'improved' the work. THE HISTORY OF A WATCH COAT is a retitled version of an earlier piece – A POLITICAL ROMANCE – which was written in 1759 and so outraged the authorities (it being a satire on ecclesiastical courts) they had it burned. It re-appeared (though the preface describes it as appearing for the first time) under the original title, in 1769.

LETTERS FROM YORICK TO ELIZA.   for G. Kearsley 1775. Sm. 8vo.

LETTERS FROM ELIZA TO YORICK.   For the Editor 1775. Sm. 8vo.
A forgery.

LETTERS SUPPOSED TO HAVE BEEN WRITTEN BY YORICK AND ELIZA.   For J. Bew 1779. 2 vols. 12mo.
Not by Sterne, but William Combe.

ORIGINAL LETTERS OF THE LATE REVEREND MR. LAURENCE STERNE;   never before published. Logographic Press 1788.
Another spurious collection, probably by Combe.

STEVENSON, Robert Louis (1850–1894)

From the checklist, I have excluded some of the ornate little 'first separate editions', some limited editions and most of the pamphlets. As far as the latter are concerned, if they are early they are rare and valuable, and this certainly applies to all the pieces printed by Samuel Osbourne in Davos-Platz. The following were Wise/Forman forgeries – On The Thermal Influence of Forests (q.v.), The Story of a Lie, 1882, Some College Memories, 1886, Thomas Stevenson, 1887, Ticonderoga, 1887, War in Samoa, 1893, Familiar Epistle in Verse and Prose, 1896.

THE PENTLAND RISING. Edinburgh: Andrew Elliott 1866. Foolscap 8vo. 32pp. Green wrappers, the front wrapper acting as title-page.

Very few copies were printed – probably not many more than the 20 copies released by the Stevensons in 1899. And yet, in addition to a copy in the Phillips sale of November 12, 1992, there was another at Bloomsbury on January 14, 1993.

THE CHARITY BAZAAR: An Allegorical Dialogue. 4pp. Pamphlet without imprint, printed and distributed at a charity bazaar in Edinburgh in 1868. It does not bear the printed name of the author, but all copies issued at the time were signed. Any which are not, are assumed to be remainders.

Even the remainders are rare, but naturally the signed copies are the ones most in demand. There were five copies together in a mixed lot of juvenilia at the sale of material from Stevenson's mother and her niece, at Phillips, November 12, 1992. The lot went for £1350.

NOTICE OF A NEW FORM OF INTERMITTENT LIGHT FOR LIGHTHOUSES. From the Transactions of the Royal Scottish Society of Arts. Edinburgh: Printed by Neill and Company 1871. 7pp. Pamphlet. Probably less than 50 copies.

The piece was included in volume 8 of the Society's Transactions, published in 1873.

ON THE THERMAL INFLUENCE OF FORESTS. Edinburgh: Printed by Neill and Company 1873. 14pp Pamphlet. Pale blue wrappers with the title-page reproduced on the front.

Prideaux, Stevenson's bibliographer, agonises over the number of copies printed, suggesting 26 or 27. What he did not know was that the piece was a forgery of T. J. Wise. A 'second impression' was issued in the same year, with the addition of 'From the Proceedings of the Royal Society of Edinburgh' on the title-page, in unlettered dark blue wrappers. There may have been 50 of these (according to Prideaux), that being the number of extra copies subsequently ordered by Stevenson. It should be noted that, unlike the INTERMITTENT LIGHT pamphlet, this one (both impressions) did not precede the Society's volume of Transactions, and is therefore only a First Separate Publication.

AN INLAND VOYAGE. C. Kegan Paul & Co. 1878. Frontispiece by Walter Crane. Blue cloth, bevelled, with gold and black river scene on front. First Illustrated: Chatto 1902. Frontispiece & 11 plates from photographs by J. B. Carrington. Printed in New York and issued in green imitation leather.

Stevenson's first substantial publication. The dedication copy (inscribed to his mother) got £8500 at the Phillips sale of November 12, 1992.

EDINBURGH: PICTURESQUE NOTES. Seeley, Jackson, and Halliday 1879. (December 1878). Folio. Blue cloth, arms of the City of Edinburgh embossed on front.

TRAVELS WITH A DONKEY IN THE CEVENNES. C. Kegan Paul & Co. 1879. Frontispiece by Walter Crane. Green cloth, bevelled, with mountain scene on front.

DEACON BRODIE. By Stevenson and William Ernest Henley. 1880. Mauve wrappers. No publisher given on the title-page. Printed by T. and A. Constable, Edinburgh (imprint after text). Revised Edition: printed for private circulation 1888. Cream wrappers.

VIRGINIUS PUERISQUE AND OTHER PAPERS. C. Kegan Paul & Co. 1881. Orange cloth, bevelled. 1000 copies printed. Remaining sheets bought by Chatto & Windus in 1884.

FAMILIAR STUDIES OF MEN AND BOOKS. Chatto and Windus 1882. Green cloth.

NEW ARABIAN NIGHTS. Chatto & Windus 1882. 2 vols. Green cloth. First issue: volume one (only) has yellow endpapers.

THE SUICIDE CLUB AND THE RAJAH'S DIAMOND. Chatto & Windus 1894. Blue cloth.
> Described on the title-page as 'A New Edition', this is in fact a separate printing of the first portion of New Arabian Nights.

THE SILVERADO SQUATTERS. Chatto & Windus 1883. Green cloth. Earliest issues: 32pp. publisher's catalogue at end, dated October 1883.
> The book apparently sold slowly, later issues of the first edition having catalogues dated November 1887. And yet, a 'New Edition' was published in 1886 and of this, some copies have catalogues dated January 1886, others having catalogues dated March 1886. This surely highlights the danger of using dated adverts to deduce priorities.

TREASURE ISLAND. London, Paris & New York: Cassell 1883. Frontispiece map. 2000 copies. Green or blue (later crimson) cloth. Misprints: p. 197 'worse' for 'worst'; p. 2 and p. 7 'dead man's chest' later given initial capitals. First issue has '7' of p. 127 slightly misaligned. Later, the '7' is missing. First U.K. Illustrated Edition: Cassell 1885. Red cloth. The illustrations are by various artists. U.S.: Boston 1884. Illustrated.

PRINCE OTTO. Chatto & Windus 1885. Green cloth decorated with brown flowers.

A CHILD'S GARDEN OF VERSES. Longman's Green, and Co. 1885. Blue cloth, bevelled, with The Sign of the Ship stamped in gold on top left corner of front cover. Some copies have gilt edges. Not illustrated.
> In 1892, Longmans published A CHILD'S GARLAND OF SONGS GATHERED FROM 'A CHILD'S GARDEN OF VERSES', set to music

by C. Villiers Stanford. SONG FLOWERS FROM 'A CHILD'S GARDEN OF VERSES' with music by Katherine M. Ramsay, and with illustrations, followed in 1897. The First Illustrated Edition of the complete work, with illustrations by Charles Robinson, was published by John Lane (& Scribners of New York) in 1896. This was a small 8vo in dark green cloth decorated in gold on the spine and covers. The American edition is dated 1895 and was issued in both red and green cloth.

MORE NEW ARABIAN NIGHTS / THE DYNAMITER. By Robert Louis Stevenson and Fanny Van de Grift Stevenson. Longmans, Green, and Co. 1885. Green wrappers. A few copies were issued in crimson cloth.

STRANGE CASE OF DR JEKYLL AND MR HYDE. Longmans, Green, and Co. 1886. Salmon-coloured cloth, lettered in black, with The Sign of the Ship in the top left corner of the front cover. Also issued in fawn wrappers lettered in red and blue. This has the title, author, publisher and date on the front wrapper, the date having been altered by pen from 1885 to 1886. U.S.: Scribner 1886.
The issue in wrappers appears to be scarcer than the cloth issue.

KIDNAPPED. Cassell 1886. Cloth – blue, red, brown, or green. First Illustrated Edition: Cassell 1887. Cloths of various colours.

THE MERRY MEN and Other Tales and Fables. Chatto & Windus 1887. Blue cloth with a flower-spray and five stars on the front.

MEMORIES AND PORTRAITS. Chatto and Windus 1887. F'cap 8vo. Blue buckram.

UNDERWOODS. Chatto & Windus 1887. Green cloth.

MEMOIR OF FLEEMING JENKIN. New York: Scribner 1887. Crimson cloth. (A copy is known in grey boards.). U.K.: Longmans, Green and Co. 1912. Black buckram.
The U.S. edition has a Preface by R.L.S. not included in the U.K. edition.

THE BLACK ARROW. New York: Scribner 1888. Red cloth. U.K. (three months later): Cassell 1888. Red cloth. First Illustrated Edition: Cassell 1891.

THE MASTER OF BALLANTRAE. Cassell 1889. Illustrated red cloth. Cassell adverts (20pp) at end – 4pp. on thick paper, 16 on thin.

THE WRONG BOX. By Stevenson and Lloyd Osbourne. Longmans, Green, and Co. 1889. Red cloth.
There is reason to believe that preliminary pages i-iv were reprinted at an early stage, resulting in the word 'Contents' which had been in the same

size type as the heading opposite (i.e. The Wrong Box) being reset in a smaller type.

FATHER DAMIEN. Privately Printed in Sydney, Australia 1890. 32pp Pamphlet. Another Edition: Privately printed in Edinburgh. Vellum with silk ties. According to the limitation notice, 30 copies (forming the second edition) were for subscribers and the rest (forming the third edition) were for the public.
Chatto & Windus published an edition in brown wrappers, in 1890.

BALLADS. Chatto & Windus 1890. Dark blue buckram.

AMERICAN NOTES By Rudyard Kipling / THE BOTTLE IMP By Robert Louis Stevenson. New York: M. J. Ivers & Co n.d. (1891). Blue wrappers with Colgate advert on back. The rare first issue has the publisher's address at the foot of the title-page, as '86 Nassau Street'.

ACROSS THE PLAINS. Chatto & Windus 1892. Dark blue buckram.

DAVID BALFOUR. Atlanta 1892. see CATRIONA.

THE WRECKER. By Stevenson & Lloyd Osbourne. Cassell 1892. Blue cloth.

A FOOTNOTE TO HISTORY. Cassell 1892. Dark blue cloth, also dark green cloth.

THREE PLAYS. By W. E. Henley and R. L. S. David Nutt 1892. Green cloth, 1000 ordinary copies, 100 large paper, and 30 on Japanese vellum.
In 1906 Heinemann published THE PLAYS OF W. E. HENLEY AND R. L. STEVENSON in red buckram. This added one play to the three of 1892.

THE BEACH OF FALESA. Cassell 1892. Red cloth. Only a few copies issued for copyright purposes.

ISLAND NIGHTS' ENTERTAINMENTS. Cassell 1893. Cloth (various colours). Before the half-title is a list of Works by R.L.S. In the earliest copies, the book is priced in the list at 5/- amended by ink pen to 6/-. It was issued in America four days earlier.

CATRIONA. Cassell 1893. Dark blue cloth.
This is the first U.K. edition and the first under this title. It was issued in Atlanta under the title DAVID BALFOUR, in 1892.

THE EBB-TIDE. By Stevenson & Lloyd Osbourne. Chicago & Cambridge:

Stone & Kimball 1894. Green cloth. U.K.: Heinemann 1894. Copper-coloured imitation silk.
   The American edition was published in July, the U.K. Edition in September.

VAILIMA LETTERS.   Methuen 1895. Terra-cotta buckram. U.S.: Stone & Kimball 1895. 2 vols. Green buckram.

WEIR OF HERMISTON.   Chatto & Windus 1896. Dark blue buckram.
   This is the First Published Edition. In the same year, Stone & Kimball of Chicago brought out a 'Copyright Edition' and a 'Preparatory Issue'.

SONGS OF TRAVEL and other verses.   Chatto & Windus 1896. Dark blue buckram.

IN THE SOUTH SEAS.   New York: Scribner 1896. Red cloth. U.K.: Chatto 1900. Black buckram.

ST. IVES.   New York: Scribner 1897. Brown cloth. U.K.: Heinemann 1898. Grey cloth.

A LOWDEN SABBATH MORN.   Illustrated by A. S. Boyd. Chatto & Windus 1898. Square 8vo. Dark blue cloth.

THE LETTERS OF ROBERT LOUIS STEVENSON TO HIS FAMILY AND FRIENDS.   Methuen 1899. 2 vols. Crimson buckram, paper labels on spine. Uniform with the Edinburgh Edition of the Works.
   The 4th and Cheaper Edition of 1901 contains additional letters.

THE LETTERS OF ROBERT LOUIS STEVENSON.   A New Edition with 150 new letters. Methuen (1911). 4 vols. Red leather with 'RLS' monogram on front.

PRAYERS WRITTEN AT VAILIMA.   New York: Scribner 1904. Sm. 8vo. Grey boards. U.K.: Chatto & Windus 1905. Grey boards, also in leather.
   The First Separate Edition.

THE STORY OF A LIE and other Tales.   Boston: Turner & Co. 1904.

TALES AND FANTASIES.   Chatto 1905. Blue buckram.
   This is the first U.K. edition of THE STORY OF A LIE and Other Tales.

ESSAYS OF TRAVEL.   Chatto 1905. Blue buckram.

THE ART OF WRITING.   Chatto 1905. Blue buckram.

LAY MORALS and Other Papers.   Chatto 1911. Blue buckram.

RECORDS OF A FAMILY OF ENGINEERS. Chatto 1912. Blue buckram.
First separate publication.

POEMS AND BALLADS. Complete Edition. New York: Scribner's 1913. Demy 8vo.

STOKER, Bram (i.e. Abraham Stoker 1847–1912)

His most famous work, DRACULA, is notoriously difficult to find in fine condition. A genuinely fine copy would almost certainly be priced at something in excess of £1000. Poor copies are not so difficult and generally fetch no more than a few hundred pounds. Signed copies are not particularly rare. His DUTIES OF THE CLERKS was a standard reference book, is not rare, and is not much sought after (perhaps worth £20 or so).

THE NECESSITY FOR POLITICAL ACTION. An address delivered to Trinity College Historical Society, November 13, 1872. By Abraham Stoker. Dublin: James Charles 1872. 60pp. Pamphlet.
An extremely rare ephemeral item – few copies can have survived.

THE DUTIES OF THE CLERKS OF PETTY SESSIONS IN IRELAND. Dublin: John Falconer 1879.

UNDER THE SUNSET. Sampson Low 1882 (1881). Illustrations by W. Fitzgerald & W. V. Cockburn. Imitation cream vellum, a.e.g.
A volume of eight stories for children. The Second Edition, also dated 1882, has additional illustrations. It has the same binding as the first edition, but later copies were in green cloth.

A GLIMPSE OF AMERICA. Sampson Low 1886. Brown wrappers.

THE SNAKE'S PASS. Sampson Low 1891 (1890). Pictorial cloth.
His first novel.

THE WATTER'S MOU. Constable 1895. Acme Library series. Decorated cloth, also in wrappers.

THE SHOULDER OF SHASTA. Constable 1895.
A Colonial Edition was issued by Macmillan.

DRACULA. Constable 1897. Yellow cloth, red lettering. No adverts at end. At least 3000 copies were published. Later issues have the original title page, but also have adverts at the end – 8pp or 16pp. U.S.: Doubleday & McClure 1899.

Archibald Constable & Co. issued the novel in pictorial wrappers in 1901, priced at 6d.

MISS BETTY.   Pearson 1898.

THE MYSTERY OF THE SEA.   New York: Doubleday Page 1902 (March). U.K.: Heinemann 1902 (July).

THE JEWEL OF SEVEN STARS.   Heinemann 1903.

THE MAN.   Heinemann 1905.
Issued in America, greatly abridged, as THE GATES OF LIFE.

PERSONAL REMINISCENCES OF HENRY IRVING.   Heinemann 1906. 2 vols.

LADY ATHLYNE.   Heinemann 1908.

SNOWBOUND.   Collier 1908. Wrappers.

THE LADY OF THE SHROUD.   Heinemann 1909.

FAMOUS IMPOSTERS.   Sidgwick & Jackson 1910.

THE LAIR OF THE WHITE WORM.   Rider 1911. Six coloured plates. Decorated red cloth. First issue has copyright notice dated 1911 on verso title, and 16pp adverts at end. Second issue lacks the copyright date and has no adverts at the end.

DRACULA'S GUEST AND OTHER WEIRD STORIES.   Routledge 1914.

THE DUALITISTS.   Edinburgh: Tragara Press 1986. Wrappers.
A horror story reprinted from The Theatre Annual, 1887.

STOWE, Harriet Beecher (1811–1896)

Her most famous book is worth $3000-$4000 in its rare earliest form and in very good condition. The various U.S. and U.K. cloth issues are worth far less – in the range of $300-$1000.

UNCLE TOM'S CABIN; or, Life among the Lowly.   Boston: John P. Jewett 1852. 2 vols. 8vo. Title vignette & 6 plates. The first issue has the slug of

Hobbart & Robbins on the verso title. This was later changed to George C. Rand. First issued in pictorial wrappers, then various cloths including a gift binding of pictorial brown cloth. U.K.: Cassell 1852. Illustrated by George Cruikshank. First issued in 13 parts in pictorial wrappers. As a book, with edges uncut, in black cloth, and later, in brown cloth.

STRACHEY, Lytton (1880–1932)

His first published work was a poem included in PROLUSIONES ACADEMICAE, from C.U.P. 1902. This is rare. With two others, he was the author of a volume of poems published in Cambridge in 1905 by Elijah Johnson, entitled EUPHROSYNE. (The poems in this volume however, are not ascribed.) It too is rare. None of Strachey's remaining books are especially hard to find, although the first issue of LANDMARKS can be difficult. His most valuable books are the signed limited editions, though even these can often be obtained for less than £100.

LANDMARKS IN FRENCH LITERATURE.   Williams & Norgate. Home University Library series (1912). First Issue: Bright green cloth, top edges green, spine lettered in gilt. At end, 8pp adverts for Home University Library, the last title given being 'Rome' by W. Warde Fowler. On p. 4 'Landmarks' is listed as No. 35 in the series. Second Issue: p. 3 of ads includes an extract from the Times review of 'Landmarks', and No. 58 in the series is announced. Third Issue; Green cloth, black lettering, top edge uncoloured. At front, a 4pp list giving No. 107 as the latest volume in the series. U.S.: Holt 1912.

EMINENT VICTORIANS.   Chatto & Windus 1918. U.S.: Putnam 1918.

QUEEN VICTORIA.   Chatto & Windus 1921. U.S.: Harcourt 1921.

BOOKS AND CHARACTERS.   Chatto & Windus 1922. U.S.: Harcourt 1922.

POPE.   C.U.P. 1925. Wrappers.

ELIZABETH AND ESSEX.   Chatto & Windus 1928. U.S.: Harcourt Brace/ Crosby Gage 1928. Also, a signed limited edition.

PORTRAITS IN MINIATURE.   Chatto & Windus (1931). Also, a signed limited edition. U.S.: Harcourt 1931.

CHARACTERS AND COMMENTARIES.   Chatto & Windus 1933. U.S.: Harcourt 1933.

VIRGINIA WOOLF AND LYTTON STRACHEY: LETTERS.   Hogarth Press 1956.

SPECTATORIAL ESSAYS. Chatto & Windus 1964. U.S.: Harcourt 1965.

ERMYNTRUDE AND ESMERELDA. Blond 1969. 4to. Also, a limited edition of 250 copies. U.S.: Stein & Day 1969.

SURTEES, Robert Smith (c. 1803–1864)

His first published work, apart from contributions to the Sporting Magazine, was a collection of pieces culled from the Law Reports and entitled THE HORSEMAN'S MANUAL, published in 1831. In that same year, he founded the New Sporting Magazine, in which his celebrated Cockney Sportsman, John Jorrocks appeared in the issues from July 1831 to September 1834.

The works of Surtees are perhaps collected as much for their hand-coloured plates as for their texts. However, the illustrations in the first edition of JORROCKS were not coloured, and the first editions of HANDLEY CROSS and HILLINGDON HALL were not illustrated at all. These last two were done in three volumes, and no doubt the circulating libraries took many copies. So that today, the first editions are scarce, but especially so in good condition and in the original bindings. The editions with hand-coloured plates, which have always been popular and carefully preserved, are not so scarce, although a continuing strong demand for them keeps them fairly expensive.

JORROCKS'S JAUNTS AND JOLLITIES. Walter Spiers 1838. 12 illustrations by H. K. Browne. Pictorial cloth. First Alken Edition: Ackermann 1843. Illustrated title and 14 coloured plates by Henry Alken. Pictorial cloth. New, Augmented Edition, with three additional 'papers', and the same coloured plates by Alken: Routledge 1869. Cloth.
    The first edition was reprinted in 1839. The edition of 1874 had an additional coloured plate by Alken.

HANDLEY CROSS. By the Author of 'Jorrocks's Jaunts and Jollities' etc. Henry Colburn 1843. 3 vols. Cloth. Not illustrated. First Illus. Edition: Bradbury & Evans 1854.

HILLINGDON HALL. By the Author of 'Handley Cross' etc. Henry Colburn 1845. 3 vols. Cloth. Not illustrated. First Edition with coloured plates: Bradbury, Agnew & Co. (1888). Cloth. With 12 coloured plates by Wildrake, Heath, and Jellicoe.

THE ANALYSIS OF THE HUNTING FIELD. Ackermann 1846. Oblong 8vo. Cloth. Coloured pictorial title-page, 6 coloured plates and many woodcuts by Henry Alken.

HAWBUCK GRANGE. By the Author of 'Handley Cross; etc.'. Longman, Brown, Green & Longmans 1847. Scarlet cloth. 8 full-page illustrations by Phiz. New Edition: Bradbury, Agnew. n.d. (1888). With coloured plates by Wildrake, Heath, and Jellicoe.

MR. SPONGE'S SPORTING TOUR. By the Author of 'Handley Cross'. Originally issued in 13 monthly parts, with 13 coloured plates and numerous wood engravings by John Leech. Book: Bradbury & Evans 1853. Same Leech illustrations. Pictorial cloth. New Edition: Bradbury, Agnew & Co. n.d. (1888). With coloured plates by Wildrake, Heath, and Jellicoe.

HANDLEY CROSS. By the Author of 'Mr. Sponge's Sporting Tour'. Originally issued in 17 monthly parts, in red wrappers, with 17 coloured plates and numerous wood engravings by John Leech. Book: Bradbury & Evans n.d. (1854). Same Leech illustrations. Red cloth. New Edition: Bradbury, Agnew & Co. n.d. (1888). With coloured plates by Wildrake, Heath, and Jellicoe.

ASK MAMMA. By the Author of 'Handley Cross'. Originally issued in 13 monthly parts, in red wrappers, with 13 coloured plates and numerous wood engravings by John Leech. Book: Bradbury & Evans 1858. Same Leech illustrations. Cloth. Reprinted by Bradbury, Agnew & Co. n.d. (1888) with the same coloured plates.

PLAIN OR RINGLETS? By the Author of 'Handley Cross'. Originally issued in 13 monthly parts, in red wrappers, with 13 coloured plates and numerous wood engravings by John Leech. Book: Bradbury & Evans 1860. Same Leech illustrations. Red cloth. Reprinted by Bradbury, Agnew & Co. n.d. (1888) with the same illustrations

MR. FACEY ROMFORD'S HOUNDS. By the Author of 'Handley Cross'. Originally issued in 12 monthly parts, in red wrappers, with 24 coloured plates (14 by Leech, and 14 by 'Phiz'). Book: Bradbury & Evans 1865. Same illustrations. Cloth.
Both Surtees and Leech died during publication of the parts issue. 'Phiz' was brought in to complete the illustrations.

SWIFT, Jonathan (1667–1745)

The earliest work of Swift is to be found in the Athenian Society SUP-PLEMENT TO THE FIFTH VOLUME (1691), to which he made some small contributions, and in the 1700 edition of Sir William Temple's Letters, which he edited and for which he wrote a Preface. Almost all of his many works were published anonymously or pseudonymously. In fact, only one authorized edition was published under his name, during his lifetime (see below).

A DISCOURSE ON THE CONTESTS AND DISSENTIONS BETWEEN
THE NOBLES AND THE COMMONS IN ATHENS AND ROME ...
Printed for John Nutt 1701. Small 4to.

His first original publication. Since 1949, it has been recognized that there
are two states of the 1701 text, perhaps amounting to two distinct editions.
Both are extremely rare and are valued in the range of £5000–£10,000.

A TALE OF A TUB. Written for the Universal Improvement of Mankind.
To which is added, An Account of a Battel between the Ancient and Modern
Books in St. James's Library. London: for John Nutt 1704. 8vo. Advert leaf
before the title (scarce). Page 320, line 10, should contain the word 'uterinus'.
In later issues, this becomes a blank.

Two of his better known pieces within a single first edition.

A PROPOSAL FOR CORRECTING, IMPROVING AND ASCERTAIN-
ING THE ENGLISH TONGUE; in a letter to the most Honourable Robert
Earl of Oxford and Mortimer, Lord High Treasurer of Great Britain. Printed
for Benj. Tooke ... 1712. 8vo.

This appeal for consistency in the English language, was the only authorized
edition published in his lifetime, under his real name.

(GULLIVER'S TRAVELS) TRAVELS INTO SEVERAL REMOTE
NATIONS OF THE WORLD. In Four Parts. By Lemuel Gulliver, First a
Surgeon, and then a Captain of several ships. London: for Benj. Motte 1726.
2 vols. 8vo. Portrait frontispiece in volume I, six plates in all.

There are different states of the portrait and different states of the text. Over
the years, this has led to different assessments of the book in terms of editions
and issues. And even now, there is some confusion. At the risk of adding to
it, I give here a brief summary of the main factors.

In its earliest state (referred to as 'Teerink A'), the four parts of the book
have separate pagination. Not all the prelims are actually numbered, but the
parts collate thus:

Part I. (Portrait) pp. xvi & pp. 148 (1 plate).
Part II. pp. vi & pp. 164 (1 plate)
Part III. pp. vi & pp. 155 (3 plates)
Part IV. pp. viii & pp. 199 (1 plate).

The next earliest state ('Teerink AA') is very similar to the above, but there
are only xii prelims in Part I, and Part III ends on page 154.

Of the numerous words in the text which vary between the two earliest
states, I give just a few examples for comparison:

Part I, page 3, line 19, has the word 'too'. This later becomes 'two'.
Part II, page 163, line 16, has 'Goose'. This becomes 'Gooss'.

Part III, page 79, line 5, has 'Abstinence'. This becomes 'Abstience'.
Part IV, page 89, line 19, has 'Tincture'. This becomes 'tinture'.

After the two earliest states, the pagination is continuous through Parts I &
II, and (restarting at page 1) continuous through Parts III & VI. In the past
this later state of the 1726 book, was usually called the Second Edition, and
is now sometimes described as the Third Issue of the First Edition (or
'Teerink B'). It is properly called the Third Edition.

The publisher's 'Second Edition' was also in two vols by Motte, but is dated
1727. This is sometimes called the 'First 12mo' edition. Alas, there are
variants of this too. For all the details of this and other editions, there is no
substitute for the revised Teerink-Scouten Bibliography.

DIRECTIONS TO SERVANTS IN GENERAL; and in particular to the
Butler, Cook, Footman, Coachman, Groom, House-Steward, and Land-Stew-
ard, Porter, Dairy-Maid, Nurse, Laundress, House-Keeper, Tutoress, or
Governess.   Printed for R. Dodsley ... and M. Cooper ... 1745.
This celebrated prose satire was included in Vol. VIII of Faulkner's WORKS
OF SWIFT, published in Dublin, 1746. The type for this edition might
have been set earlier than the London edition, but the London edition is in
any case the First Separate Edition.

SWINBURNE, Algernon Charles (1837–1909)

Swinburne contributed four pieces to the Oxford University collection
UNDERGRADUATE PAPERS, published by Mansell in 1858. He found
success and became a celebrity quite early in his career, with ATALANTA
IN CALYDON, first published in 1865. Thus it is only his few very early
pieces (along with a few ephemeral publications) which are genuinely rare,
the majority of his first editions after 1865 being comparatively common.

THE QUEEN-MOTHER. ROSAMOND. Two Plays.   Basil Montagu Pickering 1860. Slate cloth, paper label on spine. The author's name given as 'A.
G. Swinburne' on the label. Second issue, same year, with Moxon title-page
on a cancel-leaf.

THE CHILDREN OF THE CHAPEL. A tale.   By the author of 'Mark
Dennis'. Joseph Masters 1864. A later issue has the imprint 'J. Masters and
Co.' and is dated 1865. Red cloth.
Swinburne contributed 'The Pilgrimage of Pleasure'.

DEAD LOVE.   John W. Parker & Son 1864. 15pp. Red wrappers.
A Wise/Buxton Forgery.

ATALANTA IN CALYDON. A Tragedy. Edward Moxon 1865. 4to. Cream buckram. 100 copies printed. Second Edition: same year, in red cloth. U.S.: Boston: Ticknor & Fields 1866. Green cloth.
  The first edition is rarely priced at over £100, but the Kelmscott Press edition of 1894 is more like £500.

CHASTELARD; A Tragedy. Moxon & Co. 1865. Blue cloth or red cloth. Later issue has Hotten imprint dated 1866 on a cancel title-page, and again is in either blue cloth or red cloth.

LAUS VENERIS. Moxon 1866. 28pp. Pamphlet or in wrappers.
  A Wise/Buxton Forgery.

POEMS AND BALLADS. Moxon 1866. First issue has a quotation from The Edinburgh Review on page 8 in the publisher's adverts. In the second issue, it is on p. 4.

CLEOPATRA. John Camden Hotten 1866. 17pp. Wrappers.
  A Wise/Buxton Forgery.

NOTES ON POEMS AND REVIEWS. John Camden Hotten 1866. 23pp. Pamphlet.

THE ROYAL LITERARY FUND REPORT ON THE ANNIVERSARY. Printed by John James Metcalfe 1866. Green wrappers.

A SONG OF ITALY. John Camden Hotten 1867. Green cloth, also blue cloth.
  Carter's Variant 'A' binding is sand-grained green cloth, with 'Hotten' at foot of spine. His second binding is smooth blue cloth with gilt-lettered spine, with the date 1867 at the foot. There was a later binding of blue ribbed cloth dated 1868 at the foot of the spine.

DOLORES. John Camden Hotten 1867. 23pp. Pamphlet.
  A Wise/Buxton Forgery.

AN APPEAL TO ENGLAND . . . CONDEMNED FENIANS. Reprinted from the Morning Star 1867. Wrappers.
  A Wise/Buxton Forgery.

SIENA. John Camden Hotten 1868. 15pp. Cream wrappers. 6 copies only. A later reprint was in wrappers with an orange tint. Unlike the earlier 6 copies, the reprint has no period after the publisher's address – Piccadilly – on the title-page.
  A Wise/Buxton Forgery.

WILLIAM BLAKE: A Critical Study. John Camden Hotten 1867. 6 copies only of the first issue. There were three further issues. Second issue: has a vignette followed by 'Ithuriel'. Third issue: 'Ithuriel' becomes 'Zamiel'. Fourth issue: 'Ithuriel' becomes 'Going to an fro in the Earth'.

ODE ON THE PROCLAMATION OF THE FRENCH REPUBLIC. F. S. Ellis 1870. 23pp. Wrappers.

SONGS BEFORE SUNRISE. F. S. Ellis 1871. Blue-green cloth. Also 25 copies on large paper.

UNDER THE MICROSCOPE. D. White 1872. Wrappers. First issue: pp. 41–42 is a cancel-leaf.

BOTHWELL.   Chatto & Windus 1874. Purple (dark blue?) cloth.

GEORGE CHAPMAN.   Chatto & Windus 1875. Green cloth.

SONGS OF TWO NATIONS.   Chatto & Windus 1875. Green cloth.

ESSAYS AND STUDIES.   Chatto & Windus 1875. Green cloth.

THE DEVIL'S DUE . . .   By Thomas Maitland 1875. For Private Circulation. 11pp. Pamphlet.
   A Wise/Buxton Forgery.

ERECHTHEUS.   Chatto & Windus 1876. Green cloth.

NOTE OF AN ENGLISH REPUBLICAN ON THE MUSCOVITE CRUSADE.   Chatto & Windus 1876. 24pp. Wrappers.

A NOTE ON CHARLOTTE BRONTË.   Chatto & Windus 1877. Blue cloth. First issue does not have a dedication to Theodore Watts between sigs. A2 and B1.

POEMS AND BALLADS.   Second Series. Chatto & Windus 1878. Green cloth. Also some large paper copies.

A STUDY OF SHAKESPEARE.   Chatto & Windus 1880. Green cloth.

SONGS OF THE SPRINGTIDES.   Chatto & Windus 1880. Green cloth.

STUDIES IN SONG.   Chatto & Windus 1880. Green cloth.

SPECIMENS OF MODERN POETS . . .   Chatto & Windus 1880. Green cloth.

MARY STUART. A Tragedy.   Chatto & Windus 1881. Green cloth.

TRISTRAM OF LYONESSE AND OTHER POEMS. Chatto & Windus 1882. Green cloth.

A MIDSUMMER HOLIDAY AND OTHER POEMS. Chatto & Windus 1884. Green cloth.

MARINO FALIERO. Chatto & Windus 1885. Blue-green cloth.

A STUDY OF VICTOR HUGO. Chatto & Windus 1886. Green cloth.

MISCELLANIES. Chatto & Windus 1886. Blue-green cloth.

LOCRINE. A Tragedy. Chatto & Windus 1887. Cloth.

GATHERED SONGS. Charles Ottley, Landon & Co. 1887. Green wrappers.
   A Wise/Buxton Forgery.

THE JUBILEE MDCCCLXXXVII. Charles Ottley, Landon & Co. 1887. Green wrappers.
   A Wise/Buxton Forgery.

THE QUESTION MDCCCLXXXVII: A Poem. Charles Ottley, Landon & Co. 1887. Green wrappers.
   A Wise/Buxton Forgery.

A WORD FOR THE NAVY: A Poem. Charles Ottley, Landon & Co. 1887. Green wrappers.
   A Wise/Buxton Forgery.

A STUDY OF BEN JONSON. Chatto & Windus 1889.

THE BALLAD OF DEAD MEN'S BAY. Privately Printed 1889. Buff wrappers.
   A Wise/Buxton Forgery.

THE BRIDE'S TRAGEDY. Privately Printed 1889. Buff wrappers.
   A Wise/Forman Forgery.

THE BROTHERS. Printed 1889. Blue wrappers.
   A Wise/Forman Forgery.

A SEQUENCE OF SONNETS ON THE DEATH OF ROBERT BROWNING. Printed for Private Circulation 1890. Blue wrappers.
   A Wise/Forman Forgery.

MUSIC: An Ode. Single sheet folded to make 4pp. 4to. Printed rectos only. No place or publisher, dated Christmas, 1892. Copies of the first edition, presumably for private circulation, have 'Private and Confidential' printed at top left of each recto. Only a few copies are known in this form.

Copies have recently been offered at £1000 and at £2200.

THE SISTERS.   Chatto & Windus 1892. Blue cloth.

GRACE DARLING.   Printed Only for Private Circulation. 1893. Vellum boards.
A Wise/Buxton Forgery.

THE BALLAD OF BULGARIE.   Printed for Private Circulation 1893. Pamphlet.
A Wise/Forman Forgery.

STUDIES IN PROSE AND POETRY.   Chatto & Windus 1894. Cloth.

ASTROPHEL AND OTHER POEMS.   Chatto & Windus 1894. Blue cloth. First issue has adverts dated Feb. 1894.

ROBERT BURNS. A Poem.   Printed for Members of the Burns Centenary Club, Edinburgh 1896.
A Wise/Buxton Forgery.

THE TALE OF BALEN.   Chatto & Windus 1896.

ROSAMUND, Queen of the Lombards.   Chatto & Windus 1899. U.S.: Dodd, Mead 1899. Blue boards.

LOVE'S CROSS CURRENTS. A Year's Letters.   New York & London: Harper 1905. Mauve cloth.

THE DUKE OF GANDIA.   Chatto & Windus 1908. Also 110 on large paper. Blue cloth.

THE AGE OF SHAKESPEARE.   Chatto & Windus 1908. Blue cloth.

LETTERS . . . TO A. H. BULLEN.   Thomas J. Wise for Private Circulation 1910. 20 copies. Wrappers.

CHARLES DICKENS.   Chatto & Windus 1913. Green cloth.

POSTHUMOUS POEMS.   Heinemann 1917. Blue cloth, d/w.

WEARIESWA': A Ballad.   Printed (for T. J. Wise) 1917. 30 copies. Green wrappers.

THE TWO KNIGHTS AND OTHER POEMS. Printed (for T. J. Wise) 1918. 30 copies. Green wrappers.

THE LETTERS. Edited by Gosse and Wise. Heinemann 1918. 2 vols. Blue cloth.

THE LETTERS. Edited by Hake & Compton-Rickett. Murray 1918. Red cloth.

THE SPRINGTIDE OF LIFE. Heinemann (1918). Illustrated by Rackham. 4to. U.S.: Lippincott 1918.

T

TENNYSON, Alfred, Lord (1809–1892)

Tennyson's first editions up to about 1850, have always been seriously collected. His later works however, were produced in enormous numbers and have been very common indeed throughout the 20th Century. That is now changing, and at last they are starting to disappear from the bookshops.

Early reprints of this author's works are of some interest, for Tennyson was an habitual reviser. A poem reprinted was often a poem extensively revised, and the second edition of a volume was sometimes very different from the first. Thus the Tennyson collector needs to pay close attention to the texts.

His first book is one of the highlights of Victorian Poetry and is rare and expensive. A decent copy at less than £1000 would be a bargain. His most famous single poem is probably THE CHARGE OF THE LIGHT BRIGADE. This was first published in the 'Examiner' for December 9, 1854. It was first issued separately as a single sheet, folded once to make a foolscap 4to and printed on three sides, dated at the bottom of page 3 '8th of August, 1855'. 1000 copies were printed (at London) and sent to the troops in the Crimea. In this form (not surprisingly) it is rare, and I have seen a copy (a few years ago) offered at £1000. The poem, much revised, was later included in the collection MAUD.

As the most celebrated poet of the century, Tennyson was inevitably a prime target for pirates and forgers, including the notorious T. J. Wise. The latter's known productions (having some value) are included (and identified) in the checklist below. It should be noted however that 'Trial' or 'Proof' issues of a number of Tennyson's works were produced legitimately. All the major items, and a small selection of illustrated editions (of which there are very many) are included in the checklist.

POEMS BY TWO BROTHERS. (i.e. Alfred & Charles Tennyson). Printed for W. Simpkin & R. Marshall, Stationers' Hall Court, and J. & J. Jackson, Louth 1827. 12mo and also 8vo. (large paper copies). Drab boards with paper label, but some copies were also issued in cloth. Remaindered in yellow wrappers.

> Macmillan reprinted the book in 1893, in the familiar green cloth format of the later works. This was not the only publication of Tennyson's brother Charles. He published several volumes of sonnets, though of course he never achieved the fame of Alfred.

TIMBUCTOO . . . A Poem which obtained the Chancellor's Medal at the Cambridge Commencement, MDCCCXXIX. By A. Tennyson of Trinity College. n.d. (1829). Demy 8vo. Wrappers. There were several reprints, differing from the original edition in that the words 'ravished sense' are changed to 'lavished sense' near the end of the poem. Remaindered in drab wrappers.

POEMS CHIEFLY LYRICAL. Effingham Wilson 1830. 12mo. Drab boards, also pink boards, with paper label on spine. First Issue: page 91 is numbered '19', and there is a misprint on page 72 – 'caronet' instead of 'carcanet'. Copies are known with the mis-numbered page, but with 'carcanet' correctly spelt.

POEMS BY ALFRED TENNYSON. Edward Moxon 1833. (December 1832). Foolscap 8vo. Drab boards with paper label on spine, also issued in cloth.

THE LOVER'S TALE. Edward Moxon 1833.
> Printed for inclusion in POEMS (1833) but suppressed from that volume. A few copies survived (given to friends). A revised version of the work got to proof stage again in 1868, but was again suppressed, with only a handful of proofs surviving (without title-page). These proofs, or trial printings, are extremely rare. In 1879, Kegan, Paul & Co published a completely revised/rewritten version, which counts as the first trade edition. Other earlier editions are forgeries.

MORTE D'ARTHUR: DORA: AND OTHER IDYLLS. Edward Moxon 1842. Stitched but without covers. A forgery.

POEMS. Edward Moxon 1842. 2 vols. Foolscap 8vo. Drab boards, paper label on spine. 800 copies were printed.
> Differs substantially from the Moxon 1833 volume. Contains some pieces published previously, some revised, and some entirely new. The second edition of 1843 (also in 2 vols) contains further revisions, and the third edition of 1845 (2 vols) still further revisions.

THE PRINCESS. Edward Moxon 1847. Foolscap 8vo. Green cloth. A volume in the 'Parchment Library'. Also, 50 large paper copies.
The third edition (1850) contains several new pieces, the fourth edition contains some new and some revised pieces. In the fifth edition a passage was added to the Prologue. A folio illustrated edition was published in 1850, with 10 plates by Mrs S. C. Lee. Moxon also published a 4to edition with illustrations by Maclise in 1866.

IN MEMORIUM. Edward Moxon 1850. Foolscap 8vo. Deep purple cloth. A volume in the 'Parchment Library'. Also, 50 Large Paper copies. First Issue: page 2, line 13, has the words 'the sullen tree' instead of 'thee, sullen tree'; and page 198, line 3, has the word 'baseness' instead of 'bareness'.
The fourth edition of 1851 contains a new stanza (number 58).

ODE ON THE DEATH OF THE DUKE OF WELLINGTON. Edward Moxon 1852. 16pp. in slate-coloured wrappers.

THE LADY OF SHALOTT. Illustrated by 'A Lady'. 1852. Folio.

MAUD AND OTHER POEMS. Edward Moxon 1855. Green cloth.
According to Schwartz, there was a 'pre-natal' edition entitled MAUD; or, the Madness. He goes on to say that this is exceedingly rare – something of an understatement, because no copy is known.

DORA. Illustrated by Mrs Mildmay. 1856. Folio.

POEMS. Edward Moxon 1857. F'cap 4to. Green cloth.
The contents differ from earlier editions with the same title.

THE MILLER'S DAUGHTER. Illustrated by A. L. Bond. 1857. 4to.

IDYLLS OF THE KING. Edward Moxon 1859. 8vo. Blind-stamped green cloth gilt. First Issue: verso title-page blank (no printer's name); 4 leaves of adverts dated July 1859.
A folio edition illustrated by Gustave Dore was published in 1868.

THE MAY QUEEN. Illustrated by 'E.V.B.' (Hon. Mrs Boyle). Sampson, Low 1860. Post 8vo. Another Edition: Illustrated by Mrs W. H. Hartley. 1861. Crown 4to. And Another Edition: Illustrated by W. R. Thomms. Day & Son 1861. Small sq.4to.

HELEN'S TOWER. Clandeboye . . . Privately Printed. n.d. (1861). 4to. Pink wrappers. 8pp.
Rare.

THE SAILOR BOY. Emily Faithfull & Co., Victoria Press 1861. 8pp. in cream stiff wrappers. A forgery.

ODE FOR THE OPENING OF THE INTERNATIONAL EXHIBITION. Edward Moxon 1862. 8pp. pamphlet. A forgery.

POEMS MDCCCXXX–MDCCCXXXIII. Privately printed 1862. F'cap 8vo. Green wrappers. 112pp.
> Includes poems (published earlier) which the author wished to suppress. The work was compiled by James Dykes Campbell and printed at his expense (probably in Toronto). Reputedly 50 copies were imported into the U.K. and John Camden Hotten attempted to distribute some of them. An injunction was obtained and distribution was forbidden by the Court of Chancery. Hotten was obliged to surrender his copies. The book is scarce, but by no means impossible to get nowadays.

MARIANA. Illustrated by Mary Montgomerie Lamb. 1863. Wrappers.

A WELCOME. Edward Moxon 1863. 4pp. pamphlet. There are different states, all rare. In the same year, there was an illuminated edition by Owen Jones (which ran to three printings). This consists of 8 leaves printed on rectos only. The piece was also forged by T. J. Wise (1874).

ENOCH ARDEN. Edward Moxon 1864. Green cloth. U.S.: Boston. Ticknor & Fields 1864. Illustrated edition: Moxon 1866. 25 vignettes by Arthur Hughes.
> The original title was IDYLLS OF THE HEARTH, but this was abandoned before publication. Copies with the 'original' Idylls title-page were forged by T. J. Wise. Unlike ENOCH ARDEN, these are rare.

PROPERTY. An 8pp. pamphlet, not dated (1864). Only a few copies were printed.

THE WINDOW, or The Loves of the Wrens. (Privately Printed by Sir J. & Miss Guest). Canford Manor 1867. Folio. Limp red cloth. Text on one side only of 15 leaves (not numbered). Only six copies were printed. The first published edition was set to music by Sullivan, and issued as a quarto in 1871.

THE VICTIM. (Privately Printed by Sir J. & Miss Guest). Canford Manor 1867. Folio. Mottled grey paper boards. Also, in limp red French morocco, boards. Text on one side only of six leaves (not numbered). Only a few copies were printed.

ELAINE. Illustrated by Gustave Dore. 1867.

ENID. Illustrated by Gustave Dore. 1867.

LUCRETIUS. Cambridge, Mass.: Printed for Private Circulation 1868. 27pp. in brown cloth. A forgery.

GUINEVERE. Illustrated by Gustave Dore. 1867.

VIVIEN. Illustrated by Gustave Dore. 1869.

THE HOLY GRAIL, and Other Poems. Strahan 1870. Green cloth. The first issue does not have 'All Rights Reserved' at the foot of the title-page.

ENGLAND AND AMERICA IN 1782. Strahan & Co. 1872. 6pp. pamphlet. A forgery.

GARETH AND LYNETTE &c. Strahan 1872. Green cloth gilt.
This volume includes The Last Tournament, a trial issue of which was forged by T. J. Wise ('Strahan 1871').

TO THE QUEEN. 1873. 8pp. pamphlet. 50 copies were printed.

A WELCOME TO HER ROYAL HIGHNESS MARIE ALEXAN-DROVA. Henry S. King 1874. An 8pp pamphlet. A forgery.

QUEEN MARY, A Drama. Henry S. King 1875. Green cloth. The earliest issue has the misprinted word 'Behled' on page 126, and no printers' imprint on p. 278.

THE NEW TIMON AND THE POETS, With Other Omitted Poems. Privately Printed 1876. A forgery (Richard Herne Shepherd & T. J. Wise).

HAROLD, A Drama. Henry S. King 1877 (1876). Green cloth.

CHILD-SONGS. Kegan Paul 1880. 8pp. pamphlet. A forgery.

BALLADS AND OTHER POEMS. Kegan Paul 1880. Green cloth. U.S.: Boston. Osgood 1880.

THE PROMISE OF MAY. Printed for the Author 1883. Wrappers. A forgery.

BECKETT, A Tragedy. Macmillan 1884. Green cloth.
Copies dated 1879 were forged.

THE FALCON. Printed for the author 1879. Wrappers. A forgery.

THE CUP. Printed for the author 1881. Wrappers. A forgery.

THE CUP AND THE FALCON. Macmillan 1884. Green cloth.
Editions of the plays in this volume, dated prior to 1882 are forgeries (see above). There was, however, a genuine proof in 1882.

TIRESIAS AND OTHER POEMS. Macmillan 1885. Green cloth.

LOCKSLEY HALL SIXTY YEARS AFTER. Macmillan 1886. Green cloth.

ODE ON THE OPENING OF THE COLONIAL AND INDIAN EXHIBITION. Clowes 1886. Pamphlet. A forgery.

CARMEN SAECULARE. Printed for Private Distribution 1887. Wrappers. A forgery.

DEMETER AND OTHER POEMS. Macmillan 1889. Green cloth.

THE DEATH OF OENONE, AKBAR'S DREAM, AND OTHER POEMS. Macmillan 1892. Published in America by the same publisher, same year.

THE FORESTERS, ROBIN HOOD AND MAID MARIAN. Macmillan 1892. Green cloth.

THE DEATH OF THE DUKE OF CLARENCE AND AVONDALE. 1892. Pamphlet. A forgery.

THE ANTECHAMBER. Printed for private circulation 1906. 24pp in orange wrappers. A forgery.

THACKERAY, William Makepeace (1811–1863)

Thackeray's earliest literary efforts appeared in two Cambridge University journals, both published by W. H. Smith, entitled THE SNOB (11 numbers published in 1829) and its successor THE GOWNSMAN (17 numbers in 1830). He was also, in those early years (and indeed later), active as an illustrator, and some of his earliest published works were his illustrations. These are not included in the checklist below, for though his illustrations have their admirers, he is principally known as a novelist, and in particular, as the author of one of the classics of English Literature – VANITY FAIR. This is offered by booksellers at wildly varying prices, depending on issue and binding; but on the whole, prices fall in the range of £200–£500.

The pseudonym Mr Titmarsh or Michael Angelo Titmarsh was used for many of his publications. These are given in the checklist without comment.

THE PARIS SKETCH-BOOK. By Mr. Titmarsh. John Macrone 1840. 2 vols. Cloth.

AN ESSAY ON THE GENIUS OF GEORGE CRUIKSHANK. Henry Hooper 1840. Cloth. Reprinted from the Westminster Review, Vol 34. Of the 17 plates, that entitled 'Philoprogenitiveness' is (I understand) often missing.

THE SECOND FUNERAL OF NAPOLEON. By Mr M. A. Titmarsh. Hugh Cunningham 1841. Small 4to. Wrappers.
    Very scarce

COMIC TALES AND SKETCHES. Edited and Illustrated by Mr. Michael Angelo Titmarsh. Hugh Cunningham 1841. 2 vols. Dark brown cloth. Unsold copies were issued later (after the success of Vanity Fair) with a new title-page, not dated and crediting the author with Vanity Fair.

THE IRISH SKETCH BOOK. By Mr. M. A. Titmarsh. Chapman & Hall 1843. 2 vols. Cloth.

NOTES OF A JOURNEY FROM CORNHILL TO GRAND CAIRO, BY WAY OF LISBON. By Mr. M. A. Titmarsh. Chapman & Hall 1846. Pictorial cloth. Some copies contain a coloured frontispiece, but most do not.

MR PERKINS' BALL. By M. A. Titmarsh. Chapman & Hall. No date on title-page (1847 on front board). Crown 4to. Pink boards. The earliest of three editions in the same year (all in the same binding) has no letterpress below the frontispiece. The book was issued in two forms – with coloured plates, and with uncoloured plates.

OUR STREET. By Mr. M. A. Titmarsh. Chapman & Hall 1848. Foolscap 4to. Pink boards. Coloured plates. Second edition (same year): uncoloured plates.

THE BOOK OF SNOBS. By W. M. Thackeray. Punch Office 1848. Green pictorial wrappers.

VANITY FAIR: a Novel without a Hero. By William Makepeace Thackeray. With Illustrations on Steel and Wood by the Author. Originally issued in 20 monthly parts, from January 1847, in yellow wrappers. Book Edition: Bradbury & Evans 1849 (1848). Green cloth. Contains two title-pages, each dated 1848, and an illustrated advert for 'The Great Hoggarty Diamond'. First Issue: has the short title 'Vanity Fair' on page I in small rustic open lettered type, has a woodcut of the Marquess of Steyne on page 336, and has 'Mr Pitt' (later, 'Sir Pitt') on p. 453, the 19th line from the bottom. U.S.: Harper 1848. 2 vols. Green wrappers. Also, one volume in cloth.
    Altogether, there were five issues of the first edition in book form.

THE HISTORY OF PENDENNIS. Originally issued in 24 monthly parts, in yellow wrappers, from November 1848. Book Edition: Bradbury & Evans 1849 (Vol 1) & 1850 (Vol 2). Cloth.

THE HISTORY OF SAMUEL TITMARSH AND THE GREAT HOGGARTY DIAMOND. Bradbury & Evans 1849. Pictorial boards or wrappers.

DOCTOR BIRCH AND HIS YOUNG FRIENDS. By Mr. M. A. Titmarsh. Chapman & Hall 1849. Crown 4to. Pink boards.

AN INTERESTING EVENT. By M. A. Titmarsh. David Bogue 1849. Pink wrappers.
A Wise Forgery.

REBECCA AND ROWENA. By Mr. M. A. Titmarsh. Illustrated by Richard Doyle. Chapman & Hall (1850). Crown 4to. Pictorial boards.

THE KICKLEBURY'S ON THE RHINE. By Mr. M. A. Titmarsh. Smith, Elder (1850). Pink boards. Second Edition: With a new Preface: 1851. Pink boards.

THE HISTORY OF HENRY ESMOND, ESQ. . . . Written by Himself. Smith, Elder 1852. 3 vols. Olive-brown cloth with paper labels.

THE ENGLISH HUMOURISTS OF THE EIGHTEENTH CENTURY. London: Smith, Elder (&) Bombay: Smith, Taylor 1853. Cloth.

PUNCH'S PRIZE NOVELISTS: The Fat Contributor and Travels in London. New York: Appleton 1853. Dark brown cloth.

THE NEWCOMES. Edited by Arthur Pendennis, Esq. Illustrated by Richard Doyle. Originally issued in 24 monthly parts in yellow wrappers, from October 1853. Book Edition: Bradbury & Evans 1854. 2 vols, slate-coloured cloth.

SKETCHES AFTER ENGLISH LANDSCAPE PAINTERS. By L. Marvey. (The text by Thackeray). David Bogue, n.d. (1854). Blue cloth. Also issued in the same year (undated) by Griffin & Co.

THE ROSE AND THE RING. By Mr. M. A. Titmarsh. Smith, Elder 1855. Square 8vo. Pink boards.

THE VIRGINIANS. Originally issued in 24 monthly parts, in yellow wrappers, from November 1857. Book Edition: Bradbury & Evans 1858 (Vol 1) & 1859 (Vol 2). Cloth.

LOVEL THE WIDOWER. Smith, Elder 1861. Violet cloth.

THE FOUR GEORGES. Smith, Elder 1861. Green cloth. First Issue: has

'Sketches of Manners, Morals, Court and Town Life' on the title-page. Subsequent Issues: the same words appear on the half title, but not on the title-page.

A LEAF OUT OF A SKETCH-BOOK.   Emily Faithful & Co. Victoria Press 1861. Green wrappers.
A Wise Forgery.

ADVENTURES OF PHILIP.   Smith, Elder 1862. 3 vols. There are three cloth bindings, with uncertain priority – two brown and the other violet-blue. Sadleir defines them as issue i – brown cloth with 'Smith, Elder & Co.' on the spine. Copies in this binding have a catalogue dated July 1862 at the end of volume 3; issue ii – brown cloth with 'Smith & Elder' on the spine; issue iii – violet-blue cloth with 'Smith & Elder' on the spine.
   Sadleir's 'issue i' conforms with the copy in the B. M. and he regards this as the first officially published version. He conjectures that the violet-blue copies were bound first but rejected as unsatisfactory. Essentially, the mystery is that the imprint 'Smith & Elder' was abandoned at least 36 years before the publication of the book.

ROUNDABOUT PAPERS.   Smith, Elder 1863. (1862). Cloth. 4 plates (not 2 as listed).

THE STUDENTS' QUARTER.   John Camden Hotten n.d. (1864). 5 coloured illustrations. Cloth.

DENIS DUVAL.   Smith, Elder 1867. Cloth.

THAKERAYANA.   Chatto & Windus 1875 (1874). Pictorial red cloth. Pp. xx–492. Suppressed for a time, but reissued with altered text and five coloured plates.

THE ORPHAN OF PIMLICO . . .   By Miss M. T. Wigglesworth . . . and other Sketches, Fragments, and Drawings. By William Makepeace Thackeray. Smith, Elder 1876. Large 4to. Slate-coloured boards, lettered in dark red. Some copies were issued with coloured illustrations. Later Issues: in blue cloth.

THOMAS, Dylan (1914–1953)

Firmly established now as one of the most important British poets of the twentieth century. Thomas remains a strong favourite with collectors. He achieved a kind of celebrity quite early on and this did not go unnoticed by collectors, who quickly gathered up his early first editions. His wider fame began just after the war, with the publication of DEATHS AND

ENTRANCES. Thus his first editions from that point on (c. 1946) are not rare, but the earlier ones have now become very scarce.

18 POEMS. Sunday Referee & The Parton Bookshop 1934. Black cloth, grey d/w. First issue has a flat spine. The second issue has a rounded spine. Second Edition: Fortune Press (1942). 'First Published in 1934' on verso title-page. First issue in red boards, yellow d/w.

TWENTY-FIVE POEMS. Dent (1936). Grey boards & d/w.

THE MAP OF LOVE. Dent 1939. Mauve cloth, grey & purple d/w. Gold lettering on front and spine, publishers imprint in blind. Top edges dark purple. Second issue: in a deeper mauve (plum) cloth. Third issue: blocked in blue, and top edges purple. Fourth issue: top edges plain.

THE WORLD I BREATHE. U.S.: New Directions (1939). Some copies have two stars on each side of the author's name (on the title-page and spine), other copies (later?) have five stars on each side.
 Selections from works previously published in the U.K., but including two previously unpublished stories.

PORTRAIT OF THE ARTIST AS A YOUNG DOG. Dent (1940). Green cloth, d/w. U.S.: New Directions (September 1940). Red cloth, d/w.

NEW POEMS. New York: New Directions 1943. Mauve boards, d/w. Also issued in wrappers.

DEATHS AND ENTRANCES; poems. Dent 1946. $5\frac{1}{2} \times 4\frac{1}{2}$ ins. Orange cloth, d/w.

SELECTED WRITINGS. New York: New Directions (1946). Pink cloth, d/w.
 Reprints are identifiable only from the flap of the dust wrapper.

TWENTY-SIX POEMS. Dent & New Directions (1950). Limited to 150 signed, including 10 on Jap vellum. (50 copies for sale in Great Britain).
 This volume was printed in 1939, but publication was delayed by the war. The British copies sold out on the day of publication (31st August 1950).

IN COUNTRY SLEEP. New York: New Directions 1952. Also 100 signed.

COLLECTED POEMS 1934–1952. Dent 1952. Also 65 signed copies. U.S.: New Directions 1953. First printing has 'daughter' mis-spelt on p. 199.
 Dent issued 68 proof copies a few weeks before publication. The proofs lack the Author's Prologue, but include the poem 'Paper and Sticks' which was left out of the published volume. (It appeared earlier in DEATHS AND ENTRANCES).

THE DOCTOR AND THE DEVILS.   Dent 1953. U.S.: New Directions 1953.

TWO EPIGRAMS OF FEALTY.   by Dylan Thomas Duke of Gweno. Thirty memorial copies privately printed for Members of the Court. Not for Sale. (1953). 16mo. 8pp. Pamphlet. Title, author, and limitation notice (with copy number) on front.
  Not in Rolph's Bibliography.

GALSWORTHY & GAWSWORTH.   Privately Printed (1953). 16mo. 8pp. Pamphlet. Limited to 30 numbered copies.
  Matching the preceding item, and again not in Rolph.

UNDER MILK WOOD.   Dent (1954). U.S.: New Directions (1954).

QUITE EARLY ONE MORNING.   Dent (1954). U.S.: New Directions 1954.

CONVERSATION ABOUT CHRISTMAS.   New York: New Directions 1954. (2000 copies). Wrappers. 6 leaves, stapled, with an envelope.

ADVENTURES IN THE SKIN TRADE AND OTHER STORIES.   New York: New Directions 1955. U.K. (without 'other stories'): Putnam 1955.

A PROSPECT OF THE SEA.   Dent 1955.

LETTERS TO VERNON WATKINS.   Faber/Dent 1957. U.S.: New Directions 1957.

THE BEACH OF FALESA.   U.S.: Stein & Day 1963. U.K.: Cape 1964.

TWENTY YEARS A-GROWING.   Dent 1964.

REBECCA'S DAUGHTERS.   Triton 1965. U.S.: Little Brown 1965.

ME AND MY BIKE.   New York: McGraw-Hill (1965) and U.K.: Triton (1965). 4to.
  Proof pages of the first (limited) edition were dated 1964 and bore a limitation notice, stating that 1000 copies were issued. The published book was dated 1965 on the verso title-page, and the limitation was given as 500 copies.

SELECTED LETTERS.   Dent 1966. U.S.: New Directions 1967.

THE NOTEBOOKS.   New York: New Directions 1967. U.K.: Dent 1968.

EARLY PROSE WRITINGS.   Dent 1971. U.S.: New Directions 1972.

THE DEATH OF THE KING'S CANARY. By Thomas & Davenport. Hutchinson 1976.

THOMAS, Edward (1878–1917)

His first prose work THE WOODLAND LIFE is the most expensive, at two or three hundred pounds. After that, the prose up to 1904 and the much later poetry volumes are most in demand.

The early poetry was published under the pseudonym Edward Eastaway (to distinguish the poet from the hack prose writer). His earliest poems appeared in James Guthrie's quarterly journal ROOT AND BRANCH, Volume 1, no. 4, 1915. This includes two poems by Thomas. Two more appeared in the anthology THIS ENGLAND, O.U.P. 1915. And an important item is the anthology AN ANNUAL OF NEW POETRY published by Constable in 1917, which contains 18 poems by Thomas. The anthology TWELVE POETS, Selwyn & Blount 1918, includes a selection of poems by Thomas. The first dust wrapper for this book carries the misprint 'Charles on Holiday', subsequently changed to 'Clerks on Holiday'. I understand that only 12 copies had the misprinted d/w.

THE WOODLAND LIFE. Blackwood 1897. Red cloth, gilt panel with red floral design on the front. Second binding: blue-green buckram, dark green panel and green lettering on the front. Second Issue: smooth green cloth, black panel with green floral design on the front, lettering black.
Eckert describes the first two bindings listed above as 'states' of the first issue, with no definite priority. The red binding, he says, represents a 'deluxe style'. Gwendolyn Murphy (earlier) gave a blue-green version as the first edition. There are other variants, some not described by either Eckert or Murphy.

HORAE SOLITARIE. Duckworth 1902. Green cloth, gilt. U.S.: Dutton n.d. Red cloth. Title leaf and dedication leaf pasted onto p. vii.
Eckert gives no date for the Dutton edition. I believe it was 1902 and made up from U.K. sheets with the cancels noted above. It was Thomas's first book to be published in America.

OXFORD. A. & C. Black (1903). Illustrations by Fulleylove. Blue cloth. First issue: 'A. & C. Black' at foot of spine. Second issue: 'Black' at foot of spine. Also a de luxe edition of 300 copies.

ROSE ACRE PAPERS. Printed by Lanthorn Press, Published by Brown Langham 1904. Blue cloth spine with paper label, blue and white boards. New Edition: Duckworth 1910. Green cloth.
The 1910 edition differs substantially from the 1904 edition, and is in effect a different book with the same title.

BEAUTIFUL WALES. A. & C. Black 1905. Dark green cloth.

THE HEART OF ENGLAND. Dent 1906. 4to. White cloth, d/w. U.S.: Dutton (1906).

RICHARD JEFFERIES. Hutchinson 1909. Blue cloth. Folding map at end. U.S.: Boston: Little, Brown 1909. Blue cloth. Folding map at front.

THE SOUTH COUNTRY. Dent 1909. Green cloth. Heart of England series.

REST AND UNREST. Duckworth 1910. Dark green cloth with 'Duckworth & Co.' at foot of spine. Second issue (Remainder): has simply 'Duckworth' at foot of spine. U.S.: Dutton 1910.
A variant (of the second issue) has pictorial endpapers by Will G. Mein.

FEMININE INFLUENCE ON THE POETS. Secker 1910. Blue cloth, d/w. First issue: gilt-lettered on front; title and publisher printed in blue on the title-page, which is dated, with Ballantyne's imprint on verso. Second issue: black-lettered front cover, title-page lettered in black only, not dated, lacking imprint on verso. U.S.: John Lane 1911. Cancel title-page.

WINDSOR CASTLE. Blackie & Son 1910. Grey boards. Beautiful England series. Blackie imprint foot of p. 56. Second Edition: almost identical to the first edition, but no imprint on p. 56, and the adverts (after title-page) give 9 vols ready in the series, as opposed to 6 in the first edition.

THE ISLE OF WIGHT. Blackie & Son 1911. Grey boards. Beautiful England series, with adverts for 16 vols ready, and 4 vols in the Beautiful Ireland series.
Eckert suspects an earlier issue, advertising fewer vols in series.

LIGHT AND TWILIGHT. Duckworth 1911. Green cloth, d/w; later, in bluish-green or plum cloth, d/w.

MAURICE MAETERLINCK. Methuen (1911). Red cloth.

CELTIC STORIES. Clarendon Press 1911. Green cloth.

THE TENTH MUSE. Secker (1911). First issue: cream buckram with t.e.g., also red cloth with top edges red. Second issue (c. 1916): red cloth, top edges plain, front cover lettered in white. Third issue (1917): blue cloth. No frontispiece.

ALGERNON CHARLES SWINBURNE. Secker 1912. Blue cloth. First issue: at end, 2pp. notes and references pasted in, followed by adverts dated September 1912. Second issue: lacks 2pp. notes. Third issue: lacks 2pp. notes and has adverts dated autumn 1914.

GEORGE BORROW. Chapman & Hall 1912. Purple cloth. Second issue: corrigendum slip bound in after p.xii, and lacks gilt ornament at top of spine.

LAFCARDIO HEARN. Boston & New York: Houghton Mifflin 1912. Green cloth. U.K.: Constable 1912. Green cloth. Second issue: Leaf, with adverts, pasted on half-title (in 1913).
   The U.S. edition preceded the U.K. edition by six days.

NORSE TALES. Clarendon Press 1912. Blue cloth.

THE ICKNIELD WAY. Constable 1913. Green cloth, t.e.g. Second issue: top edges plain.

THE COUNTRY. Batsford (1913). Blue cloth, gilt. Fellowship Books series. Dated imprint on p. (61).

THE HAPPY-GO-LUCKY MORGANS. Duckworth 1913. Green cloth. Frontispiece. Second issue: lacks frontispiece, and has undated title-page tipped in.

WALTER PATER. Secker 1913. Dark blue cloth, t.e.g. Adverts dated 1913. Second issue: has a frontispiece, but no adverts, t.e.g. Third issue: has a frontispiece, but no adverts, and top edges plain.

IN PURSUIT OF SPRING. Nelson (1914). Blue cloth, t.e.g. Second issue: top edges plain.

FOUR-AND-TWENTY BLACKBIRDS. Duckworth (1915). Light blue cloth, black lettering and ruling, d/w. Second issue: gilt-lettering, gilt and blind ruling, and 16pp adverts at end.

THE LIFE OF THE DUKE OF MARLBOROUGH. Chapman & Hall 1915. Red cloth. Second issue: green cloth.

SIX POEMS. By Edward Eastaway (pseud.). Flansham, Sussex: Pear Tree Press (1916, although printed and bound over a period of several years). 100 copies, signed by James Guthrie (the printer). Small folio. Boards or wrappers. Earliest copies printed on Jap vellum; later copies on handmade paper with a label bearing the author's true name on p. 17. Second Edition: same press 1927.
   His first volume of poetry, and the only one seen by him.

KEATS. London & Edinburgh: Jack. New York: Dodge (1916). The People's Books series. Green cloth. Second issue: in yellow wrappers.

POEMS. By Edward Thomas ('Edward Eastaway'). Selwyn & Blount 1917.

Grey boards, paper label on spine. 525 copies. U.S.: Holt 1917. Blue cloth spine, blue boards. 525 copies.
> There were two proof copies giving the author as Edward Eastaway. The U.K. and U.S. editions were simultaneous.

A LITERARY PILGRIM IN ENGLAND. New York: Dodd, Mead 1917. Grey-blue cloth. U.K.: Methuen (1917). Dark blue cloth, gilt-lettered spine. 31pp adverts dated 5/1/16 at end. Second state: adverts dated 4/10/16. Second Issue: royal blue cloth. Second issue/second state: blue cloth of vertical weave, adverts dated 4/10/16.
> The U.S. edition preceded the U.K. edition by 12 days, and consisted of U.K. sheets with a cancel title-page. No priority can be safely attributed to the date of the adverts in the U.K. edition. A later U.K. issue (not mentioned by Eckert) is bound in blue cloth with the spine lettered in pale blue, and has no adverts.

LAST POEMS. Selwyn & Blount 1918. Cream boards, paper label.

COLLECTED POEMS. Selwyn & Blount 1920. Blue cloth, paper label. Also De Luxe Edition of 100 copies. U.S.: Seltzer 1921.

CLOUD CASTLE. Duckworth (1922). Blue cloth. First issue: gilt-lettered spine. Second issue: black-lettered spine. U.S.: Dutton (1923). Light blue cloth. U.K. sheets with new title-page.

ESSAYS OF TODAY AND YESTERDAY. Harrap (1926). Black wrappers. Second state: brown dermatoid binding, red and gold border on front. Second Issue: bound in imitation leather. Second Issue, second state: dermatoid binding, blue and gold border on front.

CHOSEN ESSAYS. Gregynog Press 1926. Limited to 350 copies.

AUGUSTAN BOOKS OF MODERN POETRY – EDWARD THOMAS. Benn (1926). Wrappers.

SELECTED POEMS. Gregynog Press 1927. Limited to 275 copies.

TWO POEMS. Ingpen & Grant 1927. Limited to 85 copies.

THE LAST SHEAF. Cape (1928). Green linen.

THE CHILDHOOD OF EDWARD THOMAS. Faber 1938.

THE FRIEND OF THE BLACKBIRD. Pear Tree Press 1938.

THE PROSE OF EDWARD THOMAS. Falcon Press 1948.
> Includes some letters printed for the first time.

LETTERS TO GORDON BOTTOMLEY.   O.U.P. 1968.

THOMAS, Helen

AS IT WAS.   Heinemann 1926. Second issue has pp. 53/4 tipped in, following the removal of a description of love-making which today seems perfectly innocuous. U.S.: Harper 1926. Unexpurgated text.

WORLD WITHOUT END.   Heinemann 1931.
The above two books were first combined in one volume in 1935.

THOMPSON, Flora (1876–1947)

Her first published work, apart from journalism, was a little-known volume of verse entitled BOG-MYRTLE AND PEAT published in 1921. The well-known book LARK RISE TO CANDLEFORD was originally published as three separate volumes, as follows:

LARK RISE.   Oxford University Press 1939.

OVER TO CANDLEFORD.   O.U.P. 1941.

CANDLEFORD GREEN.   O.U.P. 1943.

LARK RISE TO CANDLEFORD.   O.U.P. 1945.
The first edition of the trilogy in one volume.

STILL GLIDES THE STREAM.   O.U.P. 1948.
Unlike the LARK RISE Trilogy, this work was entirely fictional.

THOMSON, James (1700–1748)

THE SEASONS.   Originally published in parts, 1726–1730. Collected Form: printed by Samuel Richardson for Miller 1730. 4to. Also 8vo.

THE CASTLE OF INDOLENCE: An Allegorical Poem.   Miller 1748. 4to.

THOREAU, Henry David (1817–1862)

Thoreau published only two books during his lifetime – the first two listed below. They made no impact at the time, but the second, WALDEN, has come to be regarded as a masterpiece and one of the most important books in American Literature. It has a current value of about $3000. His first book is scarcer but not such a seminal work, and has a similar value.

A WEEK ON THE CONCORD AND MERRIMACK RIVERS. Boston & Cambridge: Munroe / New York: Putnam / Philadelphia: Lindsay & Blacksiton / London: Chapman 1849. 16mo. Brown cloth (also known in black). Only 294 copies were sold. The last 3 lines of p. 396 were missing, and in some copies, the author inserted the lines in pencil. Remaining sheets were used for a new edition with a new title-page, published by Ticknor & Fields of Boston in 1862. 16mo.

WALDEN. Boston: Ticknor & Fields 1854. Brown cloth. Adverts variously dated from April to December, 1854. Errors: first two leaves not numbered; 'post' for 'port', p. 24; 'single spruce' for 'double spruce', p. 137; 'white spruce' for 'black spruce', p. 217.

EXCURSIONS. Boston: Ticknor & Fields 1863. Green cloth. Eng. portrait.

THE MAINE WOODS. Boston: Ticknor & Fields 1864. Green cloth. First Issue: advert leaf for 'Atlantic Monthly' at end, reads, 'The Thirteenth Volume' and 'January, 1864' (but the British Museum copy has no advert). Some copies have adverts dated April 1864.

CAPE COD. Boston: Ticknor & Fields 1865. Variant cloth bindings – green, purple, or brown.

LETTERS TO VARIOUS PERSONS. Boston: Ticknor & Fields 1865. Issued in cloth of various colours. Later bindings have 'James R. Osgood & Co.' on the spine.

A YANKEE IN CANADA. Boston: Ticknor & Fields 1866.

EARLY SPRING IN MASSACHUSETTS. Boston: Houghton, Mifflin 1881.

SUMMER: FROM THE JOURNAL. Boston: Houghton, Mifflin / New York: Riverside Press 1884. Cloth.

WINTER: FROM THE JOURNAL. Boston & New York: Houghton, Mifflin, etc. 1888. Cloth.

AUTUMN: FROM THE JOURNAL. Boston & New York: Houghton, Mifflin, etc. 1892. Cloth.

MISCELLANIES. Boston & New York: Houghton, Mifflin, etc. 1894. Cloth.

FAMILIAR LETTERS. Boston & New York: Houghton, Mifflin, etc. 1894. Cloth. Also, Edition de-luxe of 150 copies.

POEMS OF NATURE. Boston & New York: Houghton, Mifflin / London: John Lane 1895. Cloth.

SOME UNPUBLISHED LETTERS. Printed on the Marion Press / Jamaica, Queensborough, New York 1899. 150 copies.

THE SERVICE. Boston: Goodspeed 1902. Cloth.

THE FIRST AND LAST JOURNEYS. Boston: Bibliophile Society 1905. 2 vols.

SIR WALTER RALEIGH. Boston: Bibliophile Society 1905.

TOLKIEN, J. R. R. (1892–1973)

THE HOBBIT and LORD OF THE RINGS, the cornerstones of his reputation, are among the most sought after first editions in the whole of twentieth century literature. Inevitably, they have become very difficult to obtain, and of course, very expensive. Of the two, the much earlier HOBBIT is the scarcer, but each of them currently costs in excess of £2000 in fine condition, and can be considerably more than that.

In compiling the checklist below, I have not had the benefit of the Bibliography of Tolkien by Wayne Hammond, announced for publication in the winter of 1993. The seemingly endless stream of posthumous publications, revamped editions, and spin-offs, have been excluded.

OXFORD POETRY 1915. Basil Blackwell 1915.
This anthology includes Tolkien's poem 'Goblin Feet'. It should not be confused with the later collection entitled OXFORD POETRY 1914–16 which contains the same poem.

A MIDDLE ENGLISH VOCABULARY. O.U.P. 1922. U.S.: O.U.P. 1922.

A NORTHERN VENTURE. Leeds: Swan Press 1923.
This contains three poems by Tolkien.

SIR GAWAIN AND THE GREEN KNIGHT. Edited by Tolkien and E. V. Gordon. O.U.P. 1925. Should have an errata slip. U.S.: O.U.P. 1925.

BEOWULF: THE MONSTER AND THE CRITICS. British Academy 1936. Grey wrappers. U.S.: Folcroft Editions 1972.

SONGS FOR THE PHILOLOGISTS. University College 1936.
  Contains 13 poems by Tolkien.

THE HOBBIT; or There and Back Again. Allen & Unwin 1937. Black & white illustrations by the author. Rear flap of d/w carries a blurb with the misprint 'Dodgeson'. Most copies have the 'e' deleted by pen, but a number were sent out before the error was noticed. U.S.: Houghton Mifflin 1938.
  For the second impression (1938) four coloured plates were added. The second edition (1951) was revised. The third edition (1966) contains further revisions. De-Luxe editions were issued in 1976 and 1987. All the foregoing were published by Allen & Unwin, but some sheets of the 1976 edition were issued by the Folio Society under their imprint and in their own binding.

THE REEVE'S TALE. Oxford 1939. Pamphlet.

SIR ORFEO. Oxford 1944. Pamphlet.

FARMER GILES OF HAM. Allen & Unwin 1949. U.S.: Houghton Mifflin 1950.

THE FELLOWSHIP OF THE RING. Allen & Unwin 1954. Red cloth, grey d/w. U.S.: Houghton Mifflin 1954.

THE TWO TOWERS. Allen & Unwin 1954. Red cloth, grey d/w. U.S.: Houghton Mifflin 1955.

THE RETURN OF THE KING. Allen & Unwin 1955. Red cloth, grey d/w. U.S.: Houghton Mifflin 1956.

LORD OF THE RINGS. The above three works were first issued together as 3 vols in one slipcase, by Allen & Unwin in 1962. Revised Editions (3 vols): Allen & Unwin 1966.
  The first one vol edition was issued as a paperback in 1968. There was a De-Luxe edition on India Paper (one vol in slipcase) in 1969, and the Folio Society Edition, illustrated by Eric Frazer, came out in 1977.

THE ADVENTURES OF TOM BOMBADIL. Allen & Unwin 1962. U.S.: Houghton Mifflin 1963.

TREE AND LEAF. Allen & Unwin 1964. U.S.: Houghton Mifflin 1965.

THE ROAD GOES EVER ON. New York: Houghton Mifflin 1967. U.K.: Allen & Unwin 1968. 4to.

SMITH OF WOOTON MAJOR. Allen & Unwin 1967. Glazed boards. Issued without dust wrapper. U.S.: Houghton Mifflin 1967.

THE FATHER CHRISTMAS LETTERS. Allen & Unwin 1976. U.S.: Houghton Mifflin 1976.

THE SILMARILLION. Allen & Unwin 1977. U.S.: Houghton Mifflin 1977. The U.K. edition was printed by Billing & Sons. A Commonwealth Issue was printed by William Clowes. Copies of this latter are sometimes offered at a premium price, on the dubious basis that it is scarcer in the U.K. than the issue printed by Billing.

PICTURES BY J. R. R. TOLKIEN. Allen & Unwin, 1979. Cloth and slipcase. U.S. (THE PICTURES OF . . .): Houghton Mifflin 1979.

THE LETTERS. Edited by H. Carpenter and C. Tolkien. Allen & Unwin 1981. U.S.: Houghton Mifflin 1981.

TRAHERNE, Thomas (1637–1674)

He published only one book during his lifetime. This was ROMAN FORG-ERIES, 1673. His CHRISTIAN ETHICKS was prepared for publication before his death, but appeared posthumously in 1675. The bulk of his poems, including his best pieces, were only discovered in the winter of 1896–97, when Mr W. T. Brooke purchased a notebook (for a few pence) at a London bookstall and showed it to the bookseller Bertram Dobell. Dobell identified the contents as the work of Traherne, and edited and published them in 1903 and 1908. The notebook is now in the Bodleian. Subsequently, further poems (prepared for publication by Traherne's brother) were discovered in a manuscript in the British Museum, and these were published in 1910. And since then, yet more of his work has been discovered in the J. M. Osborne collection.

POETICAL WORKS. 1903.

CENTURIES OF MEDITATION. 1908.

POEMS OF FELICITY. Edited by H. I. Bell. Oxford: Clarendon Press 1910.

TROLLOPE, Anthony (1815–1882)

Enthusiasm for Trollope's works is now as great as it has ever been – with both readers and collectors. His earliest works were not a commercial success, but with the publication of THE WARDEN in 1855, his fortunes began to change and during the 1860s his works became very popular indeed – especially the Barsetshire novels, which remain firm favourites to this day. However, by the time of his death in December 1882, his popularity had waned again.

It was not until the early years of this century, and especially during the 1920s, that collectors began to take a keen interest in his first editions. By then, some had become very scarce, but many others were still readily obtainable in their original form and in reasonable condition. Now, as we near the end of the twentieth century, they are pretty well all scarce and rapidly getting scarcer, while interest in his works continues to grow. A collector starting out today with the aim of getting all Trollope's first editions in their original bindings and in fine condition, has a very long road ahead of him. Collectors can no longer afford to ignore rebound copies, although many issue points will have been lost in the rebinding.

Trollope's first work THE MACDERMOTS OF BALLYCORAN is one of the rarest books in the entire field of nineteenth century fiction. Only 400 copies were printed, and not all of those were put out with the original 1847 title page (first issue). It appears that very few copies have survived.

The several novels which followed the first were, as will be seen from the list below, also published in small numbers, and they too are rare.

In general, the identification of Trollope first editions is not too great a problem. They are at least all dated on the title-page. However, those not familiar with Sadleir's Bibliography should be warned that it describes many issues and binding variants, which I have not had space to include in the following summary.

THE MACDERMOTS OF BALLYCORAN. Thomas Cautley Newby 1847. 3 vols. Brown cloth. Second issue dated 1848. 400 copies in all were printed.

THE KELLYS AND THE O'KELLYS. Henry Colburn 1848. 3 vols. Half cloth and boards. 375 copies printed.

LA VENDEE. Henry Colburn 1850. 3 vols. Half cloth and boards, also green cloth. Second issue, same year, with cancel title pages giving the author's previous works. 500 copies printed.

THE WARDEN. Longman, etc. 1855. Adverts on endpapers. Pale brown cloth with horizontal grain. Second Binding has the Second Edition of Johnston's New Dictionary of Geography advertised on the front endpaper and Roget's Thesaurus on the back endpaper; and (sometimes) a catalogue dated March 1856 bound in. Third binding has catalogue dated October 1858. In all, 1000 copies were printed.

BARCHESTER TOWERS. Longman, etc. 1857. 3 vols. Pale brown cloth. Brick red endpapers with adverts. Second binding has liver-brown endpapers with adverts.

THE THREE CLERKS. Bentley 1858. 3 vols. Quarter grey cloth, brown boards; also, dark grey-purple cloth.

DOCTOR THORNE. Chapman & Hall 1858. 3 vols. Dark grey-purple cloth.

THE BERTRAMS. Chapman & Hall 1859. 3 vols. Dark grey-purple cloth.

THE WEST INDIES AND THE SPANISH MAIN. Chapman & Hall 1859. Maroon cloth.

CASTLE RICHMOND. Chapman & Hall 1860. 3 vols. Dark grey-purple cloth. First Issue: On the spine, no line between 'Trollope' and 'Vol 1'; 16pp. catalogue dated Feb. 1860; on verso title, imprint is 'William Clowes & Sons'. Second Issue: On the spine, a line between 'Trollope' and 'Vol 1'; 32pp. catalogue dated May 1860; on verso title, imprint is 'William Clowes & Sons'. (Sadleir lists many other differences.). Secondary Binding: 3 vols, dark green cloth, no author on spine. Copies are known with first issue points, in the secondary binding.

FRAMLEY PARSONAGE. Smith, Elder 1861. 3 vols. Grey-purple cloth. Subsequently issued, same year, in one vol without illustrations, violet cloth.

TALES OF ALL COUNTRIES. Chapman and Hall 1861. Blue cloth. Some copies have a 32pp. catalogue dated November 1861, some do not – no priority established.
   Remaining sheets of this first series, along with those of the second series (1863) were issued (with the original title pages) as a single volume in green cloth.

ORLEY FARM. Chapman and Hall. 20 monthly parts from March 1861, in buff wrappers. Book Edition, First Issue: Bound from parts (stabholes throughout). 1862. 2 vols. Brown-purple cloth.
   There were three further issues. The issue points in these are complicated by the fact that the volumes were not published simultaneously. See Sadleir's Bibliography.

NORTH AMERICA. Chapman and Hall 1862. 2 vols, pinkish-maroon cloth. Pirated by Harper 1862, one vol. Authorized U.S. Edition (4 days after the Harper pirate): Lippincott 1862. 2 vols.

THE STRUGGLES OF BROWN, JONES, AND ROBINSON. New York: Harper 1862. Buff wrappers. (Pirated). U.K.: Smith, Elder 1870. Brown cloth.

TALES OF ALL COUNTRIES. Second Series. Chapman & Hall 1863. Blue cloth, uniform with the binding of the first series.
   The remaining sheets of the first and second series (including title pages), were bound up and issued as a single volume in green cloth.

RACHEL RAY. Chapman and Hall 1863. 2 vols. Pinkish maroon cloth – the dominant lines of the pattern being horizontal and 'VOL I' and 'VOL II' on the spine being in roman capitals with serifs.
   The first six editions were issued within six months, and all dated 1863. Sadleir takes the view that 3000 copies were printed in the first place and issued at the rate of 500 copies per edition, the original title page being over-printed with the edition number. And this, he suggests, is why Rachel Ray is one of the scarcer Trollope first editions. Sets of mixed editions may have been sold originally.

THE SMALL HOUSE AT ALLINGTON. Smith, Elder 1864. 2 vols. Green cloth.

CAN YOU FORGIVE HER? Chapman and Hall. 20 Monthly Parts from Jan. 1864, in buff wrappers. Book: Chapman and Hall 1864 (Vol 1) & 1865 (Vol 2). 2 vols. Crimson cloth.

MISS MACKENZIE. Chapman and Hall 1865. 2 vols. Green cloth. Also, maroon cloth (earlier, but probably a trial binding).

HUNTING SKETCHES. Chapman and Hall 1865. Red cloth, bevelled edges. 32pp catalogue dated May 1865.
   Catalogues dated October 1864 – i.e. earlier than the book itself – are not unknown, but are not accepted as denoting an earlier issue.

THE BELTON ESTATE. Chapman and Hall 1866. 3 vols. Red cloth. 24pp. catalogue dated December 1, 1865.

TRAVELLING SKETCHES. Chapman and Hall 1866. Red cloth, uniform with HUNTING SKETCHES. 24pp. catalogue dated February 1866.

CLERGYMEN OF THE CHURCH OF ENGLAND. Chapman and Hall 1866. Red cloth, uniform with HUNTING SKETCHES. 24pp. catalogue dated March 30, 1866.

NINA BALATKA. Edinburgh & London: Blackwood 1867. 2 vols. Red-brown cloth. 8pp. catalogue at end of vol 2.

THE LAST CHRONICLE OF BARSET. 32 weekly parts from December, 1866, in white wrappers. 32 Illustrations by George H. Thomas. Book: Smith, Elder 1867. 2 vols. Powder blue cloth with gold church porch on front and spire on spine. The first issue was bound from the parts and has stab holes throughout.

Beyond that, issue points are complex – see Sadleir for details.

THE CLAVERINGS. Smith, Elder 1867. 2 vols. Green cloth, gold scales on front. Some copies have a blind border on front and back, others have the border in black. (Priority uncertain.). U.S.: Harper 1866. One vol.

The date 1866 on the Harper volume is dubious, but this edition may still have preceded the U.K. edition by a few weeks.

LOTTA SCHMIDT, AND OTHER STORIES. Strahan 1867. Maroon cloth.

LINDA TRESSEL. Edinburgh & London: Blackwood 1868. 2 vols. Red-brown cloth.

PHINEAS FINN. Virtue 1869. 2 vols. Green cloth. Author's name not on the binding.

HE KNEW HE WAS RIGHT. 32 weekly numbers in pale grey-green wrappers, published by Virtue, from 17th October, 1868. Also published in 8 monthly parts, in buff wrappers, from November 1869 (but not dated). And also issued in 2 parts in wrappers by Harper, in U.S.A. during 1869. U.K. Book Edition: Strahan 1869. 2 vols. Green cloth.

THE VICAR OF BULHAMPTON. 11 monthly parts in blue-grey wrappers, published by Bradbury, Evans, from July, 1869. Book Edition: Bradbury, Evans 1870. Brown cloth.

AN EDITOR'S TALES. Strahan 1870. Pinkish brown cloth with author and title on the front, also in dark brown cloth with publisher's device (only) on front. (No priority established.)

THE COMMENTARIES OF CAESAR. Edinburgh & London: Blackwood 1870. Brown cloth. A school book in the series 'Ancient Classics For English Readers'.

Reprinted several times with the same date and binding. The first edition is identified by the presence of 2 leaves of publisher's adverts at end (i.e. following page 182), and by only three other titles in the series being advertised (within the book) as already published.

SIR HARRY HOTSPUR OF HUMBLETHWAITE. Hurst and Blackett 1871. Orange-red cloth. U.S.: 500 sets of English sheets issued (later) by MacMillan in New York, dated 1871.

RALPH THE HEIR. 19 Monthly Parts published by Strahan from January, 1870, in buff wrappers. Also issued as a stitched-in Supplement to Saint Paul's

Magazine, from January 1870. Book: Hurst and Blackett 1871. 3 vols. Brown cloth.

THE GOLDEN LION OF GRANPERE. Tinsley Brothers 1872. Red brown cloth. Also in a later, secondary binding of dark brown cloth.

THE EUSTACE DIAMONDS. Chapman and Hall 1873. 3 vols. Salmon-brown cloth, lettered in gold on spine. Also a dubious secondary binding of brown cloth, lettered in black on the spine. U.S.: Harper 1872. One vol.
  The Harper edition preceded the U.K. edition by two months.

AUSTRALIA AND NEW ZEALAND. Chapman and Hall 1873. 2 vols. Red brown cloth with blind decoration on back, and black decoration on front. A later binding, also of brown cloth, was plainer, having only blind frames and centre ornament on back and front.
  An 'Authorized Australian Edition' was published by George Robertson in Melbourne in the same year, in six parts in blue wrappers, and also in one vol bound in red cloth.

PHINEAS REDUX. Chapman and Hall 1874. 2 vols. Blue cloth. U.S.: Harper 1874. One vol. With 26 illustrations – 2 more than the U.K. Edition.

LADY ANNA. Chapman and Hall 1874. 2 vols, red-brown cloth. There is a secondary binding, similar to the first, but of a cheaper quality.

HARRY HEATHCOTE OF GANGOIL. Sampson, Low 1874. Red cloth, also blue. U.S.: Harper 1874.
  The Harper edition preceded the U.K. edition. A Tauchnitz edition, dated 1874, may also have preceded the U.K. edition.

THE WAY WE LIVE NOW. 20 Monthly Parts in blue wrappers. Chapman and Hall from February 1874. Book: Chapman 1875. 2 vols. Green cloth, also blue cloth.

THE PRIME MINISTER. 8 Monthly Parts in grey wrappers. Chapman and Hall from November 1875. The parts were also issued (simultaneously) in brown cloth, with the wrappers bound in. Book: Chapman 1876. 4 vols. Red-brown cloth.

THE AMERICAN SENATOR. Chapman and Hall 1877. 3 vols. Pinkish ochre cloth. Secondary bindings: blue, brown, or green cloth.

CHRISTMAS AT THOMPSON HALL. New York: Harper 1877. Drab Wrappers.
  The story (and the illustrations) originally appeared in the Graphic Christmas Number, December 1876. The first separate U.K. Edition, entitled

THOMPSON HALL (still with the same illustrations) was done by Sampson, Low in 1885.

SOUTH AFRICA.   Chapman and Hall 1878. 2 vols. Red cloth.
The Abridged version of 1879, contains some material not in previous editions.

IS HE POPENJOY?   Chapman and Hall 1878. 3 vols. Red-brown cloth.

THE LADY OF LAUNAY.   New York: Harper 1878. Drab wrappers.

AN EYE FOR AN EYE.   Chapman and Hall 1879. 2 vols. Green-ochre cloth.

THACKERAY.   Macmillan 1879. English Men of Letters series. Cream cloth, paper label on spine.
The ninth book in the series and followed by Church's SPENSER. The vols already published, and the planned SPENSER are listed in a publisher's advert at the end. Copies in ochre or red cloth are generally not first editions, being of later issue, but those carrying the appropriate advertisement are (rightly or wrongly) frequently offered as First Issues.

JOHN CALDIGATE.   Chapman 1879. 3 vols. Grey cloth, later in green cloth.

COUSIN HENRY.   Chapman 1879. 2 vols. Blue cloth, also brown cloth.

THE DUKE'S CHILDREN.   Chapman 1880. 3 vols. Blue-green cloth.

THE LIFE OF CICERO.   Chapman 1880. 2 vols. Maroon cloth. Darker maroon cloth used a little later, with fancy (as opposed to plain) capitals used in the lettering (e.g. the 'V' of 'VOL' on the spine, curls over the 'O').

DR WORTLE'S SCHOOL.   Chapman 1881. 2 vols. Greenish grey cloth.

AYALA'S ANGEL.   Chapman 1881. 3 vols. Orange cloth, also blue-grey.

WHY FRAU FROHMANN RAISED HER PRICES, and Other Stories.
Isbister 1882. Green cloth, also blue, also red. Also issued (a little later) in 2 vols with a cancel title page in vol 1.

THE FIXED PERIOD.   Edinburgh & London: Blackwood 1882. 2 vols. Red cloth.

LORD PALMERSTON.   Isbister 1882. English Political Leaders series. Red-brown cloth.

MARION FAY. Chapman 1882. 3 vols. Yellow ochre cloth, also blue cloth.

KEPT IN THE DARK. Chatto 1882. 2 vols. Olive-brown cloth.

MR SCARBOROUGH'S FAMILY. Chatto 1883. 3 vols. Green-blue cloth.

AN AUTOBIOGRAPHY. Edinburgh and London: Blackwood 1883. 2 vols. Red cloth (smooth early, ribbed later).

THE LANDLEAGUERS. Chatto 1883. 3 vols. Green cloth.

AN OLD MAN'S LOVE. Edinburgh and London: Blackwood 1884. 2 vols. Smooth red cloth, also (probably later) in red cloth with embossed broad lines.

THE NOBLE JILT, a comedy. Constable 1923. Red patterned cloth, cream d/w.

LONDON TRADESMEN. London & New York: Elkin Mathews & Scribner's 1927. Red linen spine, marbled boards, plain glacine d/w. Limited to 530 copies. Unlimited edition in 1928.

TWAIN, Mark (Samuel Langhorne Clemens, 1835–1910)

Samuel Langhorne Clemens obtained the pseudonym 'Mark Twain' from the leadsman's call on the Mississippi, on which he worked as a pilot from 1857 to 1861. His memories of those years are contained in LIFE ON THE MISSISSIPPI. TOM SAWYER and HUCKLEBERRY FINN (both first published in London) are rare and of course valuable, fetching prices in excess of £1000. His first book, published in New York, cannot normally be obtained for under $2000 (often considerably more). A full checklist of the major works is given below.

THE CELEBRATED JUMPING FROG OF CALVALERAS COUNTY, AND OTHER SKETCHES. New York: Webb. 1867. First Issue has yellow advert leaf before title, perfect 'i' in 'this' on p. 198 (last line) and perfect 'life' on p. 66 (last line). Issued in cloth, various colours – plum-coloured is generally preferred nowadays. U.K.: Routledge 1867. Wrappers.

THE INNOCENTS ABROAD. Hartford: American Pub. Co. 1869. First Issue: numerals on right of pp. xvii & xviii are missing, 'conclusion' missing from foot of p. xviii, and no portrait of Napoleon III on p. xviii. U.K.: Hotten (1870). U.K. (Revised): Routledge 1872.

Both the Hotten edition (unauthorized) and the Routledge edition were in 2 vols, entitled THE INNOCENTS ABROAD (vol 1) and THE NEW PILGRIM'S PROGRESS (vol 2). Hotten also issued the whole work in a single volume entitled MARK TWAIN'S PLEASURE TRIP ON THE CONTINENT (also in 1870).

MARK TWAIN'S (BURLESQUE) AUTOBIOGRAPHY AND FIRST ROMANCE. New York: Sheldon (1871). Cloth, also wrappers. First Issue: No advert of Ball, Black & Co. on verso title. U.K.: Hotten (1871) Wrappers. Unauthorized. U.K. (authorized. 2 weeks after Hotten): Routledge (1871). Wrappers.

MEMORANDA FROM THE GALAXY. Toronto: Backas 1871. Buff wrappers. Pirated.

EYE OPENERS / GOOD THINGS... Hotten (1871). Cloth, also yellow wrappers.

SCREAMERS / A GATHERING... Hotten (1871). Cloth, also yellow wrappers.

ROUGHING IT. Routledge 1872 (about 2 weeks before the U.S. edition). U.S.: Hartford: American Pub. Co. 1872. Black cloth, also leather. 'Issued by Subscription only'. Early impressions have perfect 'M' in first line of Contents, and perfect 'y' in first word of Chapter 1.

THE INNOCENTS AT HOME. 'Copyright Edition'. Routledge (1872). Cloth, also boards, also yellow wrappers.
   This is the second half of ROUGHING IT which appeared a week earlier in the U.S.

A CURIOUS DREAM... Selected and Revised... Routledge (1872).

SKETCHES. Selected and Revised... Copyright Edition. Routledge 1872. Pictorial boards.

SKETCHES. Authorized Edition. New York: American News Co. (1874). Green wrappers. First Issue: Plain back wrapper.

THE GILDED AGE. By Twain & Warner. Hartford: American Publishing Co. 1874 (December 20 1873). First Issue lacks illustration on p. 403. Later issues usually have 2 leaves of publisher's lists at end. U.K.: Routledge 1874 (same day as U.S.). 3 vols.

SKETCHES, NEW AND OLD. Hartford & Chicago: American Pub. Co. 1875. First issue: p. 299 has paragraph 'From Hospital Days' and erratum slip regarding the piece; also duplicated 'Note' on pp. 119/120.

OLD TIMES ON THE MISSISSIPPI.   Toronto: Belford 1876. Maroon cloth, also wrappers.

INFORMATION WANTED.   Routledge (1876). Yellow boards.

THE ADVENTURES OF TOM SAWYER.   Chatto & Windus 1876 (June). Red cloth. First Illustrated Edition: Chatto 1876 (December 16). U.S.: American Publishing Co. / Roman & Co. 1876 (end December). On wove paper, later on cheap rough paper. First Issue: Blank leaves before & after Preface. Blue cloth. In the second printing the frontispiece appears on the verso half-title.

A TRUE STORY. . . .   Boston: Osgood 1887. Maroon cloth, also green cloth.

PUNCH, BROTHER, PUNCH . . .   New York: Slote, Woodman (1878). Red wrappers, also green and blue cloth. First issue: author's name in Roman caps on title-page (not script).

A TRAMP ABROAD.   Hartford: American Pub. Co. / London: Chatto 1880. Black cloth. First issue: lines of engraved frontispiece vertical (later, oblique). U.K. Edition: later in 1880 in 2 vols.

THE PRINCE AND THE PAUPER.   Chatto 1881. Red cloth. Catalogue at end dated November 1881. U.S.: (Boston) 1882 (December 13 1881). Franklin Press imprint on verso title. Also in U.S., a De-Luxe edition of 20 copies in vellum.

THE STOLEN WHITE ELEPHANT.   Chatto 1882. Red cloth. U.S.: Boston: Osgood 1882 (2 days after U.K.). Tan cloth.

DATE 1601 / CONVERSATION . . .   Ye Acadamie Presse 1882. 11pp. Pamphlet.
    Much pirated.

LIFE ON THE MISSISSIPPI.   Chatto & Windus 1883. Red cloth. U.S.: later in 1883. First issue has plate of Mark Twain in flames on p. 441.

THE ADVENTURES OF HUCKLEBERRY FINN.   Chatto & Windus 1884. 32pp adverts dated October 1884. The first issue has '[preparing]' beside this title in the adverts. Red cloth. U.S.: New York: Webster 1885. Green cloth, also (later) in blue cloth. (Various points and states).

LIBRARY OF HUMOR.   Chatto & Windus 1888. Red cloth.

A CONNECTICUT YANKEE IN KING ARTHUR'S COURT.   New York: Webster 1889. Green cloth. U.K.: Chatto & Windus 1889.

MERRY TALES.   New York: Webster 1892. Blue-grey cloth. First bound up without portrait frontispiece, and with figured endpapers.

THE AMERICAN CLAIMANT.   New York: Webster 1892. Blue-grey cloth, also tan cloth. U.K.: Chatto & Windus 1892.

THE $1,000,000 Bank Note.   New York: Webster 1893. U.K.: Chatto & Windus 1893.

TOM SAWYER ABROAD.   Chatto & Windus 1894. Red cloth. U.S.: later in 1894.

PUDD'NHEAD WILSON.   Chatto & Windus 1894. Red cloth. U.S.: later in 1894.

TOM SAWYER ABROAD / TOM SAWYER, DETECTIVE / AND OTHER STORIES . . .   New York: Harper 1896. Red cloth. First issue has 'MT' in gilt on front.

TOM SAWYER, DETECTIVE . . .   Chatto & Windus 1897.

HOW TO TELL A STORY.   New York: Harper 1897. Red cloth.

FOLLOWING THE EQUATOR.   Hartford: The American Pub. Co. 1897. Blue cloth, also leather. First issue has photo of elephant on cover.

MORE TRAMPS ABROAD.   Chatto & Windus 1897. Maroon cloth.
   The U.K. edition of FOLLOWING THE EQUATOR.

QUEEN VICTORIA'S JUBILEE.   Privately Printed 1897. Cloth spine, cream boards.

THE MAN THAT CORRUPTED HADLEYBURG . . . Stories and Essays.   New York & London: Harper 1900. Red cloth. First issue on thick paper. U.K.: Chatto & Windus 1900. Has 'Sketches' in title, not 'Essays'.

TO THE PERSON SITTING IN DARKNESS.   Reprinted . . . February, 1901. 16pp. Pamphlet.

EDMUND BURKE ON CROKER & TAMMANY.   (1901). 15pp. Grey wrappers.

A DOUBLE BARRELLED DETECTIVE STORY.   New York & London: Harper 1902. Red cloth.

MY DEBUT AS A LITERARY PERSON.   Hartford: American Publishing Co. 1903. Leather.

A DOG'S TALE.   National Anti-vivisection Society (1903). Yellow wrappers.

EXTRACTS FROM ADAM'S DIARY.   New York & London: Harper 1904. Red cloth.

KING LEOPOLD'S SOLILOQUY.   Boston: Warren 1905. Paper covers, printed in green. Black covers indicate second issue.

THE $30,000 BEQUEST.   New York & London: Harper 1906. Red cloth.

WHAT IS MAN?   (anonymous) New York: De Vinne Press 1906. Grey boards. 250 copies.

A HORSE'S TALE.   New York & London: Harper 1907. Red cloth. Also, an edition in wrappers, published by the S.P.C.A.

CHRISTIAN SCIENCE.   New York & London: Harper 1907. First issue has perfect 'W' in 'Why' on p. 5, line 14.

IS SHAKESPEARE DEAD?   New York & London: Harper 1909.

THE MYSTERIOUS STRANGER.   1916.

WHO WAS SARAH FINDLAY?   Privately Printed by Clement Shorter 1917. Grey wrappers. 25 copies.

U

UPDIKE, John Hoyer (b. 1932)

Many of Updike's stories first appeared in the periodical the 'New Yorker' before being collected into volume form. The following list includes all his major works, and many lesser ones, to 1984. The more recent works are still very common indeed. The earliest works are just becoming scarce, and demand is strong.

THE CARPENTERED HEN AND OTHER TAME CREATURES.   New York: Harper (1958). 'First Edition' on verso title.

HOPING FOR A HOOPOE.   Gollancz 1959.

The U.K. edition of THE CARPENTERED HEN AND OTHER TAME CREATURES. Has 'Author's Note' added.

THE POORHOUSE FAIR. New York: Knopf 1959. 'First Edition' on verso title. U.K.: Gollancz 1959.

THE SAME DOOR. New York: Knopf 1959. 'First Edition' on verso title. U.K.: Deutsch 1962.

RABBIT, RUN. New York: Knopf 1960. 'First Edition' on verso title. U.K.: Deutsch 1961.
   The Penguin paperback edition of 1964 was revised.

PIGEON FEATHERS. New York: Knopf 1962. 'First Edition' on verso title. U.K.: Deutsch 1962.

THE MAGIC FLUTE. New York: Knopf (1962).

THE CENTAUR. New York: Knopf 1963. 'First Edition' on verso title. U.K.: Deutsch 1963.

TELEPHONE POLES. New York: Knopf 1963. 'First Edition' on verso title. U.K.: Deutsch 1963.

OLINGER STORIES. New York: Vintage Books (1964). Wrappers. 'First Vintage Edition, September, 1964' on verso title.

THE RING. New York: Knopf (1964).

ASSORTED PROSE. New York: Knopf 1965. 'First Edition' on verso title. U.K.: Deutsch 1965.

ON THE FARM. New York: Knopf 1965. 'First Edition' on verso title. U.K.: Deutsch 1973.

A CHILD'S CALENDAR. New York: Knopf (1965).

DOG'S DEATH. (Cambridge, Mass.: Scott) 1965. Broadside. 100 signed.

VERSE. Greenwich, Conn.: Crest Book / Fawcett Publications (1965). 'First Crest Printing, February 1965' on verso title.

THE MUSIC SCHOOL. New York: Knopf 1966. 'First Edition' on verso title. First Issue: On page 45, lines 15 & 16 read 'The state of both his universities / The King, observing with judicious eyes,'. Later, the lines were reversed on a tipped-in leaf, and later still the correction was made on an integral leaf. U.K.: Deutsch 1973.

COUPLES. New York: Knopf, 1968. 'First Edition' on verso title. U.K.: Deutsch 1968.

BATH AFTER SAILING. (Stevenson, Conn.: Country Squires Books 1968). A few copies (around 18) were issued as a broadside (some printed in Roman, some in Italic), and 125 signed copies were issued in wrappers.

THE ANGELS. Pensacola, Fla.: King & Queen Press 1968. Wrappers. 150 copies.

THREE TEXTS FROM EARLY IPSWICH. Ipswich, Mass.: The 17th Century Day Committee 1968. Wrappers. 1000 copies, including 50 numbered and signed.

ON MEETING AUTHORS. Newburyport, Mass.: Wickford Press 1968. Wrappers. 250 copies.

MIDPOINT. New York: Knopf, 1969. 'First Edition' on verso title. Also 350 signed copies, boxed. U.K.: Deutsch 1969.

BOTTOM'S DREAM. New York: Knopf (1969).

BECH. New York: Knopf 1970. 'First Edition' on verso title. Also 500 signed copies, boxed. U.K.: Deutsch 1970.

THE DANCE OF THE SOLIDS. (New York: Scientific American c. 1970). Wrappers.

THE INDIAN. The Blue Cloud Quarterly, XVII, 1. (1971). Wrappers.

RABBIT REDUX. New York: Knopf 1971. 'First Edition' on verso title. Also 350 signed copies, boxed. U.K.: Deutsch 1972.

A CONVERSATION WITH JOHN UPDIKE. (Schenectady, N.Y.: Union College 1971). Special Issue of THE IDOL, Spring 1971. Wrappers.

MUSEUMS AND WOMEN. New York: Knopf 1972. 'First Edition' on verso title. Also 350 signed copies. U.K.: Deutsch 1973.

WARM WINE. New York: Albondocani Press 1973. Wrappers. 276 signed copies.

A GOOD PLACE. (New York): Aloe Editions 1973. Wrappers. 126 signed.

SIX POEMS. (New York): Aloe Editions 1973. Wrappers. 126 signed.

BUCHANON DYING.   New York: Knopf 1974. 'First Edition' on verso title. U.K.: Deutsch 1974.

CUNTS.   New York: Hallman (1974). 276 signed.

QUERY.   (New York: Albondocani / Ampersand 1974). Wrappers. 400 copies.

A MONTH OF SUNDAYS.   New York: Knopf 1975. 'First Edition' on verso title. Also, 450 signed copies, boxed. U.K.: Deutsch 1975.

SUNDAY IN BOSTON.   (Derry, Penn.: Rook Press 1975). Broadside. 300 copies, of which 100 were signed by the author, and 100 were signed by both author & illustrator.

PICKED-UP PIECES.   New York: Knopf 1975. 'First Edition' on verso title. Also 250 signed copies, boxed. U.K.: Deutsch 1976.

MARRY ME.   New York: Knopf 1976. U.K.: Deutsch 1977.

TOSSING AND TURNING.   New York: Knopf 1977. U.K.: Deutsch 1977.

THE COUP.   New York: Knopf 1978. U.K.: Deutsch 1979.

FROM THE JOURNAL OF A LEPER.   Lord John Press 1978.

16 SONNETS.   Ferguson 1979.

THREE ILLUMINATIONS IN THE LIFE OF AN AMERICAN AUTHOR.   Targ Editions 1979.

PROBLEMS AND OTHER STORIES.   New York: Knopf 1979. U.K.: Deutsch 1980.

TOO FAR TO GO.   Fawcett 1979.

RABBIT IS RICH.   New York: Knopf 1981. U.K.: Deutsch 1982.

BECH IS BACK.   New York: Knopf 1982. U.K.: Deutsch 1983.

THE BELOVED.   Lord John Press 1983. Limited signed.

HUGGING THE SHORE.   New York: Knopf 1983. U.K.: Deutsch 1984.

THE WITCHES OF EASTWICK.   New York: Knopf 1984. U.K.: Deutsch 1984.

WALPOLE, Horace, Earl of Orford (1719–1797)

The interest of collectors in Walpole's output covers a number of different fields – principally art, literature, and private printing. The short checklist below gives only his original literary publications. His most celebrated work of literature was of course the Gothic novel THE CASTLE OF OTRANTO. This was given to the world under a double-pseudonym of author and translator. The truth was simply that Walpole wrote it, as he readily admitted when it proved to be a success. His memoirs and letters are of great interest to collectors in all fields. The former were left by the author in a sealed chest and not opened until 21 years after his death. They were published in 1822 (2 vols) and 1845 (4 vols). There have been several editions of his letters (some appeared in the WORKS of 1798) but the definitive edition, is the Yale edition – a monumental work, published over the period 1937–1981 in 42 volumes, followed by a further 6 volumes of corrections, additions, and an index.

THE BEAUTIES. An Epistle to Mr. Eckhardt, the Painter. Printed for M. Cooper . . . 1746. Folio.
His anonymous second book (pirated) and the first edition of his first poem. Extremely rare.

A CATALOGUE OF THE ROYAL AND NOBLE AUTHORS OF ENGLAND, with Lists of their Works. Engraved frontispiece & vignettes. Printed at Strawberry-Hill 1758. 2 vols, sm. 8vo. 300 copies were printed. Second Edition, corrected and enlarged: Dodsley 1759 (5 December 1758). 2000 copies.

FUGITIVE PIECES IN VERSE AND PROSE. Printed at Strawberry-Hill 1758. Sm. 8vo. 200 copies printed.

THE MAGPIE AND HER BROOD: A Fable. (Strawberry-Hill 1764). 4pp. 4to. 200 copies printed.

THE CASTLE OF OTRANTO, a Story. Translated by William Marshall, Gent. From the Original Italian of Onuphrio Muralto, Canon of the Church of St. Nicholas at Otranto. London: for Thomas Lowndes 1765. Sm. 8vo.
A classic of the Gothic genre, now worth about £2000.

THE MYSTERIOUS MOTHER. A Tragedy. Printed at Strawberry-Hill: 1768. 8vo. Only 50 copies printed. Second Edition: Dodsley 1781.

The first edition, as might be expected, is very rare. The second edition is not common, but might be obtained for something close to £100.

WORKS.   Robinson 1798. 5 vols. 4to.
The first collected edition.

WALTON, Isaak (1593–1683)

Though Walton's fame rests almost entirely on THE COMPLEAT ANGLER, he did write some other works of literary interest – namely, biographies of Donne (1640), Wotton (1651), Hooker (1665), Herbert (1670), and Sanderson (1678).

Bibliographically, THE COMPLEAT ANGLER is an extremely interesting work. To begin with, the first edition is not the 'best' edition nor the definitive edition, and certainly not the only edition of interest to collectors. All the early editions, and some later ones, are very keenly sought after, and are valuable. Substantial additions were made to the second edition, which runs to 355 pages of text, as opposed to 246 in the first. The fifth edition, being the last published in Walton's lifetime, saw the substantial addition of Charles Cotton's 'Instructions how to angle for a Trout or Grayling, in a clear stream'. That edition, with Cotton's contribution and another by Col. Robert Venables, provided the basis for practically all future editions and the text as we know it today. However, the collective title for that edition, namely THE UNIVERSAL ANGLER, has not achieved the fame of the original. And on that point, be it noted, the spelling of 'Compleat' appears thus only on the engraved title-page, and as 'Complete' elsewhere in the volume.

Two editors have made an impact on the book. Firstly, Moses Brown, who tinkered with the text but gave the book a new lease of life in 1750. And secondly, Sir John Hawkins, whose editorial work on the book is highly regarded, and who wrote the first life of Walton. Hawkins did, however, create a small hazard for the unwary collector, by numbering his own editions as though no others had been published. A full list of all the collected editions of THE COMPLEAT ANGLER would be a very long list. I therefore give only the earliest ones below.

THE COMPLEAT ANGLER OR THE CONTEMPLATIVE MAN'S RECREATION.   (The title within a decorative cartouche). Printed by T. Maxey for Rich. Marriot 1653. Pages between 69 and 80 are mis-numbered. On p. 245 in the final couplet of a verse by Donne, the word 'contentment' appears incorrectly as 'contention'. Second Edition 1655, Third Edition 1661. (Reissued in 1664), Fourth Edition 1668, Fifth Edition (The Universal Angler) 1676, Sixth (First Browne) Edition 1750, Eighth Edition (First Hawkins) 1760. U.S.: Wiley & Putnam 1847.

In rebound copies of the first edition, the trimming of the edges is often found to have caused some loss on page 245, at the end of the line 'These guests . . . dearly loves,'. Copies with no such loss are at a premium. Page 217, bearing the bass part of 'The Angler's Song' appears upside down, and this was intentional, the opening being designed for two singers facing each other.

WAUGH, Evelyn (1903–1966)

Along with Graham Greene, Waugh has been the most popular of the collected 'literary' writers, during the last decade or so. As might be expected, the several very small editions of Waugh's work, such as the editions of 12 copies put out by Chapman & Hall in 1937, are the rarest and most expensive – in excess of £1000. Those apart, the usual rule applies – namely, that the earliest works are the rarest and most valuable.

THE WORLD TO COME: A POEM IN THREE CANTOS. Privately Printed 1916.

PRB: AN ESSAY ON THE PRE-RAPHAELITE BROTHERHOOD. Privately Printed 1926. Half cloth.

DECLINE AND FALL. Chapman & Hall 1928. 'Originally Published . . . September 1928' on the verso title-page. In the first issue: on page 168 appears 'Martin Gaythorne-Brodie' who becomes 'The Hon. Miles Malpractice' in the second issue. Similarly, on page 169, 'Kevin Saunderson' becomes 'Lord Parakeet'. In 1937, the same publisher issued an edition of only 12 copies. U.S.: Doubleday, Garden City 1929. Remaindered by Farrar & Rinehart with a cancel title, still dated 1929.

ROSSETTI. Duckworth 1928. U.S.: Dodd 1928.

LABELS. Duckworth 1930. Trade Edition, also 110 signed with page of holograph manuscript tipped-in.

VILE BODIES. Chapman & Hall 1930. In 1937, the same publisher issued an edition of only 12 copies. U.S.: Farrar 1930.

REMOTE PEOPLE. Duckworth 1931.

A BACHELOR ABROAD. New York: Farrar 1930.
    The U.S. edition of LABELS.

THEY WERE STILL DANCING. New York: Farrar 1932.
    The U.S. edition of REMOTE PEOPLE.

BLACK MISCHIEF. Chapman & Hall (1932). Black cloth, d/w; but also known in a greyish blue cloth, d/w. Also, 250 signed. Also, in 1937 an edition of 12 copies. U.S.: Farrar 1932.

A HANDFUL OF DUST. Chapman & Hall 1934. Same publisher: edition of 12 copies in 1937. U.S.: Farrar 1934.

NINETY-TWO DAYS. Duckworth 1934. U.S.: Farrar 1934.

EDMUND CAMPION. Longman 1935. U.S.: Sheed 1935.

MR LOVEDAY'S LITTLE OUTING. Chapman & Hall 1936. U.S.: Little Brown 1936.

WAUGH IN ABYSSINIA. Longman 1936. U.S.: Farrar 1936.

SCOOP. Chapman & Hall (1938). In the second issue, on page 88, last line, the 's' of 'as' is dropped out. The first issue d/w has the 'Daily Beast' logo on the front. U.S.: Little Brown 1938.

ROBBERY UNDER LAW. Chapman & Hall 1939.

MEXICO: AN OBJECT LESSON. New York: Little Brown 1939.
 The U.S. edition of ROBBERY UNDER LAW.

PUT OUT MORE FLAGS. Chapman & Hall 1942. U.S.: Little Brown 1942.

WORK SUSPENDED. Chapman & Hall 1942. Limited to 500 copies.

WORK SUSPENDED AND OTHER STORIES. Chapman & Hall 1948. Limited to 500 copies.

BRIDESHEAD REVISITED. Chapman & Hall 1945. Also 50 copies in wrappers, for private circulation. U.S.: Little Brown 1945.

WHEN THE GOING WAS GOOD. Duckworth 1946. U.S.: Little Brown 1947.
 Selections from previously published works.

WINE IN PEACE AND WAR. Saccone & Speed (1947).

SCOTT-KING'S MODERN EUROPE. Chapman & Hall 1947. U.S.: Little Brown 1949.

THE LOVED ONE. First published in Horizon magazine, February 1948.

Wrappers. Book: Chapman & Hall 1948. Also, 250 signed. U.S.: Little Brown 1948.

HELENA.   Chapman & Hall 1950. U.S.: Little Brown 1950.

MEN AT ARMS.   Chapman & Hall 1952. U.S.: Little Brown 1952.

THE HOLY PLACES.   Queen Anne Press 1952. Limited Edition. 900 copies in red buckram and d/w; also 50 specials, signed.

LOVE AMONG THE RUINS.   Chapman & Hall 1953. Also 350 signed.

OFFICERS AND GENTLEMEN.   Chapman & Hall 1955. U.S.: Little Brown 1955.

THE ORDEAL OF GILBERT PINFOLD.   Chapman & Hall 1957. Also a large paper edition for private distribution. U.S.: Little Brown 1957.

RONALD KNOX.   Chapman & Hall 1959. U.S.: Little Brown 1960.

A TOURIST IN AFRICA.   Chapman & Hall 1960. U.S.: Little Brown 1960.

UNCONDITIONAL SURRENDER.   Chapman & Hall 1961.

THE END OF THE BATTLE.   New York: Little Brown 1961.
   The U.S. edition of UNCONDITIONAL SURRENDER.

BASIL SEAL RIDES AGAIN.   Chapman & Hall 1963. Limited to 750 signed. U.S.: Little Brown 1963. 1000 signed copies.

A LITTLE LEARNING.   Chapman & Hall 1964. U.S.: Little Brown 1964.

DIARIES.   Weidenfeld 1976. U.S.: Little Brown 1976.

A LITTLE ORDER.   Methuen 1977. U.S.: Little Brown 1981.

THE LETTERS.   Weidenfeld 1980. U.S.: Ticknor & Fields 1980.

CHARLES RYDER'S SCHOOLDAYS AND OTHER STORIES.   New York: Little Brown 1982.

THE ESSAYS, ARTICLES AND REVIEWS.   Methuen 1983. U.S.: Little Brown 1984.

WEBB, Mary (1881–1927)

Her books were not greatly appreciated until after her death, thus the earliest first editions are now scarce. Her first two, and her most famous (being her sixth book) were:

THE GOLDEN ARROW. Constable 1916.

GONE TO EARTH. Constable (1917). Dark red cloth.

PRECIOUS BANE. Cape (1924).

WEBSTER, John (c. 1578–c. 1632)

Listed below are the works definitely by Webster, either solely or with others, along with those ascribed to him and generally accepted as his. The two masterpieces on which his great reputation rests are certainly by him, and they are THE WHITE DIVEL (sic) and THE DUCHESSE OF MALFY. The play THE THRACIAN WONDER, 1661, has been ascribed to him, but is generally not accepted as his. Some plays by Webster have been lost.

THE MALCONTENT. Augmented by Marston . . . Written by John Webster 1604. At London. Printed by V. S. for William Apsley and are to be sold at his shop in Paules Church-yard.

THE FAMOUS HISTORY OF SIR THOMAS WYAT . . . Written by Thomas Dickers and John Webster. London, printed by E. A. for Thomas Archer and are to be sold at his shop in the Pope's Head Pallace, near the Royal Exchange 1607.

WESTWARD HOE . . . written by Thomas Decker and John Webster. Printed at London and are to be sold by John Hodges dwelling in Paules Churchyard 1607.

NORTHWARD HOE . . . written by Thomas Decker and John Webster. Imprinted at London by G. Eld 1607.

THE WHITE DIVEL . . . Written by John Webster . . . London, printed by N. O., for Thomas Archer, and are to be sold at his Shop in Pope's Head Pallace, near the Royal Exchange 1612.

'A MONUMENTAL COLUMN' . . . By John Webster. London, printed by N. O. for William Wolby, dwelling in Paules Church-yard at the sign of the Swan 1613.

CHARACTERS. By Thomas Overbury. The sixth edition of 1615, includes New Characters (Drawn to the Life) of Severall Persons, in Several Qualities . . . (By Webster).

THE TRAGEDY OF THE DUCHESSE OF MALFY . . . Written by John Webster . . . London. Printed by Nicholas Okes, for John Waterson, and are to be sold at the sign of the Crown, in Paules Church-yard 1623.

THE DEVIL'S LAW CASE . . . Written by John Webster . . . London. Printed by A. M. for John Grismand, and are to be sold at his shop in Pauls Alley at the sign of the Gunne 1623.

MONUMENTS OF HONOR . . . invented and written by John Webster, Merchant Taylor . . . Printed at London by Nicholas Okes 1624.

APPIUS AND VIRGINIA. By John Webster. London, printed for Rich. Marriott in St Dunstan's Church-yard, Fleet Street 1654.

A CURE FOR A CUCKOLD . . . Written by John Webster and William Rowley . . . Printed by Thomas Johnson and are to be sold by Francis Kirkman at his shop at the sign of John Fletcher's Head, over against the Angel-Inne on the Backside of St Clements, without Temple Bar 1661.

WELLS, H. G. (1866–1946)

Much of Wells' vast and varied output attracts only modest interest from collectors. By far the most popular today, are the science fiction works, which are among the earliest in the genre. These are listed below. But one other work currently attracting much interest is FLOOR GAMES first published by Frank Palmer (1911):

THE TIME MACHINE. Heinemann 1895. 16pp adverts. Purple-stamped grey cloth with sphinx on the front. Also issued in bluish wrappers.
    U. S. edition (same year) has the author as 'H. S. Wells' on the title-page.

THE STOLEN BACILLUS. Methuen 1895. Dark blue cloth gilt.

THE ISLAND OF DOCTOR MOREAU. Frontispiece. Heinemann 1896. Brown pictorial cloth, lettered and blocked on the front in black and red. Earliest binding has publishers monogram on back cover.

THE INVISIBLE MAN. Pearson 1897. Black-stamped red cloth. First issue has page 1 numbered '2'.

THE PLATTNER STORY. Methuen 1897.

THE WAR OF THE WORLDS. Heinemann 1898. 16pp adverts (later 32pp). Black-lettered grey cloth.

WHEN THE SLEEPER WAKES. Harper 1899.

TALES OF SPACE AND TIME. Harper 1900 (1899). Olive cloth.

THE FIRST MEN IN THE MOON. Newnes 1901. Dark blue cloth gilt. Later, black-lettered light blue cloth.

TWELVE STORIES AND A DREAM. Macmillan 1903.

THE FOOD OF THE GODS. Macmillan 1904.

A MODERN UTOPIA. Chapman & Hall 1905.

IN THE DAYS OF THE COMET. Macmillan 1906.

THE WAR IN THE AIR. George Bell 1908. Pictorial blue cloth, lettered and stamped in gold. 'George Bell & Son' at foot of spine.

THE COUNTRY OF THE BLIND. Nelson (1911). Dark blue cloth.

THE WORLD SET FREE. Macmillan 1914.

THE DOOR IN THE WALL. New York: 1911. 600 copies. U.K.: Grant Richards 1915. Limited to 60 signed copies, from the American sheets of 1911.

MEN LIKE GODS. Cassell 1923.

THE SHAPE OF THINGS TO COME. Hutchinson 1933.

WHITE, T. H. (1906–1964)

As Timothy White, he contributed six poems to CAMBRIDGE POETRY, Hogarth Press 1929 – No. 8 in the series of Hogarth Living Poets. This was his first appearance in print. The following is a selection of his many works.

LOVED HELEN AND OTHER POEMS. Chatto & Windus 1929. U.S.: Viking 1929.
His scarce first book.

THE GREEN BAY TREE. Cambridge: Heffer 1929. Songs for Sixpence No. 3. Pamphlet.

DEAD MR NIXON. By White & McNair Scott. Cassell 1931.

DARKNESS AT PEMBERLEY. Gollancz 1932.

THEY WINTER ABROAD. By James Aston (pseudonym). Chatto 1922. U.S.: Viking 1922.

FIRST LESSON. By James Aston (pseudonym). Chatto 1922. U.S.: Knopf 1933.

THE GODSTONE AND THE BLACKYMOR. Cape 1959. Green cloth, d/w. Also in striped boards with a picture of the Godstone on the front, d/w. No priority has been established.

A WESTERN WIND. New York: Putnam 1959.
The U.S. edition of THE GODSTONE AND THE BLACKYMOR.

WHITMAN, Walt (1819–1892)

Whitman's most famous work, LEAVES OF GRASS, had a complicated publishing history. The basic details of the early editions are given below. They are all important collectors items. There were only 12 poems in the first edition. 21 poems were added to the Second Edition, and 122 were added to the Third Edition, including the important suite of poems entitled CALAMUS. There were six further editions during the poet's lifetime, and each one was revised and augmented. Most of his lifetime publications are rare. He did not meet with the approval of the general public in America, and his importance was only widely recognized after his cause was taken up in England by Rossetti, Swinburne and others.

FRANKLIN EVANS;   or The Inebriate. An extra to 'The New World', New York, November 1824, No. 34. pp31, without covers. New Edition in the same year, in wrappers.

LEAVES OF GRASS. Brooklyn, New York 1855. No publisher. pp.xii +95. Green cloth. First issue: no adverts or reviews; marbled endpapers, both front and back covers with triple gilt-stamped line, frontis portrait on plain paper.

Second Edition: Brooklyn, New York 1856. No publisher (but a leaf of adverts by Fowler & Wells at end). Green cloth. 1000 copies.

Third Edition: Boston: Thayer & Eldridge, Year '85 of The States. (May, 1860). Orange cloth. Various issues exist, including pirates.

Fourth Edition: New York 1867. No publisher & no author on title. Issued in cloth, also walnut half-morocco. (Printed for the author by William E. Chopin). pp.[iv]+338. Later issues have 'Drum-Taps' and other pieces added with separate pagination.

(Fifth Edition): Washington, D.C. 1871.

Sixth Edition: 'Author's Edition'. New Jersey: Camden 1876. Another 'Author's Edition' from Camden 1882.

(Seventh Edition): Boston: Osgood 1881–82.

'First Philadelphia Edition': Rees, Welsh 1882.

DRUM-TAPS.   New York 1865. Brown cloth, pp.iv+72. Some copies issued before addition of the sequel 'When Lilacs Last . . .' etc. (pp.24 separately paginated).

POEMS.   Edited by W. M. Rossetti. London 1868. Cloth gilt. First issue has no price on the spine.

MEMORANDA. DEMOCRATIC VISTAS.   Washington, D.C. 1871. Green wrappers. First issue: no author on title-page.

LEAVES OF GRASS. PASSAGE TO INDIA.   Washington, D.C. 1871. Green wrappers.

AFTER ALL, NOT TO CREATE ONLY.   11 folio sheets printed by Pearson (on one side only). Washington 1871. Regular Edition: Boston: Roberts Bros. 1871. 8vo. Green cloth, also maroon or brown cloth.

LEAVES OF GRASS. AS A STRONG BIRD ON PINIONS FREE.   And other Poems. Washington, D.C. 1872. Green cloth.
    The presence of LEAVES OF GRASS on the title-page is misleading. This is simply the first edition of AS A STRONG BIRD . . . etc.

MEMORANDA DURING THE WAR.   Author's Publication. Camden, N. J. 1875–76. Red-brown cloth. 2 portraits. Signed at beginning below 'Remembrance Copy'. Secondary issue lacks the portraits and the 'Remembrance Copy' leaf.

TWO RIVULETS.   Author's Edition. Camden, N. J. 1876. Half leather.

THE POETRY OF THE FUTURE.   From The North American Review. 1881. Pamphlet.
    Very few copies issued.

SPECIMEN DAYS & COLLECT.   Philadelphia: Rees, Welsh 1882–83. Blue wrappers or yellow cloth. Second issue has imprint of David McKay. Revised Edition: Walter Scott, London 1887.

NOVEMBER BOUGHS. Philadelphia: David McKay 1888. Maroon cloth, also green cloth. Also a large paper edition: green, red or blue cloth.

COMPLETE POEMS & PROSE OF WALT WHITMAN. 1855–1888. Printed by Ferguson, Philadelphia (1888–1889). Half cloth, also half leather, also grey buckram. 600 copies, signed.

LEAVES OF GRASS with SANDS AT SEVENTY . . . (etc). May 31, 1889. Black morocco. 300 copies, all signed.

FANCIES AT NAVESINK. Single folio sheet. (c. 1889).

GOOD-BYE, MY FANCY. Philadelphia: McKay 1891. Green or maroon cloth. Also, some large paper copies.

LEAVES OF GRASS, including SANDS AT SEVENTY . . . (etc.). Philadelphia: McKay 1891–92. Brown wrappers (about 50 copies). Also green cloth or grey wrappers.

COMPLETE PROSE WORKS. Philadelphia: McKay 1892. Green cloth.

AUTOBIOGRAPHIA. New York: Webster 1892. Grey cloth.
  Scarce – the publisher failed.

IN RE WALT WHITMAN. Published by the editors via David McKay, Philadelphia 1893. Green cloth. 1000 copies.

CALAMUS. A Series of Letters . . . Boston: Laurens Maynard 1897. 12mo. Cloth spine with paper label, boards: first issue of 35 numbered copies on large paper. Ordinary issue in cloth.

WALT WHITMAN AT HOME. Critic Pamphlet No. 2. New York 1898.

THE WOUND DRESSER . . . LETTERS . . . Boston: Small, Maynard 1898. Red buckram. Also 60 large paper copies.

NOTES AND FRAGMENTS. Printed for private distribution 1899. 250 copies, signed by the Editor (R. M. Bucke). Blue cloth.

LETTERS . . . TO HIS MOTHER. New York & London: Putnam 1902. Wrappers. 5 copies only.

THE COMPLETE WRITINGS. New York & London: Putnam 1902. 10 vols. Various bindings.

WILDE, Oscar (1854–1900)

Most of Wilde's works are scarce to say the least – and not only in first edition form. Some of the early reprints are also scarce. Many of them (firsts and reprints) were issued in very small editions. Practically nothing can be obtained for under £100. A notable exception is the first issue of DE PROFUNDIS of which 10,000 copies were published. Wilde's first appearance in print was in the Dublin University Magazine in 1875, to which he contributed an ode entitled 'Chorus of Cloud Maidens.'

NEWDIGATE PRIZE POEM / RAVENNA. Oxford: Thos. Shrimpton & Son 1878. 16pp. Green wrappers. The title page and front wrapper bear the arms of Oxford University. A pirated edition, printed in 1904, does not bear the University arms.

VERA; OR, THE NIHILISTS. Ranken & Co., Printers 1880. 52pp. Grey wrappers. The new edition of 1882 has a prologue added. The New York edition of 1883 has corrections and a typewritten introduction by Robert Ross.

POEMS. David Bogue 1881. White parchment. 750 copies printed and issued as three 'editions' in 1881. New Edition: Elkin Mathews 1892. 220 copies signed by the author. Made up from David Bogue's remaining fifth edition sheets, with a new title page, and bound in violet cloth.

OP.II / THE DUCHESS OF PADUA. New York: Privately Printed as Manuscript. 1883. 122pp. Grey-green wrappers. 20 copies only. U.K.:Methuen 1907.

THE HAPPY PRINCE AND OTHER TALES. Illustrated by Walter Crane and Jacomb Hood. D(avid) N(utt) 1888. Sm. 4to. Japanese vellum. 1000 copies. Also 75 signed copies on large paper. New Edition, illus. Charles Robinson: Duckworth 1913. 5000 copies. Also 250 signed, on Japanese vellum.

THE PICTURE OF DORIAN GRAY. First published in Lippincott's Monthly Magazine, 1890 (July issue). Book: London, New York & Melbourne: Ward Lock & Co. n.d. (1891). Crown 8vo. Grey paper-covered boards (bevelled), gilt butterfly designs. 8 lines from the bottom of page 208, the word 'and' is misprinted 'nd'. An edition of 250 signed copies was issued a few months later. This does not contain the misprint.

Carrington of Paris issued several editions during the first decade of the 20th Century, including the First Illustrated Edition dated 1908 (in fact, 1910). Vellum spine, grey boards & d/w.

INTENTIONS . . . Osgood, McIlvaine 1891. Green cloth, gilt. 1500 copies. Second Edition: 1894. 1000 copies.

LORD ARTHUR SAVILLE'S CRIME, and other stories. Osgood, McIlvaine and Co. 1891. Salmon boards.

A HOUSE OF POMEGRANATES. Design & Decoration by Ricketts & Shannon. Osgood, McIlvaine & Co. 1891. Cream linen with green linen spine.

'SALOME / Drama en un Acte'. Paris: Librairie de L'art Independant (and) Londres: Elkin Mathews et John Lane 1893. 84pp. Silver-lettered purple wrappers. Also 50 tall copies on Van Gelder hand-made paper.

SALOME. Illustrated by Aubrey Beardsley. Elkin Mathews 1894. Small 4to. Limited to 875 copies. There were '500' ordinary copies (but in fact, 750). Blue canvas boards.
> The First Edition in English, and the first illustrated edition. Beardsley's contribution was a pictorial title-page border, 10 full-page plates, a tailpiece, and a small cover design. Lane's edition of 1907 (the 5th U.K. edition) includes three plates suppressed from the 1894 edition.

LADY WINDERMERE'S FAN. Elkin Mathews and John Lane 1893. Reddish brown linen. Also, a De Luxe edition of 50 copies on handmade paper.

THE SPHINX. Decorations by Charles Ricketts. Elkin Mathews and John Lane (and) Boston: Copeland & Day 1894. Sm.4to. (44pp). Vellum spine, boards. Also full vellum. 200 ordinary copies, and a De Luxe Edition of 50 copies, signed by Ricketts.
> The number of copies stated is doubtful. It is thought that there were 328 in all.

A WOMAN OF NO IMPORTANCE. John Lane 1894. Red linen. Also a De Luxe Edition of 50 copies on handmade paper.

PHRASES AND PHILOSOPHIES FOR THE USE OF THE YOUNG. London: Privately Printed for Presentation 1894. 8vo. Wrappers. Limited to 75 copies.
> This first separate edition of Wilde's aphorisms, all of which had been printed before in various publications, was pirated by the bookseller A. Cooper, who was later prosecuted for his piracy. The date of publication was not 1894 as given, but 1902. Reprints were issued in the years following the original publication.

THE SOUL OF MAN. Privately Printed. Arthur L. Humphries 1895. 98pp. Light brown wrappers, red lettering. 50 copies. New Edition: Humphries 1907. Post 8vo. Cloth (various colours).

OSCARIANA. Privately Printed. Arthur Humphries 1895. 50 copies. Buff wrappers. Both the text paper and the wrappers are hand-made paper. New

Edition: Humphries 1910. Vellum wrappers, 200 copies, also 50 printed on vellum.

According to Mason, there are forgeries of the first printing.

THE BALLAD OF READING GAOL by C.3.3. Leonard Smithers 1898. Cinnamon linen, with white linen spine. 800 copies on handmade paper (2 impressions), in 2-tone cloth. Also a De Luxe Edition of 30 copies on Japanese vellum.

An edition of 99 signed copies, was issued in 1898. Wilde's name first appeared on the title page in the 7th edition, 1899.

CHILDREN IN PRISON AND OTHER CRUELTIES OF PRISON LIFE. Murdoch & Co. n.d. (1898). 16pp. Wrappers.

THE IMPORTANCE OF BEING EARNEST. Leonard Smithers and Co. 1899. Reddish brown linen. Also 12 copies on Japanese vellum and 100 De Luxe copies, signed.

AN IDEAL HUSBAND. Leonard Smithers & Co. 1899. Brownish red linen. Also 12 signed copies on Japanese vellum and 100 numbered De Luxe copies.

THE PORTRAIT OF MR. W. H. Original version: in Blackwood's Magazine, July 1889. Much longer rewritten version: Portland, Maine: T. B. Mosher 1904. Limited edition. U.K.: Smithers 1904. Pirated. 200 copies. Green wrappers.

Duckworth published an edition of 10 copies in 1921.

ESSAYS, CRITICISMS AND REVIEWS. Wright & Jones 1901.

A pirated collection of contributions to Woman's World.

POEMS ... together with his LECTURE ON THE ENGLISH RENAISSANCE. Paris 1903. (Published by Leonard Smithers and/or 'Wright & Jones'). 250 copies. Cream buckram, boards.

THE HARLOT'S HOUSE. Mathurin Press 1904.

A pirated poem, issued in various forms. Mathurin Press was an imprint of Leonard Smithers.

POEMS IN PROSE. Paris: Carrington 1905. 50 copies on paper, 50 on vellum.

Pirated.

DE PROFUNDIS. Methuen n.d. (1905). Blue buckram. At the back, a 40pp Catalogue dated February 1905. 10,000 copies. Also 50 copies on Japanese vellum, and 200 copies on handmade paper.

WILDE AND WHISTLER. An Acrimonious Correspondence in Art. Smithers 1906. 400 copies in yellow wrappers.
  Pirated.

THE SUPPRESSED PORTION OF 'DE PROFUNDIS'. Now for the first time published . . . by Robert Ross. New York: Paul R. Reynolds 1913. Grey linen.
  Rare – only a few copies printed.

AFTER BERNEVAL. Letters of Oscar Wilde to Robert Ross. Beaumont Press 1922. Limited Edition.

SOME LETTERS FROM OSCAR WILDE TO ALFRED DOUGLAS 1892–1897. San Francisco: Printed for William Andrews Clark, Jr. by John Henry Nash 1924. 4to. Parchment spine, sage green boards, slipcase. 225 copies for private distribution only.
  A fine example of book production, financed by a millionaire bibliophile.

WILLIAMSON, Henry (1895–1977)

Of the 15 volumes comprising THE CHRONICLE OF ANCIENT SUNLIGHT, two volumes are comparatively scarce – A FOX UNDER MY CLOAK and THE GALE OF THE WORLD (second state). Their scarcity probably arises merely from the fact that only 6000 copies were printed in each case. There were 10,000 copies of the first volume in the series (DARK LANTERN), and the numbers gradually declined to the low point of 6000 (A FOX UNDER MY CLOAK), then steadily rose again, only to fall back to 6000 at the end (THE GALE OF THE WORLD).

THE BEAUTIFUL YEARS. Collins 1921. Red-lettered dark blue cloth. 750 copies issued. New Edition (Revised): Faber 1929. Red cloth. 2580 copies. Also 200 signed, in blue buckram.

THE LONE SWALLOWS. Collins 1922. Black cloth spine, straw boards, paper label. No d/w. 500 copies issued. Second Edition (Less two pieces, for schools): Collins 1924. New World Series. New Edition (with changes): Collins (1928). Kings Way Classic. Brown cloth with green leather label on spine. U.S.: Dutton (1926). Patterned boards, d/w.

DANDELION DAYS. Collins 1922. Red-lettered dark blue cloth. 600 copies issued. New Edition (slight alterations): Faber 1930. Blue cloth. 2500 copies. Also 200 signed, in yellow buckram.

THE PEREGRINE'S SAGA. Collins 1923. Green cloth, gilt. 600 copies.

SUN BROTHERS.   New York: Dutton (1925).
  The U.S. edition of THE PEREGRINE'S SAGA.

THE DREAM OF FAIR WOMEN.   Collins 1924. Red-lettered dark blue cloth. 750 copies. New Edition: with a valediction to the Flax of Dream. Faber 1931. Chocolate cloth. 3500 copies. Also 200 signed, in terra-cotta buckram.

THE INCOMING OF SUMMER.   Collins Clear Type Press (1924). New World series. A school book, issued in two bindings – blue cloth boards, and blue cloth flush.
  A selection of stories from THE LONE SWALLOWS.

MIDSUMMER NIGHT.   Collins Clear Type Press (1924). A school book, issued in two bindings – blue cloth boards, and blue cloth flush.
  A selection of essays from THE LONE SWALLOWS.

THE OLD STAG.   London & New York: Putnam's Sons 1926. Red cloth, gilt. 1500 copies.

STUMBERLEAP.   Putnam's (1926). Brown wrappers.
  First separate edition of a story from THE OLD STAG.

TARKA THE OTTER.   Privately printed at the Chiswick Press (and sold by the author) 1927. Limited to 100 signed copies. Vellum with leather label. A further 1000 copies were issued (same year) by Putnam in brown cloth with a cream buckram spine and leather label. $9\frac{1}{2} \times 6\frac{1}{2}$ inches. A cheaper (crown 8vo) edition was issued by Putnam later that year (October). Slightly revised edition: Putnam (June 1928). First Illustrated Edition (with illustrations by Tunnicliffe): Putnam (1932).

THE PATHWAY.   Cape 1928. Green cloth, d/w with misprint 'Last Generation' for 'Lost Generation'. 2000 copies. Limited Signed Edition: 1931. 200 copies. Green buckram.

THE ACKYMALS.   1929. Edition of 225 signed printed at The Windsor Press. Cloth spine, dec. boards.

A SOLDIER'S DIARY OF THE GREAT WAR.   (Anon. Originally by D. H. Bell). Faber & Gwyer 1929. Red cloth.
  Williamson, who served with Captain Bell in 1914, extensively revised the work and provided an introduction.

THE WET FLANDERS PLAIN.   Beaumont Press 1929. 80 signed copies in decorative boards with vellum spine & 320 copies with holland spine. Trade Edition: Faber 1929. Black cloth. 2990 copies.
  Of the Faber edition, there are apparently three issues, arising from misprints

on page 62. In what must be the first issue, the first word on line 5 is
'neither' and the first word on line 6 is 'keepers'. These misprints were
subsequently corrected so that 'neither' appears in line 6 and 'keepers' in
line 5. In what must be the second issue, the alterations are on a cancel leaf.
In what must be the third issue, the leaf is integral. (See Ulysses Bookshop
Catalogue 3, 1930 and Clearwater Books 'The Henry Williamson
Catalogue'). The work originally appeared in serial form in the Daily Express
newspaper – 4 issues, July 1929.

THE LINHAY ON THE DOWNS. Elkin Mathews, Woburn Books 1929.
530 initialled copies. Dec. boards, d/w. THE LINHAY ON THE DOWNS
And Other Adventures . . . Cape (1934).

THE PATRIOT'S PROGRESS. Geoffrey Bles 1930. Red buckram. 3000
copies. Also 350 signed.

THE VILLAGE BOOK. Cape 1930. Brown cloth. Also 504 signed in green
cloth with vellum spine.

THE WILD RED DEER OF EXMOOR. Faber 1931 (August). Limited
Edition of 75 copies. Trade Edition one month later.

THE LABOURING LIFE. Cape 1932. Also 122 signed.

AS THE SUN SHINES. New York: Dutton 1933.
  The U.S. edition of THE LABOURING LIFE.

THE STAR-BORN. Faber 1933. Illus Tunnicliffe. Also 70 signed copies.
Revised Edition: Faber 1948. Illus Eldridge.
  Of the signed edition, 16pp unbound first signatures exist, bearing the signed
  limitation notice of '50' copies – evidence presumably of a late decision to
  increase the number to 70.

THE GOLD FALCON. (anonymous). Faber 1933. Revised Edition: Faber
1947.
  The revised edition appeared under the author's name.

ON FOOT IN DEVON. Maclehose 1933.

SALAR THE SALMON. Faber (1935). First Illustrated Edition (Tunnicliffe):
Faber (1936).

DEVON HOLIDAY. Cape 1935.

GOODBYE WEST COUNTRY. Putnam 1937.

THE CHILDREN OF SHALLOWFORD.   Faber 1939. Revised Edition: Faber 1959.

GENIUS OF FRIENDSHIP: T.E. LAWRENCE.   Faber 1941. The first binding was light brown cloth, the second was chocolate-brown buckram.

THE STORY OF A NORFOLK FARM.   Faber 1941.

AS THE SUN SHINES.   Faber 1941.

NORFOLK LIFE.   By Williamson & Haggard. Faber 1943.

LIFE IN A DEVON VILLAGE.   Faber 1945.
   A collection of previously published stories.

TALES OF A DEVON VILLAGE.   Faber 1945.
   A collection of previously published stories.

THE SUN IN THE SANDS.   Faber 1945.

THE PHASIAN BIRD.   Faber 1948.

SCRIBBLING LARK.   Faber 1949.

THE DARK LANTERN.   Macdonald 1951.

DONKEY BOY.   Macdonald 1952.

YOUNG PHILLIP MADDISON.   Macdonald 1953.

TALES OF MOORLAND AND ESTUARY.   Macdonald 1953.

HOW DEAR IS LIFE.   Macdonald 1954.

A FOX UNDER MY CLOAK.   Macdonald 1955.

THE GOLD VIRGIN.   Macdonald 1957.

A CLEAR WATER STREAM.   Faber 1958.

LOVE AND THE LOVELESS.   Macdonald 1958.

A TEST TO DESTRUCTION.   Macdonald 1960.

IN THE WOODS.   Llandeilo: St. Albert's Press 1960. Stiff wrappers & d/w. 950 copies. also 50 signed copies.

THE INNOCENT MOON. Macdonald 1961.

IT WAS THE NIGHTINGALE. Macdonald 1962.

THE POWER OF THE DEAD. Macdonald 1963.

THE PHOENIX GENERATION. Macdonald 1965.

A SOLITARY WAR, Macdonald 1966.

LUCIFER BEFORE SUNRISE. Macdonald 1967.

THE GALE OF THE WORLD. Macdonald 1969.
There are two states of the text. The number of typographical errors in the original printing brought complaints from the author, and copies were destroyed. Those which survived form the first state. They can be identified by the absence of the owl device from page 361, and the mis-spelling of the running headlines in Chapter 21. The number of copies in the first state is unknown, but informed opinion suggests that perhaps a few dozen copies survived. The second state copies are, of course, ones with the errors corrected (6000 copies).

THE SCANDAROON. Macdonald 1972. Also, 250 signed.

WODEHOUSE, P. G. (1881–1975)

Wodehouse, almost completely neglected by collectors until around 1970, is one of the most fashionable authors of recent years and consequently now one of the most expensive of the 'moderns'. The early works are very hard to find and competition is intense. His first book easily gets about £2000 in its earliest form, and his other early works are priced at around £1000.

I give here a comprehensive checklist of his major works. Where the American and U.K. editions have different titles, each is listed separately in priority sequence.

THE POTHUNTERS. Black 1902. Blue cloth with silver cup on front and spine. Later binding: pictorial boards. Later issue: has 8pp adverts. U.S.: Macmillan 1924.

A PREFECT'S UNCLE. Black 1903. Red cloth with lilac & pink decoration; cricketer on spine. U.S.: Macmillan 1924.

TALES OF ST. AUSTINS. Black 1903. Red cloth with lilac & pink decoration, or (no priority established) green cloth with black & blue decoration. U.S.: Macmillan 1923.

THE GOLD BAT.   Black 1904. Pictorial cloth. U.S.: Macmillan 1923.

WILLIAM TELL TOLD AGAIN.   Black 1904. Brown cloth, with green, yellow & black decoration. No publisher's address on title page.

THE HEAD OF KAY'S.   Black 1905. Red cloth with grey, yellow & black decoration. U.S.: Macmillan 1922.

LOVE AMONG THE CHICKENS.   Newnes 1906. Pictorial cloth. New Edition 'Entirely rewritten for this edition' Jenkins, 1921. Blue cloth, blue lettering. List on verso title should consist of 6 titles only, the last being 'Indiscretions of Archie'. U.S.: Circle 1909.

THE WHITE FEATHER.   Black 1907. Decorated tan cloth. U.S.: Macmillan 1922.

NOT GEORGE WASHINGTON.   By Herbert Westbrook & P. G. Wodehouse. Cassell 1907.

THE GLOBE BY THE WAY BOOK.   By Herbert Westbrook & P. G. Wodehouse. Globe 1908. Pictorial wrappers.

THE SWOOP.   Alston Rivers 1909. Pictorial wrappers.

MIKE.   Black 1909. Green pictorial cloth. U.S.: Macmillan 1924.

THE INTRUSION OF JIMMY.   New York: Watt 1910. Black cloth, circular label.

A GENTLEMAN OF LEISURE.   Alston Rivers 1910. Blue cloth.
   The U.K. edition of THE INTRUSION OF JIMMY with minor textual changes.

PSMITH IN THE CITY.   Black 1910. Pictorial cloth.

THE PRINCE AND BETTY.   New York: Watt 1912. Black cloth. U.K.: (Rewritten). Mills and Boon 1912. Red cloth.

THE LITTLE NUGGET.   Methuen 1913. Red cloth. U.S.: Watt 1914.

THE MAN UPSTAIRS.   Methuen 1914. Brown cloth.

SOMETHING NEW.   New York: Appleton 1915.

SOMETHING FRESH.   Methuen 1915.
U.K. edition of SOMETHING NEW, with minor changes.

PSMITH JOURNALIST.   Black 1915.
A rewrite of THE PRINCE AND BETTY.

UNEASY MONEY.   New York: Appleton 1916. U.K.: Methuen 1917.

PICCADILLY JIM.   New York: Dodd, Mead 1917. U.K.: Jenkins 1918.

THE MAN WITH TWO LEFT FEET.   Methuen 1917.
The 1933 U.S. edition from Burt & Co. has three additional stories.

MY MAN JEEVES.   Newnes 1919. Small 8vo. Red cloth. 1/9d Novels series.

THEIR MUTUAL CHILD.   New York: Boni & Liveright 1919.

THE COMING OF BILL.   Jenkins 1920.
U.K. edition of THEIR MUTUAL CHILD.

A DAMSEL IN DISTRESS.   New York: Doran 1919. U.K.: Jenkins 1919.
Red cloth or blue cloth (no priority established).

THE LITTLE WARRIOR.   New York: Doran 1920.

JILL THE RECKLESS.   Jenkins 1921. Blue cloth.
U.K. edition of THE LITTLE WARRIOR.

INDISCRETIONS OF ARCHIE.   Jenkins 1921. U.S.: Doran 1921.

THE CLICKING OF CUTHBERT.   Jenkins 1922.

GOLF WITHOUT TEARS.   New York: Doran 1924.
U.S. edition of THE CLICKING OF CUTHBERT with minor changes.

THREE MEN AND A MAID.   New York: Doran 1922.

THE GIRL ON THE BOAT.   Jenkins 1922. On verso title, list of 8 earlier
works, the last being THE CLICKING OF CUTHBERT.
U.K. edition, revised, of THREE MEN AND A MAID.

THE ADVENTURES OF SALLY.   Jenkins 1923 (1922).

MOSTLY SALLY.   New York: Doran 1923.
U.S. edition of THE ADVENTURES OF SALLY.

. THE INIMITABLE JEEVES.   Jenkins 1923. Verso title lists 10 earlier works, the last being THE CLICKING OF CUTHBERT.

JEEVES.   New York: Doran 1923.
   U.S. edition of THE INIMITABLE JEEVES.

LEAVE IT TO PSMITH.   (novel) Jenkins 1923 U.S.: Doran 1924.
   The play of the same name, with Ian Hay: French 1932. Grey wrappers.

UKRIDGE.   Jenkins, 1924. 13 titles listed on verso half-title.

HE RATHER ENJOYED IT.   New York: Doran 1926.
   The U.S. edition of UKRIDGE.

BILL THE CONQUEROR.   Methuen 1924. U.S.: Doran 1925..

CARRY ON, JEEVES.   Jenkins 1925. U.S.: Doran 1927.

SAM THE SUDDEN.   Methuen 1925.

SAM IN THE SUBURBS.   New York: Doran 1925.

THE HEART OF A GOOF   Jenkins 1926.

DIVOTS.   New York: Doran 1927.
   The U.S. edition of THE HEART OF A GOOF

HEARTS AND DIAMONDS.   With Laurie Wylie. Prowse 1926.

THE PLAY'S THE THING.   New York: Brentano's 1927.

THE SMALL BACHELOR.   Methuen 1927. U.S.: Doran 1927.

MEET MR. MULLINER.   Jenkins 1927. U.S.: Doran 1928.

GOOD MORNING BILL.   Methuen 1928.

MONEY FOR NOTHING.   Jenkins 1928. U.S.: Doran 1928.

MR. MULLINER SPEAKING.   Jenkins 1929. U.S.: Doubleday 1930.

FISH PREFERRED.   New York: Doubleday 1930.

SUMMER LIGHTNING.   Jenkins 1929.
   U.K. edition of FISH PREFERRED with new Preface.

A DAMSEL IN DISTRESS.   With Ian Hay. French 1930. Blue wrappers.

BAA, BAA, BLACK SHEEP. With Ian Hay. French 1930. Blue wrappers.

VERY GOOD, JEEVES. New York: Doubleday 1930. U.K.: Jenkins 1930. New Preface.

BIG MONEY. New York: Doubleday 1931. U.K.: Jenkins 1931.

IF I WERE YOU. New York: Doubleday 1931. U.K.: Jenkins 1931.

JEEVES OMNIBUS. Jenkins 1931.

LOUDER AND FUNNIER. Faber 1932. Yellow cloth. Later Issue: Green cloth.

DOCTOR SALLY. Methuen 1932.

HOT WATER. Jenkins 1932. Simultaneously issued by Doubleday in New York.

NOTHING BUT WODEHOUSE. New York: Doubleday 1932. Reprinted material.

MULLINER NIGHTS. Jenkins 1933. U.S.: Doubleday 1933.

HEAVY WEATHER. Boston: Little Brown 1933. U.K.: Jenkins 1933.

CANDLELIGHT. New York: French 1934. Grey wrappers.

METHUEN'S LIBRARY OF HUMOUR: P.G. WODEHOUSE. Methuen 1934. Reprinted material.

THANK YOU, JEEVES. Jenkins 1934. U.S.: Little Brown 1934.

RIGHT HO, JEEVES. Jenkins 1934.

BRINKLEY MANOR. Boston: Little Brown 1934.
  US edition of RIGHT HO, JEEVES.

MULLINER OMNIBUS. Jenkins 1935.

BLANDINGS CASTLE. Jenkins 1935. U.S.: Doubleday 1935.

THE LUCK OF THE BODKINS. Jenkins 1935. U.S. (rewritten): Boston: Little Brown 1935.

ANYTHING GOES. (with others). French 1936. Wrappers.

YOUNG MEN IN SPATS. Jenkins 1936. U.S.:New York: Doubleday 1936. 2 stories omitted, 3 added.

LAUGHING GAS. Jenkins 1936. U.S.: Doubleday 1936.

THE THREE MUSKETEERS. (with Grey & Grossmith). Chappell (U.K.) & Harms (U.S.) 1937.

LORD EMSWORTH AND OTHERS. Jenkins 1937.

CRIME WAVE AT BLANDINGS. New York: Doubleday 1937.
  The U.S. edition of LORD EMSWORTH AND OTHERS.

SUMMER MOONSHINE. New York: Doubleday 1937. U.K.: Jenkins 1938.

THE CODE OF THE WOOSTERS. Jenkins 1938. Published simultaneously in New York by Doubleday.

WEEK-END WODEHOUSE. Jenkins (London) & Doubleday (New York) 1939. Reprinted material.

UNCLE FRED IN THE SPRINGTIME. New York: Doubleday 1939. U.K.: Jenkins 1939.

WODEHOUSE ON GOLF. New York: Doubleday 1940.

EGGS, BEANS AND CRUMPETS. Jenkins 1940. U.S. (different stories): Doubleday 1940.

QUICK SERVICE. Jenkins 1940. U.S.: Doubleday 1940.

MONEY IN THE BANK. New York: Doubleday 1942. U.K.: Jenkins 1946.

JOY IN THE MORNING. New York: Doubleday 1946. U.K.: Jenkins 1947.

FULL MOON. New York: Doubleday 1947. U.K.: Jenkins 1947.

SPRING FEVER. Jenkins 1948. Published simultaneously in New York by Doubleday.

UNCLE DYNAMITE. Jenkins 1948. U.S.: Didier 1948.

THE BEST OF WODEHOUSE. New York: Pocket Books 1949.

THE MATING SEASON. Jenkins 1949. U.S.: Didier 1949.

NOTHING SERIOUS. Jenkins 1950. U.S.: Doubleday 1951.

THE OLD RELIABLE. Jenkins 1951. Orange cloth, lettered in black. Issued later in red boards. U.S.: Doubleday 1951.

BARMY IN WONDERLAND. Jenkins 1952.

ANGEL CAKE. New York: Doubleday 1952.
  The U.S. edition of BARMY IN WONDERLAND.

PIGS HAVE WINGS. New York: Doubleday 1952. U.K.: Jenkins 1952.

MIKE AT WRYKYN. Jenkins 1953. Part of MIKE (1909), rewritten.

MIKE AND PSMITH. Jenkins 1953. 'Reissued . . . 1953' on verso title. Part of MIKE (1909), rewritten.

RING FOR JEEVES. Jenkins 1953.

THE RETURN OF JEEVES. New York: Simon & Schuster 1954.
  U.S. edition, altered, of RING FOR JEEVES.

BRING ON THE GIRLS. (With Guy Bolton). New York: Simon & Schuster 1953. U.K. (rewritten): Jenkins 1954.

PERFORMING FLEA. Jenkins 1953.

AUTHOR! AUTHOR! New York: Simon & Schuster 1962.
  Revised version of PERFORMING FLEA.

JEEVES AND THE FEUDAL SPIRIT. Jenkins 1954.

BERTIE WOOSTER SEES IT THROUGH. New York: Simon & Schuster 1955.
  U.S. edition of JEEVES AND THE FEUDAL SPIRIT.

CARRY ON JEEVES. (Play written with Guy Bolton). Evans 1956.

FRENCH LEAVE. Jenkins 1956. U.S.: Simon & Schuster 1959.

AMERICA, I LIKE YOU. New York: Simon & Schuster 1956.

OVER SEVENTY. Jenkins 1957.
  Revised version of AMERICA, I LIKE YOU.

SOMETHING FISHY. Jenkins 1957.

THE BUTLER DID IT.   New York: Simon & Schuster 1957.
  The U.S. edition of SOMETHING FISHY.

SELECTED STORIES.   New York: Modern Library 1958.

COCKTAIL TIME.   Jenkins 1958. U.S.: Simon & Schuster 1958.

A FEW QUICK ONES.   New York: Simon & Schuster 1959. U.K.: Jenkins
1959.

THE MOST OF P.G. WODEHOUSE.   New York: Simon & Schuster 1960.

HOW RIGHT YOU ARE JEEVES.   New York: Simon & Schuster 1960.

JEEVES IN THE OFFING.   Jenkins 1960.
  The U.K. edition of HOW RIGHT YOU ARE JEEVES.

THE ICE IN THE BEDROOM.   New York: Simon & Schuster 1961. U.K.:
Jenkins 1961. (Entitled simply ICE IN THE BEDROOM).

SERVICE WITH A SMILE.   New York: Simon & Schuster 1961. U.K.:
Jenkins 1962.

STIFF UPPER LIP, JEEVES.   New York: Simon & Schuster 1963. U.K.:
Jenkins 1963.

BIFFEN'S MILLIONS.   New York: Simon & Schuster 1964.

FROZEN ASSETS.   Jenkins 1964.
  U.K. edition of BIFFEN'S MILLIONS

THE BRINKMANSHIP OF GALAHAD THREEPWOOD.   New York:
Simon & Schuster 1965.

GALAHAD AT BLANDINGS.   Jenkins 1965.
  U.K. edition of THE BRINKMANSHIP OF GALAHAD
  THREEPWOOD.

PLUM PIE.   Jenkins 1966. U.S.: Simon & Schuster 1967.

THE WORLD OF JEEVES.   Jenkins 1967.

THE PURLOINED PAPERWEIGHT.   New York: Simon & Schuster
1967.

COMPANY FOR HENRY.   Jenkins 1967.
  U.K. edition of THE PURLOINED PAPERWEIGHT.

DO BUTLERS BURGLE BANKS. New York: Simon & Schuster 1968. U.K.: Jenkins 1968.

A PELICAN AT BLANDINGS. Jenkins 1969.

NO NUDES IS GOOD NUDES. New York: Simon & Schuster 1970.
  U.S. edition of A PELICAN AT BLANDINGS.

THE GIRL IN BLUE. Barrie & Jenkins 1970. U.S.: Simon & Schuster 1971.

MUCH OBLIGED, JEEVES. Barrie & Jenkins 1971.

JEEVES AND THE TIE THAT BINDS. New York: Simon & Schuster 1971.
  U.S. edition of MUCH OBLIGED, JEEVES.

THE WORLD OF MR MULLINER. Barrie & Jenkins 1972. U.S.: Taplinger 1974.

PEARLS, GIRLS, AND MONTY BODKIN. Barrie & Jenkins 1972.

THE PLOT THAT THICKENED. New York: Simon & Schuster 1973.
  U.S. edition of PEARLS, GIRLS, AND MONTY BODKIN.

THE GOLF OMNIBUS. Barrie & Jenkins 1973. U.S.: Simon & Schuster 1974.

BACHELORS ANONYMOUS. Barrie & Jenkins 1973. U.S.: Simon & Schuster 1974.

THE WORLD OF PSMITH. Barrie & Jenkins 1974.

AUNTS AREN'T GENTLEMEN. Barrie & Jenkins 1974.

THE CAT-NAPPERS. New York: Simon & Schuster 1974.
  U.S. edition of AUNTS AREN'T GENTLEMEN.

THE WORLD OF UKRIDGE. Barrie & Jenkins 1975.

THE WORLD OF BLANDINGS. Barrie & Jenkins 1976.

THE UNCOLLECTED WODEHOUSE. U.S.A.: Seabury Press 1976.

VINTAGE WODEHOUSE. Barrie & Jenkins 1977.

SUNSET AT BLANDINGS. Chatto & Windus 1977. U.S.: Simon & Schuster 1977.

WODEHOUSE ON WODEHOUSE. Hutchinson 1980.

TALES FROM THE DRONES CLUB. Hutchinson 1982.

WODEHOUSE NUGGETS. Hutchinson 1983.

THE WORLD OF UNCLE FRED. Hutchinson 1983.

FOUR PLAYS. Methuen 1983.

WOLLSTONECRAFT, Mary (1759–1797)

A VINDICATION OF THE RIGHTS OF WOMAN: with Strictures on Political and Moral Subjects. Printed for J. Johnson 1792. Vol I (all published). Boards, paper label.

WOOLF, Virginia (1882–1941)

The Hogarth Press was founded by Virginia and Leonard Woolf in 1917 and was based initially at their home Hogarth House in Richmond, Surrey. In 1924, the press moved to Tavistock Square, London. The imprint became part of the Chatto & Windus group in 1947.

THE VOYAGE OUT. Duckworth 1915. U.S.: Doran 1920. Revised text.

TWO STORIES. (One by Virginia & one by Leonard Woolf). Hogarth Press 1917. 150 copies. Wrappers.
The first publication of the Hogarth Press.

KEW GARDENS. Hogarth Press 1919. 150 copies. Wrappers.

NIGHT AND DAY. Hogarth Press 1919. 'Second Edition'. White wrappers.
The first separate edition of her contribution to TWO STORIES.

NIGHT AND DAY. Duckworth 1919. Cloth, d/w. U.S.: Doran 1920.

MONDAY OR TUESDAY. Hogarth Press 1921. Illustrated boards, cloth spine, no d/w. 1000 copies. U.S.: Harcourt Brace 1921.

JACOB'S ROOM. Hogarth Press 1922. Yellow cloth. Also about 40 signed copies were issued to subscribers. U.S.: Harcourt Brace 1923.

MR BENNETT AND MRS BROWN. Hogarth Press 1924. Hogarth Essays series no. 1. White wrappers.

THE COMMON READER. Hogarth Press 1925. Cloth spine, white boards. U.S.: Harcourt Brace 1925.

MRS DALLOWAY. Hogarth Press 1925. U.S.: Harcourt Brace 1925.

TO THE LIGHTHOUSE. Hogarth Press 1927. U.S.: Harcourt Brace 1927.

ORLANDO. New York: Crosby Gaige 1928. Limited Edition of 851 (800 for sale) signed. Unlimited Edition: Hogarth Press 1928. Brown cloth, also (perhaps later) orange cloth. U.S.: Harcourt Brace 1928.

A ROOM OF ONE'S OWN. Fountain Press (U.S.) & Hogarth Press 1929. Limited Edition of 492 (450 for sale) signed. Unlimited Edition: Hogarth Press & Harcourt Brace 1929.

STREET HAUNTING. San Francisco: Westgate Press 1930. Limited Edition of 500 signed. Morocco spine (blue or green), boards, & slipcase.

ON BEING ILL. Hogarth Press 1930. Limited Edition of 250 signed. Vellum spine, cloth sides, d/w.

BEAU BRUMMELL. New York: Rimington & Hooper 1930. Quarter cloth, boards, glassine d/w & slipcase. Limited Edition of 550 signed.

THE WAVES. Hogarth Press 1931. U.S.: Harcourt Brace 1931.

A LETTER TO A YOUNG POET. Hogarth Press 1932. Hogarth Letters series no. 8.

THE COMMON READER: SECOND SERIES. Hogarth Press 1932. U.S.: Harcourt Brace 1932.

FLUSH. Hogarth Press 1933. U.S.: Harcourt Brace 1933.

WALTER SICKERT. Hogarth Press 1934.

THE ROGER FRY MEMORIAL EXHIBITION. Bristol 1935. 125 copies printed.

THE YEARS. Hogarth Press 1937. U.S.: Harcourt Brace 1937.

THREE GUINEAS. Hogarth Press 1938. U.S.: Harcourt Brace 1938.

REVIEWING.   Hogarth Press 1939. Hogarth Sixpenny Pamphlets series, no. 4.

ROGER FRY.   Hogarth 1940. U.S.: Harcourt Brace 1940.

BETWEEN THE ACTS.   Hogarth Press 1941. U.S.: Harcourt Brace 1941.

THE DEATH OF THE MOTH.   Hogarth Press 1942. U.S.: Harcourt Brace 1942.

A HAUNTED HOUSE.   Hogarth Press 1943. U.S.: Harcourt Brace 1944.

THE MOMENT AND OTHER ESSAYS.   Hogarth Press 1947. U.S.: Harcourt Brace 1948.

THE CAPTAIN'S DEATH BED.   New York: Harcourt Brace 1950. U.K.: Hogarth Press 1950 (a week later than New York).

A WRITER'S DIARY.   Hogarth Press 1953. U.S.: Harcourt Brace 1954.

VIRGINIA WOOLF & LYTTON STRACHEY: LETTERS.   Hogarth Press 1956. U.S.: Harcourt Brace 1956.

GRANITE AND RAINBOW.   Hogarth Press 1958. U.S.: Harcourt Brace 1958.

HOURS IN A LIBRARY.   New York: Harcourt, Brace 1958. Blue and black cloth. 1800 copies, issued by the publishers as a New Year greeting gift.
    The piece first appeared in the T.L.S., November 1916.

CONTEMPORARY WRITERS.   Hogarth Press 1965. U.S.: Harcourt Brace 1966.

NURSE LUGTON'S GOLDEN THIMBLE.   Hogarth Press 1966.

MRS DALLOWAY'S PARTY.   Hogarth Press 1973.

THE FLIGHT OF THE MIND: LETTERS . . . 1888–1912.   Hogarth Press 1975. U.S.: Harcourt Brace 1975.

MOMENTS OF BEING.   Sussex U.P. 1976.

THE QUESTION OF THINGS: LETTERS . . . 1912–1922.   Hogarth Press 1976. U.S.: Harcourt Brace 1976.

FRESHWATER.   Hogarth Press 1976.

THE DIARY . . . Volume I: 1915–1919.   Hogarth Press 1977. U.S.: Harcourt Brace 1977.

BOOKS AND PORTRAITS.   Hogarth Press 1977. U.S.: Harcourt Brace 1977.

A CHANGE OF PERSPECTIVE: LETTERS . . . 1923–1928.   Hogarth Press 1977. U.S.: Harcourt Brace 1977.

THE PARGITERS.   Hogarth Press 1977. U.S.: Harcourt Brace 1977.

THE DIARY . . . Volume II: 1920–1924.   Hogarth Press 1978. U.S.: Harcourt Brace 1978.

A REFLECTION OF THE OTHER PERSON: LETTERS . . . 1929–1931.   Hogarth Press 1978. U.S.: Harcourt Brace 1978.

THE SICKLE SIDE OF THE MOON: LETTERS . . . 1932–1935.   Hogarth Press 1979. U.S.: Harcourt Brace 1979.

THE DIARY . . . Volume III: 1925–1930.   Hogarth Press 1980. U.S.: Harcourt Brace 1980.

LEAVE THE LETTERS TILL WE'RE DEAD: LETTERS . . . 1936–1941. Hogarth Press 1980. U.S.: Harcourt Brace 1980.

THE DIARY . . . Volume IV: 1931–1935.   Hogarth Press 1982. U.S.: Harcourt Brace 1982.

THE LONDON SCENE.   Hogarth Press 1982. U.S.: Random House 1982.

THE DIARY . . . Volume V: 1936–41.   Chatto & Windus 1984. U.S.: Harcourt Brace 1984.

WORDSWORTH, William (1770–1850)

Most of Wordsworth's first editions are scare to say the least, and always in great demand. The LYRICAL BALLADS, which includes poems by Coleridge, is a key book of English poetry and is very rare. A collector who obtained one of the first three books for less than £5000, could count himself fortunate. The fourth book, the 2-volume POEMS, has a current value of about £1000. The more run of the mill later volumes can still be had for sums varying between £50 and £300.

AN EVENING WALK.   Printed for J. Johnson 1793. 27pp. Boards. No half-title.
> The bibliographer T. J. Wise thought that no more than seven or eight copies could now exist. Current thinking puts the figure at perhaps a dozen copies; but either way, this is clearly a very rare book indeed.

DESCRIPTIVE SKETCHES.   Printed for J. Johnson 1793. 55pp. Boards. No half-title.
> This work appears to be just as rare as AN EVENING WALK, with probably no more than a dozen copies in existence.

LYRICAL BALLADS.   Bristol: Printed by Biggs and Cottle for T. N. Longman . . . London 1798. Pink boards. No half-title. Uncancelled leaf at page 97–98. Second issue: London: Printed for J. & A. Arch . . . 1798. Page 97–98 is a cancel. Errata leaf at end.
> Poems by Wordsworth and Coleridge. The Second Edition of 1800, contains additional poems.

POEMS, in Two Volumes.   for Longman, Hurst, Rees, and Orme 1807. 2 vols. Small 8vos. Boards.

CONCERNING THE CONVENTION OF CINTRA.   for Longman, Hurst, Rees and Orme 1809. First issue: on page 97, the sentence beginning on line 14 'For what punishment' ends with the words 'the unremovable contempt and hatred of their countrymen?' In the second issue, those final words read 'the sentence passed upon them by the voice of their countrymen?'.
> Only a few copies of the first issue are known.

THE EXCURSION.   Being a Portion of The Recluse, for Longman, Hurst, Rees, Orme, and Brown 1814. Boards. The Errata & Summary of Contents, on pp. xv–xxii, are between pp. 424 & 425. (Not an issue point).

POEMS.   Including Lyrical Ballads . . . with additional poems, a new Preface, and a Supplementary Essay. for Longman, Hurst, Rees, Orme, and Brown 1815. 2 vols. Blue-grey boards, drab paper-covered spine with a paper label. Frontispiece in each volume. No half-titles.

THE WHITE DOE OF RYLSTONE.   for Longman, Hurst, Rees, Orme, and Brown . . . By James Ballantyne and Co. 1815. Frontispiece. Demy 4to. Boards, paper label on spine.

A LETTER TO A FRIEND OF ROBERT BURNS.   for Longman, Hurst, Rees, Orme, and Brown 1816. 37pp. Plain wrappers.

THANKSGIVING ODE.   Printed by Thomas Davison . . . For Longman, Hurst, Rees, Orme, and Brown 1816. 52pp. Green wrappers.

PETER BELL. Printed by Strahan and Spottiswoode ... For Longman, Hurst, Rees, Orme, and Brown 1819. Frontispiece. Wrappers, paper label on spine.

THE WAGGONER ... SONNETS. Printed by Strahan and Spottiswoode ... for Longman, Hurst, Rees, Orme, and Brown 1819. 68pp. Wrappers, paper label on spine.

THE RIVER DUDDON. A series of Sonnets ... A Topographical Description of the Country of the Lakes. for Longman, Hurst, Rees, Orme, and Brown 1820. Boards.

THE LITTLE MAID AND THE GENTLEMAN; or, We are Seven. (Anonymous) York: J. Kendrew (1820). 16mo. 16pp including yellow wrappers. With 14 woodcuts. (First Sep. Edn.)

MEMORIALS OF A TOUR ON THE CONTINENT. 1820. for Longman, Hurst, Rees, Orme, and Brown 1822. Boards.

THE MISCELLANEOUS POEMS. Longman 1820. 4 vols. 12mo. (First Collected Ed.).

ECCLESIASTICAL SKETCHES. for Longman, Hurst, Rees, Orme, and Brown 1822. Blue-grey boards.

YARROW REVISITED. for Longman, Hurst, Rees, Orme, and Brown ... and Edward Moxon 1835. 12mo. Errata slip after page xvi. Boards, paper label on spine.
    Second Edition: Longman 1836.

EPITAPH. (Anonymous). No publisher or date (1835). 4pp. Pamphlet. 4to.
    A poem on Charles Lamb.

ODE TO THE MEMORY OF CHARLES LAMB. (Anonymous). No publisher. No title page. 7pp. Plain lavender wrappers.

THE SONNETS OF WILLIAM WORDSWORTH. Edward Moxon 1838. Green cloth.
    This collection includes a few previously unpublished sonnets.

POEMS, CHIEFLY OF EARLY AND LATE YEARS. Edward Moxon 1842. Cloth.

VERSES COMPOSED AT THE REQUEST OF JANE WALLAS PENFOLD. No publisher. (1843). 4pp. Pamphlet, approximately $12\frac{1}{2} \times 10$ inches.

GRACE DARLING.   Carlisle: Printed at the Office of Charles Thurnam (1843). Single sheet folded to make 4pp.

> The imprint appears on the last page. There was a reprint, in which the imprint appears on the third page, thus: Newcastle: Printed by T. & J. Hodgson, Union Street.

KENDAL AND WINDERMERE RAILWAY.   Kendal: Printed by R. Branthwaite & Son. (1845). 23pp. Pamphlet. Second issue has 'Four Pence' on the title-page.

> The contents consist of two letters reprinted from the Morning Post, with revisions and additions.

TO THE QUEEN.   Dedicatory Verses . . . Printed for the Author By R. Branthwaite & Son, Kendal 1846. 7pp. Pamphlet.

> A Wise forgery.

ODE,   Performed in the Senate House, Cambridge. Printed at the University Press 1847. 8pp. Pamphlet.

> This Cambridge issue is the first. Subsequent issues were printed in London by Vizitelly Bros. and published by George Bell.

THE PRELUDE, OR GROWTH OF A POET'S MIND.   Edward Moxon 1850. Claret cloth. U.S.: Appleton 1850.

WORDSWORTH'S POEMS FOR THE YOUNG.   Strahan 1866. Sm.4to. Illus Macwhirther & Pettie.

> First edition of this selection.

THE RECLUSE.   Macmillan 1888. Fcap 8vo. Yellowish green cloth.

WYCHERLEY, William (1641–1715)

MISCELLANY POEMS;   as Satyrs, Epistles, Love-Verses, Songs, Sonnets, &c. Printed for C. Brome, J. Taylor, and B. Tooke, 1704. Mezzotint portrait. Folio in 4's.

> The only collected edition of his miscellaneous verse.

Y

YEATS, William Butler (1865–1939)

To exclude limited editions from a checklist of Yeats' publications would be to exclude a very large portion of his total output. I have therefore included limited editions more freely in this list than in others. Nevertheless, it represents only a good selection of his numerous works.

MOSADA. Dublin: Printed by Sealy, Bryers and Walker 1886. Frontispiece Portrait. Brown wrappers.
Only 100 copies were printed. It is an extremely rare book, worth in the region of £50,000.

FAIRY AND FOLK TALES OF THE IRISH PEASANTRY. Edited by Yeats. Walter Scott 1888. Camelot series, no. 32. Red cloth. Also issued in blue cloth (no priority). An undated later issue has the publisher's device in blind on the front and a medallion on the spine.

THE WANDERINGS OF OISIN AND OTHER POEMS. Kegan, Paul, Trench & Co. 1889. Blue cloth.

JOHN SHERMAN AND DHOYA. By 'Ganconagh'. T. Fisher Unwin 1891. 12mo. Yellow wrappers (1664 copies) and in brown linen (356 copies).

THE COUNTESS KATHLEEN AND VARIOUS LEGENDS AND LYRICS. T. Fisher Unwin 1892. Green boards with vellum spine. Also 30 special copies on Jap vellum.

THE CELTIC TWILIGHT / MEN AND WOMAN, DHOULS AND / FAIRIES. Lawrence and Bullen 1893. Green cloth, with the lettering in capitals. Later bindings have lettering (publisher's name at foot of spine) in lower case. Revised & Enlarged: Bullen 1901.

THE LAND OF HEART'S DESIRE. T. Fisher Unwin. 1894. 48pp in lilac wrappers with design by Beardsley. 500 copies. U.S.: Chicago: Stone & Kimball 1894. Drab boards, paper label on the spine. 450 copies. Frontispiece by Beardsley.

POEMS. T. Fisher Unwin. 1895. Cream cloth. First issue does not have the top edges gilt, later issues do. Also 25 signed copies on Japanese vellum. Second edition, revised: Fisher Unwin 1899. Blue cloth. Copies are also known (inexplicably) in the cream binding of the 1895 edition.

THE SECRET ROSE.   Illustrations by J. B. Yeats. Lawrence & Bullen 1897. Gilt dec blue cloth.

THE TABLES OF THE LAW / THE ADORATION OF THE MAGI. Privately Printed 1897 (but with the press mark of Lawrence & Bullen on the title-page) 48pp. Cloth. 110 numbered copies. Trade Edition: Elkin Mathews 1904. Wrappers.

THE WIND AMONG THE REEDS.   Elkin Mathews 1899. Blue cloth.

THE SHADOWY WATERS.   Hodder and Stoughton 1900. 60pp. Blue cloth. U.S.: Dodd, Mead 1901. Grey boards, label.

IS THE ORDER OF R.R. AND A.C. TO REMAIN A MAGICAL ORDER?   By D.E.D.I. Privately Printed 1901. Wrappers.
    A POSTSCRIPT . . . was privately printed in the same year.

THE CELTIC TWILIGHT.   A. H. Bullen 1902. Cloth.

CATHLEEN NI HOULIHAN.   Caradoc Press for A. H. Bullen 1902. 12mo. 34pp in white boards, leather spine. Limited to 308, including 8 copies on vellum.

WHERE THERE IS NOTHING.   Being Volume One of Plays for an Irish Theatre. John Lane 1902. Grey wrappers. 15 copies printed for copyright purposes. A second edition of 30 numbered copies was printed on large paper, from the same type (with corrections) in the same year, but without the publisher's imprint. Trade Edition: A. H. Bullen 1903. Green cloth spine with paper label, grey boards.
    The play was issued in Dublin as a 4pp supplement to 'The United Irishman' dated 'Samhain 1902'. It was probably issued on 30th October 1902.

THE HOUR GLASS.   Heinemann 1903. 16pp. Only 12 copies were printed for copyright purposes. First published edition: HOUR GLASS, CATHLEEN NI HOULIHAN, THE POT OF BROTH: Being Volume Two of Four Plays for an Irish Theatre. A. H. Bullen 1904. Green cloth spine with paper label, boards.

IDEAS OF GOOD AND EVIL.   A. H. Bullen 1903. Green boards.

IN THE SEVEN WOODS.   The Dun Emer Press, Dundrum 1903. 325 copies. Linen, with paper label.
    This was the first book from the Dun Emer Press. Copies are known in various special bindings, produced in the bindery of 'Dun Emer Industries'.

THE KING'S THRESHOLD.   New York. Printed for Private Circulation 1904. 100 signed copies. Boards, glassine d/w, slipcase.

THE KING'S THRESHOLD: AND ON BAILES' STRAND: Being Volume Three of Plays for an Irish Theatre. A. H. Bullen 1904. Boards with cloth spine. Also in 1904 in New York, an edition was privately published by John Quinn.

STORIES OF RED HAURAHAN. The Dun Emer Press, Dundrum 1904. Boards with linen spine.

POEMS 1899–1905. London: A. H. Bullen (and) Dublin: Maunsel & Co. 1906. Blue cloth gilt.
   Contains new versions of some works, some new poems, and a new Preface.

DEIRDRE. Being Volume Five of Plays for an Irish Theatre. London: A. H. Bullen (and) Dublin: Maunsel & Co. 1907. Boards, cloth spine.
   Copies are occasionally found with 'Alterations in "Deirdre" ' (4pp leaflet) loosely inserted.

DISCOVERIES. Dun Emer Press, Dundrum 1907. Blue boards, linen spine.

THE GOLDEN HELMET. John Quinn, New York 1908. Grey boards. 50 copies.

THE UNICORN FROM THE STARS AND OTHER PLAYS. by William B. Yeats and Lady Gregory. New York: Macmillan 1908. Blue cloth.

THE COLLECTED WORKS. Stratford-on-Avon: Shakespeare Head Press 1908. 8 vols. Olive brown buckram.

THE GREEN HELMET. Dublin: Cuala Press 1910. Limited to 400. Linen spine, boards, label.

SYNGE AND THE IRELAND OF HIS TIME. With a note . . . by Jack Butler Yeats. Dundrum: Cuala Press 1911. Grey boards.

THE CUTTING OF AN AGATE. New York: Macmillan 1912. Green boards.

THE HOUR GLASS. Dublin: Cuala Press 1912. Limited to 50. Wrappers.

POEMS WRITTEN IN DISCOURAGEMENT 1912–1913. Dundrum: Cuala Press 1913. 8pp. Grey wrappers. 100 copies.

REVERIES OVER CHILDHOOD. Dublin: Cuala Press 1915. Linen spine, boards, label. 425 copies. Issued with a Portfolio of Plates. U.K.: Macmillan 1916. U.S.: Macmillan 1916.

RESPONSIBILITIES AND OTHER POEMS. Macmillan 1916.

Macmillan's American edition was published 10 days after the London edition.

EIGHT POEMS. Morland Press 1916. Wrappers. 200 copies.

PER AMICA SILENTIA LUNAE. Macmillan 1918. Pictorial gilt cloth.

THE CUTTING OF AN AGATE. Macmillan 1919. Blue cloth, gilt.

FOUR PLAYS FOR DANCERS. Illustrations by Dulac. Macmillan 1921. 4to. Cloth spine, illustrated boards & d/w. 1000 copies.

FOUR YEARS. Dundrum: Cuala Press. Linen spine, boards. 400 copies.

THE CAT AND THE MOUSE AND CERTAIN POEMS. Dublin: Cuala Press 1924. Limited to 500.

EARLY POEMS AND STORIES. Macmillan 1925. Also 250 signed.

THE BOUNTY OF SWEDEN. Dublin: Cuala Press 1925. Limited to 400. Linen spine, boards, label.

ESTRANGEMENT. Dublin: Cuala Press 1925. Limited to 300. Linen spine, boards, label, glassine d/w.

OCTOBER BLAST. Dublin: Cuala Press 1927. Limited to 350. Linen spine, boards, label.

AUTOBIOGRAPHIES: Reveries Over Childhood and Youth and The Trembling of the Veil. New York: Macmillan 1927. 250 signed. Cloth & boards, without d/w.

THE DEATH OF SYNGE. Dublin: Cuala Press 1928. Limited to 400. Linen spine, boards, label.

THE TOWER. Macmillan 1928. Green cloth gilt. 2000 copies.

THE WINDING STAIR AND OTHER POEMS. New York 1929. U.K.: Macmillan 1933. Includes new material.

A PACKET FOR EZRA POUND. Dublin: Cuala Press 1929. 425 copies.

THE COLLECTED POEMS. Macmillan 1933. Also, a leather bound issue.

THE COLLECTED PLAYS. Macmillan 1934.

THE KING OF THE GREAT CLOCK TOWER. Dublin: Cuala Press 1934. Limited to 400. U.S.: Macmillan 1935.

WHEELS AND BUTTERFLIES. New Plays. Macmillan 1934. Pale green cloth.

A FULL MOON IN MARCH. Macmillan 1935.

DRAMATIS PERSONAE. Dublin: Cuala Press 1935. Limited to 400. Linen spine, boards, label.

A VISION. Macmillan 1937. Black buckram spine, patterned boards, d/w.

NINE ONE-ACT PLAYS. Macmillan 1937.

NEW POEMS. Dublin: Cuala Press 1938. Limited to 450. Linen spine, boards, label.

ON THE BOILER. Dublin: Cuala Press (1939). Wrappers.

IF I WERE FOUR AND TWENTY. Dublin: Cuala Press 1940. Limited to 450.

LETTERS OF POETRY FROM W. B. YEATS TO DOROTHY WELLESLEY. O.U.P. 1940.

LAST POEMS AND PLAYS. Macmillan 1940.

PAGES FROM A DIARY WRITTEN IN NINETEEN HUNDRED AND THIRTY. Dublin: Cuala Press 1944. 280 copies.

THE LETTERS. Hart-Davis 1954.